The Dragon, the Lion, & the Eagle

AMERICAN DIPLOMATIC HISTORY
Lawrence S. Kaplan, Editor

Aftermath of War: Americans and the Remaking of Japan, 1945–1952
Howard B. Schonberger

The Twilight of Amateur Diplomacy: The American Foreign Service and Its Senior Officers in the 1890s
Henry E. Mattox

Requiem for Revolution: The United States and Brazil, 1961–1969
Ruth Leacock

American Historians and the Atlantic Alliance
edited by Lawrence S. Kaplan

The Diplomacy of Pragmatism: Britain and the Formation of NATO, 1942–1949
John Baylis

Uses of Force and Wilsonian Foreign Policy
Frederick S. Calhoun

The Dragon, the Lion, and the Eagle: Chinese-British-American Relations, 1949–1958
Qiang Zhai

The Dragon, the Lion, & the Eagle

CHINESE / BRITISH / AMERICAN

RELATIONS, 1949–1958

Qiang Zhai

THE KENT STATE UNIVERSITY PRESS

Kent, Ohio, & London, England

© 1994 by The Kent State University Press
Kent, Ohio 44242
ALL RIGHTS RESERVED
Library of Congress Catalog Card Number 93-36348
ISBN 0-87338-490-3
Manufactured in the United States of America

Library of Congress Cataloging–in–Publication Data
Zhai, Qiang, 1958–
    The dragon, the lion, and the eagle: Chinese-British-American relations,
    1949–1958 / Qiang Zhai.
       p.   cm.—(American diplomatic history)
       Revision of thesis (Ph. D.)—Ohio University, 1991.
       Includes bibliographical references and index.
       ISBN 0-87338-490-3 (cloth: alk.) ∞
1. United States—Foreign relations—China. 2. China—Foreign relations—
United States. 3. Great Britain—Foreign relations—China. 4. China—Foreign
relations—Great Britain. 5. United States—Foreign relations—1945–1953.
6. United States—Foreign relations—1953–1961. 7. Great Britain—Foreign
relations—1945-. 8. China—History—1949-1976. I. Title. II. Series.
E183.8.C5Z42 1994   93-36348
951.05—dc20   CIP

British Library Cataloging-in-Publication data are available.

To Hui and Ye

Contents

Acknowledgments

This study had its origins in my doctoral dissertation completed at Ohio University in 1991. I am greatly indebted to several members of the faculty of that institution. First of all, I owe particular thanks to John Lewis Gaddis. As dissertation adviser, he supervised my research and writing. A disciplined scholar, incisive critic, and keen analyst, he provided me with immeasurable guidance and insight. As participants on my dissertation committee, Alonzo L. Hamby, Donald A. Jordan, and Stephen M. Miner suggested ways to improve the style and content of my work. To them, I am grateful. I also wish to thank Charles C. Alexander, Robert H. Whealey, and Lyle A. McGeoch of Ohio University for their encouragement and assistance during my study there. My fellow graduate students, Mark Benbow, Derrick Smith, and Philip Nash, also helped me in various ways.

In revising my dissertation for publication, I benefited from the advice of many friends. Drawing on his own familiarity with the subject, William Stueck of the University of Georgia made many helpful suggestions for revisions. Michael H. Hunt of the University of North Carolina at Chapel Hill read a portion of my manuscript and provided a thoughtful critique that reflected his vast knowledge of the subject. Chen Jian and Wang Xi have my appreciation for sharing Chinese material with me. The Auburn University at Montgomery History Department has provided me with the most excellent intellectual and personal company that a historian could ask for.

I wish to record my gratitude to Mr. and Mrs. David Wallbridge for their hospitality during my stay in London while researching in the Public Record Office. The staffs of libraries and archives which I visited in the course of my research were extremely helpful in furthering my work. For financial assistance that supported my research and writing, I wish to thank the Harry S. Truman Library Institute, the Eisenhower World Affairs Institute, the John Foster Dulles Program of Princeton University, and the United States Institute of Peace.

I would also like to thank the *China Quarterly* and *Chinese Historians* for permission to reproduce here my articles entitled, "China and the

Geneva Conference of 1954," and "Britain, the United States, and the Jinmen-Mazu Crisis, 1954–55 and 1958," which first appeared in their journals. I wish to extend appreciation to John Hubbell and Linda Cuckovich of the Kent State University Press for their assistance in producing this book.

My wife, Hui, and my son, Ye, have both been deprived of countless hours of a husband and father as a result of this study. The book is therefore dedicated to them.

I adopt the pinyin system of romanization for Chinese personal names, place names, and sources, with a few exceptions. Sun Yat-sen, Chiang Kai-shek, T.V. Soong, Kuomintang, Taipei, Quemoy-Matsu, and Yangtse River are used because of their familiarity to Western readers. All translations from Chinese materials are mine.

Abbreviations

ANZUS	Australia-New Zealand-United States Alliance
CAT	Civil Air Transport
CATC	Central Air Transport Corporation
CCP	Chinese Communist Party
CIA	Central Intelligence Agency
CINCPAC	Commander in Chief, Pacific
CMAG	Chinese Military Advisory Group
CNAC	China National Aviation Corporation
CPV	Chinese People's Volunteers
DRV	Democratic Republic of Vietnam
EDC	European Defense Community
ICBM	intercontinental ballistic missile
JCS	Joint Chiefs of Staff
KMT	Kuomintang
NATO	North Atlantic Treaty Organization
NSC	National Security Council
OSS	Office of Strategic Services
PLA	People's Liberation Army
POW	Prisoners of War
PPS	Policy Planning Staff
PRC	People's Republic of China
SCAP	Supreme Commander for the Allied Powers
SEATO	Southeast Asia Treaty Organization
U.N.	United Nations
UNC	United Nations Command
U.S.	United States
USSR	Union of Soviet Socialist Republics

Introduction

The establishment of the People's Republic of China (PRC) in 1949 and the subsequent conclusion of the Sino-Soviet Alliance Treaty were epoch-making events in post–World War II history. They destroyed the old balance of power in East Asia and introduced new forces into the international system. These developments had major implications for Great Britain and the United States, both of which possessed important interests in the region. I examine here Anglo-American policy toward the PRC between 1949 and 1958 and the reaction of the Chinese Communist party (CCP) to that policy.

I first compare Anglo-American approaches to China on such major issues as recognition, the PRC's representation in the United Nations, Tibet, Taiwan, the Korean War, the Geneva Conference of 1954, and the Quemoy-Matsu crises of 1954–55 and 1958; second, analyze the objective of dividing the Sino-Soviet alliance as a goal of Anglo-American policies; and third, investigate Chinese foreign policy initiatives as well as responses to Western challenges.

The PRC's relations with Western countries during its formative years, especially with the United States, attracted much attention during the 1970s and 1980s.[1] Most of those studies, however, were bilateral, focusing on either Sino-American or Sino-British relations. Edwin Martin's *Divided Counsel: The Anglo-American Response to Communist Victory in China* is the only monograph that compares the two Western countries' attitudes toward China during the early Cold War. In it, he discusses Anglo-American policies toward the Chinese revolution between 1949 and 1954. But as a former State Department official, he writes with a Cold War bias and uses no Chinese materials. The result is a one-sided view of a complex subject.[2]

In this work, I use recently declassified British and American documents as well as new Chinese sources to explore the interactions between a revolutionary state and two established Western powers between 1949 and 1958. I stress mutual influences and mutual constraints in the formation of

I

Anglo-American policies, examining how considerations of each other's reactions affect decisions. A comparative and multinational approach better elucidates the dynamics and intricacy of the triple relationship.

In 1949, both Washington and London had to confront the reality of a Communist government in China. They agreed that the establishment of the PRC changed the balance of power in the Far East and constituted a great challenge to Western interests in the region. But they differed widely in their assessments of Beijing's intentions and capabilities. Their differences were reflected in their respective attitudes toward recognition and containment of China. Their policies toward the PRC were, in turn, reflections of the perceptions and idiosyncracies of the top policymakers, of distinct strategic concerns, of different considerations involving their respective Asian allies, of divergences in political structures, public opinion, interest groups, and diplomatic traditions.

During the period in question, the Anglo-American relationship was often marked by tension and distrust. Washington's tendency to rely on nuclear deterrence against China during the Korean War and the two offshore island crises disturbed the British. Controversies over such issues as U.S. strategy in concluding the fighting in Korea and the American commitment to the defense of Quemoy and Matsu in 1954–55 seriously strained relations between Britain and the United States. To study these disputes and discords enriches one's understanding of the nature of the Atlantic alliance in the post–World War II world and contributes to the literature on the Anglo-American "special relationship."[3]

The goal of driving a wedge into the Sino-Soviet partnership constituted an important aspect of Anglo-American policies toward China. As a result of newly opened American and British archives, historians have begun to appreciate the complexity and subtlety of Western attitudes toward international communism during this period. In the past, because of the unavailability of documents, historians used to take literally the rhetoric of "monolithic communism" uttered by such policymakers as John Foster Dulles. The new literature has begun to portray Dulles as a shrewd and sophisticated leader, who understood the potential differences within the world Communist movement and devised policies aimed at stimulating those differences.[4] But until the early 1990s there was no treatment of the "wedge" policy from the British perspective. Newly declassified British documents show that, like their American counterparts, London policymakers were also conscious of potential trouble within the Sino-Soviet alliance and were eager to encourage it.

When the CCP took over China in 1949, it confronted enormous problems at home and hostility abroad. After many decades of continuous warfare, the country's economy was in shambles. The new government had not yet gained control of the entire country. Its domestic agenda was full and urgent: the consolidation of its position, the recovery of the economy, and the implementation of many political, social, and economic reform programs. By declaring itself as "leaning to one side," the CCP involved itself in the intensifying Cold War even before the founding of the PRC. By examining Chinese leaders' perceptions of and reactions to Western policies, one overcomes the conventional problems of studying international relations "according to Washington," or "according to London."[5]

In the past, the paucity of documentation hampered analysis of Chinese Communist foreign policy. Nonetheless, conditions for research on the CCP's foreign relations have changed significantly over the 1980s owing to the availability of inner-party documents, the publication of memoirs by many party leaders and the People's Liberation Army (PLA) commanders, as well as books and articles based on privileged access to archives and interviews with individual leaders.[6] These fresh materials shed much new light on CCP foreign policy-making by revealing perceptions and misperceptions of individual leaders about international affairs in general and the United States in particular and by illuminating the domestic influences as well as international constraints that helped shape Beijing's choices. For the first time, it is possible to describe in detail the role of individual policymakers such as Mao Zedong, Liu Shaoqi, and Zhou Enlai in such major decisions as China's entry into the Korean War, the CCP's assistance to Ho Chi Minh in his struggle against the French in the early 1950s, Beijing's preparations for and performance at the Geneva Conference of 1954, and the shelling of the offshore islands in 1954–55 and 1958. Together with traditional staples of research (the contemporary party press and the selected works of party leaders), the new sources greatly enrich understanding of the CCP's foreign policy.

Perceptions and images of decision makers are an important determinant in policy-making. As the political scientist Robert Jervis has argued, it is impossible to explain important foreign policy decisions without understanding decision makers' beliefs about the world and the motives of other actors in it. These beliefs, organized as "images," determine the way in which policymakers respond to outside events. He suggests that the principal source of images is stereotyped interpretations of significant historical incidents, particularly wars and revolutions. These upheavals have especially strong effects upon the thinking of younger people, whose views about the world are still highly impressionable. He points out: "People pay more attention to what has happened than to why it has happened. Thus learning is superficial, overgeneralized, and based on post hoc ergo propter hoc reasoning. As a result, the lessons learned will be applied to a wide variety of situations without a careful effort to determine whether the cases are similar on crucial dimensions."[7] I aim here to apply these insights to the decision-making process of the three countries in question. It is my conviction that Sino-Anglo-American relations can be best appreciated by understanding the nature of policymakers, by studying their fixations and misperceptions, and by analyzing their unspoken assumptions.

Although I emphasize perceptions, images are not the only sources of decision making in foreign policy. I refer to alternative approaches such as rational choice, organizational and bureaucratic models, and a focus on domestic politics in my discussion of Sino-Anglo-American policy formation. Images and perceptions do not necessarily lead to misperception or distortions of reality, and it is quite possible that images are susceptible to modification over time in the face of challenging information and experience.

In chapter 1, I describe the formative experience of major CCP leaders and its impact upon their perceptions of the United States and Britain, highlighting misperceptions and stereotypes in their thinking. An analysis of the nature of CCP-Soviet relations during the 1940s helps explain the reasons for Mao Zedong's decision to lean to the side of the Soviet Union in an emerging Cold War world.[8] In chapter 2, I examine the perceptions of Anglo-American policymakers about the Chinese Communists and the Sino-Soviet relationship together with the strategies they devised aimed at undermining that partnership and compare Anglo-American differences over recognition within the context of the "wedge" strategy. In chapter 3, I discuss Anglo-American perceptions of and policies toward Tibet within the context of their general China policy in the 1949–50 period.

China's decisions to enter the Korean War and divergent Anglo-American responses to Beijing and the Sino-Soviet alliance constitute the subject of chapter 4. In chapter 5, I deal with the effects of the hostilities on the issues of Taiwan, Chinese representation in the United Nations, and China's aircraft properties in Hong Kong. I investigate the reasons for the lack of progress in Sino-British negotiations to establish diplomatic relations following British recognition of China in early 1950 and Beijing's increasing criticism of London and hostility toward Washington.

In chapter 6, I address the Churchill government's attitude toward China, compare Anglo-American efforts toward the conclusion of the Korean War, and discuss China's reasons for concluding the Korean conflict. In chapter 7, I examine Zhou Enlai's diplomacy at the Geneva Conference and Anglo-American attitudes toward China in 1954 and in chapters 8 and 9 investigate Beijing's decisions to initiate the Quemoy-Matsu crises of 1954–55 and 1958, respectively, and Anglo-American reactions to them.

1 Perception and Alliance: The CCP's Foreign Policy in 1949

THE BACKGROUND OF CHINESE COMMUNIST LEADERS

Born at the turn of the twentieth century when China was in a ferment of antifeudal and anti-imperialist movements, most of the CCP leaders were imbued with a strong sense of nationalism and revolutionary spirit. They were determined to shed the humiliation China had suffered at the hands of foreign imperialists, to "save the motherland," and to restore the country to the status of a world power. They found themselves drawn into the vortex of a burgeoning revolution. Their formative experiences were Dr. Sun Yat-sen's Revolution of 1911 and its failure, the Paris Peace Conference and Japan's humiliating treatment of China, the May Fourth Movement, and, most significantly, the Russian October Revolution. These events were to have enormous effects on their later perceptions and foreign policy-making.

Communism in China was born out of the nationalist movement. Those young Chinese intellectuals who sought answers to China's problems in Marxism and Leninism were also motivated by existing social and economic circumstances, which helped to make the Communist cause a popular one. China was very much a peasant country, and the endorsement of the rural population was to prove essential for the Chinese Communist movement. The Chinese Communist leaders were Marxist and nationalist at the same time. The party's road to victory was full of twists and turns. Setbacks, sacrifices, and defeats in the course of party history made its leaders tough, pragmatic, and perseverant.

Many of the CCP leaders had educational backgrounds higher than those of ordinary Chinese, and some of them had even studied abroad. Before 1917, they had been exposed to various intellectual trends current in China. Mao's reading covered a wide range from Chinese reform thinkers such as Kang Youwei and Liang Qichao to translated foreign works such as Adam Smith's *The Wealth of Nations,* Charles Darwin's *Origin of Species,* and writings by John Stuart Mill, Jean-Jacques Rousseau, and Charles de Secondat de Montesquieu. Mao told Edgar Snow that when he was a student at the Changsha Normal College between 1912 and 1918, his mind was "a curious mixture of ideas of liberalism, democratic reformism, and Utopian Socialism." It was the Bolshevik Revolution that finally attracted him. "The salvos of the October Revolution," Mao later wrote, "brought us Marxism-Leninism. The October Revolution helped progressives in China, as throughout the world, to adopt the proletarian world outlook as the instrument for studying a nation's destiny and considering anew their own problems."[1]

Zhou Enlai was also a voracious reader of Kang Youwei, Liang Qichao, Rousseau, and Montesquieu. In September 1917, he went to Japan hoping to learn how to save and rebuild China. At the time, he thought that militarism might be a way out, but he was soon to be disillusioned. World War I was raging, and Japan, determined to make the most of it while the other powers were preoccupied in Europe, stepped up its aggression against a weak China. Zhou very much resented Japanese militarism. He plunged into anti-Japanese rallies and demonstrations staged by Chinese students in Japan. Zhou was first introduced to Marxism in a serious way in Japan through reading *Studies of Social Problems,* a journal edited and published in Tokyo by Professor Kawakami Hajime of the Imperial University, who first brought Marxist teachings to Japan. It was also in that country that Zhou learned about the October Revolution. He shared the general excitement and tried to comprehend what the dictatorship of the proletariat meant. He read John Reed's *The Ten Days That Shook the World* and immersed himself in the press, reading all he could lay his hands on about developments in the world's first socialist regime. He began a serious study of the principles underlying this world-shaking occurrence and finally became a Marxist three years later when he was a work-study student in France.[2]

Before 1949, except for Zhou Enlai and a few others, most of the Chinese Communist leaders had not had much experience in foreign affairs. Mao himself had never traveled abroad before his visit to Moscow early in 1950. For many of his other comrades, a spell in the Soviet Union represented their only overseas excursion. When the People's Republic of China was founded in 1949, a majority of the party's politburo members had spent some time either as students or as visitors in Russia. Among the thirteen members of the politburo elected at the first plenary session of the Seventh Central Party Committee in June 1945, only Mao, Gao Gang, Peng Zhen, and Peng Dehuai had not studied in the Soviet Union. Both Liu Shaoqi and Ren Bishi had enrolled in the Communist University of the Toilers of the East in Moscow in the early 1920s. After returning to China, Liu began his political career as a major CCP labor organizer and Ren became one of the most important leaders of the Communist Youth League. Later, Ren Bishi, Chen Yun, and Kang Sheng served as CCP representatives to the Comintern in the 1930s. After brief study in the United States, Zhang Wentian went to Moscow in 1926, where he attended Sun Yat-sen University and taught at the Lenin School. Lin Baiqu was also a graduate of Sun Yat-sen University (1930) and taught politics at the Far Eastern Industrial University at Vladivostok. Gao had forged close ties with the Russians when he was the head of the party's Northeast Bureau in Manchuria. Therefore, a majority of the CCP leaders in 1949 had close connections with the Soviet Union, but their experiences overseas were unbalanced and almost completely confined to Russia.[3]

The lessons of the Russian Revolution and subsequent Soviet history had a profound influence on these people, building images that shaped their perceptions and reactions to external stimuli. For instance, in the wake of the defeat of the Nanchang Uprising in 1927, Zhu De used the analogy of the Russian Revolution to encourage his remnant troops not to lose heart: "After the failure of the 1905 Russian Revolution, some 'dregs' remained, who later became the backbones of the October Revolution. Our present situation resembles the Russian Revolution of 1905. So long as we retain some people, we can play a great role in a future revolution." In a speech to the Shenyang workers' representatives on January 5, 1949, Chen Yun said: "Not until after the three Five-Year Plans following the success of the October Revolution did people's life in Russia begin to change for the better with each passing day. After we win the victory over the Nationalists in the country, we must also work hard and engage in large-scale construction before our children can enjoy the fruit of a comfortable life."[4]

THE CCP'S VIEW OF THE UNITED STATES

Both Marxist ideology and historical experience shaped the basic assumptions about the United States held by CCP decision makers in the postwar decades. As students of Marx and Lenin, they had a rather rigid opinion of America. To them, Washington was the leader of the reactionary camp in the world, which was "against the Soviet Union, against the People's democracies in Europe, against the workers' movements in the capitalist countries, against the national movements in the colonies and semi-colonies and against the liberation of the Chinese people." Washington harbored a wild scheme for "converting China into a U.S. colony."[5]

As believers in Marxist dialectical materialism and historical materialism, Mao Zedong and his lieutenants were convinced that imperialism represented the decadent and dying phase of capitalism and would be replaced by communism, which constituted the highest stage of social development. Therefore, they kept telling their people that American imperialism, although momentarily powerful and frightening, was, in fact, weak and vulnerable in the long run because it did not reflect the trend of history and lacked popular support. Furthermore, it was constantly threatened by political and economic crises. Its difficulties were historically inevitable and determined by its capitalist system.[6]

In an analysis of the post–World War II international situation, Mao elaborated this idea most graphically: "People's democratic forces" within America "are getting stronger every day." "The economic power of U.S. imperialism," Mao continued, "is confronted with unstable and daily shrinking domestic and foreign markets. The further shrinking of these markets will cause economic crises to break out." Wartime prosperity in America was "temporary" and U.S. strength was only "superficial and transient." "Irreconcilable domestic and international contradictions," Mao concluded, "like a volcano, menace U.S. imperialism every day. . . . This situation has driven the U.S. imperialists to draw up a plan for enslaving the world, to run amuck like wild beasts in Europe, Asia and other parts of the world."[7]

Imperialist forces, Mao reasoned, tended to take precisely those actions that would lead to their own doom, to paraphrase a Chinese saying, "lifting a rock only to drop it on one's own feet." The stress on the long-term and inherent weaknesses of U.S. imperialism also informed Mao's well-known metaphor that America was a paper tiger.[8] Although this characterization of the United States reflected Mao's ideological convictions, it also served as a psychological device to boost morale when the CCP was still in a weak position in its struggle to win national power. Resembling Lenin's previous description of imperialism as a "colossus with clay feet," Mao's paper tiger thesis constituted the most vivid example of the Chinese concept of despising the enemy strategically but taking full account of it tactically.

To the Chinese Communists, U.S. imperialism had committed aggression against China ever since the mid-1840s. America had been one of the first Western powers to force China to cede extraterritoriality and to open ports for trade and missions. It participated in the eight-power Allied expedition to suppress the Boxer Uprising in 1900 and later supported Chiang Kai-shek's Nationalist government in the civil war against the CCP.[9]

After the end of the Marshall Mission in China in early 1947 and the total eruption of civil war in which America supported the Kuomintang (KMT, or Nationalists), the CCP drew bitter lessons and abandoned illusions about American neutrality in Chinese internal conflict.[10] In the world arena, the United States and the Soviet Union became increasingly locked in a Cold War confrontation. In this context, Mao made a series of speeches clarifying the CCP's position in the emerging bipolar world. The basic tenets of Mao's theory were the "two camps" and the "intermediate zone." Mao viewed the postwar world as divided into two hostile camps represented by the United States and the Soviet Union. Between these two camps, Mao contended, lay "a vast zone which included many capitalist, colonial and semi-colonial countries in Europe, Asia, and Africa." "Before the U.S. reactionaries have subjugated these countries," Mao believed, "an attack on the Soviet Union is out of the question." Therefore, the major contradictions in the world were those between the peoples of the "intermediate zone" and U.S. imperialism, especially those between China and the United States. China's choice in this struggle, Mao declared, was to side with the Soviet Union.[11]

As the CCP approached nationwide triumph, it repeatedly warned its cadres and soldiers against the danger of U.S. intervention. The party leadership believed that the threat from the United States could come either in the form of direct military invasion or by indirect meddling through secret agents, sabotage, and political infiltration. In perceiving this U.S. menace, the CCP leaders were influenced by the existing political context, by their ideological beliefs, and by historical analogies. In the CCP-KMT struggle for power, the United States sided with Chiang Kai-shek. Ideologically, America was the number-one imperialist power, inherently antagonistic toward national liberation movements and with many imperialist interests and prerogatives in China to protect. Historically, Washington had a tradition of intervention in foreign revolutions. In this regard, the history of U.S. intervention during the Russian Revolution sensitized the CCP leadership to the danger that the Americans might react similarly against them. This point merits close attention when analyzing Chinese Communist perceptions of the U.S. threat.

As did other human beings, CCP leaders tended to use the past to make sense of the present. This exercise often involved dipping into the grab bag of historical experience for instances that offered instructive analogies to current problems. They were prone to envision the future either as foreshadowed by past parallels or as following a straight track from what had recently gone before. Thus, it was both easy and natural for them to apply the Soviet experience to their own situation. They believed that, because Western imperialists had opposed the Bolshevik Revolution, they would not put up with the Chinese Revolution either. Mao claimed: "Make trouble, fail, make trouble again, fail again . . . till their doom; that is the logic of the imperialists and all reactionaries the world over in dealing with the people's cause, and they will never go against this logic." Imperialists never learned from their mistakes, Mao explained; instead, they invariably repeated them.[12]

It is important to point out that CCP leaders' understanding of Western intervention in the Russian Revolution was both simplistic and inaccurate. For instance, when analyzing the reason for the failure of the Allied mission, Zhou Enlai argued that this was because American soldiers "could not bear hardships." Zhou was obviously not cognizant of the complex nature of the intervention and had no idea of the lack of official determination and coordination that characterized the entire course of the action.[13]

From their misreading of the American intervention in the Russian Revolution, CCP officials developed another misperception of the United States: American soldiers were spoiled by a rich and comfortable life in a capitalist society and would not withstand hard conditions. Therefore, even if the United States did invade China, the CCP would endure simply because American troops were "spoiled" and could be defeated. Zhou Enlai expressed this notion in a 1949 speech:

> If American troops really invade China, we will surround them from the countryside, forcing them to ship all military supplies, including toilet paper and ice cream, from the United States. They would be burdened by big cities. . . . The Americans enjoy a high standard of living and are unwilling to fight. After the Russian October Revolution, the United States once intervened, but the result was "voluntary withdrawal"? Why? This was because they could not bear hardships. We have defeated the Japanese invaders. Are we to be afraid of American troops?[14]

The result was ironic. Although CCP leaders were conscious of history, they also tended to misapply history. They failed to appreciate not only changes in contexts and actors over time but also variables that changed from one situation to another. Once persuaded that Western intervention in 1918–20 was repeating itself, they tended to see only factors conforming to such an image. When referring to a past lesson, they were inclined to grab the first that came to mind. They did not pause to examine the instance and test its applicability. Merely projecting a trend, they failed to dissect the forces that gave rise to it and to ask if those factors would persist with the same effect.

Finally, the CCP's increasing criticism of American aggression in China and intense attacks on Chiang Kai-shek as the "running dog" of U.S. imperialism since 1947 served the practical function of discrediting its rivals in its struggle for national power. Here one sees the link between domestic politics and the CCP's foreign policy. By emphasizing the "master-puppet" relationship between the United States and Chiang Kai-shek, the Communists sought to tarnish the reputation of the Nationalists in the eyes of the people and to establish their own legitimacy within the country. This had been a consistent Communist tactic throughout the Chinese civil war. It had the benefit of turning disadvantages into advantages.

THE CCP'S VIEW OF GREAT BRITAIN

Throughout the late 1940s and 1950s, the Chinese Communists considered the United States the main enemy of the Chinese Revolution. Therefore, most of the foreign policy statements by the party leadership were directed at America. Great Britain did not receive as much attention and criticism as the United States, but many of the basic Communist descriptions of U.S. imperialism also applied to Britain.

The CCP regarded London as a power belonging to the reactionary camp headed by the United States. In a foreign policy comment in 1949, Mao asserted: "The U.S. and British governments belong to the type in which the bourgeoisie, and this class alone, exercise dictatorship over the people. Contrary in all respects to the people's government, this type of government practices so-called democracy for the bourgeoisie but is dictatorial toward the people." On another occasion, the CCP leader dismissed the idea of seeking help from the British and American governments as "naive." "Would the present rulers of Britain and the United States, who are imperialists, help a people's state," Mao asked. If they wanted to do business, Mao reasoned, it was not because they wanted to help the Chinese people but because "their capitalists want to make money and their bankers want to earn interest to extricate themselves from their own crises."[15]

As to the relationship between Britain and the United States, Mao told the party that since World War II a common feature of the reactionary forces in the world had been their dependence on U.S. imperialism. During the war, three big imperialist powers, Germany, Italy, and Japan, were knocked out, whereas two other powers, Britain and France, were weakened. In the whole world only one big power, the United States, "remained uninjured." This situation "reflects the severity of the blows world capitalism received in World War II," Mao explained. "It reflects the weakness of the reactionary forces in all countries, their panic and loss of confidence, and it reflects the might of the world revolutionary forces."[16]

As was the shaping of its attitude toward the United States, the CCP's perception of Britain was influenced by its reading of history. To the Communists, England was an old imperialist power that had taken the lead in encroaching upon China. Since the Opium War of 1839–42, the United Kingdom had involved itself in a series of aggressions: the Anglo-French intervention in 1856, the suppression of the Boxers, and hostility toward the Chinese Nationalist Revolution in the 1920s.

While regarding Britain as a reactionary imperialist power in principle, the CCP's actual policy toward the United Kingdom was practical and flexible. The party was satisfied that the British had not intervened in the Chinese civil war as much as the Americans had. According to British sources, in November 1948, Qiao Guanhua (alias Qiao Mu), the head of the CCP's New China News Agency in Hong Kong, told H. C. Bough, a British journalist, that the Chinese Communists had no intentions of taking Hong Kong by force and were prepared to have normal relations with the British Labor government. Qiao pointed out that the status of Hong Kong was a minor diplomatic issue. He praised the British policy of neutrality in the Chinese internal conflict and expressed the view that the CCP would understand the Hong Kong government's policy if, in the future, KMT leaders became refugees in the colony.[17]

Qiao's assurances to Britain of the CCP's policy toward Hong Kong were clearly deliberate, for the party was fully cognizant of the diplomatic and economic importance of the colony. In fact, throughout the Chinese civil war, the CCP had viewed Hong Kong as a useful base to help its struggle for power in China proper. The party's South China bureau was located in Hong Kong, headed by Liao Chengzhi and Fang Fang. The focal points of the bureau's activities were Guangdong and Guangxi provinces in southern China. The party also used the colony to promote its united front strategy against the KMT, to recruit new supporters, and to raise funds. When conducting its activities in Hong Kong, the party took care not to violate local laws. Peng Zhen, a member of the CCP Politburo, said in 1951 that to occupy Hong Kong at the moment would not only cause "unnecessary technical difficulty in the enforcement of our international policy, but also increase our burden." To keep Hong Kong in its current position, however, would be advantageous to China's economic reconstruction programs. Therefore, Peng asserted that it would be "unwise for us to deal with the problem of Hong Kong rashly and without preparation."[18]

Aside from this practical attitude toward Hong Kong, the CCP also displayed flexibility when establishing trade relations with Britain. As early as March 1948, Zhou Enlai said that the CCP welcomed British suggestions to trade with the Communist-controlled area in China. In Zhou's view, such a relationship "was beneficial to both sides."[19] On September 25, Zhou authorized Qian Zhiguang, a CCP representative in Hong Kong, to conduct unofficial negotiations with the British on the issue of trade. If the British showed sincerity in trade, Zhou told Qian, he could invite them to come to the liberated area in North China to negotiate directly with the People's Government there.[20] This willingness to trade with Britain was also designed to exploit Anglo-American differences over the issue.

Throughout the late 1940s, there was no major controversy between the CCP and Britain, except the *Amethyst* incident in April 1949, which soured their relationship for a while. On April 20, 1949, the day the PLA was preparing to cross the Yangtse River to occupy Nanjing, the *Amethyst,* a British frigate sailing up the river, was bombarded by the Communist troops. Later a Communist spokesman accused the British warship of opening fire first and causing 252 casualties.[21] The party adroitly used the event to stir up national sentiment and win popular support by connecting the incident with previous imperialist atrocities in China and by showing itself as the protector of Chinese national interests. An April 25 New China News Agency editorial claimed that "The British imperialists must understand that China is no longer the China of 1926 when British naval vessels bombarded Wan Xian. She is no longer the China of the days when Great Britain and the United States jointly bombarded Nanjing in 1927. The Yangtse River now belongs to the Chinese people and the PLA and no longer belongs to servile and weak traitors."[22]

In a public statement on the matter, Mao demanded that Britain together with the United States and France should "quickly withdraw their armed forces—their warships, military aircraft and marines stationed in the Yangtse and Whangpoo Rivers and other parts of China—from China's territorial inland waters, seas, land and air and that they refrain from helping the enemy of the Chinese people to wage civil war." In private, however, the CCP leader noted that the *Amethyst* event "seemed an accident and Britain even made no protest." Therefore, he insisted that, "except for using this incident to educate the people, we actually had no need to make too much of it."[23]

Zhou Enlai was directly involved in the resolution of the crisis. On May 5, he sent an instruction on behalf of the CCP Central Committee to the party's Nanjing Municipal Committee, asking officials there to negotiate with the commander of the *Amethyst* in the name of the PLA's Zhenjiang Front Command. If people from the British Embassy in Nanjing participated in the negotiations, Zhou continued, the party should treat them not as diplomats but as individuals assisting the wounded crew.[24]

On the whole, the CCP's policy toward Britain in the late 1940s was characterized by common sense and pragmatism. Despite occasional anti-imperialist rhetoric against the British, which was more often directed at a domestic audience, the party adopted a flexible and realistic policy in its dealings with Britain as demonstrated in the cases of Hong Kong and trade.

The difference between the CCP's attitudes toward the United States and Britain is illuminating because it shows that although ideology and historical memory helped shape the CCP's foreign policy, geopolitical and military-security calculations were of overriding significance. Although the party viewed both Washington and London as reactionary and deplored their extraction of imperialist rights from China and their intervention in the Russian Revolution, it considered America more dangerous than Britain in the late 1940s simply because the United States actively supported the Nationalists, whereas the United Kingdom remained neutral in the Chinese civil conflict.

The Marxist-Leninist teachings to exploit contradictions between capitalist countries also underscored the difference in the CCP's treatment of the two Western powers. CCP leaders had often stressed to the rank and file of the party the importance of identifying their principal enemy at any particular moment and forming the broadest possible united front against it. As early as 1940, Mao had developed the concept of "limited alliances." He contended that in dealing with China's main enemy it was necessary to unite with all possible forces, even the enemies of China's principal foe, and to treat alliances formed in the process as limited and temporary. He asked the party "to make use of contradictions, win over the many, oppose the few and crush our enemies one by one."[25]

Zhang Wentian, the party theoretician, said in August 1940 that it would be "very beneficial" for the revolutionary cause if there was disunity within reactionary forces. The Chinese Communists should "take full advantage" of contradictions inside the enemy ranks. To fail to do so would be "incorrigibly foolish." He cited Stalin's exploitation of contradictions between imperialist powers as the "best example" in this regard.[26]

In a message to the party's Northeast Bureau on November 23, 1948, Zhou Enlai contended that the purpose for not recognizing the diplomatic relationship between the KMT and such Western countries as the United States, Britain, and France was to ensure the party's initiative in foreign policy. It did not mean that the party would establish no diplomatic relations with those Western nations forever, nor did it indicate that the party would deal with them without difference.[27]

Furthermore, the CCP's united-front strategy reflected the Chinese traditional practice of "playing one barbarian off against another."[28] During the Opium Wars officials of the Qing dynasty had contemplated the possibility of pitting the Americans against other powers, especially the British. Later, in its effort to abolish extraterritoriality in the late 1920s, the Nationalist government attempted to exploit contradictions between Britain, France, and the United States. These historical parallels would be inescapable to Mao and his lieutenants, who took history seriously. The attempt to drive a wedge between the United States and Britain (also between Washington and Taipei) would be a consistent goal in the CCP's foreign policy later.

PRE-1949 CCP-SOVIET RELATIONS

The CCP's relationship with the Soviet Union before 1949 cannot be described as cordial. Stalin had long been suspicious of Chinese Communist strength and strategy. Both ideological and historical factors were behind the Soviet leader's skepticism. Stalin did not appreciate Mao's stress on the rural area as the base of revolution. Mao did not follow the Soviet pattern dogmatically; instead, he combined general Marxist-Leninist principles with particular Chinese conditions. He achieved domination within the CCP only after the disastrous leadership of the Soviet protégé Wang Ming and his Russian advisor had caused the party to lose its southern base region and to embark on the Long March. Mao's agrarian-based struggle against the Nationalists had developed and endured without Soviet endorsement. When Zhou Enlai was in Moscow in early 1940 for medical treatment, he recounted Wang Ming's errors to the Comintern leader Georgi Dimitrov, who showed surprise at Zhou's story. At the time, people in the Comintern worried that the Chinese Communists might distance themselves too far from the working class by focusing on the countryside. Zhou explained to them that, although operating in rural areas, the CCP could maintain its proletariat outlook because it had experienced a long struggle and had Mao as its leader. In a talk with American Ambassador Patrick J. Hurley in 1944, Molotov went so far as to suggest that Mao's forces "were related to Communism in no way at all. It was merely a way of expressing dissatisfaction with their economic condition and they would forget this political inclination when their economic condition improved."[29]

Stalin had been burned in the Far East in 1927 when he tried unsuccessfully to ride the tide of Asian nationalism and revolution. Soviet and Comintern mishandling of the Chinese situation had not only damaged the Communist position in China but had also colored Stalin's future perceptions to the point that he had simply precluded future defeats by refusing to reinvest Soviet energies and resources in an Asian revolution. Frustrated by his inability to achieve his goals by working with forces that eluded his total control, the Soviet leader must have decided not to attempt again any similar exercise in cooperation with unreliable Asian Nationalists and Communists. After 1927, Comintern influence declined markedly in the Chinese Communist movement.[30]

During World War II, Stalin provided substantial aid to Chiang Kai-shek in an effort to secure the safety of his eastern flank against Japan.[31] He dispatched General Vasilii Chuikov as military advisor to Chiang.[32] Meanwhile, the Comintern urged Mao to improve relations with the Nationalists. In early 1941, the Wannan incident occurred. Chiang's troops assaulted the headquarters of the Communist New Fourth Army in southern Anhui, arresting its commanders. Mao decided upon a strong reaction, but the Comintern leader Dimitrov instructed the CCP to display restraint. Soviet Ambassador Aleksandr Paniushkin and General Chuikov advised Zhou Enlai in the same vein in Chongqing, the wartime Chinese capital. Mao asked Zhou to tell Chuikov in February 1941 that the Soviet Union should not be lured into Chiang's trap and that the attacks must be retaliated against. This was the first time that Mao ever directly challenged the directions of Stalin and the Comintern.[33]

In an effort to rid the party of dogmatism and "foreign formalism" and to develop a Maoist version of Marxism independent of the Soviet model, Mao launched the Zhengfeng (rectification) Movement in 1942. The campaign had both doctrinal and practical purposes: to establish the authority of Mao Zedong thought and to develop a self-sufficient and independent party capable of survival and expansion. It represented the beginning of the cult of Mao Zedong thought as serious study of his writings became a requirement for all party cadres.[34]

In April 1945, Moscow abrogated its neutrality treaty with Japan. Soon afterward, Mao approved an important party guideline, which concluded that with the termination of the Soviet-Japanese treaty great changes could be expected in the Far East. In the past, the document pointed out, because such a treaty existed, the party had concentrated its favorable propaganda on American victories in the Pacific. This had created many illusions about the United States in the minds of party members and other people. To overcome these illusions, the party should devote more publicity to Soviet strength and assistance to China.[35]

After the Soviet entry into the Pacific War, Mao spoke in Yanan on August 13, 1945, praising the Soviet contribution to China's war against Japan. At the same time, however, the CCP leader did not predict whether Stalin would supply direct or indirect aid to the Chinese Communists. Instead, Mao stressed the importance of self-reliance. He asked the party "to rely on our own force to defeat all internal and external reactionaries."[36] Here, Mao actually was setting the basic tone for the CCP's future policy toward the Soviet Union: while seeking cooperation with Stalin, the party would base its policy upon the principle of self-reliance and not subject itself to the constraints of Soviet foreign policy.

Post–World War II Soviet policy toward China was marked by Stalin's distrust of the CCP's power and overestimation of the possibility of U.S. military intervention in China. Cold War tensions influenced Stalin's thinking. Just as the Americans tended to suspect Soviet intentions in China, the Kremlin developed a tendency to be unnecessarily wary of U.S. motives in the Far East. Stalin cooperated with the United States in efforts to bring about negotiations between the CCP and the Nationalists at the end of August 1945. In a telegram to the CCP, Stalin urged Mao to start talks with Chiang, insisting that China should adopt a road of peaceful development. At the time, the Soviet leader judged that the CCP was no match for the U.S.-backed Nationalist army and that a civil war in China would eventually involve a direct Soviet-American military confrontation. During the early stage of the Marshall Mission, the Kremlin warned the CCP that it should avoid civil war; otherwise, the American army and air force would intervene.[37]

Mao had different estimates of Chiang's strength. He claimed in December 1947: "From the day Chiang Kai-shek started his counter-revolutionary war we said that we not only must defeat him but can defeat him. . . . If we had shown weakness or given ground and had not dared to rise resolutely to oppose counter-revolutionary war with revolutionary war, China would have become a world of darkness and the future of our nation would have been forfeited."[38]

After moving his headquarters to Chengnanzhuang, Fuping County, Hebei Province in April 1948, Mao decided to visit the Soviet Union.[39] As Mao's bodyguard Li Yinqiao recalled, the CCP leader told him at Chengnanzhuang, "I want to visit the Soviet Union in order to persuade Stalin to take the lead in recognizing our new government." Regarding the creation of the new regime, Mao contended: "We should be prepared not only domestically but also internationally. The United States is behind Chiang Kai-shek, and will not support us. The Soviet Union can support us. If the Soviet Union takes the lead, other socialist countries will follow suit."[40] Mao sent a telegram to Stalin informing him of his intentions to visit Moscow. The Soviet leader replied that, since the Chinese civil war was at a critical juncture, it would be better for Mao, as commander of the Chinese Communist army, not to leave China at the moment. If there were important issues that needed to be discussed, Stalin continued, he would send a Politburo member as his representative to China. Mao accepted Stalin's suggestion.[41]

In May 1948, Mao moved to Xibaipo, Pingshan County, Hebei Province. Because the location was too close to the Nationalist-controlled Baoding, it was unsafe for the Soviet Union to send people there. Therefore, not until January 1949, when the CCP had occupied Tianjin and Baoding, did Stalin dispatch Anastas Mikoyan to Xibaipo. During his stay in China from January 31 to February 7, the Soviet visitor held discussions with Mao, Liu Shaoqi, Zhou Enlai, Zhu De, and Ren Bishi. Mao explained to Mikoyan China's internal situation and his plans for the new government. Zhou discussed with the Soviet official a wide range of issues, including his preparations for post-civil-war economic reconstruction, transportation recovery, foreign relations, and international trade.[42] This encounter left a deep impression on Mikoyan, who later remarked that "Zhou will be an excellent premier for China's new government."[43]

"LEANING TO ONE SIDE"

On June 30, 1949, Mao proclaimed that China would lean to one side in his famous "On the People's Democratic Dictatorship" speech: "Externally, unite in a common struggle with those nations of the world which treat us as equal and unite with the peoples of all countries. That is, ally ourselves with the Soviet Union, with the People's Democratic countries, and with the proletariat and the broad masses of the people in all other countries."[44]

Western scholars have different interpretations of Mao's "leaning to one side" policy. Peter Van Ness argues that Mao's statement represented "an essentially black and white—with us or against us—view of world politics."[45] Robert R. Simmons disagrees with this view of a clear-cut CCP policy. Stressing implied and potential Sino-Soviet problems, Simmons contends that, "rather than being a black-and-white presentation of reality," the speech actually tried to create "a middle road between wholeheartedly joining with the seemingly logical ally (Russia) and rejecting it in favor of Western aid."[46]

As to the role of ideology in the making of Mao's policy, Tang Tsou points out, "Ideology convictions . . . combined with hostility toward the United States [led] Mao to make a sharp break with the age-old Chinese policy of using barbarians to control barbarians."[47] David Allan Mayers, however, tends to downplay the importance of principles. In his view, Mao's pronouncement "constituted only cautious acceptance of Soviet leadership and limited dependence on Moscow . . . flexibility informed by economic and diplomatic requirements rather than rigid adherence to principles or unqualified devotion to ideology would characterize Chinese policy."[48]

I argue that a blend of ideological idealism, practical realism as well as historical experience, underlined Mao's choice. Doctrinal factors can not be underrated in understanding Mao's decision. The strategy of "leaning to one side" represented a logical evolution in the CCP's policy over past years. For a long time, Mao and other CCP leaders had been emphasizing that the Chinese revolution was an inseparable part of the world proletarian revolution initiated by the Soviet Union. They regarded their struggle against Chiang and his "master," the United States, as a continuation of the anti-imperialist cause started by Lenin and Stalin. As Liu Shaoqi said, "The Great October Revolution opened up a new era in human history and began to change the face of the world. . . . The victory of the Chinese revolution further changed the face of the world . . . made a very big breach on the imperialist front in the East and dealt a fatal blow to the imperialist colonial system." To the CCP leaders, there was no "fence sitting" or "third road" between the Soviet Union and the United States.[49]

Although Communist doctrines emphasized the basic thrust of Mao's speech, realistic considerations of balancing against the perceived U.S. threat as well as economic needs played a more important role. The CCP's decision stemmed from its immediate concern with the danger of American intervention, a conviction reinforced by perceived historical lessons. Washington's long-term support of Chiang had left a deep distrust of U.S.

intentions in CCP leaders. The U.S. plan to rehabilitate Japan worried the Chinese Communists. In January 1949, Mao warned the party that Washington was fostering "the forces of aggression in Japan."[50] The economic blockade by Chiang with American acquiescence left the CCP no choice but to seek economic assistance from the Soviet Union and other socialist countries.

Mao's reading of history strengthened his determination to join the Soviet side. When explaining his position, Mao said: "The forty years' experience of Sun Yat-sen and the twenty-eight years' experience of the Communist Party taught us to lean to one side. . . . Throughout his life, Sun Yat-sen appealed countless times to the capitalist countries for help and got nothing but heartless rebuffs. Only once in his life did Sun Yat-sen receive foreign help, and that was Soviet help."[51]

Mao's address served several purposes. First, it was designed to win the trust of Stalin, who was afraid that Mao might become another Tito. The Soviet party chief had already discovered with Tito the problems he would face with a Communist neighbor who had forged victory on his own and governed without Soviet tutelage or control. As Mao revealed some years afterward, "After the victory of revolution, Stalin suspected China being a Yugoslavia, and that I would become a second Tito." It was during the Korean War in the winter of 1950, Mao recalled, that Stalin "came to believe that we were not Tito, not Yugoslavia."[52]

Second, Mao wanted to indicate to Washington that there was no chance to infiltrate politically into China. As Zhou Enlai later explained, without Mao's clear statement, the imperialists might harbor illusions about the Chinese Communists. American Ambassador John Stuart was in Nanjing at the time looking for opportunities to "Zhuankongzi" (infiltrate), Zhou said. Mao's speech poured "cold water" on these people who had illusions.[53]

Third, Mao's address was directed at those "democratic individualists," "who still cherished certain illusions about the relations between China and the imperialist countries, especially between China and the United States."[54] These were the people on whom American Secretary of State Dean Acheson had pinned his hope in his white paper on China and who, the CCP leadership feared, might act as imperialist agents or fifth columnists to subvert the Chinese Revolution.

Finally, Mao was preparing the way for Liu Shaoqi's secret visit to the Soviet Union in July. Liu's mission was to explain the Chinese situation to the Soviets to obtain their understanding and support. At the Soviet capital, Liu reported on the CCP's policies and the politburo of the Soviet

Communist party held a special meeting to discuss Liu's report. Stalin reviewed the world situation after World War II, commenting on the characteristics of current international conflicts and pointing out the danger of a new global war as well as the possibility of preventing and checking such a war. After praising the achievements of the CCP, the Soviet leader also apologized for not having helped the Chinese comrades much and admitted that he did not know China well.[55]

Liu informed Stalin that the CCP planned to form the Central People's Government in January 1950. Because the CCP was making rapid military progress in the civil war, Stalin was eager to know when and where Mao was going to establish his government. The Soviet leader claimed that "a country should not be without a government for long; otherwise foreign powers will seize the opportunity to intervene" (my translation). If that happened, Stalin warned, China "will be in a passive position." Liu notified the CCP Central Committee of Stalin's warning. Accordingly, Mao speeded up the process of creating a new government.[56]

Liu's visit produced substantial progress in CCP-Soviet relations, especially on the issues of Xinjiang (Sinkiang) and Soviet assistance to the CCP. Xinjiang is located in northwestern China, adjacent to Russian Central Asia. Historically, the Russians had regarded Xinjiang as their sphere of interest. In the late nineteenth and early twentieth centuries, there had been clashes between China and Russia in the northern part of Xinjiang. When the Bolsheviks seized power in Russia in 1917, Lenin recognized China's sovereignty over Xinjiang, but the Soviets had always been nervous about Xinjiang being controlled by a hostile force. In 1941, Sheng Shicai, the local ruler in Xinjiang, switched allegiance to the Chiang Kai-shek government and began to crack down on Communists. As a result, Moscow began to promote pro-Soviet forces in northern Xinjiang, which staged a successful revolt in 1944, establishing a revolutionary government in the area. When Liu was in Moscow, Soviet officials informed him that the United States was instigating Muslim Nationalist units in northwestern China to form an "Islamic state" in Xinjiang. If that happened, the Soviets warned Liu, China's domestic issue would become an international one. They suggested that the CCP liberate Xinjiang as soon as possible and offered to let the pro-Soviet regime in northern Xinjiang cooperate with the CCP's effort. Accordingly, Deng Liqun, a member of Liu's delegation, left Moscow on August 9 for northern Xinjiang as the CCP representative to establish contact with the revolutionary government there. The reason for Stalin's eagerness to cooperate with the CCP in Xinjiang, as Deng later recalled, was that the Soviet leader was afraid of American intervention in that area, which would threaten Soviet Central Asia.[57]

As to Liu's request for Soviet aid, Stalin promised to help the CCP modernize its armed forces and to send experts and technicians to assist in China's economic reconstruction. He agreed to let the CCP's air force and naval delegations come to Moscow to work out details regarding Soviet assistance, including the establishment of an air force academy and a naval school in China. When Liu left the Soviet capital for China on August 18, ninety-six Soviet specialists traveled with him, including Iran Vladimirovich Kovalev, the Soviet general adviser.[58]

It is clear from Liu's talks in Moscow that Stalin was apprehensive about the situation in China and was primarily concerned with the possibility that the United States would exploit the fluid Chinese conditions to intervene. He was willing to assist Mao mainly for security considerations. To some extent, Soviet perceptions of American intentions in China influenced the CCP's attitude toward the United States. Liu's trip was an important event in CCP-Soviet relations; it established the basic Sino-Soviet strategic unity in East Asia and paved the way for the later more official visit to Moscow by Mao.

After the establishment of the People's Republic of China, the Soviet Union was the first country to recognize the new nation. To further solidify Sino-Soviet solidarity, Mao himself visited Moscow between December 16, 1949, and February 17, 1950. In Mao's mind, major aims of this journey were to conclude a Sino-Soviet alliance treaty to replace the old Sino-Soviet Treaty of 1945 and to deter the perceived American threat. As Mao explained to the CCP Central Committee on January 3, 1950, his trip "would put the People's Republic in a more favorable position, forcing capitalist countries to submit to our terms, to recognize China, to abolish old treaties, and to conclude new treaties." The visit, Mao believed, "would make capitalist countries dare not to take rash actions against us."[59]

During his stay in the Soviet capital, it was Mao who first raised the issue of a Sino-Soviet alliance treaty with his Soviet hosts.[60] After securing Stalin's agreement, Mao summoned Zhou Enlai to the Soviet capital to hammer out the details of the treaty. At Zhou's insistence, the treaty included an explicit mutual military commitment: "If one side is attacked by Japan or its ally, the other side must devote all its efforts to providing military and other assistance."[61] The two countries also signed agreements on Soviet loans, the China-Changchun railroad, Lushun, Dalian, and other matters.

The Chinese leaders were satisfied with the results of their Moscow trip for it institutionalized Mao's diplomatic strategy of "leaning to one side" in the form of the Sino-Soviet Friendship and Alliance Treaty. As Zhou Enlai said at the conclusion of the Soviet visit, Sino-Soviet treaties and agreements had aborted the attempt by imperialists headed by the United States to divide Sino-Soviet relations. They would "make the Chinese people no longer feel isolated and [would] help rehabilitate and develop the Chinese economy."[62]

The formation of the Sino-Soviet alliance lends credence to Stephen Walt's theory of alliances, which posits that "balancing is far more common than bandwagoning" in alliance behavior and "ideology is less powerful than balancing as a motive for alignment."[63] Ideology played a role in the forging of the Sino-Soviet alignment, but not a decisive one, for without the perceived threat from the United States, the CCP would not have entered into an alliance with the Soviet Union despite the existence of common ideological traits between the two countries. As the CCP leadership had repeatedly claimed, they were willing to establish normal relations with the West as long as it abandoned its hostility toward the CCP. Therefore, ideology alone cannot explain the shaping of the Sino-Soviet alliance, and ideology itself can be divisive within an alliance as demonstrated by later developments in Sino-Soviet relations.

Walt also argues that "states ally to balance against threats rather than against power alone. Although the distribution of power is an extremely important factor, the level of threat is also affected by geographical proximity, offensive capabilities, and perceived intentions."[64] In this situation, however, the element of geographical closeness is less relevant than historical consciousness in affecting the extent of threat felt by the CCP. Therefore, I add historical memory to the variables that determine the level of threat.

THE CCP'S FOREIGN POLICY IN 1949

The CCP did not formulate a concrete foreign policy program until the beginning of 1949 when its victory over the Nationalists was around the corner. With the occupation of more and more big cities, the party began to encounter increasing numbers of foreign policy issues, and it began to give more thought to this area.

On January 19, 1949, Mao and Zhou drafted a "Directive on Foreign Affairs" for the party central committee in which they said that because the party had no diplomatic relations with any foreign country, it was natural that it should refuse to recognize the legal status of any foreign diplomatic representatives in China. This approach, they argued, "will enable us to maintain diplomatic initiatives and not to be restricted by any humiliating diplomatic tradition of the past." In principle, they emphasized, the party should abolish imperialist prerogatives in China and realize the independence and liberation of the Chinese nation; in practice, however, the party should treat each case individually according to its nature and circumstances. In general, they concluded, "We should combine principle and flexibility properly in foreign affairs." The guideline also laid out temporary policies on such issues as recognition, foreign trade, customs revenue, foreign business, and press in China.[65]

Mao elaborated these points in his subsequent speeches to the party during the spring and summer of 1949. His ideas can be summarized by three phrases: "to make a fresh start," "to clean the room before inviting guests," and "to lean to one side."[66] By "making a fresh start," Mao meant that the new Chinese government should "refuse to recognize the legal status of any foreign diplomatic establishments and personnel of the Kuomintang period, refuse to recognize all the treasonable treaties" concluded by Chiang Kai-shek. Mao also recommended that the CCP should "abolish all imperialist propaganda agencies in China" and "take immediate control of foreign trade and reform the custom system." After they had done so, Mao claimed, "the Chinese people will have stood up in the face of imperialism."[67]

"To clean the room before inviting guests" was directed at imperialist countries. It was designed to eliminate all vestiges of imperialist power and influence in China. Only then could the new China consider diplomatic ties with countries that were once invaders.[68] "To lean to one side" was a policy that emerged from the special historical conditions of the time when the world was divided into two camps. But to adopt this policy did not mean that the CCP would completely rely on one country and give up its independence. As Zhou Enlai put it in April 1949, "With respect to foreign relations, we have a basic stand: we uphold China's national independence and self-reliance. . . . No country may interfere in China's internal affairs."[69]

About foreign recognition, Mao said: "We are willing to establish diplomatic relations with all countries on the principle of equality. . . . As long as the imperialist countries do not change their hostile attitude, we will not grant them legal status in China." Mao also brought up the question of foreign trade. The new government, he contended, welcomed trade with both socialist and capitalist countries. In his words, "wherever there is business, we shall do it."[70]

The CCP's three slogans on foreign policy were, in a sense, a manifestation of the two main elements of the Chinese Communist movement:

nationalism and a revolutionary ideology. The fact that the CCP had not excluded establishing diplomatic and trade relations with Western countries demonstrated that the new regime's foreign policy was also based on a realistic understanding of China's position and needs.

CONCLUSION

Both Marxist ideology and historical memory influenced the Chinese Communists' basic assumptions about the United States and Great Britain. Adhering to Marxist-Leninist doctrines, which depicted international politics in dichotomous terms, they regarded the world conflict as between proletarian revolutionaries and reactionary capitalists. They viewed both America and the United Kingdom as belonging to the capitalist camp.

As avid readers of history, the Chinese Communists were aware of the Anglo-American imperialist record in China—unequal treaties, extraterritoriality, open ports, the suppression of the Boxers. The Western intervention in the Russian October Revolution sensitized Mao and his comrades to the danger of another foreign interference with their own revolution.

Although ideology and historical remembrance helped shape the CCP's foreign policy, geopolitical considerations were of paramount importance. The party's leaders were not ideologically blinkered. They were sensitive to the shifting political realities and were able to adjust their policy to them accordingly. This was demonstrated by their discriminatory policies toward the United States and Britain. Mao Zedong perceived Washington as the most dangerous threat to China's security and believed that there were three fronts—Taiwan, Korea, and Indochina—where the United States could launch an attack against his country. This sense of vulnerability was determined not only by the image of the United States as an imperialist power and an opponent of previous revolutions, especially the Russian one, but also by the current American support for Chiang Kai-shek in the Chinese civil war.

The United Kingdom had also had an imperialist past in China and had intervened in the Russian Revolution, but the Chinese Communists did not view it as a threat because London had remained neutral in the KMT-CCP conflict. Furthermore, Mao realized that Britain was a weakened power after World War II and depended on the United States to maintain its influence. This unbalanced relationship between the two Western countries provided an opportunity for the CCP to apply the Marxist principle of exploiting contradictions within the capitalist camp. The party adopted a pragmatic policy toward England by refraining from interference with Hong Kong affairs and welcoming the British proposal for trade.

It was chiefly for security reasons that Mao entered into an alliance with the Soviet Union. Ideological and economic considerations also played a role in shaping his decision. The conclusion of the Sino-Soviet alignment reinforced the stark polarization of the international system and limited the CCP's freedom of choice and room for maneuver. It increased U.S. suspicion and hostility toward the new regime.

2 *Perception and Recognition: Anglo-American Policies in 1949*

BRITISH POLICYMAKERS AND THEIR BACKGROUNDS

The British decision makers of the period shared the common experience of the 1930s and of World War II. They had gone through the ordeal of hostilities and were fully aware of the serious social, economic, and human consequences of such a global conflict. The Labor leaders who assumed power in 1945 were not unprepared or inexperienced in policy-making. At the political level, they had been in opposition during the 1930s. As D. C. Watt observes, "They shared in the view which saw 'appeasement' not as the prewar attempt to avoid a confrontation in Europe by the management and alleviation of sources of potential crises, but as a craven betrayal and abandonment for highly dubious reasons of the only system of institutions, rules, and conventions for interstate relations possible for the restraint of aggression and the suppression of tyranny, and the achievement of enduring peace."[1] They had been directly involved in the Churchill-led coalition government during the war. For them, the long wartime government service was not only a useful preparation for office but a major formative experience. The training they went through in the Churchill mode of real politik left a deep imprint on their general outlook.[2]

Of all those major people who composed the Labor cabinet in August 1945, as Raymond Smith and John Zametica observe, Clement Attlee possessed "perhaps the most significant background in foreign and defence affairs." In 1924, he had been appointed under secretary of war in Ramsay MacDonald's first government; three years later, he became a member of the Simon Commission on India. As leader of the Parliamentary Labor party from October 1935, he found himself increasingly occupied in defense and foreign policy issues. Through his contact with such international figures as Blum, Benes, and Negrín, Attlee became quite familiar with the major problems of the European diplomacy of the time. He toured the Soviet Union in 1936, acquiring valuable knowledge of Soviet preoccupations in foreign affairs. At the same time, he paid more and more attention to the development

28

of a Labor defense policy. His basic approach to international issues "was always the idea of a powerful supranational body which would not only review disputes, but which also [would] have an effective force to deter or stop potential aggressors." When he formed his own government, he had the advantage of having served for the five preceding years as a member of the war cabinet, and he presided as Churchill's deputy over its discussions during the latter's frequent trips overseas.[3]

Foreign Secretary Ernest Bevin had solid origins in labor movements. He had played a major role in the fight to commit the Labor party to rearmament and a resolute response to fascism in the 1930s. Although his involvement in foreign affairs had been episodic, the experience he brought with him was by no means irrelevant to his new job. Three decades spent in organizing the dockers and other transport workers had taught him that employment and wages in Britain were connected with the level of international trade and economic conditions overseas. His tenure as the minister of labor in Churchill's coalition government, as Bevin's private secretary Frank Roberts later said, "had given him experience of the problems of handling international affairs at the highest level in most crucial times." He enjoyed the trust of Attlee and had a dominant influence in the Foreign Office. In the words of Permanent Under Secretary Alexander Cadogan, Bevin was "the heavyweight of the Cabinet and will get his own way with them."[4]

A keen sense of power and realism was the main quality that Bevin brought with him from the trade union movement to the Foreign Office. He understood from experience that moralism and idealism were as futile in diplomatic bargains as they were in labor negotiations unless they were buttressed by force.[5] This factor undoubtedly influenced him later in his handling of China. During the immediate postwar period, however, Attlee and Bevin preoccupied themselves with the problems of Europe and the Middle East; they left China policy mostly in the hands of Far East specialists in the Foreign Office.

FOREIGN OFFICE PERCEPTIONS OF THE CCP

As a signatory to the Moscow Declaration of December 1945, Great Britain, together with the United States and the Soviet Union, promised compliance with the principle of noninterference in China and recognized the Kuomintang regime in Nanjing as the de jure government there. The declaration became the basis of British policy toward China for the following four years. Despite its doctrine of noninterference, London was more than ready to provide moral support to Chiang in an attempt "to achieve unity and to develop a strong stable Government on a broad democratic basis."[6]

Before the conclusion of World War II, people in Britain had little knowledge of the Chinese Communists. This situation stemmed partly from the CCP's inaccessibility in remote North China and partly from the blockade launched against it by the Chiang government. During the last years of the war, however, a few foreign correspondents finally found their way to Yanan, the headquarters of the CCP. Among them was a young man, Michael Lindsay, who had served as press attaché to the British Embassy in Chongqing in 1940. After his visit to Yanan, he wrote in the *Times* that Chinese communism had roots other than Marxist-Leninism and that if Mao and his comrades showed signs of becoming extremists or moving closer to the Soviet Union, it was owing to the pressures of the West, especially American policy. His views were echoed by another China specialist, the former consul, Sir John Pratt. Basing his presentation on his son's firsthand materials, the first Lord Lindsay praised the Chinese Communists and criticized U.S. and KMT policies during debates on Chinese situations in the House of Lords between 1946 and 1948.[7]

Michael Lindsay's report is said to have influenced the view of the British ambassador to China at the time, Sir Horace Seymour, who asserted: "It is clear that the Chinese Communists have no intention of abandoning Marx-Leninism, but aim rather to adapt it to present and future Chinese conditions." But the Foreign Office gave short shrift to the views of those old China hands and regarded the Lindsays as eccentric nuisances.[8]

As Mao's force spread across the China mainland from 1948 on, Foreign Office officials began to give more and more consideration to how they should react. Much, however, depended upon their analysis of the nature of Chinese communism. It is interesting to note that they rarely succumbed to the myth that characterized Mao and his associates as "agrarian reformers," a view that had much currency among some American China watchers during the 1940s. The initial widely held view within the Foreign Office was that the CCP was made up of "orthodox Marxists." A minute prepared by the Foreign Office Research Department in February 1949 referred to the "essential orthodoxy" of the Chinese Communists. It pointed out that a look at the roots, development, and methods of the CCP revealed that even if the leaders were not pure Marxists, they were directed by orthodox Communist principles under the guidance of Soviet influence. Mao's subservience to Moscow, the document continued, "was provided in the denunciation issued by the Chinese Communists of Tito and the Communist Party of Yugoslavia in phraseology totally un-Chinese."[9]

On March 4, 1949, Bevin circulated in the cabinet a Foreign Office memorandum reviewing the Chinese situation. According to the paper, a police raid on the residence of a leading Chinese Communist in Hong Kong had produced a diary and a series of notes, which "paint a revealing picture of the ruthless fervour, efficiency and cynicism of the Chinese Communists and provide abundant evidence that, far from the Chinese Communist Party being moderated by any special 'Chinese' factors, it is strictly orthodox, confident, mature, and at the highest level very well organized. There is no trace of Titoism."[10]

After the conclusion of the North Atlantic Treaty on April 4, 1949, the CCP issued a declaration voicing support to the Soviet position in the emerging Cold War. P. D. Coates of the Foreign Office Far Eastern Department pointed out that the CCP's attacks on Tito and the Atlantic Powers represented "the most outstanding examples" of the party's "rigorous orthodoxy."[11] While acknowledging Mao's allegiance to orthodox Marxism-Leninism, Foreign Office analysts predicted an eventual Sino-Soviet schism, for they were convinced that Chinese nationalism would prove more powerful than the ties of socialist solidarity. As early as December 1948, Bevin said that "Far Eastern Communism might develop on Chinese rather than Slav lines." He considered it "unwise to pursue a policy which might have the effect of gratuitously driving a Chinese Communist Government into the arms of the Soviet Union." On August 26, 1949, Bevin told the American ambassador in London, Lewis Douglas, the "Chinese Communists were first and foremost Chinese and that they were not capable of becoming Russians overnight." Later the foreign secretary said in a cabinet discussion on October 24, 1949, "It is possible that in due course friction may develop between the Russians and the Chinese, but we cannot take advantage of this unless we are in relations with the Communist Government."[12]

The protracted negotiations on the Sino-Soviet Alliance Treaty provided a chance for the Foreign Office to observe the Sino-Soviet relationship. The consensus appeared to be that although the two allies needed each other in the near future, they would have disagreements eventually. In this respect, the view of British Embassy official in Moscow Jack Nicholls was representative. To take a longer point of view, he argued on February 9, 1950: "There are encouraging prospects of 'contradictions' between the Soviet Union, which has already demonstrated that failure to accept the Moscow line in its entirety is synonymous with defection to the imperialist camp, and China with its alien civilisation and a long tradition of xenophobia. . . . The seeds of disagreement exist and may even have germinated, but it is likely to be a long time (and perhaps a very long time) before anything is visible above ground." But at present, Nicholls continued, neither side could afford "to admit even the possibility of a split," partly because Moscow needed China to get to Southeast Asia, which, aside from a prize worth having in itself, provided attractive opportunities to weaken Western Europe and the United States, and partly because Mao desired Soviet help in solving his problems of reconstruction and organization.[13]

After the conclusion of the Sino-Soviet Treaty, Nicholls reiterated his belief in the long-term prospect of Sino-Soviet estrangement. "It would be rash to assume that the Sino-Soviet honeymoon now inaugurated will prove of short duration," he asserted, but in the long run, "Chinese demands on the Soviet Union for further material assistance and Soviet expectations of loyal obedience from China will each meet with sufficient resistance from the other partner to create favourable conditions for a real divergence of opinions and interests."[14]

Charles Bateman of the Foreign Office had this to say about Mao's relationship with the Russians while the Sino-Soviet treaty talks were going on: "Except for his ideological affinity with the Russians, Mao is not really very much in their debt apart from the fact that they allowed him to get control of the Japanese arms in Manchuria. . . . We have no reason to believe that Mao would be willing to act as the conscious tool of Russia in Asia."[15]

The Foreign Office, especially its Far Eastern Department, played a major role in shaping Britain's policy toward China, but the decision-making process was not entirely limited to that agency. Other government departments with interest in China—the Chiefs of Staff, the Colonial Office, the Treasury and the Board of Trade—were also closely consulted.[16] From the beginning, Foreign Office policy planners recognized that a Communist victory in China would have far-reaching implications: it would affect British commercial interests in China, the nationalist movements in Southeast Asia, and the future position of Hong Kong. Furthermore, the China question had to be viewed within the context of the emerging Cold War. London had to consider its allies', particularly America's, opinions.

In December 1948, the Foreign Office submitted to the cabinet a position paper, "The Situation in China," which pointed out that the Communists already controlled North China and "it is merely a matter of time before this control is extended." The Chinese Communists were not just Communists in name; they "will adopt the policies of orthodox Communism." The Foreign Office worried about the political consequences of Mao's victory on British interests in the area adjacent to China. First, the spread of communism in China would enhance the political and strategic position of Japan as the most important non-Communist stronghold in the Far East. Washington no longer appeared to consider Japan as a potential threat to security but as a potential help in its Cold War confrontation with the Russians. Certain Commonwealth countries, notably Australia and New Zealand, were scrutinizing very carefully this trend in American policy because they felt threatened by the restoration of Japan unless it was kept under strict allied control. "For this reason," the Foreign Office contended, "besides its more direct effects on the United Kingdom's own interests," Britain "must also watch carefully.[17]

Second, if the Communists took control of all China, the retention of Hong Kong as a British colony, in the absence of strong British naval and military forces, might depend on whether the Communists found the presence of a well-administered British port convenient for their foreign trade. "In that event," the Foreign Office continued, "while Hong Kong might be faced with a vast refuge(e) problem, the colony could continue its life, but would be living on the edge of a volcano."[18]

The Federation of Malaya and Singapore was a third area of concern to the Foreign Office. Communist domination of China, it warned, would move militant communism closer to Malaya's northern border, with Thailand and French Indochina as "poor buffers." It would boost the morale of the Malayan Communists. The Foreign Office concluded, "There might very well be increased activity by China Communist Party agents infiltrating into Malaya." A number of them "are already reported to have reached Singapore." Furthermore, the increased Communist influence in Burma, Tibet, Nepal, and Bhutan would generate pressures on India and Pakistan. The French position in Indochina "might well become untenable" and that of the Dutch in Indonesia compromised.[19]

Apart from those political repercussions, London also feared the economic effects of a Communist triumph. The total value of British commercial property and investments in China was estimated at £300 million in 1941. For an initial period before a stable Communist government came into being, the Foreign Office calculated, "foreign commerce and business generally would be at a low ebb." In the long run, it surmised, "much depends on the attitude the Communists adopt towards foreign commercial and shipping interests, and towards Hong Kong as a foreign enclave on the one hand and as a well-run and well-organized entrepôt on the other hand." The final expropriation or expulsion of these interests, the Foreign Office believed, "may not materialise for some time" in view of their extent and essential nature.[20]

The Foreign Office realized that Britain could not do much to influence events in China. "The only power which could contribute financial, material and military resources for counter action against the Chinese Communists," the Foreign Office asserted, "is the United States, but it seems unlikely that such counter action will be taken or, if taken, will be effective." Therefore, the best hope for Britain lay in "keeping a foot in the door. That is to say that, provided there is not actual danger to life, we should endeavour to stay where we are, to have de facto relations with the Chinese Communists in so far as these are unavoidable, and to investigate the possibilities of continued trade in China."[21]

Throughout late 1948 and 1949, British diplomats conducted wide-ranging consultations with Commonwealth countries, its allies, and especially the United States about the best means of containing the Communist threat to all British interests.[22]

TRUMAN, ACHESON, AND THEIR CHINA POLICY AIDES

Like his British counterpart, Attlee, Harry S. Truman was greeted with doubts and suspicions when he first succeeded Franklin D. Roosevelt in the White House. Unlike Roosevelt, whose worldview was shaped by the events before, during, and after World War I, President Truman had a narrower sense of international affairs. As Robert L. Messer observes, Roosevelt's worldview was "cosmopolitan and international" and Truman's "more parochial and more chauvinistic."[23] Although he had served as a battery commander in the American Expeditionary Force in Europe during World War I, Truman's historical perceptions derived mostly from the 1930s, the era of totalitarian aggression. He was fully cognizant of Japanese depredations in China during that sad decade, and he felt it was crucial to undermine the Japanese and German war efforts. "I have always been in favor of cutting off the shipments of war materials to Japan," Truman wrote in 1941, "and I hope the United States and England will effectively prevent her receiving any more materials with which to murder the Chinese."[24]

Truman was an avid reader of history and biography. As one of his biographers says, Truman viewed "history as a story of men, battles, and leadership, a uniquely personal process with little room for intangible forces."[25] He once told his daughter, Margaret: "Ancient history is one of the most interesting of all studies. By it you find out why a lot of things happen today."[26] His speeches and writings were often illustrated by historical references; but he also tended to misuse history.[27]

It was from a zero-sum Cold War framework that President Truman approached East Asia in the postwar years, which witnessed, in the words of Messer, "a process of change from Roosevelt's integrationist, assimilationist approach . . . to Truman's more competitive, more simplistic doctrine of anti-Soviet, anti-Communist containment." During the early years of his first administration, Truman preoccupied himself with European affairs and showed little interest in China. In early 1946, after reading letters from various Chinese people in the United States, Truman responded, "I know very little about Chinese politics. The one thing I am interested in is to see a strong China with a Democratic form of Government friendly to us. It is our only salvation for a peaceful Pacific policy." From late 1948 on, however, the president took a more active role in China policy. Although he usually delegated it to his secretary of state, Dean Acheson, Truman intervened at several critical points in 1949.[28]

Acheson was very much a Europeanist and had little interest in Far Eastern affairs beyond a determination to integrate Japan into the West. During his tenure as secretary of state, he never set foot in East Asia. As Warren Cohen points out, Acheson's aides, Philip C. Jessup, Dean Rusk, George F. Kennan, and John Paton Davies, were uneasy with his neglect of the Far East, but they could not change his opinion very much until the Korean War. The secretary of state was convinced that major U.S. resources should be devoted to Europe without much diversion.[29]

For policy planning, Acheson relied more on Jessup and Rusk. Jessup had been a scholar of international law and served as ambassador-at-large. "To serve the secretary, either by obtaining information for him or by protecting him," was his purpose in Chinese affairs.[30] Rusk, as Acheson's deputy under secretary, had acted as deputy chief of staff in charge of military planning and intelligence to General "Vinegar Joe" Stillwell in the China-Burma-India theater during World War II. He was a faithful and obedient official and took on additional duties for East Asian affairs as a result of Acheson's lack of attention. Like many of his colleagues, Rusk's world outlook was very much influenced by the events preceding World War II. While a Rhodes scholar at Oxford in the early 1930s, the young Rusk watched Japanese aggressions in China closely and applauded when Secretary of

State Henry Stimson issued the nonrecognition notes to Tokyo. He perceived the conflict of World War II as a tragic failure that must not be allowed to take place again.[31]

Kennan was the department's leading Soviet specialist. As head of the Policy Planning Staff (PPS), he was the chief architect of the containment policy toward the Soviet Union. When planning China policy, he sought advice mostly from his associate, John Paton Davies, who was born in China of missionary parents. Unlike other China hands, Davies was often cool and detached when analyzing China. In the words of Warren I. Cohen, Davies was "much given to analyses of Chinese character reminiscent of the 19th century treaty port mentality."[32]

THE AMERICAN PERCEPTION OF THE CCP-SOVIET RELATIONSHIP

The Tito-Stalin break encouraged American policy planners as they studied the Chinese situation in the late 1940s. They believed that many similarities existed in Yugoslavian and Chinese cases and that the "Titoization" of Mao was a possibility. Kennan was most articulate in this respect. One of Kennan's major principles regarding Cold War problems in the Far East, as David Mayers has argued, was the recognition that, as in Europe, the expansion of Soviet influence in Asia relied primarily on the cooperation of indigenous Communist parties whose sense of nationalism was at least as great as their loyalty to international communism. Kennan told Naval War College students in October 1948 that Titoism "is going to spread in Asia."[33]

John Davies was another firm advocate of managing CCP-Soviet relations. Drawing upon his past observations of Chinese history and foreign relations, Davies concluded that Chinese nationalism could be used to work against the Russians. He called for careful studies of Asian communism on the ground that that phenomenon could not be appreciated simply "by applying mechanistically the European pattern to the Far Eastern scene."[34]

Drawing upon the lessons of Tito, PPS analysts concluded, "Moscow faces a considerable task in seeking to bring the Chinese Communists under its complete control, if for no other reason than that Mao has been entrenched in power for nearly ten times the length of time Tito has." In February 1949, the National Security Council pointed out that the natural points of conflict between Mao and the Soviet Union had not developed, and the "vestiges of American 'intervention' still serve the Chinese Communists as a rationalization for equating their interests with those of the USSR." The current U.S. policy was "not a happy one" because American support of the Kuomintang served to "solidify the Chinese people in support of the Communists and perpetuate the delusion that China's interests lie with the USSR." Given this situation, the NSC recommended that the United States "should avoid military and political support of any non-communist regimes in China unless the respective regimes are willing to resist communism with or without U.S. aid." The United States should seek, "while scrupulously avoiding the appearance of intervention . . . to exploit through political and economic means any rifts between the Chinese Communists and the USSR." NSC planners pointed out two ways to achieve this goal: either to isolate and eventually overthrow the Chinese Communists through economic and political warfare or to lure the CCP away from the Soviets with economic inducements. They believed the second choice was better because a tough policy would push Mao into total subservience to Moscow.[35]

To preserve his freedom of action in China, Acheson also decided to disengage from the Kuomintang government. The secretary of state found the corruption and ineptitude of Chiang's regime disgusting. He told Bevin on April 4, 1949, that the Kuomintang was doomed and that the United States had "abandoned the idea of supporting the regime and were only extending to June 2 a further 58 million dollars under the China Aid Act." It was difficult to withdraw support publicly, but he believed that Chiang's staunch supporters in Congress "were gaining a better appreciation of realities." "The U.S. henceforth will pursue a more realistic policy respecting China."[36]

On April 10, 1950, New York Governor Thomas Dewey telephoned Acheson to clear certain portions of a speech he was going to deliver at Princeton. He read to the secretary the part about China, which said that the "only flicker of hope for China and the Far East was in Formosa." Acheson answered that "the statement about the flicker of hope made him very unhappy." He considered that "the hope in the Far East is to drive a wedge between Peking and Moscow, and to reach agreement on a Japanese Peace Treaty." Dewey agreed to strike out the "flicker of hope" and it was decided to be unwise for him to mention the wedge.[37]

Much can be learned about the character of U.S. policy and policymakers by comparing their approach to the Sino-Soviet Alliance Treaty of 1950 with that of the British. Unlike the more moderate and restrained reaction of London, Washington appeared to be more eager and impatient to make an issue of the lengthy Sino-Soviet treaty negotiations between Mao and Stalin. American officials were more inclined than the British to stress the alleged mistreatment Mao had received from Stalin. In his well-known National Press Club speech on January 12, 1950, Secretary of State Acheson emphasized the imperialist nature of Soviet policy by dwelling on Russian territorial encroachments in China's northern provinces.[38]

The British, however, believed that both sides profited from the treaty and that "the Chinese emerged as winners from the long-drawn-out negotiations."[39] This assessment was closer to Mao's thinking at the time. For the CCP leader, the symbolic and psychological significance of the alliance was far more important than actual Soviet material support.[40]

The British considered that the Americans sometimes tended toward overreaction and "wishful thinking." For example, on December 28, 1949, the head of the British liaison mission in Tokyo, Sir Alvary Gascoigne, sent the Foreign Office a minute that included some information provided by the Supreme Commander for the Allied Powers (SCAP) regarding the Sino-Soviet relationship. The source of this information was American observers in Shanghai, who reported "a mounting Chinese resentment" against the Russians in which even the Communist elements joined, which was causing an apparent Soviet "disquiet over the spirit of obstructionism" among the Chinese. The Soviets, they claimed, doubted that the great efforts required to "renew the solidarity of the Chinese Communists and their faith in Moscow would be worthwhile." The Russians were either "crude and callous" in their behavior or were only thinking in terms of turning Manchuria, Outer Mongolia, and Xinjiang into "a belt of 'autonomous' states" for their protection. P. W. Scarlett of the Foreign Office commented that the American information was "full of wishful thinking" and was "designed to please the assumed views of the United States authorities." He believed that American observers in Shanghai had no opportunity of talking to the Chinese Communists, who were at present "the only people who count." The Chinese man on the street might not love the Soviet Union, but what he thought did not really matter a lot.[41]

ANGLO-AMERICAN DIFFERENCES OVER RECOGNITION

In early January 1949, British Embassy officials held a series of talks with State Department people on how to respond to the threat of a Communist victory in China. It was clear from these consultations that both sides wanted to maintain their interests in China and both recognized that the prospect of recognition and the economic deficiencies of a Communist-controlled China provided bargaining weapons the West could use in connection with the protection of its interests.

On January 6, 1949, Hubert Graves, counselor of the British Embassy, told W. Walton Butterworth of the State Department that his government, before extending recognition, would examine carefully the character of any successor government in China, paying special attention to the extent of its control and the way it would treat British interests and trade. Butterworth said that the United States shared these views, adding that the question of recognition "provided bargaining power" in dealing with the Communists. Graves agreed with this observation.[42]

As the Communists occupied most of China, the Foreign Office began to study the legal and practical problems that would arise. Invoking the policy adopted during the Spanish Civil War, the British government informed Washington of the possibility of extending de facto recognition to a Communist government and continuing de jure recognition of the Kuomintang. To assure the Americans, London stressed that it would "not wish to appear unduly precipitate in recognising the Communist regime" and that it was "anxious to proceed to recognition only on the basis of full consultation with the other powers concerned."[43]

Anglo-American differences over recognition soon began to emerge. John Leighton Stuart, the American ambassador in China, was uneasy with the British intention to grant de facto recognition to the Communist regime. He told Acheson that he objected to making any first move in establishing relations with the Communist government because its leaders were now in an "arrogant mood." He was afraid that the Communists would seek to divide the West by tempting it with economic benefits. He believed that "premature decisions on North Atlantic Community basis may prejudice flexible policy" as well as the "freedom of action of us all."[44]

Acheson agreed with this analysis of the disadvantages of initiating any moves toward recognition and emphasized the desirability that the concerned Western powers adopt a "common front." He informed Stuart on May 13, 1949, of the three principles of American recognition policy: to receive recognition, a new government should have de facto control of the territory; the ability and willingness to discharge its international obligations; the general acquiescence of the people.[45]

Conscious of Britain's large economic interests in China, the Americans worried that the British government might yield to business pressure by according "premature" recognition to the Communist regime. On June 29, 1949, Lewis Douglas, the U.S. ambassador in London, raised the concern with the Foreign Office officials, who reassured him that British business circles were content to leave matters to the government.[46]

There was little prospect of keeping the China issue in a holding pattern when the CCP approached its national victory. On August 15, Whitehall gave the American ambassador a memo that included an interdepartmental study on China. The study reaffirmed the Foreign Office's belief that the CCP leaders were "orthodox Marxist-Leninists" and argued that their current pro-Soviet policy constituted "a serious threat" to Western positions in China and Southeast Asia. But any foreign intervention in China, the Foreign Office pointed out, "would rally the traditional xenophobic Chinese behind their new rulers" and push the new regime "into the arms of Moscow." Therefore, the only hope of encouraging the appearance in China of a less anti-Western tendency was "to give the new regime time to realize both the necessity of Western help in overcoming its economic difficulties, and the natural incompatibility of Soviet imperialism with Chinese national interests." In this connection, the Foreign Office asserted, although hasty recognition was not recommended, withholding such an action from a government in effective control of a large part of China would be unwise. It would not only be "legally objectionable" but lead to "grave practical difficulties" in protecting Western interests in China.[47]

The Foreign Office prevailed over the doubts and opposition of British colonial authorities in Southeast Asia. In a letter dated August 19 to William Strang of the Foreign Office, Malcolm MacDonald, commissioner-general for the United Kingdom in Southeast Asia, warned that there were large local Chinese populations in the Federation of Malaya and Singapore and the three territories of British Borneo. Recognition would give the Chinese Communist government the right to appoint consular representatives in these five countries. The presence of these people would be "dangerous" because it would "stimulate anti-British Chinese nationalism" among the local Chinese. Therefore, MacDonald asked to postpone "as long as possible diplomatic recognition of a Communist government in China." To strengthen his case, MacDonald also enclosed a letter from the governor of Singapore, Sir Franklin Gimson, who was worried that if London recognized the Chinese Communists, the Chinese in Singapore would think that the Communists could not be that bad after all.[48]

In reply, Strang told MacDonald that the appointment of Communist representatives could not be avoided indefinitely. If Britain persisted in refusing to recognize the Chinese Communist government, "we must expect that China will become wholly and overtly hostile to us." "In that event," Strang warned, "the danger to South East Asia would be greatly increased, for there would be no means by which we could hope to induce China to live up to her obligations."[49]

In September, Bevin held official talks with Acheson in Washington. The American secretary of state insisted that the Communists should recognize international obligations in full as a prerequisite to recognition. While restating opposition to hasty recognition, Bevin reminded his American hosts that Britain had commercial and trading interests in China that the United States did not share. Therefore, London intended to stay on in China. Bevin felt that if the West were "too obdurate," it would lose an opportunity to divide the Chinese and the Russians; alternatively, with caution, the West could "weaken Russia's grip." Acheson replied that he doubted "if recognition is a strong card in keeping China out of Russian hands and they will be there anyway." Furthermore, Acheson added, recognition would produce "a discouraging effect throughout Southeast Asia."[50]

It is important to note that Bevin's decision to "stay in China" was also informed by his perceptions of British past experience in China. He told U.S. Ambassador Douglas that Britain had made "a great mistake" at the time of the Sun Yat-sen revolution "by hanging on to the Manchu dynasty." He believed that "in the long run it was better to stay in China and attempt to influence developments."[51]

At home, Bevin found his conciliatory position on China supported by the Chiefs of Staff, who had concluded their study of the Far East on September 14. The military planners believed that "it is of the first importance to maintain for as long as possible the maximum Western contact and influence behind the Asiatic Iron Curtain." The major means of doing so, they recommended, "is by maintaining the Western business community in China." Unless their positions in China became untenable, "the Government do(es) not propose to advise their wholesale evacuation."[52]

On October 1, 1949, Mao announced the founding of the PRC and expressed its willingness to establish diplomatic relations. Five days later, the first indication of a break in Anglo-American cooperation emerged when the State Department obtained the text of the British reply to the Communists. The British note had suggested that "informal relations should be established between His Majesty's Consular offices and the appropriate authorities in the territory under the control of the Central People's Government for the greater convenience of both governments and promotion of trade between the two countries." The Americans were unhappy with the British note on several accounts. First, they were "considerably disturbed" by the use of the term *People's Government*. Second, they believed that invitation to set up "informal relations" could be understood as de facto recognition. Finally, they felt betrayed because the British had not consulted them on the matter in advance. President Truman complained that London had not "played very squarely" with the Americans over this.[53]

The British government believed that because the British interest in China was much larger than that of other powers, the United Kingdom should not feel constrained by their opinions on recognition. Agreement with Commonwealth countries was desirable, however. In early November, a conference of British representatives in Southeast Asia and the Far East convened in Bukit Serene, Singapore, to consider the implications of recognition for British interests in the region.

At Bukit Serene, the previous MacDonald-Gimson line was further outweighed. The Foreign Office found itself supported by the British ambassador in China, Sir Ralph Stevenson, and the governor of Hong Kong, Sir Alexander Grantham. Stevenson favored recognition because of British interests in China. Grantham shared this position on the grounds of Hong Kong's proximity and relations with China. The conference urged that for the sake of the situation in Southeast Asia and the Far East, de jure recognition of the Chinese Communists was "desirable as early as possible and in any case by the end of the year." No formal conditions were to be attached to this recognition although the British government should state that it would assume the acceptance by the Communists of China's existing international obligations. Recognition should cause the strengthening rather than a weakening of resistance to the spread of communism in China. Efforts should be made to minimize the adverse effects of any disagreement with the United States. The British informed the Americans of the results of the conference.[54]

By mid-November, the British government had finished its consultation on China policy with the Commonwealth and Allied countries. India favored early recognition. The views of Pakistan and Ceylon generally coincided with those of London. Australia and New Zealand preferred to postpone any decision until some time after their respective elections. Canada realized that recognition was inevitable but was in no hurry to take the step because of its considerable interests in Nationalist China and its unwillingness to differ with the United States. The Netherlands wanted to delay recognition until Indonesian independence, no later than December 30. The French also wished to delay recognition until after ratification of the agreements with Bao Dai. The British government concluded that as far as Commonwealth opinions were concerned "differences are on time rather than on principle."[55]

During this period, the State Department was considering the significance of the possible development of "great strains" between the CCP and the Soviet Union. A meeting between Acheson and consultants on the Far East held on October 26 and 27 recommended that to encourage "Chinese Communist deviation from the Moscow line," the United States "should keep before the Chinese people the fact of our interest in their independence and welfare . . . should permit American business firms already in China to continue their operations and should favor the continued functioning of American philanthropical and educational missions in China in order to maintain our contacts with the Chinese people." As for recognition, those meeting concluded that it was not "to be regarded as a major instrument for sowing our interest in the Chinese people or for winning concessions from the Communist regime." The American attitude on this question should "not be an eager one, but should be realistic."[56]

The State Department Office of Chinese Affairs advised that hasty recognition by any Western power would entail "immediate and far-reaching repercussions in Southeast Asia because of the indication of a break in the democratic ranks and the aid and comfort given to local Communist movements."[57] Aside from these geopolitical considerations, the State Department was also hampered on the recognition question by Communist actions and domestic pro-Kuomintang constraints.

Angus Ward, the American consul general in Shenyang, and his staff were held incommunicado by local Communists in late 1948 and were charged with espionage and deported the next year. The case had remained an irritant in CCP-American relations. Butterworth said on November 10, 1949, that the U.S. government could "give no consideration to the question of recognition" given the Communist treatment of Ward. The British were aware that the Ward incident "remained a most serious obstacle" to U.S. recognition. The Communist seizure of American property in Beijing in early 1950 further angered U.S. officials and the public.[58]

At home, Acheson had become the target of increasing attacks by conservative Republicans and the China lobby. They laid the victory of the Chinese Communists at the door of the Democratic administration and its preoccupation with Europe. The bitterness at the failure in the 1948 election contributed to Republican partisan anger. The State Department's white paper on China was described as "a 1,054-page whitewash of a wishful, do-nothing policy which has succeeded only in placing Asia in danger of Soviet control." These domestic pressures greatly limited the range of choices available to Acheson.[59]

In December, the British decided to move ahead on de jure recognition of the PRC. Bevin put the issue to the cabinet on December 15, recommending recognition with the date left to his discretion. In a letter to Acheson, Bevin expressed his regret that they had not been able to agree: "We want to keep in close association with you, but we have to be careful not to lose our grip of the situation in Asia and to take into account the views of our Asian friends. . . . We also take the view that to withhold recognition indefinitely is to play straight into the hands of the Soviet Union. We feel that the only counter to Russian influence is that Communist China should have contact with the West, and that the sooner these contacts are established, the better."[60]

On January 6, 1950, Britain recognized the PRC as the de jure government of China and announced that it was ready to enter diplomatic relations. At the same time, it withdrew recognition from the Nationalist government. London nominated J. C. Hutchinson as chargé d'affaires ad interim. Three days later, Beijing indicated that it was prepared to establish diplomatic relations and accepted Hutchinson as the representative to conduct negotiations on this question.

CONCLUSION

The previous discussion of Anglo-American perceptions of the CCP-Soviet relationship and the question of recognition suggests that London and Washington shared the view that it was desirable to seek to drive a wedge between the CCP and the Soviet Union as a way to protect Western interests in China. Both powers recognized that Chinese nationalism was a force that could be exploited to work against the Russians. Both agreed that to keep China's contacts with the West was a way to achieve that goal, and recognition provided bargaining power to the West. But in practice differences emerged. The British appeared more consistent in carrying out their policies, whereas the State Department found implementation difficult. There was a gap in policy planning and execution on the American side. There were several reasons for this.

First, Bevin enjoyed more of a free hand than Acheson. In Britain there was nothing like the American China lobby, which vehemently opposed any conciliatory gestures toward the Chinese Communists. If there was a China lobby in the United Kingdom, it was the business community, which favored recognition in the hope that this would enable them to continue their activities there.

Second, British policy was informed by more immediate and concrete concerns, whereas American officials tended to look at China from a wider geopolitical angle. London had a larger economic stake in China and wanted to maintain Hong Kong's safety and prosperity. American economic interests in China were small. Washington was more worried about Soviet intentions in the Far East. To the Americans, Cold War confrontation with the Soviet Union colored and gave meaning to events in the Far East. Furthermore, Britain had to pay attention to the views of the Commonwealth countries, especially those of India, which advocated early recognition of China, because London wanted to use the Commonwealth as an instrument to maintain its influence in Asia.

Third, the British had a tradition of taking commonsense and legalistic approaches to recognition. They did not expect to change the behavior of another government by recognizing it. As Churchill had said, "The reason for having diplomatic relations is not to confer a compliment, but to secure a convenience."[61] The Americans, on the other hand, tended to be moralistic. To them, recognition was much more than an acknowledgment of facts. It implied a measure of faith in the capacity and willingness of a government to adhere to its international obligations, thus, Acheson's three-point criteria for recognition. The State Department was not against recognition in principle but against "premature" or "hasty" recognition. It would grant recognition to the PRC only with conditions: the Chinese Communists must "moderate" or "civilize" their international behavior.

Fourth, temperamentally, the British were more pragmatic and matter-of-fact. They were less emotional when analyzing China. The Americans, in contrast, tended to be idealistic and patronizing as far as China was concerned. They perceived that they had a "special relationship" with China and felt frustrated and perplexed when they encountered Chinese hostility.[62] This unrealistic mentality partly explained the domestic controversy over "Who lost China?" after the birth of the PRC.

3 *Controversy over Tibet, 1949–1950*

THE CCP AND TIBET

After the foundation of the PRC in October 1949, the Chinese Communists still had enormous problems to solve. Unification with Tibet and Taiwan was high on the agenda. As did the Nationalist government, the CCP viewed Tibet as Chinese territory. PLA Commander-in-Chief Zhu De declared in a speech to the People's Political Consultative Conference on September 24, 1949, that the PLA was determined to liberate the whole of China's territory, including Tibet. On June 6, 1950, Mao asserted that the party's general policy at the moment was "to eliminate the remnants of the KMT . . . to overthrow the landlord class, to liberate Taiwan and Tibet, and to struggle against the imperialists to the end."[1]

From the beginning, the CCP's strategy of unifying Tibet was to try persuasion and negotiation supplemented by military pressures. Mao and his associates realized that to defeat the Tibetan army would not be too difficult but to administer Tibet would be much more demanding, given Tibet's unique geography, culture, and religion. Therefore, the Chinese leaders stressed the principle of *politics preceding the military and logistics ahead of combat.* By implementing its goal of liberating Tibet through peaceful means, Beijing was able to exploit internal divisions within the Tibetan leadership between the Dalai Lama and the Panchen Lama. On October 1, 1949, the founding day of the PRC, Qoigyi Gyaincain, the Tenth Panchen Lama, who was not recognized by the Kashag (the Tibetan local government) as Panchen, sent a telegram to Beijing, welcoming the PLA to Tibet. The Kashag also addressed a letter to Mao on November 2. Claiming Tibet to be an "independent country," the message urged the PLA not to "cross the Tibetan frontier from the Sino-Tibetan border." "As regards those Tibetan territories annexed as part of Chinese territory some years back," the letter said, "the Government of Tibet would desire to open negotiations after the settlement of the Chinese civil war." Mao and Zhu De responded warmly to the Panchen's letter but ignored the Kashag's.[2] The Communist strategy was certainly consistent with China's traditional approach to Tibet. Officials of both the Ming and Qing dynasties had adopted the "divide and rule" policy toward the Tibetans and the Mongolians.

Mao attached great importance to the unification of Tibet and was directly involved in planning the operation. On January 2, 1950, he sent a telegram to the CCP Central Committee from Moscow, stressing the necessity of occupying Tibet as soon as possible. "Although Tibet does not have a big population," Mao pointed out, "it has great international significance. We must occupy it." Because it was very difficult to approach Tibet from Qinghai and Xinjiang, Mao instructed the party's Southwest Bureau to be responsible for "liberating and governing Tibet." Recognizing that the best time to travel to Tibet was between mid-May and mid-September because snow would block Tibetan roads for the rest of the year, Mao asked the party to accelerate preparations for the occupation. "If there are no insurmountable difficulties," the CCP leader insisted, "we should begin the Tibetan campaign in mid-April and take the whole of Tibet before October." He also emphasized the importance of conducting "special political training" among the PLA units assigned to the Tibetan operation.[3]

On January 6, the Southwest Bureau assigned the PLA Eighteenth Army the task of occupying Tibet.[4] The next day, Deng Xiaoping and Liu Bocheng, First and Second Secretaries of the Southwest Bureau, sent Mao their plan for the Tibetan campaign. When approving the scheme, Mao also contended that the recent diplomatic recognition of the PRC by Britain, India, and Pakistan made it "favorable for us to march into Tibet." He urged Deng and Liu to speed up preparations for the campaign.[5] He Long, commander of the Southwest Military Region, was in direct charge of the Tibetan operation. When mobilizing his troops, he put much emphasis on the importance of logistics and supplies. In the spring of 1950, the Eighteenth Army under the command of Zhang Guohua and Tan Guansan began to approach Tibet. Poor road conditions and bandit activities, however, hampered their progress. They first had to build the Sichuan-Xikang highway and eliminate banditry. They did not reach Lhasa until 1951.[6]

The Communist advance frightened the Kashag, which had followed closely developments in the Chinese civil war and had been extremely apprehensive about Mao's victories. To the Tibetan leaders, the godless Communists were more threatening than the Nationalists. The Thirteenth Dalai Lama had warned of the Red menace, and Mongolian monks in Lhasa feared the prohibition of religion in their land after the Communists took power there.[7] On July 8, 1949, the Kashag closed the Chinese mission and expelled all Han officials from Tibet. The move sought to forestall a future Communist takeover, for the Tibetan leaders feared that if the Nationalist government fell, the new Communist regime might first accredit the existing KMT officials in Tibet and then gradually replace them with Communist agents. The CCP immediately reacted to this event. An editorial in the New China News Agency contended: "The Tibetan local authorities' expulsion of Han people and KMT personnel was an action incited by British and U.S. imperialists. Its purpose is to separate Tibet from the motherland, to split Tibet from Chinese territory." The CCP also suspected that India was party to an Anglo-American plot to annex Tibet and had been responsible for the removal of the Chinese from Lhasa.[8]

At the same time, the Kashag stepped up its activities to seek international help. In November and December, it appealed to the British, American, and Indian governments, asking them to provide civil and military support and to assist Tibet in obtaining membership in the United Nations. In this connection, it proposed to send special missions to the two Western capitals. Beijing was very apprehensive about Lhasa's attempt to internationalize the Tibetan issue and was suspicious of Anglo-American intentions in Tibet. To preempt possible Western intervention, the CCP launched a publicity campaign in early 1950. On January 29, a public rally was held in Lanzhou to protest against "the American and British imperialist plot to encroach on Tibet, and the Lhasa Authorities' attempt to betray the interests of the Tibetan people." Speakers at the rally denounced the Lhasa government's plan to send so-called "goodwill missions" to foreign countries and pledged to mobilize the Tibetan people to support the advance of the PLA into Tibet.[9]

"PASSING THE BUCK": BRITISH ATTITUDES TOWARD TIBET

Throughout the nineteenth century, Central Asia had remained a consistent target of British colonial competition with Russia. Having first conquered India and Burma, the British persistently attempted to penetrate Tibet. Fermenting strife among local Buddhist groups and fostering separatist tendencies failed to achieve their goals, nor did the military expedition of 1880 succeed in subjugating Tibet. By the end of the century, London had succeeded in annexing only the Lamaist provinces of Sikkim and Bhutan, located south of the Himalayas. Taking advantage of the Russo-Japanese War, British troops invaded Tibet and entered Lhasa, but they were unable to stay there. In 1906, Britain was forced to renounce the "treaty" it had imposed on Tibet and to begin negotiations with China. Under the Anglo-Russian agreement of 1907, Britain undertook not to interfere in Tibetan internal affairs and to conduct its relations with Lhasa only through China. According to the Simla Convention in 1914 (although China never ratified it), the United Kingdom had recognized China's suzerainty in return for a Chinese promise to respect Tibetan autonomy. This principle had governed British policy toward Tibet ever since. On August 5, 1943, British Foreign Secretary Anthony Eden reaffirmed this principle to Chinese Foreign Minister T. V. Soong.[10]

After withdrawing from India in 1947, Britain's interest in Tibet diminished. In the wake of Indian independence, London transferred its treaty rights and obligations in Tibet to India and decided not to retain any separate representation in Lhasa. The head of the British mission in Lhasa, Hugh E. Richardson, stayed on as the head of the renamed Indian mission. But in a message sent on July 23, 1947, conveying this decision to the Tibetan government, the British promised that they would "continue to take a friendly interest in the future prosperity of the Tibetan people and the maintenance of Tibetan autonomy." Specifically, they would continue their contacts with the Tibetan government by arranging for periodical visits to Lhasa by the U.K. high commissioner in India, or by members of his staff.[11]

In this spirit, London in early 1949 planned to dispatch a goodwill mission to Tibet. In a memorandum to the Treasury Department, the Foreign Office explained the triple advantages of such action. First, although Britain had no evidence of Soviet attempts to penetrate Tibet, there was a risk that Soviet influence might spread there by way of China, particularly if the Chinese Communists extended their control over the whole of Northern China. Second, it was desirable to demonstrate that London had not lost all interest in Central Asia as a result of the transition of power in India. Third, the proposed mission might serve to pry open the door to unofficial British visitors such as botanists and mountaineers from whom "the ends of our own information as well as knowledge . . . may be served." Owing to the rapid changes in Chinese situation, however, London soon suspended this plan.[12]

In the face of Communist victories in China, British policymakers began to reassess their Tibetan policy. Although unwilling to see Tibet fall into the hands of Communist forces, they realized that they could do little to influence developments there. Furthermore, they had greater interests in China to protect, and they did not want to enrage the Communists through their actions in Tibet. The Commonwealth Relations Office calculated that "Tibet's best chances lie in the hope that Chinese Communists will have other matters to occupy their energies for [the] time being and that they may be deterred from interfering by the difficulties involved, provided that Tibetans show some spirit of resistance." London wanted to avoid direct conflict with China and ruled out any possibilities of British direct intervention to save Tibet. "We are not supplying arms to Tibet," the Foreign Office said, "but only considering selling to India certain arms to replace some of the arms she may supply to Tibet from her own stocks."[13]

British officials expected India to assume responsibility for helping Lhasa on the grounds that Tibet was now primarily an Indian concern. Furthermore, they reasoned that because India was less suspect than Britain in Chinese minds, supplies of arms should come from there and not from Britain or America. Any direct action by London or Washington could, as the Commonwealth Relations Office put it, "easily be used to rouse Chinese enthusiasm for aggression against Tibet." Thus, the British believed that India ought to be encouraged to maintain its political influence in Lhasa through its mission there and provide small arms to strengthen the Kashag's determination to resist.[14]

British diplomats in the field also suggested maintaining a low profile in Tibet. Minister in China John Hutchison told the Foreign Office on November 2, 1949, that the presence of Richardson in Lhasa lent color to the Communist allegation that the Indian government in its policy toward Tibet was "merely acting as a British puppet." New Delhi might be happy to see Britain sharing with them and America the brunt of Communist propaganda attacks against imperialist designs on Tibet. Therefore, Hutchison suggested that "it would be in our best interest to fade quickly out of the Tibetan picture and leave India to deal with affairs in Tibet where we are unable to influence developments."[15]

India, for its own part, was reluctant to take sole responsibility to support Tibet. In the words of Indian Foreign Secretary Krishna Menon, Britain was "passing the buck" to India. Interestingly enough, New Delhi, in turn, tried to pass the buck to Nepal. It suggested to the Nepalese Government that it take steps to prevent Communist infiltration. Katmandu was also unwilling to provide direct assistance to Tibet. When PLA troops entered Tibet at Qamdo (Chamdo, Kham) in October 1950, the Kashag requested help from the Nepalese Government in accordance with the Tibetan-Nepalese Treaty of 1856. The Nepalese prime minister considered that Nepal was under no obligation to give military aid to Tibet against China under the terms of the treaty.[16]

After receiving the Tibetan request for extensive civil and military aid in November 1949, Bevin sent an interim reply to the Kashag, merely acknowledging receipt of the letter and stating that the British government would give "sympathetic considerations" to it. As to Lhasa's December request for help to gain U.N. membership, Commonwealth Relations Office officials believed that at this late stage "recognition of Tibetan independence and proposal for U.N. membership must be ruled out." J. L. Taylor of the Foreign Office Southeast Asia Department argued that any direct British aid to Tibet "might involve us in difficulties with China; moreover, if it came to light, it would furnish the Communists with more effective pretexts for propaganda against alleged Imperialism in Tibet." In early 1950, Bevin further informed the Kashag that admission to the United Nations was subject to the approval not merely of the U.N. Assembly but also of the Security Council, where the veto was operative. Therefore, it would be "unrealistic in present circumstances to hope to secure Tibet's admission to the U.N.O." Bevin suggested that the proposed Tibetan mission to Britain be suspended. While rejecting the Tibetan requests, London also eagerly sought American opinions during this time with the hope that Washington "would not adopt a too discouraging attitude."[17]

AMERICAN ATTITUDES TOWARD TIBET

A basic principle of U.S. policy toward Tibet had been the recognition of China's suzerainty over Tibet. Washington did not develop much interest in Tibet until World War II. The possibility of building a motorable road through Tibet to China to transport American Lend-Lease goods prompted the Office of Strategic Services (OSS) to propose sending a covert intelligence mission to Tibet to survey the terrain. In the summer of 1942, a plan for two officers, Captain Ilia Tolstoy and Lieutenant Brooke Dolan, to travel from India to China was approved. The two agents arrived in Lhasa on December 12, 1942, where they presented President Roosevelt's letter and some gifts to the Dalai Lama. To avoid offending the Chinese government, the letter was addressed to the Dalai Lama in his capacity as the religious rather than secular leader of Tibet.[18]

In 1948, a Tibetan trade mission visited the United States. Under strong Chinese diplomatic pressures, Washington treated the mission informally with the Commerce Department acting as their hosts rather than the State Department. The Americans tried to strike a delicate balance of showing every friendliness to the Tibetans without giving the Chinese government cause to take offense.[19]

In late 1948, Loy Henderson became the American ambassador to India. A State Department Soviet and East European specialist, Henderson had first worked with the Red Cross in the Baltic States in 1919–20 and later served as a foreign service officer in the Riga observation post. After American recognition of the Soviet Union in 1933, Henderson was assigned to the U.S. Embassy in Moscow as the senior political officer. These early encounters with Soviet affairs convinced him that the Soviet system of government was a threat to world peace and stability and that the Soviet Union, as a dictatorship, had more in common with the Fascist states than with the Western democracies. It was with this·intellectual baggage that Henderson approached Tibet from his Indian post. When asked by an Indian official in 1950 for his opinion about Chinese Communist intentions in Tibet, Henderson said that, based on the actions of Communist-controlled states in the past, Beijing would continue its conquest of Tibet regardless of Indian sensibilities.[20]

In early 1949, Henderson suggested to the State Department that in view of the changing conditions in Asia, a review of American policy toward Tibet was appropriate. He proposed specifically that if the Mao forces succeeded in dominating China, the United States should be prepared to treat Tibet as independent. In response, the State Department Office of Far Eastern Affairs conducted a thorough reexamination of American policy, including a study of the pros and cons of Henderson's proposal. If the Communists took control of China proper, they pointed out, Tibet would be one of the few remaining non-Communist bastions in continental Asia, and, as a result, it would assume both ideological and strategic importance. State Department analysts noted, however, owing to its geographical remoteness, the primitive nature of its government and society and the restricted character of its contacts with the outside world, Tibet's importance both ideologically and strategically was very limited on a practical level. They believed that future developments would determine U.S. policy toward Tibet. Therefore, the Office of Far Eastern Affairs recommended a "wait-and-see" stand: the United States would "maintain a friendly attitude toward Tibet in ways short of giving China cause for offense."[21]

In the autumn of 1949, a prominent American radio commentator, Lowell Thomas of the Columbia Broadcast System, visited Tibet. According to British information, Thomas commanded "a very large audience" at home and claimed "close official contacts at very high levels." His trip provided the Kashag an opportunity to make its case known to the United States. He was given a friendly reception and allowed various privileges, including that of taking many photographs and cinema films of the Dalai Lama. During his stopover in India, Thomas made several statements to the Indian press to the effect that Tibet was strongly anti-Communist and might be willing to receive an American military mission. Upon returning to the United States on October 17, he said that he was bringing verbal messages for President Truman from both the regent of Tibet and the Dalai Lama. British diplomats observed that Thomas "is clearly an intelligent observer but seems to lack background knowledge about Asian affairs." He seemed "to know nothing of American policy towards Tibet and to be unaware that the State Department considers Tibet as part of China." [22]

The collapse of the Chiang Kai-shek regime had increased American interest in Tibet, but given the fluidity of the situation in China and the uncertainty of the Sino-Soviet relationship during the last two months of 1949, Washington was cautious in responding to Lhasa's request for help. The Americans felt that the Tibetan appeal in November for arms support had come at the wrong time. One U.S. Embassy staff member in New Delhi said that "whereas it might have been possible to do something on these lines a year ago it was now too late to get any arms to Tibet in time to be of any use." To recognize Tibet's independence at this stage, this officer argued, would be "indecent" to the Chinese Nationalist government and "provocative" to the Communists. On December 21, the U.S. Embassy conveyed to the Tibetan representative in New Delhi an oral reply to Lhasa's message regarding U.N. membership. The response pointed out that it was the State Department's conviction that "any Tibetan effort to obtain U.N. membership at this time would be unsuccessful" in view of the certain opposition of the USSR and of the Chinese delegation, both of whom possessed veto power in the Security Council. Furthermore, the Tibetan plan to send a special mission to obtain U.N. membership "may at this time serve to precipitate Chinese Communist action to gain control of Tibet." [23]

On December 22, the Kashag again approached the American government, indicating its intention of sending a special mission to Washington for the purpose of obtaining aid from the U.S. government. On January 12, 1950, Acheson instructed Ambassador Henderson to discourage the Tibetans from doing so. Acheson believed that the proposed Tibetan move "might hasten Chinese Communist action against Tibet" and considered it unlikely that the United States would be prepared at this time to extend aid to Tibet. The secretary of state asked Henderson to enlist the help of Britain and India to talk the Tibetans out of their proposed mission. Acheson thought that if the Tibetans wished to communicate with the U.S. government, it would be better for them to do so with the American Embassy in New Delhi rather than in Washington. [24]

In January, the State Department asked Henderson's judgment regarding the wisdom of sending a U.S. mission to Tibet. The ambassador listed two principal reasons against such a move: first, the dispatch of a U.S. mission under the "present delicate conditions might precipitate" a Communist incursion against Tibet; second, if the mission were sent contrary to Indian recommendations and the Chinese Communists did invade Tibet, the "Indians would be quick [to] place blame on us." Therefore, Henderson recommended that the plan be deferred for the moment. He closed his reply with the reservation that it was possible that "shifts in [the] rather fluid situation [in] this area may cause us later to change our recommendations [in] this respect."[25]

Like the British, American policymakers also expected New Delhi to take the lead in assisting Tibet, given India's location and ties to Tibet. State Department officials told British Ambassador Sir Oliver Franks in December that they considered that the question of help for Tibet was primarily for India and that the United States had no intention of giving material aid to Tibet.[26]

But to Washington's disappointment, the Indian government was unwilling to assume much of a role in helping the Tibetans. Aside from providing diplomatic support to Tibet to enable it to retain its autonomous status, India would not go beyond the point of supplying the Tibetans with small arms. For Nehru, relations with Beijing outweighed obligations inherited from Britain regarding Tibet. New Delhi did not want to alienate its Communist neighbor through its actions with Tibet. Therefore, India consistently refused to cooperate with Anglo-American suggestions that India do more to help Tibet. It objected to the American proposal to use the Indian capital as an avenue for American-Tibetan discussions. Indian Foreign Secretary Krishna Menon told Henderson that if discussions were to take place in New Delhi, there would be the danger of wide publicity. Menon feared that the Communist government would charge that Delhi was becoming the "center of [a] conspiracy" to promote the separation of Tibet from China and that Beijing might "speed up" plans to conquer Tibet.[27] Owing to the negative Anglo-American responses, the Kashag was forced to instruct the missions to the two Western countries to stop in Gyantse at the end of January 1950.

By March, the "dust" having settled in China and the Sino-Soviet alliance having taken shape, Washington began to give more consideration to the possibilities of helping Tibet. On March 1, Acheson directed Henderson to obtain through the British High Commissioner in India information on the nature and volume of Indian military assistance to Tibet, on Lhasa's plans to resist Communist incursions, and on the type of military aid Tibet required. Acheson also asked Henderson's opinions regarding probable Indian reactions to the suggestion that the United States and/or Britain collaborate with India in meeting these needs.[28]

In his reply on March 8, Henderson reported on the quantity and the type of Indian military support to Tibet. He said that the British "have constantly encouraged" the government of India to extend military assistance to Tibet and the present aid was "being given at their suggestion." They had told New Delhi that if India had difficulties sparing equipment in short supply, they would take a "sympathetic attitude" toward Indian requests for help. Henderson continued that the British doubted that Tibet had any real military plans for resisting organized Communist invasions, because the Tibetan army commanders knew almost nothing of modern warfare tactics. Therefore, London viewed the dispatch of military aid more as a "measure to raise Tibetan morale and assist in combating infiltration and subversion which they regarded as [the] greatest present danger than as [a] measure which could conceivably halt [a] full-scale invasion." As to the suggestion that the United States cooperate with India in meeting Tibetan needs, Henderson believed that the Indian reaction would likely be "somewhat unfavorable" because it was politically undesirable from the Indian point of view to collaborate with the United States in joint programs against China. Furthermore, America had been unable to meet New Delhi's own requests for U.S. military aid, such as tank spare parts.[29]

Thus, the suspicion that India would not cooperate with the United States hindered growing U.S. interest in assisting Tibet from the beginning. In April, the State Department received news that the Tibetans were so disillusioned by the failure of the West to provide effective support that they were considering turning to the Soviet Union for help. Acheson believed that this information seemed explicable either as an attempt to speed up Western action on Tibetan requests for assistance or as a reflection of the Tibetans' real intentions or both. Nevertheless, the secretary of state told Henderson that the State Department "would not wish [the] Tibetans [to] misinterpret our failure [to] accede [to] their requests as disinterest or lack of sympathy [for] their predicament or difficulties." Acheson reiterated that a primary consideration had been his belief that active or overt interest by non-Communist countries in Tibet at this time would only serve to provoke Chinese Communist action against Tibet, whereas, in the absence of such action, the cost of a full-scale Communist military invasion against Tibet in the face of geographical and logistical difficulties might lead to an indefinite delay of the Communist action, particularly, if Tibetans military capacity to resist was "quietly strengthened."[30]

On June 9, Supine Shakabpa, the head of the Tibetan mission for peace talks with Beijing, met American Ambassador Henderson in New Delhi. Henderson explained, as instructed, the reasons for Washington's negative response to the proposed mission to America. Shakabpa said that he realized that Tibet had made efforts "too late" to form close ties with the United States, but he felt confident that eventually Tibet could "rely on American friendship." He hinted that Tibet might approach America again.[31]

At about the same time the State Department discussed with the British Embassy in Washington measures that could be taken to encourage Tibetan resistance to Communist control. The British Embassy consulted the Foreign Office, which responded negatively. The Foreign Office said that "Tibet's inaccessibility makes it impracticable [to] do anything [to] stiffen military resistance to China." Past British interests in Tibet stemmed from Tibet's proximity to India, and these interests were now inherited by India. Britain no longer had representatives in Lhasa, and India had made it plain that there was no possibility of giving Tibet direct military support. "Any attempt [to] intervene would be impracticable and unwise," the Foreign Office concluded. Britain was "not sufficiently interested in [the] area to warrant embroiling itself with China and in any case can not get out of step with India."[32]

The United States did not give up. The outbreak of the Korean War provided Washington with another opportunity to approach India. In July, the State Department and "other interested agencies" (most likely the Central Intelligence Agency) were considering the advisability of approaching the Shakabpa mission currently in India with a promise of covert U.S. aid, in the hope that this would help the Tibetans to resist Communist encroachment. They asked Ambassador Henderson whether the war in Korea might have rendered the Indian authorities "more amenable to assisting Tibet." Henderson replied that in view of India's "relations with and concern about" China, he did not see any possibility of a change in New Delhi's attitudes. He reported that the Indian government "would object to any initiative by another power, particularly the United States, to extend military aid to Tibet." The ambassador added, however, that India might find it difficult to refuse if the Tibetans themselves should request India to allow them to procure in India or abroad additional supplies and equipment they might need to reinforce their defense. He favored approaching the Tibetan mission, as suggested in the State Department telegram, to inform them of the American readiness to assist them in principle.[33]

On July 22, Acheson instructed Henderson to contact the Tibetan mission. The State Department believed that the procedure should be as follows: in response to the Tibetans' approach, Henderson was to inform them that the United States was ready to assist Tibet in procurement and financing. The Tibetans then should approach the Indian government, asking whether it would agree to facilitate delivery through India of materials obtained abroad. If India's answer was an unqualified negative, the matter ended. If India gave a positive response, Henderson should raise the matter with the Indian government, explaining the Tibetan approach and the U.S. willingness to help Tibet; he should then enter into examinations concerning procedures of delivery.[34]

On July 24, the American government informed the British Embassy of the U.S. scheme to help Tibet. Hubert Graves, the British counselor in Washington, replied on July 28 "that the British Government was adopting a very passive attitude toward Tibet in favor of India which had now assumed the role of the most active power."[35]

On August 4, U.S. Counselor Lloyd Steere told Shakabpa that "if Tibet intended to resist Communist aggression and needed help, [the] U.S. government was prepared to assist in procuring material and would finance such aid." He added that Washington considered it important that prompt steps be taken because it would be extremely difficult to make aid available in time if Tibet were to wait until Communist attack had begun. Shakabpa asked whether Steere's statement meant that in the event of a Communist invasion, the United States would send troops and planes to help Tibet. The U.S. official answered that the American plan only pertained to war materials and finance and that the United States was not at war with the Chinese Communists and did not have enough troops to meet its own needs. Steere then outlined to Shakabpa the procedure laid down by the State Department, stressing the necessity of Indian cooperation for effective assistance.[36]

On September 16, the Tibetan mission met with the PRC ambassador to India, Yuan Zhongxian (Yuan Chung-xien). The Tibetans started the negotiations by restating their traditional line that there was no need to liberate Tibet because Tibet was ruled by the Dalai Lama, not by any foreign power. Yuan informed the Tibetans that the Chinese government's policy toward Tibet was that Tibet must accept that it was a part of China; Tibet's defense must be conducted by China; Tibet's political and trade affairs with foreign countries must be handled by China. He told them if Tibet accepted these three points, the Chinese troops stationed on the border would not attack Tibet and the liberation would be peaceful. If not, war was inevitable. After the talk, the Tibetan mission sent a telegram to the Kashag informing them of the meeting and advising them not to insist on full independence but, instead, to make some compromises.[37]

While pondering a reply, the Kashag also sent two representatives, Rimshi Surkhang and Lobsang Tsewang, to New Delhi in early October to discuss military assistance with the United States and India. They first called on Nehru, who told them that Tibet was making a big mistake buying arms from India, because this act might precipitate a Chinese attack. Owing to the sensitivity of the Chinese-Tibetan negotiations, the Tibetans did not ask Nehru whether India would permit them to purchase weapons from a third country such as the United States, but they received the clear impression that Nehru would not help Tibet because he desired close relations with China. Disheartened by Nehru's attitudes, Surkhang and Tsewang did not pursue the arms supply matter further with the Americans in India. The U.S. Embassy in New Delhi commented that the Tibetans had "completely lost heart" because of the attitude of the Indian government.[38]

The Tibetan Appeal to the United Nations

On October 4, the Kashag told Shakabpa that it would be very difficult to accept the three Chinese demands for to do so implied that Tibet would lose all its political rights. But, the Kashag continued, because China was so powerful and had so many troops, it was also difficult to respond negatively. Accordingly, the Kashag instructed Shakabpa to try to continue to stall, with the hope of delaying a Chinese assault until Lhasa could reassess the international situation, bring the issue before the assembly, and then communicate their decisions.[39]

Impatient with Lhasa's procrastination, Beijing increased the pressure. On October 5, the PLA launched an attack on the Tibetan positions at Qamdo in Eastern Tibet. The U.S. State Department became very much concerned about the deteriorating situation in Tibet. At his news conference on November 1, Acheson observed that very little information was available on the conditions in Tibet but the United States would view seriously any new evidence of Communist aggression in that area. Several days earlier Acheson had instructed Henderson to approach Nehru to express American readiness to cooperate with India "in every possible way" in efforts India might make to "forestall Chinese conquest [of] Tibet." It was obvious that American officials were associating Chinese behavior in Tibet with that in

Korea and Indochina. As Acheson told Henderson, the State Department believed that the Tibetan developments so soon after Chinese Communist "duplicity" in dealing with India regarding Korea and in assisting Ho Chi Minh in Indochina should leave no doubt regarding the "absence [of] moral principles" in the Beijing regime and "its cynicism" in conducting international affairs.[40]

On November 2, Henderson met with Nehru, telling him that the U.S. government "deeply regretted" Beijing's action and "agreed with India that this action was not in [the] interests of peace." The American ambassador continued that, in view of geographical and historical factors, the main burden of the Tibetan problem rested on India, and Washington did not want to say or do anything that would increase this burden. Henderson added, however, that the United States desired to do what it could to help. In this connection, he asked Nehru if he had any suggestions as to what America might do or should not do at this juncture. The Indian leader said that the United States "could be most helpful by doing nothing . . . just now. [A] series of announcements by [the] U.S. Government condemning China or supporting Tibet might lend certain . . . credence to Peking's charges that great powers had been intriguing in Tibet and had been exercising influence over India's Tibet policies." Nehru also told Henderson that he had seen reports that the Chinese Nationalist government planned to present the Tibetan issue to the United Nations. In his opinion, the United States could be of service if it could prevail on Chiang Kai-shek not to do so because Beijing had charged that the Chinese Nationalists had been active in Tibet, and the presentation of the matter by Taiwan "would give fresh ammunition to Peking." From this conversation, Henderson obtained the impression that, although Nehru was not planning to launch a crusade against Communist China, he had for the time being at least lost much of his enthusiasm for the Beijing regime.[41]

On November 17, Tibetan power was transferred from the regent to the Dalai Lama. This change of authority, as Melvyn C. Goldstein observes, "represented a victory for the faction that felt it was too early to compromise Tibet's hard-won de facto independence by accepting any of the conditions demanded by the Chinese ambassador." The hardliners felt that one more attempt should be made to obtain outside help, particularly from Washington. On November 3, Tibet notified India that it would appeal directly to the United Nations. In the meantime, Lhasa instructed Shakabpa not to go to Beijing from India but instead to forward the Tibetan appeal to the United Nations. Shakabpa sent the appeal to the U.N. secretary-general on November 7, asking the international organization to "restrain Chinese aggression."[42]

The United Nations Secretariat ruled that because Tibet was not a member of the United Nations and because the telegram was sent from a delegation outside Tibet rather than from the Tibetan government itself, it would simply record in its routine list of communications from nongovernmental organizations the fact that it had received such a message. The Secretariat, however, did distribute the Tibetan appeal to delegations on the Security Council. They also mentioned that the Tibetan message would not be issued as a Security Council document unless a Security Council member requested that it be so issued or unless a United Nations member demanded the subject be placed on the council's agenda.[43]

Tibet appealed to Britain, Canada, and the United States for help in the United Nations. The British government found it difficult to respond to the Tibetan request. It had to make sure that Tibet was qualified to appeal to the United Nations as a "state" as stipulated by the United Nations Charter. The Foreign Office's legal examination concluded that, because Chinese suzerainty was so amorphous and symbolic, it did not preclude Tibet having its own international identity. Based on this study, London decided that Tibet had the right to appeal to the United Nations. On November 10, the Foreign Office informed Sir Gladwyn Jebb, the British United Nations representative in New York, of this conclusion. Jebb had reservations about this finding. He told the Foreign Office that because India seemed to have "strong doubts regarding the 'absolute independence' of Tibet," Britain would do well to "modify" its own legal view on the subject. On the whole, the British government stressed the "preponderance of Indian interests in this matter," and, for this reason, it would not wish to take the initiative.[44] It was clear that the British government was sympathetic toward the Tibetan position, but it did not wish to run counter to the attitudes of the Indian government, which had decided not to support the Tibetan appeal. As in the case of recognition of the PRC, sensitivity to Indian reactions played an important role in British calculations regarding Tibet.

Tibet secured a sponsor for its appeal in El Salvador. On November 14, Hector David Castro, the head of the El Salvador delegation, asked the U.N. secretary-general to place the Tibetan appeal on the agenda of the current session. Castro hoped that the issue could be brought directly before the General Assembly, but the Secretariat insisted that the question first be raised before the General Committee for a discussion of whether it should be referred to the General Assembly.[45]

During the General Committee debate on November 24, both the Indian and British delegations preferred to avoid debate on the Tibetan issue. The

Indian representative claimed that there was a chance for a peaceful settlement and that the United Nations could help this not by discussing the Tibetan appeal but by dropping it. Because India was the country most closely involved in the issue, its position was very influential. After the Indian delegate's address, all the other countries fell into line. The American delegate, Ernest A. Gross, also voted for the postponement on the grounds that India had advised the committee that there was still hope for a peaceful settlement. Otherwise, as Acheson later told Ambassador Henderson, the United States would have voted to place the question on the agenda.[46] Thus, largely owing to India's opposition, Tibet's first appeal to the United Nations came to no avail.

Beijing's military assault in Eastern Tibet was designed chiefly to force Tibet to the negotiation table. Therefore, the military victories in Qamdo were followed, not by an invasion of Central Tibet but by another round of the "peaceful liberation" campaign. China continued to promise Lhasa that it would respect Tibet's traditional social and religious customs. While feigning to start negotiations with Beijing in order to gain time, Lhasa launched a second attempt to obtain United Nations support in early December. Aware of the United Nations' previous doubt about whether its first appeal was from the Tibetan government or from a private organization, Lhasa this time made it clear that the second appeal was from the Dalai Lama as the ruler of Tibet. The Tibetan note said that Lhasa was prepared "to dispatch a delegation to the United Nations to assist the Assembly in their deliberations." It also invited the international organization to send a fact-finding mission to Tibet. In connection with this effort, the Tibetan government again appealed to Britain, the United States, and Canada, requesting their assistance in the United Nations.[47]

After some deliberation, London again responded negatively to the Tibetan request. The Indian opposition remained unchanged. Washington, however, showed more interest. On December 14, Acheson directed Henderson to "explore" the possibility of a "joint US-UK-India position aiming at obstructing or halting Chinese Communist assault against Tibet." On December 18, Henderson met with Sir Girja Shankar Bajpai, secretary-general of the Indian Department of External Affairs, who told the American ambassador that India still wanted to delay action pending the outcome of its efforts to assist in achieving a cease-fire in Korea. The Indian government feared that if it now criticized China on the Tibetan issue in the United Nations, it would lose its chance to influence Beijing on the question of a Korean cease-fire. From his conversations with Bajpai,

Henderson concluded that India would not cooperate with the United States or Britain in trying to check the Chinese Communist attack on Tibet. Bajpai seemed to feel that militarily Tibet was in a hopeless position and that there was little likelihood of any foreign power being able to lend it support that would enable it to stop a Communist invasion.[48]

In a December 30 report to Acheson, Henderson expressed his dissatisfaction with the Indians. He told the secretary of state that currently India was determined to make no move in the United Nations for fear of offending China and that it seemed likely that Beijing would "have taken over Lhasa and have fastened firmly its grip on Tibet" before India would be prepared to take the lead in the United Nations. The United States, Henderson argued, seemed faced with the choice of either supporting some country other than India to take the initiative or of continuing to postpone hearing the Tibetan pleas until an "autonomous Tibet" ceased to exist. The ambassador vented his anger: "We are wondering whether this would be to [the] credit [of the] United Nations. Is it logical for [the] U.N. which gave Indonesia which was under Dutch sovereignty [a] hearing to ignore Tibet?"[49]

The American government persisted in its efforts to help Tibet. The State Department on December 30 passed an aide-mémoire to the British Embassy in Washington, summarizing the U.S. attitudes toward Tibet. It pointed out that "should the Tibetan case be introduced into the United Nations, there would be an ample basis for international concern regarding Chinese Communist intentions toward Tibet, to justify under the United Nations Charter a hearing of Tibet's case in either the UN Security Council or the UN General Assembly." The State Department also asked the American Embassy in London to approach the British Foreign Office to ascertain whether Britain considered "any action now feasible." The British reaction to the U.S. aide-mémoire was negative. One Foreign Office official commented that American policy regarding Tibet "is part of the general pattern of their policy towards China: resist Chinese pressure even if only by propaganda." Another official asserted that Washington always seemed to "think that 'action' is the panacea for everything."[50]

On January 6, 1951, Acheson instructed the American Embassy in India to inform the Tibetans that the United States government was "interested in" the continuance of Tibetan autonomy and viewed "sympathetically" the Tibetan appeal to the United Nations. The secretary of state pointed out that Chinese conquest of Tibet in the near future seemed probable unless new and unexpected factors appeared, but he believed that "every feasible effort should be made to hinder Communist occupation" and to give the Tibetan case an "appropriate hearing" in the United Nations. Acheson asked the embassy to determine the effect on Tibetan resistance of the flight of the Dalai Lama to India and whether he would have any utility as a center of support for internal resistance in the event of political turnover in Lhasa.[51]

Henderson reported one week later that he was inclined to believe that the Tibetan spirit of resistance "has been steadily ebbing," and the Dalai Lama's decision to remain temporarily in Yadong (Yatung) was "somewhat encouraging." He stressed that, unless there was an immediate future indication that Tibet might receive "moral as well as substantial military aid from abroad," the Dalai Lama might depart from Tibet and "with his departure all effective further resistance would probably collapse." As to American reaction, the ambassador put forward a three-step suggestion: first, to invite the Tibetan delegation to proceed immediately to Lake Success to present its case and to invite Beijing to present its side of the story also; second, to hear both sides of the case; and, third, to present a resolution sponsored by the United States or some other "friendly" U.N. member in case India was still unwilling to take the lead in calling for a cease-fire and to demand that negotiations be completed by a definite date. If Beijing should refuse to attend the United Nations on this issue, Henderson contended, the international body should pass a resolution "condemning Communist China for using force in endeavoring [to] deprive Tibet [of] its long established autonomy."[52]

While the U.S. government tried to generate support for Tibet, the Tibetans themselves jettisoned their U.N. initiative by yielding to Chinese pressure for negotiations. After intense internal debates, the Tibetans decided to begin serious negotiations with China. The Tibetan delegation, headed by Ngapoi Ngawang Jigmi, arrived in Beijing in April 1951, and the talks began on April 29. About one month later on May 23, the two sides signed the Agreement of the Central People's Government and the Local Government of Tibet on Measures for the Peaceful Liberation of Tibet (the Seventeen-Point Agreement). The agreement explicitly stipulated: "The Tibetan people shall return to the family of the motherland—the People's Republic of China. The local government of Tibet shall actively assist the People's Liberation Army to enter Tibet and consolidate national defense. The Central People's Government shall exercise centralized control over all external affairs of the area of Tibet."[53]

After the conclusion of the Seventeen-Point Agreement, the Central People's Government appointed Zhang Jinwu as its representative to Tibet. Before Zhang's departure, Mao Zedong and Zhou Enlai met him separately in Zhongnanhai, stressing to him the importance of persuading the Dalai Lama to return to Lhasa. On June 13, Zhang left Beijing and arrived in Yadong on July 14 where he presented Mao's letter to the Dalai Lama. On August 17, the Tibetan leader returned to Lhasa. Thus, for the moment, China completed its plan to unify Tibet peacefully.[54]

CONCLUSION

The occupation of Tibet represented an important aspect of the PRC's objective to unify all of China's territories. Given Tibet's unique geographical and cultural positions, the Beijing government adopted political measures supplemented by military coercion to overcome the resistance of the Kashag. Mao applied his united front strategy in dividing the ruling class of Tibet. The Kashag's appeal to the United States and Britain for assistance alarmed the Communist government, which was highly suspicious of Anglo-American intentions in Tibet.

In 1949 and 1950, both Britain and the United States showed concern over the prospect of Communist control of Tibet. But given their different interests, the two Western powers approached the issue differently. Since 1947, when India gained independence, London had transferred its rights and responsibilities in Tibet mostly to New Delhi and considered Tibet primarily an issue of Indian concern. British policymakers were chiefly concerned with preserving their interests in China and Hong Kong. Therefore, they did not wish to infuriate Beijing by their actions in Tibet. They looked to India to take the lead in supporting Tibet. The Indian government's reluctance to provide active support to the Tibetans influenced British attitudes.

In contrast to the British, the Americans were more eager to salvage the Tibetan cause. Initially, they also expected the Indians to do more to help Tibet. After encountering Indian reluctance and rejection, Washington began to search for alternatives to assist the Tibetans. This was especially the case with the Tibetan appeals to the United Nations. The eruption of the Korean War and the globalization of American containment policy gave impetus to Washington's policy to check Chinese actions in Tibet. But the United States was greatly hampered by the limited means available to it. After all, Tibet was such a remote and isolated place, and its major non-Communist neighbor, India, was so unwilling to alienate China by displaying too active an interest in assisting Tibet that the Americans often could not but feel frustrated and discouraged.

4 *Outbreak of the Korean War, 1950*

So far there is no conclusive evidence to show that Beijing was directly involved in the North Korean decision to launch a war against South Korea on June 25, 1950. It is generally accepted that China entered the hostilities largely for security reasons. Since its first publication in 1960, Allen S. Whiting's *China Crosses the Yalu* has remained a standard Western account of Chinese attitudes toward the Korean War. Based mainly upon contemporaneous Chinese sources, including official CCP statements, newspaper and journal editorials, as well as radio broadcasts, the book reconstructs Chinese perceptions of and reactions toward the conflict, stressing the rational character of Beijing's decision making. Owing to lack of access to Chinese internal documents, Whiting's study is weak on the inner working of Chinese policy deliberations, especially on the role of individual CCP leaders.[1]

Since the mid-1980s, however, conditions regarding Chinese sources have begun to change, thanks to the publication of memoirs, recollections, as well as party and military histories in China. Although these materials are in no way comparable to the quality and quantity of Western sources about the Korean War, they do shed much light on Chinese decision making. They all point to the fact that China's choice to enter the war was not made easily. Taken together, they add to knowledge about the role of not only top leaders, such as Mao Zedong, Zhou Enlai and Peng Dehuai, but also secondary party functionaries, such as Chen Jiakang, director of the Foreign Ministry's Asian Department, and Chai Chengwen, chargé d'affaires in Korea.[2] The following discussion of Chinese preparations for the entry into the war is largely based on these new revelations.

As Whiting has pointed out, Beijing's initial reactions to the Korean conflict were more directed at American moves in the Taiwan Strait than at the fighting in Korea. The Chinese media referred to the hostilities as a "civil war" or "war of national liberation." On June 28, Zhou Enlai issued a statement, condemning Truman's decision to send the Seventh Fleet into the

Taiwan Strait as constituting "armed aggression against the territory of China in total violation of the United Nations Charter."[3]

While concentrating its criticism of U.S. policy on Taiwan, the CCP also watched closely developments on the Korean battlefield. According to Chai Chengwen, in response to Truman's June 27 announcement that the United States would provide air and naval assistance to South Korea, the General Staff of the PLA recommended sending a military observation group to Korea. At the time, the Chinese Embassy in North Korea had not been formally established and the appointed ambassador, Ni Zhiliang, was still in China because of illness. On June 30, Chai was summoned to see Zhou Enlai, who informed him of the General Staff's recommendation. Zhou asked Chai to head the mission to Korea. He told Chai that, in his view, it would be better to send the team not as a military observation group but in the name of the Chinese Embassy. Zhou insisted that the mission should be carried out as soon as possible. To facilitate the group's task, Zhou asked Vice-Foreign Minister Zhang Hanfu to prepare a letter in Zhou's name to Kim Il Sung as an introduction for the team. The Intelligence Department of the Central Military Commission was responsible for selecting five experienced and capable people from its military attaché training class to form the group. These people would all assume embassy titles but serve as military observers.[4]

In the following week, Chai and his team found themselves in busy preparations for the trip to Korea. Chai had a long discussion with the director of the Foreign Ministry Asian Department, Chen Jiakang. The talk was significant for it revealed the perceptions of Chinese officials at the Foreign Ministry level, who viewed the American action in Korea in the broad context of Asian affairs. Chen asserted that the Korean conflict was not a simple issue because it was connected with Taiwan and the whole of Asia. Pointing to the likelihood of a world war, Chen stressed that Acheson's March 15 foreign policy address was worth noticing because it signaled that Washington intended to carry out an Asian Marshall Plan and that Truman's June 27 speech confirmed this intention. As for the general international situation, Chen contended that many countries would follow the American lead, whether willingly or not. The recent detention of Chinese airplanes by the British authorities in Hong Kong was a part of that trend.[5]

On July 8, the Chai group met with Zhou Enlai, who said that the embassy's main task was to serve as a liaison between the Chinese and North Korean Communists, maintaining close consultation with Kim Il Sung and keeping Beijing informed of latest developments there.[6] Chai and his colleagues left Beijing on the night of July 8 and arrived in Pyongyang two days later when the Chinese Embassy was officially opened. Kim Il Sung received the Chinese officials immediately, informing them that the fighting at the front was going well and that his immediate primary concern was American intervention in the name of the United Nations. To keep close contact, the Korean leader had a special telephone line installed, connecting him directly with Chai. The embassy plunged itself into studying the Korean situation at once. It had a detailed report of the fighting ready when Ambassador Ni Zhiliang arrived in the North Korean capital on August 12.[7]

Beijing worried about U.S. intervention in Korea. This anxiety was reflected in the contingency plans drawn in July. On the seventh of that month, Zhou Enlai, as vice-chairman of the Central Military Commission, held a national defense meeting, which made the decision to establish the Northeast Frontier Army (the predecessor of the Chinese People's Volunteers [CPV]). The Thirteenth Corps (consisting of the Thirty-eighth, Thirty-ninth, and Fortieth Armies) was ordered to move from Henan Province to the Northeast. Together with the Forty-second Army, which was already in the Northeast, it formed the core of the Northeast Frontier Army. General Deng Hua, who had just led the Fifteenth Corps in completing the campaign to liberate Hainan Island, was appointed the commander of the Northeast Frontier Army. Deng's troops reached the areas bordering the Yalu River toward the end of July.[8]

General Douglas MacArthur's trip to Taiwan in late July raised further unsettling questions in the minds of Chinese leaders regarding American intentions in the Far East. On August 5, acting Chief of Staff Nie Rongzhen, on behalf of Mao and the Central Military Commission, ordered Deng to finish all preparations before the end of the month. But owing to the short time and the heavy nature of the enterprise, Deng's preparations turned out to be more time-consuming than first expected. Therefore, on August 18, Nie sent another cable to Deng, stressing the "urgency" of completing all combat preparations before September 30.[9]

After examining the terrain in Korea and the fighting situations, Deng presented a report to Beijing on August 31 in which he anticipated the Inchon landing in mid-September. The report pointed out that there were two possibilities of enemy counterattack in Korea: first, the enemy might use small forces to land in North Korea for harassing and diverting operations while advancing its main troops northward along main railroads and highways; second, the enemy might employ a small force in the current position in the south to pin down the North Korean army while landing main forces at the rear of the North Koreans (Pyongyang or Seoul areas) so that it could launch an attack on Kim Il Sung's army from both the front and the rear simultaneously. In this situation, the North Koreans would be in a very difficult position. Beijing shared and attached importance to Deng's views.[10]

On September 1, Chai Chengwen was hurriedly called back to Beijing to see Zhou Enlai. Chai gave the premier a report he had prepared with Ambassador Ni about the military situation in Korea. Chai pointed out that the Korean front was in a stalemate and the North Korean army was in a vulnerable position given the geography of the peninsula and the lack of control of air and sea. When asked by Zhou for his opinions about possible difficulties should China intervene in Korea, Chai replied that the biggest problem would be transportation because Korean railroads were unreliable and the conditions of highways poor. In addition, Chai added, it was impossible to obtain supplies—food, munitions—on the spot. This created difficult conditions for military campaigns on a large scale. After the talk, Zhou distributed Chai's report to the members of the standing committee of the politburo. Chai stayed in Beijing until mid-September.[11]

On September 15, MacArthur made a successful amphibious landing at Inchon. Kim Il Sung sent two envoys to Beijing asking for help. The Chinese government decided to send another five military attachés to the embassy in Pyongyang. On September 17, Zhou received the new team and instructed Chai to take them to Korea as soon as possible. On their way to Pyongyang, the group stopped over in Shenyang, where Chai met with the party leader in the Northeast, Gao Gang, who showed him a letter from Mao in which Mao asked Gao to make urgent preparations because it appeared unavoidable that China would have to intervene.[12]

MacArthur's advance toward the thirty-eighth parallel greatly worried Beijing. On September 25, acting Chief of Staff Nie Rongzhen told K. M. Panikkar, the Indian ambassador in China, that the Chinese will not "sit back with folded hands and let the Americans come to the border." Five days later, Zhou Enlai claimed in a public statement that China desired a peaceful environment for national reconstruction, one free from external threats. But he warned that "if the American aggressors take this as a sign of the weakness of the Chinese people, they will make the same mistake as the KMT reactionaries." Zhou pointed out that "the Chinese people will absolutely not tolerate foreign aggression, nor will they sit still watching their neighbor being savagely invaded by imperialists." On the night of October 2, in a meeting with Panikkar, Zhou Enlai warned the United States not to cross the thirty-eighth parallel.[13]

According to recent Chinese materials, Mao's decision to enter the Korean War was not made lightly. He was said to have pondered "long and hard" and considered both pros and cons before making up his mind.[14] There were different opinions within the leadership regarding the wisdom of intervention. The Central Party Committee held many discussions debating advantages and disadvantages of joining the war. Those who opposed intervention or stood for postponing involvement worried about consequences of war. They pointed to the following obstacles: first, the country had not recovered from many years of warfare; second, the land reform had not been completed; third, Taiwan and Tibet remained to be liberated, and bandits and KMT remnant troops on the mainland needed to be cleared out; fourth, the Chinese army was insufficiently equipped and trained; fifth, among some portion of the population and the army, there was a sentiment against war. Therefore, they believed that, unless absolutely necessary, it would be better to avoid war, or China should at least wait for three to five years until it was well prepared to intervene.[15]

Mao, Zhou, and Peng Duhuai, however, were advocates of early intervention. Recognizing the difficulties involved, they saw more advantages in joining the war. The U.S dispatch of the Seventh Fleet into the Taiwan Strait and intervention in Korea confirmed Mao's worst assumptions about American threats. During the final stage of the Chinese civil war, he had included measures against U.S. intervention in his contingency plans. Now he was convinced that Washington had finally decided to commit itself to the rescue of Chiang Kai-shek.

During a Politburo meeting on October 13, Mao said that it was necessary to intervene because "If we do not send troops and allow the enemy to march to the Yalu river, it will encourage reactionary morale both at home and abroad. It will be detrimental to all sides, especially to the Northeast, because the Northeast Frontier Army will be pinned down and the electricity supply for South Manchuria will be controlled. All in all, we believe that we should enter the war and we must enter the war."[16]

In a speech to the Eighteenth Standing Committee of the First National Committee of the Chinese People's Consultative Conference on October 24, Zhou Enlai contended that "if American imperialism prevails over Korea, there will be no peace and stability in China's Northeast. Because half of our heavy industry is located in the Northeast and half of the Northeast's industry in the southern part, they will all be within the range of enemy bombing threats." "If American imperialists fight to the Yalu river," Zhou asked, "how can we continue production peacefully? . . . American imperialism is

carrying out MacArthur's policy in the East."[17] Zhou's remarks are revealing because they betray his misunderstanding of American policy in Korea.
By equating MacArthur's behavior to Washington's policy, Zhou was
clearly ignorant of the working of the U.S. political system and blind to the
disagreements between the general and the Truman administration over
policy in the Far East.

Both Mao and Zhou believed that a war with the United States was
ineluctable. With the American fleet in the Taiwan Strait and MacArthur's
bellicose statements against China, Mao was convinced more than ever that
such a conflict was only a matter of time. He envisaged three possible fronts
where the United States might launch an attack on China: Korea, Vietnam,
and Taiwan. Of the three locations, the CCP leader believed, Korea was the
most favorable battleground for China because of its proximity to China's
industrial bases and to the Soviet Union.[18]

Zhou later expounded Mao's calculation to the CPV's ranking officers:

With the decisive duel between China and the U.S. imperialists being
inevitable, the question is where to do it; of course it is decided by the
imperialists, but in some sense, also by us. Korea as a battleground chosen by the imperialists is favorable to us. . . . Looking at the three battle
fronts, it is easy to understand that it would be much more difficult to
wage a war against America in Vietnam, not to mention on the offshore
islands, than here [Korea]. Here, we have the most favorable terrain, the
closest communication to China, the most convenient material and manpower backup . . . and the most convenient way for us to get indirect
Soviet support.[19]

China's concern about Korea's security had a historical dimension. For a
long time in history, Korea had been a tributary state to the Central Kingdom.
Their relationship had been described as that of an older brother and a
younger brother. Just as an older brother had an obligation to protect his
younger sibling, so Chinese emperors would assist Korean rulers if their
authority were threatened by either internal uprisings or external invasions.[20]
Given its strategic location, Korea had also been a traditional route of foreign
intrusions against China. As early as 1592, Toyotomi Hideyoshi, after having
unified Japan, planned to invade China by way of Korea. The Chinese court
decided to fulfill its suzerain duty to help Korea in order to protect Manchuria
and North China. The Chinese intervention forced the Japanese to withdraw
from Korea in 1598.[21] About three hundred years later, China again clashed

with Japan over Korea between 1894 and 1895, but this time the corrupt Qing government proved no match for a dynamic, ambitious, and rapidly industrializing Japan. Subsequently, through its occupation of Korea, Japan was able to encroach upon China's territorial integrity in the early twentieth century. It was with this history in mind that Zhou Enlai remarked on October 24, 1950: "By using the bases in Japan and inheriting the mantle of Japanese militarism, the United States is following the history since the Sino-Japanese War of 1895, namely, to conquer the Northeast before annexing China and to occupy Korea before taking the Northeast. The difference lies in that it took Japanese imperialism more than forty years to accomplish its goal while American imperialism intends to realize its aim within four to five years."[22]

Aside from the paramount security concern, the fulfillment of revolutionary obligations constituted another important reason for Beijing's intervention. During his meeting with Chai Chengwen on July 8, 1950, Zhou mentioned the North Koreans' past assistance to the CCP. In addition to their help during the Anti-Japanese war, Zhou pointed out, the North Koreans had assisted the CCP in the course of the Chinese civil war. This help was especially valuable during 1946–47 when, under KMT attack, the CCP had to send families into North Korea so that it could wage guerrilla warfare in the Northeast. "We should not forget at any time," Zhou continued," the help our Korean comrades have given us when we were in difficult times. Now they are at the front of struggle; we should support them."[23]

In a meeting with Lu Zuofu (Lu Tso-fu), the manager of the Ming Sung Industrial Company, in late August 1950, Mao also dwelt on this theme of meeting obligations: "In view of the long association of North Korean Communists with the Chinese Communist Party when they had their headquarters in Yenan and because of the military assistance given the Chinese Communists by Korean volunteers in fighting the Japanese and later the Nationalists in Manchuria the Chinese Communist Party owed a debt of gratitude to the Korean Communists which they could not ignore."[24]

Mao further asserted to the Politburo on October 13 that "if the Americans occupy the whole of Korea, the Korean revolutionary force will suffer a fundamental loss, and American imperialists will be even more aggressive. This will be harmful to the entire East. If we adopt an active policy, it will be extremely beneficial to China, to Korea, to Asia and to the whole world."[25] Both Communist ideology and Chinese culture informed this sense of obligation. International proletarianism is an important tenet in the Marxist-Leninist doctrine. The concept of loyalty to friends and repayment of past favors is deeply rooted in Chinese traditional practice and teaching.

Mao initially wanted Lin Biao to command the CPV, because Lin, as commander of the Fourth Field Army, had fought in the Northeast during the civil war and the Thirteenth Corps and the Forty-second Army were all his troops. But Lin refused to accept the job on the grounds of ill health. Actually, according to Nie Rongzhen, Lin was against intervening in Korea.[26] Instead, Mao summoned Peng Dehuai from Xian to Beijing to be the commander of the CPV. As chairman of the Northwest Military and Administrative Committee, Peng had been preoccupied with overseeing bandit elimination, land reform, and economic recovery in Shaanxi, Gansu, and Ningxia provinces.[27]

Arriving in Beijing on October 4, Peng immediately found himself in the middle of a meeting of the party Central Committee in the Zhongnanhai compound. According to his autobiography, Peng was told that Mao had asked those attending the meeting to list the disadvantages involved in sending troops to Korea. After hearing their presentations, Mao said: "You have reasons for your arguments. But at any rate, once another nation is in a crisis, we would feel bad if we stand idly by." Peng did not speak at the meeting because he had arrived late. But he thought to himself that troops should be dispatched to rescue Korea. During the resumption of the Central Committee meeting the next day, Peng made his voice heard: "It is necessary to send troops to aid Korea. If China is devastated in war, it only means that the Liberation War will last a few years longer. The United States will find a pretext at any time to invade China if its troops are poised on the bank of the Yalu River and in Taiwan."[28]

On October 8, Mao appointed Peng as commander of the CPV, and the general immediately flew to Shenyang where he was briefed by Korean representatives about situations at the battlefront and convened a meeting of PLA army commanders. He conveyed to them the party Central Committee's decision to send troops to Korea, ordering the completion of preparations for entering Korea within ten days. On October 9, Peng went to Dandong, a town close to the Yalu River, to check on front preparations. Upon learning that the enemy strength in Korea totaled more than 400,000 and the front force had about 130,000 troops, Peng immediately sent a cable to Mao recommending changes in the war plan. Initially, Beijing was prepared to send two armies and two artillery divisions to Korea first. As Yao Xu reveals, this plan was made according to the suggestion of Stalin. Peng recommended that all four armies plus three artillery divisions and three antiaircraft artillery regiments be sent to Korea at once to ensure the victory of the first battle. Mao approved this recommendation.[29]

On October 11, however, Peng received a telegram from Mao, who asked him to suspend army movements temporarily and to return to Beijing to see him. Mao's sudden change of mind was caused by the news he had received from the Soviet Embassy in China that the Soviet Union could not, as had been agreed, send air force units to coordinate the entry of the Chinese army into Korea on the grounds of lack of preparation. While summoning Peng back to Beijing for further discussion, Mao also sent Zhou Enlai to Moscow to talk to Stalin. On the early morning of October 13, however, the CCP Politburo decided again to send troops to Korea immediately without waiting for a firm commitment from Stalin. On the same day, Peng returned to Shenyang, passing the Politburo's message to commanders of the CPV and political and military leaders of the Northeast region. On the next day, he held a mobilization meeting of the CPV commanders above the division level. On October 18, the CCP Central Military Commission ordered that the Northeast Frontier Army become the Chinese People's Volunteers. At the same time, Mao cabled Peng the following instruction: starting from the next night (October 19), the troops should begin to cross the Yalu River; to ensure strict secrecy, the troops should begin crossing at dusk each day and stop the operation at four o'clock the following morning. To establish contact with Kim Il Sung so as to coordinate military actions as early as possible, Peng crossed the Yalu River on October 18, a day ahead of his troops' scheduled crossing. He met Kim Il Sung two days later. From October 25 to November 5, the CPV successfully waged its first campaign against American and South Korean forces.[30]

Once it decided to intervene, the Central Committee also began to calculate possible outcomes of such an operation. On October 2, Mao mentioned in a telegram two likely results: first, the CPV would "annihilate and expel out of Korea the aggressive forces of the United States and other countries"; second, once the fighting began, China should be prepared for an American declaration of war, for air attacks on its major cities and industrial bases and for a naval assault on its coastal areas. Of the two outcomes, Mao believed that the first one was better because so long as China was destroying the American troops in Korea, the war would not last long there even if the United States did declare war on China. The second outcome, the Chinese leader reasoned, would be worse because if China could not knock out the American forces and became locked in a stalemate, China's plan of economic reconstruction would be endangered, "causing discontent among national bourgeoisie and other portions of the population."[31]

In a telegram to Peng Dehuai on October 23, Mao pointed to a third possible outcome. He argued that, although the American army had superior air support and advanced equipment and the CPV was hampered from attacking urban areas because they lacked air cover, the Chinese army could take advantage of night marches and fighting, and wipe out the enemy separately in movement battles. "In this way," Mao asserted, "we would have the possibility of forcing the United States to start diplomatic negotiations with us."[32]

After the success of the first two campaigns, which blunted MacArthur's attempt to occupy the whole of Korea, the Central Committee telegraphed Peng on December 4, further elaborating on the likelihood of this third development. The message said: "It is very likely that the enemy will ask for a ceasefire. Our position is that they must withdraw from Korea. First of all, they must retreat to the south of the 38th parallel before we agree to negotiate. If we can occupy not only Pyongyang but also Seoul and destroy the enemy, primarily the puppet army [referring to the South Korean army], we will be in a more forceful position to force the American imperialists to withdraw their troops."[33]

These communications make it clear that during the early phase of Chinese entry into the war, the Chinese leadership foresaw three likely possibilities: (1) to annihilate the enemy in Korea; (2) to force the enemy to withdraw south of the thirty-eighth parallel and to settle the Korean dispute through negotiations; (3) to bog down in a stalemate in Korea while the United States used its superior air and naval forces to disrupt Chinese economic rehabilitation. Mao's basic attitude was to strive to realize the first possibility, to be prepared for the second, and to try to avoid the third.

It is important to note that Chinese policymakers were aware of the problems between the United States and its allies regarding the Korean fighting. Zhou Enlai pointed out on October 24, 1950, that if China did not resist America, it would be in a vulnerable position; if it beat the Americans and bogged them down in the Korean "quagmire," it would make them unable to attack China and even disrupt their plan to send troops to Western Europe. Thus, "contradictions within the enemy rank would occur." In sum, the Chinese premier contended, "if we compromise, we will only alleviate the enemy's internal contradictions; if we intervene, we will deepen their contradictions." Later in the war, on April 30, 1952, Zhou further argued that it was important to adopt a discriminatory attitude toward the enemy camp: "There are fifteen countries joining the United States on the Korean battleground. But, if the war took place in China, would there be so many countries participating? This is very doubtful. After all, only a minority of the countries dares to be hostile to us and confront us on the battleground. The capitalist world is not a monolith. We should treat it differently."[34]

Like his earlier effort to exploit Anglo-American differences over trade with China, Zhou's statement was another demonstration of his intention to exploit the contradictions between capitalist countries. It represented a consistent theme in the CCP's handling of the Western countries. This Chinese version of the "wedge" strategy would find its fullest manifestation at the Geneva Conference in 1954 when Zhou conducted imaginative diplomacy with British and French officials to break Dulles's isolation of the PRC.

In sum, a combination of geopolitical, historical, and ideological factors determined Beijing's decision to intervene in the Korean fighting. Concern with China's security constituted the primary motive. Historical memory reinforced the determination of Beijing's leaders. The desire to help the North Koreans out of revolutionary obligations and past friendship also played a role. Mao did not make the decision to intervene in Korea without listening to different arguments. He fully considered them before he made up his mind. Once he had made the decision, though, he carefully weighed the posssible outcomes of Chinese intervention. Together with Zhou and Peng, he was the primary mover in the decision-making process.

Sino-Soviet Relations during the Korean War

Given available sources, a complete picture of Sino-Soviet cooperation during the Korean fighting is not possible, but recent Chinese materials do begin to reveal insights showing the limitation of the Sino-Soviet alliance in times of crisis. Although the Soviet Union in general supported Chinese intervention, it showed hesitation and reluctance in providing the assistance the Chinese requested, partly because of its fear of war with the United States and partly because of its own inadequacies and inabilities.

Stalin's unwillingness to provide air cover for the CPV in mid-October 1950 was one demonstration of this Soviet fear and reluctance. According to recent Chinese accounts, Stalin became hesitant about the Korean fighting after MacArthur's landing at Inchon. He had no confidence in the strength of the Chinese force. He was afraid that Chinese intervention would cause a world war. On October 8, Zhou Enlai, together with his interpreter, Shi Zhe, went to the Soviet Union. They met Stalin at Sochi in southern Russia. After reaffirming to the Soviet leader China's decision to enter Korea, Zhou related China's problems in ammunition, equipment, transportation, and, especially, air support. At the time, the Chinese air force had just been established, and pilots were undergoing training. They were unprepared for combat. The Chinese premier asked Stalin for assistance in these areas.[35]

Stalin expressed to the Chinese visitors his fear of a world conflict as a result of Chinese interference in Korea. He even went so far as to say that if Kim Il Sung suffered a defeat in Korea, he might evacuate to the Northeast of China to establish an "exile government" there. After receiving Zhou's report about his talks with Stalin, the CCP Politburo held an emergency meeting on October 13 at which the decision to enter Korea was reaffirmed. Thus, China finally committed itself to help Korea without securing a Soviet pledge of air support.[36]

Soviet unwillingness to meet Chinese demands further manifested itself during the course of the Korean War. According to Xu Xiangqian, chief of staff of the PLA at the time, in May 1951, Mao asked him to lead a secret military delegation to Moscow with two aims: first, to purchase Soviet arms that could equip sixty Chinese divisions; second, to introduce Soviet technology in order to develop China's own arms industry. The delegation arrived in Moscow on June 4 and was later assisted by Gao Gang, who came to Moscow in late June with the formal equipment shopping list. The negotiations lasted more than four months, partly because of China's constantly changing requests in response to Korean battle needs and partly because of Moscow's lack of resources to assist the Chinese. First, the Soviets told the Chinese that, owing to the limitation of Soviet transportation facilities, they could help to arm sixteen Chinese divisions in 1951 and would equip the rest of the forty-four divisions in the next three years. Later, the Russians said that they could only arm ten Chinese divisions in 1951. As to technical transfer, the Soviets agreed to provide some help to build the Chinese arms industry.[37]

Xu's general impression in the Soviet Union was that, in principle, the Russians supported the Chinese cause in Korea and were willing to provide some help; but they did not want to risk war with the United States. Furthermore, the Soviet Union was still recovering from the damage of World War II and really had difficulty in meeting every demand of the Chinese. During the negotiations, Xu noticed impatience, rudeness, and ill temper on the part of Soviet negotiators.[38]

Aside from problems of getting logistical support from the Soviet Union, the Chinese also encountered differences with the Russians over military operations in Korea. For instance, after the Chinese second campaign of late November 1950, which recovered Pyongyang and pushed the Americans all the way back to the thirty-eighth parallel, Peng Dehuai decided to stop pursuing the enemy. Terenty F. Shtykov, the Soviet ambassador in Pyongyang, however, according to Yao Xu, wanted the Chinese to advance southward. Peng reported his dispute with Shtykov to Mao, cautioning against the danger of "a quick victory and blind optimism." He argued that the war in Korea would be "long, protracted, and tortuous" and there would be risks to the CPV should the enemy forces be able to consolidate their strength. Mao agreed with Peng's assessment, contending that "the view of a quick victory is harmful." Mao also told Peng that Stalin believed that his leadership of the CPV was "correct."[39]

After a short period of rest and resupply, Mao decided on December 13 to start the third campaign with the aim of "crossing the 38th parallel" to deny the enemy the chance to consolidate its position. Peng initially wanted to delay a third campaign for a longer period so that his army could have sufficient rest. Nie Rongzhen concurred in Peng's sober judgment. But Mao took a more political view of the issue because he desired to coordinate military movements with political ones. At the time, Wu Xiuquan was heading a special Chinese delegation attending the United Nations to present the Chinese case. Undoubtedly, Mao wanted to strengthen Wu's position with battlefield successes.[40]

On December 31, Peng launched the third campaign, and the CPV soon captured Seoul, reaching the thirty-seventh parallel in early January 1951. Afraid to be lured into an enemy trap, Yao writes, Peng halted his troops at the parallel. Peng calculated that the enemy's main force remained strong and enjoyed superior equipment, whereas the CPV suffered from fatigue and lack of supplies. The enemy's southward retreat, he assumed, was deliberate, designed to draw the CPV deeper into the South, thereby creating additional logistic problems for them. There was the risk of another enemy amphibious landing at the rear if the CPV advanced further South. Soviet Ambassador Shtykov again intervened, insisting that the CPV continue advancing southward and take the opportunity to liberate all of Korea. Peng rejected his suggestion firmly. Stalin again sided with the Chinese general and recalled Shtykov back to Moscow.[41]

DRAWING THE LINE: THE AMERICAN RESPONSE

The United States reacted decisively to the outbreak of the Korean War. On June 25, the United Nations Security Council adopted an American-sponsored resolution (with the Soviet Union absent and Yugoslavia abstaining) branding the North Koreans as aggressors, demanding a cessation of hostilities, and requesting a withdrawal behind the thirty-eighth parallel. Two days later, Truman announced that the United States would interpose the Seventh Fleet in the Taiwan Strait, increase aid to the French in Indochina, and provide air and sea support to South Korean troops. In the meantime, the United Nations passed another resolution recommending that its members aid South Korea to repel the armed attack and restore peace. On June 30, Truman stated that he had authorized the use of American ground troops in Korea and ordered the Air Force to conduct missions against specific targets in North Korea.

The reasons for this swift and resolute response should be understood within the general international and domestic context of the time. As Burton I. Kaufman has observed, the Korean War arrived "amid a climate of crisis in the United States highlighted by fear of Communist aggression throughout the world and compounded by apprehension about internal Communist subversion reaching the highest levels of government."[42]

Several considerations determined the American reaction. First, American officials believed that the Soviet Union was behind the North Korean aggression and that the West should "draw the line" against Communist expansion in Korea. Alan Kirk, the American ambassador in the Soviet Union, told Acheson on June 25 that the North Korean action represented a "clear-cut Soviet challenge" that the United States "should answer firmly and swiftly." At the same time, the State Department Office of Intelligence Research estimated that the North Korean Government was "completely under Kremlin control and there is no possibility that the North Koreans acted without prior instructions from Moscow." In an intelligence memorandum dated June 28, the Central Intelligence Agency stated that Kim Il Sung's invasion "was undoubtedly undertaken at Soviet direction and Soviet material support is unquestionably being provided." "The Soviet objective," the CIA believed, "was the elimination of the last remaining anti-Communist bridgehead on the mainland of northern Asia, thereby undermining the position of the US and the Western Powers throughout the Far East."[43]

Second, the historical memory of Manchuria and Munich informed the American decision to stand firm in Korea. Very much in the minds of American policymakers, including Truman and Acheson, was the fear that if Western democracies showed hesitation or inaction in Korea, it would encourage Communist expansion elsewhere, such as Indochina and the Middle East. Truman later wrote in his memoirs that, when he learned the news of the North Korean attack, he "recalled some earlier instances: Manchuria, Ethiopia, Austria . . . " and "remembered how each time that the democracies failed to act it had encouraged the aggressors to keep going ahead. Communism was acting in Korea just as Hitler, Mussolini, and the Japanese had acted ten, fifteen, and twenty years earlier."[44]

Connected with this desire to prevent another Munich tragedy was Washington's determination to maintain its credibility in the world. As the historian William W. Stueck has argued, although the United States did not consider Korea significant in a military sense, the country became increasingly important in terms of America's credibility worldwide. In the words of Charles M. Dobbs, by the late 1940s, Korea had become a "symbol" of the United States' resolve to defend the free world against Communist expansion.[45]

Finally, concern over domestic politics prompted the Truman administration to move decisively. The "loss of China," as well as a series of other international developments, had rendered the administration vulnerable to the attacks of the China lobby and the Republican right-wingers. Truman feared that if he did not do anything, he would encounter further partisan tirades.[46]

The Korean fighting appeared to confirm the conclusions of NSC 68, a policy document prepared in April 1950, which contended that the Communist "assault on free institutions is worldwide and in the context of the present polarization of power a defeat of free institutions anywhere is a defeat everywhere."[47]

The Korean conflict also changed American perceptions of the wedge strategy in the sense that U.S. officials no longer believed that a Sino-Soviet division was imminent. Instead, they relegated that possibility to the distant future. For the moment, as Charles E. Bohlen explained to British and French diplomats in Paris in August, it could be assumed that in general foreign policy China would adhere to the Soviet line. Divisions between the two Communist countries might emerge eventually, Bohlen continued, but "we could not afford to predicate our policy on the expectation of Communist China splitting away from the Soviet world." Furthermore, such intra-Communist differences were "not likely to be brought about by Western attempts to wean Communist China from Kremlin control." "If a break should come," Bohlen argued categorically, "it may be expected to come from within." The British official, Sir Maberly Dening, however, did not see eye-to-eye with Bohlen's assessment. He asserted that he did not expect the Chinese always to play "for the 'beax yeux' of Russia" when their national interests were at stake.[48]

On July 7, MacArthur was appointed commander-in-chief of the U.N. Command. From then on, the "Far Eastern General" played a major role in the developments of the Korean War until his dismissal by President Truman in April 1951. The controversy surrounding his relief has obscured certain issues. Although MacArthur was certainly to blame for provoking Chinese intervention through his arrogance and disregard of Beijing's warnings, Truman and the Joint Chiefs of Staff in Washington also must bear some responsibility, for they either shared with MacArthur the general misunderstandings of Chinese intentions or failed to provide explicit and unambiguous instructions.[49]

As early as July 31, the Defense Department had pondered three possible military objectives in Korea. The first was a "minimum offensive effort" to drive the enemy out of South Korea. The second was an "intermediate objective" aimed at occupying Pyongyang and important communications points between the thirty-ninth and fortieth parallels. "An unoccupied demilitarized zone might then be set up in depth along the Chinese and Soviet frontiers to allay their suspicions." These two options were dismissed on the ground that they both left Korea disunited and with the possibility of a renewal of hostilities. The third course was a "maximum effort" designed to occupy the whole of Korea and to arrange elections under U.N. auspices. This alternative, the military planners believed, would ensure a satisfactory political solution in Korea.[50]

After MacArthur's successful landing at Inchon in mid-September, which quickly turned the tide of the war, the Joint Chiefs of Staff (JCS) sent him a directive based on NSC 81/1. Approved by Truman, Acheson, and Secretary of Defense George C. Marshall, the instruction authorized the U.N. commander to advance beyond the thirty-eighth parallel to destroy the North Korean troops "provided that at the time of such [an] operation there has been no entry into North Korea by major Soviet or Chinese Communist forces, no announcement of intended entry, nor a threat to counter our operations militarily in North Korea." The message cautioned the general that "under no circumstances . . . will your forces cross the Manchurian or USSR borders of Korea." "As a matter of policy," the JCS continued, no non-Korean ground troops were to be employed in the regions of Korea bordering the Soviet Union or China. If the Russians intervened militarily, MacArthur should "assume the defense, make no move to aggravate the situation and report to Washington." In the event of Chinese military intervention, MacArthur should "continue the action" so long as it "offered a reasonable chance of successful resistance."[51] It should be noted that this directive was not forceful enough to prevent MacArthur from interpreting it to his advantage. The phrase "as a matter of policy" was ambiguous and gave the general room to manipulate its meaning.

Two days later, Marshall sent MacArthur an "eyes only" message inform-ing him that he should "feel unhampered tactically and strategically to proceed north of the thirty-eighth parallel."[52] Washington's green light must have emboldened the already cocky general. Beijing's warnings at the end of September did not seem to worry the administration and General MacArthur. The British representative in Tokyo, Alvary Gascoigne, reported on October 3 that MacArthur dismissed Zhou Enlai's warning to Panikkar as "pure bluff."[53] The first encounter with the Chinese troops in late October failed to alert MacArthur to the seriousness of the situation, and on November 24, the general launched his disastrous "end the war" offensive.

The Americans neglected China's warnings for several reasons. First, difficulties of communications, misperceptions, and distrust of the Chinese posed a problem. Administration officials had little faith in the credibility of Panikkar, who had passed misinformation before. Truman dismissed Beijing's messages as "a bald attempt to blackmail the United Nations," which was considering a resolution authorizing U.N. forces to cross the thirty-eighth parallel.[54]

More importantly, as Burton Kaufman observes, American officials shared "a curiously bifurcated image of China." On the one hand, they believed that Chinese leaders were more nationalists than Communists; on the other hand, they held that Moscow controlled the Chinese Communist movement. Therefore, they tended to be obsessed with Soviet intentions when they were reacting to Chinese attitudes. Once convinced that Stalin was behind the whole operation in Korea, they paid no attention to how China saw the war and what its leaders wanted. That was why Acheson had contended that, so long as Moscow did not desire to expand the conflict into a world war, China would not intervene.[55]

Similarly, with an eye on the Soviet Union, Truman contended that if China failed to understand America's peaceful intentions, "it can only be because they are being deceived by those whose advantage it is to prolong and extend hostilities in the Far East against the interest of all Far Eastern people."[56] Thus, wishful thinking replaced reality, and illusion prevailed over actuality.

The Wake Island meeting of October 15 between Truman and MacArthur further dispelled any lingering doubts about the possibility of Chinese and Soviet intervention in Korea. The U.N. commander told the president that "formal resistance will end throughout North and South Korea by Thanksgiving," and that he expected to withdraw the Eighth Army to Japan by Christmas. As to the possibility of Chinese or Soviet interference, MacArthur believed that the chances were "very little." Beijing had no air force, he continued. The United States had air bases in Korea, and "if the Chinese tried to get down to Pyongyang there would be the greatest slaughter." The Russians had no ground forces available for North Korea. The possible combination "would be Russian air support of Chinese ground troops." In this respect, MacArthur asserted that the Sino-Soviet coordination "would be so flimsy" that Russian planes "would bomb the Chinese as often as they bomb us." Therefore, "it just wouldn't work" with the Chinese ground and the Russian air. The general claimed: "We are the best."[57]

LOCALIZING THE WAR: THE BRITISH REACTION

These developments in U.S. policy alarmed the British. Throughout the Korean War, and especially in the winter of 1950–51, they exerted pressures on Washington to moderate American behavior. The basic British approach to the Korean hostilities was to check North Korean aggression but confine the conflict to the Korean peninsula. The British shared with the Americans the belief that the Soviet Union was responsible for the North Korean attack. London held the view that the Kremlin "had connived at" if it had not really "instigated" Kim Il Sung's invasion. On June 26, the Foreign Office argued that "all possible action should . . . be taken to prevent the aggressors from attaining their object, both in order to safeguard the future of the United Nations Organization, and to deter the Soviet Union from attempting aggression elsewhere." British military leaders contended that the defeat of South Korea would bring about a serious loss of prestige and credibility for the West, whereas an Allied success in South Korea would "undoubtedly have a salutary effect on all non-Communists in Malaya."[58] Given these considerations, London supported the American representative in the Security Council in calling on members of the United Nations to aid the South Koreans. It placed its Far Eastern fleet at Washington's command and sent troops from Hong Kong to Korea.

Although endorsing American policy to stop North Korean aggression, the British had reservations about the sweeping nature of American policy-making and were uneasy with the American tendency to expand the war to China. They were afraid that Washington would be bogged down in "the wrong war" in Asia, leaving the Russians a free hand in Europe. As Attlee wrote to Truman on July 6, "A particular aspect of the situation in Korea which is causing us concern is that the Russians have involved the Western Powers in a heavy commitment without themselves playing an overt part."[59]

Anglo-American communications in July revealed different perceptions about China's threat in the Far East. In a letter to Bevin on July 10, Acheson said that "there can be little doubt that Communism, with Chi[na] as one spearhead, has now embarked upon an assault against Asia with immediate objectives in Korea, Indochina, Burma, the Philippines and Malaya and with medium-range objectives in Hong Kong, Indonesia, Siam, India and Japan." The United States doubted, Acheson continued, that the Chinese "will be deflected from their purpose by temporary accommodation, particularly if this accommodation is obtained by them at a time when their own conduct is aggressive and in violation of the [U.N.] Charter."[60]

On July 15, Bevin asked Sir Oliver Franks, the British ambassador in Washington, to deliver a message to Acheson, in which the foreign secretary expressed a different assessment of China's intentions in Asia and reiterated the British belief that the best way to separate China from the Soviet Union was to maintain China's contact with the West. Bevin asserted that he did not believe for the moment that China "would embark on adventures further afield from Formosa." Therefore, in his view, the West "must be careful not to accuse China of what she has not yet done, or to give her the impression that she is already so much beyond the pale that she has no hope of re-establishing her position with the West." Once Beijing became convinced that the West would have nothing to do with her, Bevin continued, she would switch further to the Russians, who would be out to exploit such a development to the detriment of the West.[61]

During the Anglo-American discussions held in Washington July 20–24, British representatives again stressed this theme of promoting Sino-Soviet tensions by avoiding conflict with China. They pointed to the "advantages of localizing any possible conflict between the U.S. or the U.K. on the one hand and the Chinese Communists on the other" so that "a possible gradual drift of the Chinese communist regime away from Moscow might not be interrupted."[62]

Although uneasy with U.S. policy in Korea, the British, however, made sure that they did not push the Americans too hard. This was especially true of Bevin, who put a high premium on the importance of the Anglo-American partnership. Reluctant to challenge U.S. decisions outright, the British made no sustained efforts to prevent American troops from crossing the thirty-eighth parallel. The Labor government also refrained from pressing vigorously for the creation of a demilitarized zone along the Chinese-Korean border as a way of reassuring Beijing that U.S.-U.N. intentions were not harmful. This British inclination not to press Washington too strongly did not change until late November when the Chinese army in overwhelming numbers attacked MacArthur's troops and President Truman unintentionally suggested that he might retaliate against Beijing with nuclear weapons during a press conference on November 30.[63]

These developments alarmed the Europeans, especially the British. The Indians had been urging on the British the importance of admitting Beijing into the United Nations and the danger of its intervention in Korea.[64] Representing European and Commonwealth views, Attlee hurried to Washington in early December 1950. His chief purposes were to persuade the Americans that they should be prepared to negotiate with China, to consider admitting it into the United Nations, and to include the future of Taiwan as well as Korea on the agenda to be discussed with Beijing.[65]

Attlee urged the Americans to look at the matter from the Chinese point of view. The Chinese attitude, the prime minister said, "seems to include an element of fear, a genuine fear of the United States and of the European nations generally. So long as they are not in the United Nations . . . they feel they are entitled to come in." He added that he "had been thinking whether there was some approach by way of discussion." The Americans regarded the British suggestion of negotiating with the Chinese as appeasement, declaring it to be politically unfeasible to sell to Congress or the American public. Acheson said that not many Americans would want an all-out war against China, but they were pessimistic about the possibilities of negotiation. He called it the worst time to negotiate with the Communists since 1917.[66]

Attlee's discussions with American officials revealed again Anglo-American differences about how to deal with the Chinese and how to judge the prospect of a Sino-Soviet split. Attlee argued that despite Chinese intervention in the Korean War, significant divergences remained between Beijing and Moscow, which would, in time, produce hostility between them. He pointed out that "it was quite true that the Chinese are hard-shelled Marxists-Leninists but it was quite possible that they were not Soviet imperialists. There was a chance of Titoism." "The Russians have not given very much help to China," Attlee continued. "The Chinese do not owe them very much. There is a strong mixture of Chinese nationalism in their Communist attitude. Chinese civilization is very old and is accustomed to absorbing new things. They may wear the Red flag with a difference." Was it wise, the prime minister wondered, "to follow a policy which without being effective against China leaves her with Russia as her only friend?"[67]

Acheson acknowledged that he would not find much disagreement among the president's advisers on Attlee's analysis of China. He himself had been more "bloodied" by putting it forward than anyone else. But the problem was, as Acheson saw it, "not whether this was a correct analysis but whether it was possible to act on it" at the moment. One obstacle, the secretary of state explained, was that the Sino-Soviet split was still a long-term prospect, while military exigencies in the Far East were more immediate. "Perhaps in ten or fifteen years we might see a change in the Chinese attitude but we do not have that time available. . . . If in taking a chance on the long future of China we affect the security of the United States at once, this is a bad bargain, especially if our security would be affected by the influence of these steps on Japan, the Philippines and other countries." Moreover, the attitude of the American public had to be considered. Truman said that the problem of Taiwan "was quite a political issue in the United States since Chiang had many converts here."[68]

George Kennan, who had left the government in August 1950, was "distressed" with the administration's handling of the talks with the British. He criticized the State Department's preoccupation with plans for a U.N. resolution condemning the Chinese as aggressors. In a letter to Charles Bohlen on December 5, he said: "What was really disturbing and dangerous . . . was our situation in the United Nations and our insistence on making a public demonstration of the state of our unity with our allies at this particular moment. Our only possible course at this moment was to get the United Nations out of the Korean business as rapidly and painlessly as possible." "Every time we tried to get one more of these resolutions in the United Nations," the veteran diplomat continued, "we insisted on making public show of the state of our relations with our friends, but without further practical purpose."[69]

Attlee's trip to Washington represented the beginning of a two-month period of intense British attempts to rein in an administration that London perceived to be on the verge of a dangerous war in China. In late January 1951, when Bevin was seriously ill with pneumonia, the British government modified an American draft of a U.N. resolution condemning China, securing a delay in the implementation of additional measures against Beijing.[70]

On April 11, President Truman relieved General MacArthur as commander of the U.N. forces and appointed General Matthew B. Ridgway to succeed him. On May 18, the U.N. General Assembly adopted a resolution recommending an embargo on the shipment of arms, ammunition, and other materials of strategic value to China and North Korea. In May and June, when the battlefront became a stalemate, the way was open for private

Soviet-American discussions at the end of May, which led ultimately to the opening of armistice negotiations at Kaesong in mid-July between the U.N. command and China and North Korea.

CONCLUSION

The American dispatch of the Seventh Fleet into the Taiwan Strait and intervention in the Korean War confirmed Mao's belief that the United States was the most dangerous enemy of China. Convinced that a Sino-American conflict was inevitable and an early war was better than a later one, Mao decided to confront the Americans in Korea. Security considerations were the principal reason for China's intervention. The obligation to assist a fellow Communist party and to repay past friendship also shaped the decision.

The Chinese Communists achieved a remarkable victory by driving U.N. forces out of North Korea. Their anti-American campaign at home successfully mobilized nationalist sentiment among the population to the advantage of the regime. Their performance in Korea helped to legitimize the new government's domestic position as the protector of China's national interests and to promote its international prestige abroad.

Beijing reacted to American threats to its security by interfering in the war in force, but it found cooperation and assistance from its ally, the Soviet Union, both inadequate and unsatisfactory. The Korean fighting revealed to the Chinese the limitations of their alliance with the Russians and underscored the importance of developing an independent defense force. Although unhappy with the quality and quantity of Soviet assistance, Beijing still emphasized the general value of the Sino-Soviet solidarity as a deterrent. It should be remembered that their differences were those between two allies opposing a common foe.

It was clear that Stalin behaved cautiously during the Korean conflict for fear of triggering a war with the United States. During the Geneva Conference in 1954, Soviet Foreign Minister Vyacheslav M. Molotov told the American representative, Walter Bedell Smith, that during the Korean War the Soviet Union had acted as a restraining influence on China.[71] But it is still not clear what kind of restraints the Russians placed upon the Chinese during the war.

Both Britain and the United States reacted resolutely to the North Korean invasion. Sharing the conviction that the Soviet Union was accountable for the North Korean behavior, Anglo-American policymakers stressed the importance of standing firm against aggression. But serious differences soon emerged between the two powers regarding how to deal with the Chinese and how to disrupt Sino-Soviet relations. Although both parties recognized the ultimate possibility of a Sino-Soviet split, they disagreed with each other on how soon that prospect would become fact and how best to promote it. Although the British remained convinced that keeping China's contact with the West was still the best way to exacerbate Sino-Soviet differences, the Americans, however, had given up the moderate approach. They believed that, given the Korean fighting, a Sino-Soviet rift was a long-term possibility and was not likely to be influenced by Western actions at the moment.

On the whole, British influence on American policy during the war was limited. This reflected Britain's dependent position on the United States after 1945. London regarded the Anglo-American alliance as essential to its foreign policy, a tendency that had been especially strong when Bevin was in charge of the Foreign Office.

The Korean War had an adverse impact on Sino-British relations. Before the outbreak of the conflict, London had been moving in the direction of voting for PRC entry in the United Nations and demanding more trade with Beijing. The war, however, cut short these developments. While Britain strove to moderate American policy during the hostilities, it had to yield to Washington pressure on trade control and Chinese representation in the United Nations in order to preserve Western unity. "After 1950," as Robert Boardman comments, "Western China policy was tilted in an American rather than, as previously, in a British direction."[72] Beijing was very unhappy with British participation in the U.N. command in Korea. The Chinese press increased its criticism of British domestic and foreign policies during the war. Sino-British negotiations for establishment of diplomatic relations stalled until 1954.

The Sino-American confrontation in Korea marked the failure of the Truman administration's efforts to separate China from the Soviet Union and froze Sino-American relations for the next twenty years. The war had several serious consequences for U.S. policy in Asia. First, the American government came to perceive China as the major threat to U.S. interests in the Far East. Thus, it tried to contain China through a tough policy of military encirclement, economic embargoes, and political isolation. Second, Washington began to attach more importance to the strategic value of Taiwan as an indispensable link in its offshore island chain in the West Pacific. Accordingly, the American government strengthened its ties with the KMT regime on Taiwan, thus precluding an early conclusion of the Chinese civil war. Third, China's intervention in Korea raised fears in Washington of a similar plunge across the border into Vietnam. The Truman administration undertook to increase American military assistance to the French fighting the Vietminh in Indochina.

One positive outcome of the Korean hostilities, however, was that China and the United States never again engaged in massive combat. The fighting in Korea had sobering effects on the Chinese and American leaders, especially when they later confronted the war in Vietnam. One reason for Beijing's reluctance to support Ho Chi Minh in his efforts to unify Vietnam in 1954 was the Chinese policymakers' memory of the Korean experience (see chap. 7). Mao and his colleagues did not desire another full-scale confrontation with the Americans and were anxious to avoid U.S. intervention in Vietnam.

Similarly, when Washington considered its military options against Vietnam in the 1960s, one of the major constraints limiting the range of its intervention was the awareness of Korea. As William P. Bundy, assistant secretary of state for East Asian and Pacific affairs in the Johnson administration, later recalled, "We thought that there was a [potential] flash point of Chinese intervention. We certainly had the Yalu on our minds very, very strongly."[73]

5 *Effects of the Korean War, 1950–1952*

U.S. POLICY TOWARD TAIWAN

The onset of the Korean War hardened American attitudes toward Taiwan. As early as late-1948, when a Communist victory in China became increasingly likely, American officials had begun to debate the implications of a Communist conquest of Taiwan. On November 24, 1948, upon the request of Acting Secretary of State Robert M. Lovett, the Joint Chiefs of Staff prepared an appraisal of the strategic ramifications to U.S. security of the loss of Taiwan to "Kremlin-directed Communists." The Communist occupation of mainland China, the JCS pointed out, would "enhance, from the strategic viewpoint, the potential value to the United States of Formosa as a wartime base capable of use for staging of troops, strategic air operations and control of adjacent shipping routes." The capture of Taiwan by Moscow-dominated Communists would be "very seriously detrimental to our national security" because it would give America's enemy the capability to control sea lines of communication between Japan and Malaya and to threaten the Philippines, the Ryukyus, and ultimately Japan itself.[1]

The State Department agreed that it was in American strategic interest to deny Taiwan to the Communists,[2] and so did MacArthur. In early 1949, the general stated that if the Chinese Communists took Taiwan, "our whole defensive position in the Far East [would be] definitely lost," and it could only bring eventually a retreat of "our defensive line back to the west coast of the continental United States."[3]

The Central Intelligence Agency drew a similar conclusion in its December 1948 "Review of the World Situation," in which it contended that

> At the moment, one element in the situation stands out as of immediate and practical concern to U.S. security. This is the possible status of Taiwan . . . when the Chinese mainland is controlled by a Communist-dominated government. On the assumption that such a development sets the stage for an expansion of the Soviet strategic position in the Far East,

Taiwan, from the U.S. point of view, is strategically divorced from China and becomes one of the group of off-shore islands on which the U.S. position will then automatically rest. Soviet penetration of an island thus situated would have an adverse effect on the U.S. position on the periphery of China somewhat similar to that which a Soviet penetration of Greece would have on the Anglo-American position in the Eastern Mediterranean.[4]

As for the means to deny Taiwan to the Chinese Communists, the consensus in the U.S. government was to use "diplomatic and economic steps."[5] The JCS and MacArthur advocated this approach largely out of military considerations. Referring to the current gap between the military capabilities and global obligations of the United States, the chiefs objected to military intervention on the grounds that it might "lead to the necessity for relatively major effort there, thus making it impossible then to meet important emergencies elsewhere."[6]

The State Department based its position primarily on political calculations. Acheson told the NSC in March 1949 that military efforts to detach Taiwan from China would risk arousing Chinese nationalism and might interfere with his strategy of trying to drive a wedge between the Chinese Communists and the Soviet Union. "We are most anxious," the secretary of state asserted, "to avoid raising the specter of an American-created irredentist issue just at the time we shall be seeking to exploit the genuinely Soviet-created irredentist issue in Manchuria and Sinkiang."[7]

To keep Taiwan out of both Nationalist and Communist hands, the State Department tried to encourage an independence movement on the island. Acheson sent Livingston Merchant, then counselor at the American Embassy in Nanjing, to contact authorities on Taiwan. As Merchant later recalled, his original instructions were "top secret." Washington believed at the time that the Nationalists would not be able to move to Taiwan "in sufficient force and power to dominate the island," which "would be run by the native Taiwanese leaders unless and until the Communists were able to mount an invasion." Merchant was asked to establish "a personal relationship with the Taiwanese underground," and cultivate "mutual confidence with them."[8]

In March, Merchant reported to Washington that independence groups on Taiwan were "disunited, politically illiterate, imperfectly organized and in general worthy [of] little reliance." Two months later, he told the State Department that "there is no new evidence that local independence groups are sufficiently numerous, well-organized, well-armed and well led to . . . successfully establish [an] anti-Communist pro-U.S. native Formosan government."[9]

While stressing the importance of detaching Taiwan from the Chinese Communists through political and economic means, Acheson did not rule out the possibility that the United States eventually might deem it necessary to use military force to defend the island. In an NSC meeting on March 1, the secretary of state asked the military not to exclude from its planning "the possibility that it might later be called upon to employ modest military strength in Formosa in collaboration with other friendly forces."[10]

The military leaned toward the position that in case of war with the Soviet Union, provision would be made for "denial to the Soviets of the use of Formosa as a base for offensive operations." The JCS told the NSC in early 1949 that "there can be no categorical assurance that other future circumstances extending to war itself might not make overt military action eventually advisable from the overall standpoint of our national security."[11] In December 1949, the JCS concluded that "a modest, well-directed, and closely supervised program of military aid to the anti-Communist government of Taiwan would be in the security interest of the United States."[12]

But the State Department remained unwilling to deny Taiwan to the PRC by measures other than political or economic. Acheson still hoped to play off Chinese nationalism against the Soviet Union. To the secretary of state, the "dust" in China had not finally settled. Furthermore, Acheson wanted the Nationalists to make "energetic efforts on their own part if they were to be successful in denying the island to the Chinese Communists." With this purpose in mind, Acheson in November had authorized the U.S. consul general in Taipei to tell Chiang Kai-shek that the U.S. government had no intention of using its armed forces for the defense of Taiwan.[13]

In early 1950, largely as a result of political considerations, the administration excluded Taiwan from the U.S. "defensive perimeter." On January 5, Truman announced that the United States had "no predatory designs on Formosa" and would not use forces to defend the island or to provide military assistance and advice. A week later, Acheson spoke at the National Press Club, outlining an American "sphere of strategic concern," which included Japan, the Philippines, and the surrounding islands but not Taiwan and South Korea.[14]

The administration's decision elicited an outcry from Chiang Kai-shek's supporters in the United States, who charged that the State Department was pursuing "a fatal policy . . . which we would live to rue and regret."[15]

Actually, the administration had not abandoned Taiwan in case of war with the Soviet Union. At a news conference on January 5, Acheson had called attention to the wording "at this time" in Truman's statement to whit that "the United States has no desire to obtain special rights or privileges or to establish military bases on Formosa at this time." The phrase, Acheson indicated, represented "a recognition of the fact that, in the unlikely and unhappy event that our forces might be attacked in the Far East, the United States must be completely free to take whatever action in whatever area is necessary for its own security."[16]

During the next few months, some members in the State Department began to push for a revision in this policy. Included in their number was Dean Rusk, who succeeded W. Walton Butterworth as assistant secretary of state for Far Eastern affairs. John Foster Dulles was another influential force within the government who favored protecting Taiwan. On May 18, Dulles presented a memorandum to Rusk and Paul Nitze, director of the State Department's Policy Planning Staff, in which he argued that the Communist victory in China had shifted the world balance of power in favor of the Soviet Union and "to the disfavor of the United States." If America continued to allow "doubtful areas" to fall under Soviet control, a "series of disasters" to Washington's position could be expected in such critical places as Japan, the Philippines, and Indonesia. Even the oil-rich Middle East would be "in jeopardy." To forestall these developments, Dulles contended that it was necessary that the United States "quickly take a dramatic and strong stand that shows our confidence and resolution." The best place to do so was Taiwan. "If the United States were to announce that it would neutralize Formosa, not permitting it either to be taken by the Communists or to be used as a base of military operations against the mainland, that is a decision which we could certainly maintain, short of open war by the Soviet Union."[17] In this suggestion, Dulles anticipated a policy Truman was to adopt after the outbreak of the Korean War.

The Korean fighting made Washington even more unwilling to see Taiwan fall into Communist hands. Truman's decision to send the Seventh Fleet into the Taiwan Strait was a logical outgrowth of the administration's thinking in the preceding months. In early August, Truman approved a plan to send a mission to examine KMT military needs and to give aid to Chiang Kai-shek. Later in the month, he authorized the allocation of more than $14 million for assistance for Taiwan.[18]

In sum, even before the outbreak of the Korean War, demand had been growing within the administration for U.S. defense of Taiwan. Washington's resolve to prevent the island from falling into Communist hands was an aspect of its Cold War confrontation with the Soviet Union in the Far East, a factor that was present both before and after the Korean War. Although Acheson remained dubious of American commitment to Taiwan, the increasing pressures within his department, from the Pentagon, and by Congress made U.S. intervention almost inevitable after the onset of the Korean hostilities on June 25, 1950. The American action regarding Taiwan greatly worried its allies, especially Britain, which did not want to see an expansion of the war to China. In the months following the eruption of the Korean fighting, British and American officials held a constant exchange of views about the Taiwan issue.

British Policy toward Taiwan

The British never attached as much importance to Taiwan as did the Americans. Lewis Douglas, the U.S. ambassador in London, told Acheson on May 25, 1949, that "very little attention has been given in British official and unofficial circles to the various problems of Taiwan." Maberly Dening, British assistant under secretary for foreign affairs (Far East), told Douglas at the time that should a refugee Chinese government be established on Taiwan, the British government would simply appoint a British consulate in Tamsui as an office of the British Embassy in China.[19]

During this period, Foreign Office officials argued that the legal status of Taiwan was uncertain. The Cairo Declaration, they pointed out, had been merely a "statement of intention" that the island should be returned to China after World War II, but this had not happened because of the Chinese civil war and the absence of a Japanese peace treaty. Therefore, Taiwan was "not yet legally Chinese territory." In a discussion with American and French diplomats in Paris on August 4, 1950, Dening said that the island, "juridically speaking, belongs neither to Chiang nor to the Peking Government, and that the question of its juridical disposition can only be resolved by a peace treaty with Japan."[20]

Regarding Taiwan's strategic significance, the British agreed with the Americans that it was desirable to keep it from Communist hands, but they did not advocate the use of military means to achieve that aim. When it seemed certain that the Chinese Communists were to conquer the whole country in late 1949 and to take Taiwan in the near future, London appeared ready to reconcile itself to the inevitable. Dening told the Americans on

September 9 that "there is a strong probability that Formosa will in any event fall into the hands of the Communists and, since this eventuality cannot very well be prevented, all that can be done is to hope that occupation of [the] island by the Communists will not prove disastrous."[21]

It is interesting to note that in this same conversation, the British also showed interest in promoting a non-Communist, non-Nationalist autonomous movement on Taiwan. Dening mentioned the Formosan League for Reemancipation, an independent group on the island. Although the leaders of the organization "were unsavory characters," Dening pointed out, they at least "appeared to oppose Communism." The British official also referred to "the possibility of an appeal by the Formosans to the UN with a view to holding a plebiscite or establishing a mandate under the UN." While agreeing with Dening in principle, Butterworth argued, however, that "the possibility of such an appeal was remote, particularly as long as Chiang Kai-shek remained in control of the Government on Formosa."[22]

In late 1949, when large quantities of U.S. military supplies found their way into Taiwan, London became very uneasy because it was afraid that if the Chinese Communists later captured these weapons, especially tanks and planes, they might use them against Hong Kong. On December 6, British Counselor Hubert Graves expressed this fear to Merchant in a memorandum in which he wondered why the U.S. government continued shipments of military equipment to the island if it "had concluded that no practical steps could be taken to prevent Formosa [from] falling into Communist hands." The document concluded that the British government "feel much concern at the above circumstances and hope that the United States Government will feel able to take steps to stop or restrict the flow of arms from the United States to Formosa." In a conversation with Acheson two days later, British Ambassador Oliver Franks again conveyed London's concern about American military support to Taiwan.[23]

Truman's decision to send the Seventh Fleet into the Taiwan Strait greatly worried the British. As noted in chapter 4, while supporting American efforts to stop North Korean aggression, London opposed expanding the war to China. In a letter to Acheson on July 7, 1950, Bevin said that the United States could expect "the whole-hearted backing of world opinion" in its "courageous initiative" in dealing with aggression in Korea, but this would not be the case with American policy toward Taiwan. This was because, the foreign secretary explained, many countries, especially Asian nations, would "dislike the prospect of an extension of the dispute which might follow" if Beijing were to attack Taiwan. Furthermore, some countries would feel that, since the PRC was in control of all Chinese territory, it would not be justified, in view of the pledge under the Cairo Declaration, to take actions that might undermine the eventual transferring of the island to China. India in particular, Bevin continued, was "very sensitive on this aspect of United States policy." In general, Bevin concluded that "the United States Government would be wise in their public statements to concentrate on the Korean issue and play down the other parts of the President's statement of 27th June, otherwise there may be a risk of a breach in the international solidarity happily achieved over Korea."[24]

The Truman administration, nonetheless, did not yield to British pressure on the Taiwan question. In his reply to Bevin on July 10, Acheson said that he did not see any possibility of "harmonizing" American policy toward China by any significant change in the basic attitudes on which that policy rested. At the same time, the secretary of state assured his British counterpart that the U.S. goal was to neutralize Taiwan, not to take possession of it, but Washington was not prepared to see hostile forces seize it and use it as a base against the United States. "We are not willing to see it go involuntarily to Peiping in the present state of affairs in Asia." Acheson emphasized to Bevin that his reply had been "approved here at highest levels [and] represents both my own strong personal views and has [the] fullest concurrence of all official quarters here."[25]

Acheson's uncompromising attitude irritated Foreign Office officials. The minister of state, Kenneth Younger, whose influence increased as a result of Bevin's long illness, complained that "military minds seem to have the upper hand in the United States at the moment." "We should stress," he told Bevin, "that India and Burma, and possibly other Asian states, would certainly refuse to support American policy on Formosa and that the effect of this on Asian minds would be to transform the Far Eastern operations from a measure of collective security into an act of imperialism by white troops."[26]

Sensing the gravity of Anglo-American differences over Taiwan, Ambassador Douglas wrote to Acheson on July 24, urging upon him the necessity of reaching "some common understanding" with the British. He pointed out that "there are a great many evidences of a substantive division of opinion in Britain on [the] question of Formosa. . . . Altogether they indicate we may be in serious trouble should the Chinese Communists attack Formosa and should there not be an agreed position with the UK."[27]

In his reply on July 28, Acheson expressed agreement with Douglas on the "high desirability [of] reaching [a] common grounding with [the] UK on Formosa." He instructed the ambassador to discuss the matter with Bevin for

the purpose of (1) securing an Anglo-American joint position on the immediate aspects of the problem, (2) exploring the UN-related aspects of the
issue, and (3) assuring Bevin that the United States would welcome a further
exchange of views over the longer term of the questions on which the two
countries might not be able to agree currently.[28]

Reporting on his meeting with Bevin on August 28, Douglas said that the
conversation "got no further than the benefits of having an understanding,
for Bevin took the position that, while it was very necessary to arrive at an
agreed position if possible, the discussion should be held preferably in
Washington." The British foreign secretary believed that the Taiwan issue
"was in a very real sense a problem of the Far East. The Eastern questions
of policy were being discussed in Washington."[29]

Throughout September and October, British and American officials conducted many discussions on the possibility of a U.N. resolution of the
Taiwan issue, but they could not agree on the objectives of such a solution.[30]
In November, the State Department abandoned its plan for a U.N.-sponsored
neutralization of Taiwan because of China's intervention in the Korean War,
domestic political sensitivities, and the lack of agreement with the allies.[31]

Although agreeing with the Americans on the desirability of denying the
island to the Communists, the British were not ready to go as far as employing military force to reach that goal. Washington's decision to send the
Seventh Fleet into the Taiwan Strait alarmed London, which was apprehensive about an expansion of war in Asia. As a result, the British pressured the
Americans to tone down their rhetoric regarding Taiwan. This allied nudg-
ing obviously contributed to the Truman administration's willingness to
explore the possibility of a U.N. solution of the Taiwan issue.

BEIJING'S REACTION TO TRUMAN'S JUNE 27 DECISION

Even before the establishment of the PRC in October 1949, the CCP had
given thought to liberating Taiwan. In the summer of 1949, Mao instructed
the Third Field Army to begin preparations for an invasion of Taiwan.[32] In
July, Zhou Enlai suggested that as a preparation for occupying the island in
the summer of 1950, the CCP send three to four hundred people to the
Soviet Union to receive air force training and to purchase one hundred airplanes from Moscow.[33]

Xiao Jingguang, former commander of the Chinese navy, recalled in his
memoirs that in October 1949 Mao asked him to lead the navy, explaining

he had chosen Xiao because he had studied the military in the Soviet Union. It was necessary, Mao said, to learn from the Soviets in order to develop China's own navy. According to Mao, the PRC needed a navy mainly for two purposes: to defend China's coast against imperialism and to liberate Taiwan. Before his departure for the Soviet Union in December, Mao met Xiao again, asking him what sort of equipment he wanted for the navy. Mao said that the main goal of his trip was to consolidate Sino-Soviet friendship; at the same time, he would ask the Soviets for assistance, including naval and air force supplies.[34]

In early 1950, Xiao found himself fully preoccupied with the preparations for the Taiwan campaign. He talked with former KMT naval officers to find out the conditions of Chiang's fleet. In March, he discussed with Su Yu, first deputy commander of the East China Military Region, the PLA's planning for attacking the island.[35]

Truman's decision to dispatch the Seventh Fleet into the Taiwan Strait after the onset of the Korean War greatly angered the Chinese leadership and confirmed the worst fears they had entertained about the United States since the failure of the Marshall Mission. Early in 1949 when the PLA was preparing to cross the Yangtse River, Mao's distrust of the United States had become so intense that he had made contingency plans against possible U.S. intervention in China. The Chinese leader was convinced that Washington had finally decided to involve itself in the Chinese civil war to rescue Chiang Kai-shek, just as he had always expected it to be.[36]

The war in Korea had three major effects on Mao's military planning. First, it disrupted his plan to occupy Taiwan. While waging a media campaign against American "armed aggression against the territory of China," Mao had to postpone his Taiwan campaign. Zhou Enlai told Xiao Jingguang on June 30, 1950, that, given the situation in Korea, the party Central Committee had decided to defer the attack on Taiwan.[37]

Second, the Korean fighting affected Mao's general defense arrangements and priorities. Now the Chinese leader had to consider the constant threat of an attack from the U.S.-KMT forces on Taiwan. In the months following June 1950, Mao paid a lot of attention to the defense of the China coast. On November 11, 1950, he wrote to the CCP's East China Bureau with the instruction that all the party's work in East China "should be based on the premise of a U.S.-KMT landing attack." On the same day, he also telegraphed the CCP's Middle and South China Bureau, instructing them to consider Guangdong and Guangxi provinces as "a single unit against [an] Imperialist-KMT landing assault."[38]

According to Xiao Jingguang, before the Korean fighting, the focus of attention for the Chinese navy was on the East China Sea, directed at Taiwan. With the war in Korea and the American fleet around the peninsula, Beijing's leaders began to worry about China's coast and ports in the north, such as Tianjin and Qingdao. Accordingly, they shifted their navy's priority to the North China Sea.[39]

Mao involved himself directly in planning for coastal defense. His strategy was "active defense," namely defense with concentration and depth instead of an all-out defense, as advocated by the Soviet military advisers in China at the time. According to Mao's thinking, if the U.S.-KMT troops attacked the mainland, China would let them come inland and then surround and eliminate them with superior force.[40] This was in line with Mao's traditional strategy of relying on geographical and numerical strength to defeat his more technically advanced enemy.

Third, the Korean hostilities influenced the way Mao used the $300 million Soviet loan he had secured during his visit to Moscow early in the year. Initially, the Chinese leader had planned to allocate half of that money to the purchase of Soviet naval supplies for China's new fleet in order to speed the preparations for the Taiwan invasion. After China's entry into the Korean War, Mao became increasingly aware of the importance of air force cover for his troops. As a result, he used most of the loan to purchase Soviet planes at the expense of delaying the modernization of his navy.[41]

The Taiwan issue was one major area affected by the Korean War. The question of Chinese representation in the United Nations was another principal area in which the war exacerbated Beijing's conflict with the United States and Great Britain.

CHINESE REPRESENTATION IN THE UNITED NATIONS

British recognition of China in January 1950 did not bring about an immediate formation of diplomatic ties between the two countries as had been expected by London. On February 14, John Hutchison, the British representative in Beijing, made his first call at the Foreign Ministry. He told the Chinese that the British government believed that the exchange of notes between Bevin and Zhou Enlai "constituted establishment of diplomatic relations."[42]

The Chinese government, however, did not share this view. It insisted that, before the exchange of ambassadors, "preliminary and procedural questions must first be discussed." By this, Beijing meant that Britain must first sever all its relations with the KMT government on Taiwan. On this account, Chinese leaders believed that the British attitude was ambivalent. In replying to British demands for establishing diplomatic relations, Foreign Ministry officials cited as examples Britain's abstention from voting in the United Nations Security Council on a Soviet resolution to expel the KMT representative together with similar actions taken in other U.N. organizations, the continued presence of a British consul in Taiwan, British permission for KMT agencies to continue operation in Hong Kong, and London's failure to help Beijing settle issues relating to Chinese national property in the colony, namely, that of the two Chinese airlines, the China National Aviation Corporation (CNAC) and the Central Air Transport Corporation (CATC). Among these issues, the U.N. question and the two airline disputes were most irritating to the Chinese Communists.[43]

The CCP had a positive view of the United Nations from its very inception. In 1945, the party had appointed its own representative, Dong Biwu, to China's delegation to the San Francisco Conference, where he participated in the proceedings and signed the United Nations Charter. Thus, the CCP had been directly involved in the founding of the international organization. In a speech commenting on the conference, Mao claimed, "The Chinese Communist Party fully agrees with the proposals of the Dumbarton Oaks conference and the decisions of the Crimea conference on the establishment of an organization to safeguard international peace and security after the war."[44]

After its founding in October 1949, eager to secure international recognition of its legitimacy, the PRC immediately sought to represent China in the United Nations. On November 15, Premier Zhou Enlai sent a message to Carlos Romulo, president of the General Assembly, and Trygve Lie, secretary-general of the United Nations, demanding that the world organization "expel the illegitimate delegates of the KMT reactionary remnant clique."[45]

Sino-Soviet coordination was close on the issue of Chinese representation in the United Nations during Mao's visit to Moscow in early 1950. On January 7, Soviet Foreign Minister Andrei Vyshinsky suggested to Mao that the PRC send a statement to the U.N. Security Council denying the legitimacy of Jiang Tingfu, the Nationalist representative to that body. If Beijing did so and Jiang continued to represent China at the Security Council, Vyshinsky continued, the Soviet Union would refuse to attend that organization. Mao immediately sent a telegram to Beijing asking Zhou Enlai to issue a statement to the Security Council.[46]

On January 13, Yacov Malik, the Soviet representative to the United Nations, introduced a resolution requesting expulsion of the Chinese

Nationalist representative from the Security Council. His motion was defeated by a vote of 6 to 3. The United States cast a negative vote, and Britain abstained. As a result, Malik walked out of the chamber.[47] On that night, Vyshinsky told Mao that, given the situation at the Security Council, it was necessary for the PRC to reassert its position. He suggested that Beijing announce its own representative to the United Nations to replace the Nationalist envoy. Accepting Vyshinsky's suggestion, Mao sent a cable to Liu Shaoqi instructing him to select the chief representative for the PRC's delegation to the United Nations.[48] On January 19, Zhou Enlai announced that China had appointed Zhang Wentian as chairman of its mission to the United Nations.

Beijing was unhappy with London's decision to abstain from the vote. The Foreign Office asked Hutchison to explain to the Chinese that Britain's abstention did not indicate support for the KMT over the PRC. The decision had been taken because there had been no likelihood of a majority decision and it was, accordingly, premature for the issue to be raised. The Foreign Office went on to say that "the problem of Chinese representation in the United Nations can not be solved unilaterally by individual states on the basis of their own wishes or views about the Chinese Government and that a collective decision of some sort must be taken."[49]

Britain was eager to improve relations with Beijing. In March 1950, in order to break the deadlock in the Security Council, the British began to work behind the scenes to secure a majority on the issue of admitting the PRC into the United Nations. At this time, conditions appeared favorable for Beijing's admission because five out of thirteen members of the Security Council, the USSR, India, Yugoslavia, Great Britain, and Norway, had already recognized the PRC. Two more votes for Beijing would constitute a majority. Bevin instructed British diplomats to approach Egypt, Ecuador, and Cuba. At the same time, Bevin realized that the key to his success rested with the Americans.[50]

Washington had refused to recognize the PRC and wanted to isolate Beijing from the United Nations. In public, the American government insisted that the China seat question was "procedural" rather than "substantive," therefore, that its negative vote should not be construed as a veto. The United States would accept any Security Council decision by a seven-vote majority.[51] But behind the scenes, Washington put pressure on small countries to prevent the formation of a majority in favor of admitting the PRC into the United Nations.

On January 18, the U.S. ambassador in Quito, as instructed by the State Department, presented to the Ecuadoran Foreign Office a memorandum which stated that, while the U.S. government understood that international political decisions regarding recognition were for each country to make independently, it wished to point out that termination of relations with the KMT government by Ecuador would have an "important effect" upon the voting situation in the Security Council in connection with Soviet efforts to unseat the KMT representative. The message added that the "Ecuadoran Government might wish to consider deferring, at least for [the] present, breaking relations with" the Chinese Nationalist regime.[52]

U.N. Secretary-General Trygve Lie was very unhappy with American pressure on Ecuador. On February 25, he told John C. Ross, the deputy U.S. representative on the Security Council, that he did not like the American action because, in his view, it was not "essential" to U.S. policy, whereas it "very seriously damaged" the effective execution of his own responsibilities. Throughout January and February, Lie had been lobbying various Security Council members to vote for the seating of the PRC. The secretary-general was afraid that Moscow would depart from the United Nations permanently and, together with China, establish a rival world organization.[53]

As a result of American opposition, the British initiative failed to secure a majority in the Security Council in favor of admitting China. Sino-British diplomatic negotiations in Beijing continued to be fruitless. During May, Hutchison kept urging the Foreign Office to take new measures on the U.N. issue, which, in his view, was one problem area in which something could be done to improve Anglo-Chinese relations.[54]

In June, the British government decided to adopt a new policy on voting in the United Nations: it would support China's admission. It was assumed that the next opportunity to carry out this new policy would be July 3 when the U.N. Economic and Social Council convened in Geneva.[55]

The outbreak of the Korean War, however, torpedoed the British plan, and instead, London decided to postpone voting in favor of Beijing. The hostilities made the American attitude more uncompromising. Washington insisted that the Security Council should not be diverted from its fundamental task of stopping aggression in Korea. On July 3, Acheson instructed Warren R. Austin, the U.S. representative to the United Nations, to state, if the question of Chinese representation were raised, that, in view of the Korean situation, the U.S. government considered it "undesirable" to discuss the issue.[56]

In addition to complicating the question of Chinese representation in the United Nations, the Korean fighting aggravated Anglo-American differences over the issue. This dispute was shown in the response of Washington and London to a Soviet attempt to end the war in early July. On July 6, Soviet

Deputy Foreign Minister Andrei Gromyko approached the British ambassador in Moscow, Sir David Kelly, proposing a peaceful settlement in Korea. Before reacting to the Soviet move, officials in London and Washington exchanged views. The Americans suspected that one of the prices that Moscow would demand for using its influence to bring about the withdrawal of the North Korean forces would be Western agreement that China be admitted into the United Nations. If Beijing became a member of the Security Council, Lewis Douglas, the U.S. ambassador in London, believed, "its claim to Formosa would be difficult to refute and the U.S. position would be made extremely difficult." Washington emphasized the connection between the Korean fighting and the China issue in the United Nations.[57]

In a message to Bevin on July 10, Acheson said that the question of Chinese representation in the United Nations should not be dealt with "until the aggression against Korea is resolved." The U.S. government, the secretary of state continued, did not believe that the United Nations could "deal with the matter on its merits under the coercion of (a) Communist aggression against Korea or (b) Russian absence, with Peiping seating as the price of return."[58]

Both Attlee and Bevin believed, however, that the question of Korea and the problem of admitting China into the United Nations were unrelated and that the China issue could be considered on its own merits. Bevin told Ambassador Douglas that he had never doubted the wisdom of Britain's decision to recognize China. It turned out, though, that when Gromyko and Kelley discussed the Korean issue on July 11, they did not mention China.[59] Anglo-American debates about the Chinese representation issue continued into August. In a note to British ambassador Oliver Franks on August 4, Acheson reiterated American opposition to the seating of the PRC in the United Nations. Responding to a Bevin message, the secretary of state contended that it was difficult to see how the question of Chinese representation could be raised "purely on its merits" while the Korean fighting was going on. The heart of the problem, Acheson explained, was "how the separation of Peiping and Moscow could be accomplished." The United States doubted that the Chinese Communists would respond to Western favors under the current circumstances or that the foreign policy of either China or Russia "would be affected by the seating of Peiping in the United Nations." On the contrary, Acheson concluded, "such increment of prestige and influence" would be "another stimulus to communist aggression in Asia."[60]

In his reply to Acheson on August 11, Bevin reaffirmed his belief that a separation of the Korean issue and the Chinese representation problem was possible. He asserted that the latter might be raised in the United Nations "in its own context, and not in the context of Korea." He told Acheson that, if the question were put to the vote in this circumstance, the British government would "feel obliged to vote for" the PRC. The reasons for this position, Bevin explained, had to do with London's sensitivity to Asian opinions. The British attitude toward China, he said, had been determined from the beginning by the fact "that any question relating to China is essentially an Asian problem. . . . I have always regarded Asia as a whole and I believe that we must not regard our attitudes toward one country in Asia in isolation without considering what the effect is going to be on the whole land mass."[61]

As for the problem of separating China and the Soviet Union, Bevin invoked the Tito analogy: "We must ask ourselves whether Tito would have broken from Moscow if he had had no hope whatever of any friendly association with the West and if Yugoslavia had not been a member of the United Nations. If China continues to be excluded from the United Nations, and if the attitude of the West continues to be coldly hostile, must she not come to the conclusion, even when the moment arrives when she would like to move away from Moscow, that she has no other course but to maintain her association?"[62] It is interesting to note that American Secretary of State John Foster Dulles would later draw the same Tito parallel to justify his tough policy toward China.[63]

Before the opening of the Fifth Session of the General Assembly on September 19, Zhou Enlai addressed a letter to the United Nations, again requesting the replacement of the "illegitimate delegates of the Chinese Kuomintang reactionary remnant clique" by the PRC representatives. He announced that the Chinese government had appointed a delegation headed by Zhang Wentian to attend the session.[64]

At the opening of the meeting on September 19, the British delegation voted for an Indian resolution to admit the PRC into the United Nations but abstained on a Soviet motion to expel the KMT representative. Both resolutions, however, were defeated. Canada then called for the establishment of a special committee consisting of seven members nominated by the president and confirmed by the Assembly to consider the question of Chinese representation and to report back with recommendations to the current session of the General Assembly. Pending decisions by the Assembly, the KMT representatives would remain in the United Nations. The General Assembly adopted this resolution.[65]

Britain had finally cast its affirmative vote for China although the Indian motion had not been adopted. Beijing, nonetheless, was not satisfied.

Zhou Enlai was angry at being rejected again by the United Nations. He told Indian ambassador Pannikar that China's patience for the international organization was running out. The Chinese premier was not impressed by Britain's vote for the Indian resolution and considered London's abstention on the Soviet resolution as a demonstration of British duplicity.[66]

Britain continued its policy of voting for China in the United Nations until mid-1951 when the American government proposed a moratorium on any discussion of the question of Chinese representation. The purpose of this action, as Acheson explained to British Foreign Secretary Herbert Morrison on May 25, 1951, was to prevent the reemergence of the China issue when Malik became president of the Security Council on June 1. The United States understood, Acheson continued, that the British delegation would, under its current instructions, have to vote for the seating of the PRC if the issue were raised in the Security Council.[67]

Partly from frustration over the procrastination of the Sino-British diplomatic talks and the Chinese refusal to accept a settlement of the Korean dispute on Western terms and partly out of a desire to improve Anglo-American relations, Britain supported the U.S. proposal. The moratorium first became operative at the U.N. Trusteeship Council meeting on June 5. Because it was a motion to defer discussion, it was given precedence over the Soviet resolution to admit the PRC.[68]

Thus, Britain's policy toward Chinese representation in the United Nations zigzagged over two years. It underwent a change from abstaining to voting, and then from voting to putting off the question. When the Conservative government assumed power in October 1951, it continued this practice of postponing a resolution to the China question. The Anglo-American moratorium in the United Nations would last for ten years until 1961. It was clear that, from the beginning, the British had not expected the issue of the Chinese seat to become a serious stumbling block in the improvement of Sino-British relations. London had failed to appreciate the sensitivities of the Chinese Communists and their determination to be the sole representative of China in the United Nations. Before the outbreak of the Korean War, the British had anticipated the imminent fall of Taiwan into CCP hands, which, of course, would have resolved the issue of KMT representation. But the Korean fighting dashed that prospect. The British would find themselves in a constant dilemma of accommodating Beijing's pressures without alienating its ally, the United States.

THE CNAC AND CATC DISPUTE

The China National Aviation Corporation (CNAC) was a Hong Kong-based firm, incorporated under Chinese law. The KMT government owned a majority of its shares and Pan American Airways the rest. The Central Air Transport Corporation (CATC) was an official agency controlled by the Nationalist regime. The CNAC and CATC case was the second major area in which the PRC believed that the British had failed the test for sincerity in establishing diplomatic relations. On November 9, 1949, the general managers and staff members of the two airlines flew to Beijing from Hong Kong and issued a statement announcing the termination of relations with Chiang Kai-shek and offering their service to the PRC. They left behind seventy-one transports, including modern Convairs and DC-4s, on the ground in Hong Kong. Beijing immediately claimed the airplanes as the "sacred property" of the PRC.[69]

Afraid that the Communists might use the aircraft to attack Taiwan, Chiang Kai-shek asked the Hong Kong authorities to impound them. In his efforts to prevent Beijing from obtaining the airplanes, the KMT leader received support from his American friends, General Claire Chennault and Whiting Willauer, associates of the Civil Air Transport (CAT), who were also alarmed at the defection and worried about the prospect of Beijing assuming control of the airplanes. They realized that the incident not only placed Taiwan in danger of invasion but also represented a political blow to Nationalist morale. Willauer rushed to Taipei on November 10 to discuss with Chiang's government how to cope with the situation. They first arrived at the idea of using the CAT to act as an agent for the KMT government, with full authority to transfer title of the airplanes or adopt any other measures necessary to prevent Communist possession of the transports. Failing to implement this scheme, Chennault and Willauer realized that their only remaining alternative was to hand over the equipment to the Americans. On December 10, it was disclosed in Taipei that the CAT would purchase the two airlines.[70]

Local courts in Hong Kong, however, refused to allow the CAT access to the aircraft, despite pressures by Chennault and Willauer. With the support of the U.S. government, the CAT pressed the Hong Kong authorities to influence court proceedings or to adopt executive measures in its favor. During a meeting with Hong Kong Governor Alexander Grantham on January 4, 1950, in the presence of American Consul-General Karl Rankin, the CAT's representatives, General William Donovan, former chief of the OSS, and Richard Heppner, wartime head of the OSS in China, demanded that the planes be handed over to the CAT "without further ado." Donovan said that "if it had not been for the United States, Britain would have lost the war." If the governor failed to satisfy his request, Donovan threatened, he would "make it hot" for him with authorities in London. Unmoved, Grantham insisted that the matter be settled in the courts.[71]

In Washington, State Department officials warned the British ambassador that if London failed to keep the aircraft in Hong Kong, the continuation of Marshall Plan aid to Britain might be jeopardized. Across the Atlantic, Arthur Ringwalt, First Secretary of the American Embassy, had "endless hours" with the Foreign Office, pressing the British for a favorable solution of the dispute.[72]

On January 14, Chennault wrote to Clark Clifford, Truman's closest adviser, spelling out his reasons for buying the two airlines. The general referred to the aircraft as "a modern Far East air fleet which in strategic importance in the Far Eastern situation constitutes the equivalent during World War II of the British fleet, or the French fleet at Oran which the British felt compelled to destroy." With these planes, the former "Flying Tiger" pilot claimed, the Communists could consolidate their power in China, attack Taiwan, or support guerrilla warfare against the Philippines, Indochina, Indonesia, or any area in Asia. He related the difficulties he had encountered with the Hong Kong authorities in obtaining the aircraft and expressed his determination to keep the planes from China.[73]

According to the diary of Wang Shijie (Wang Shih-chieh), secretary-general of the Presidential Office of Chiang Kai-shek, Donovan lobbied congressmen in Washington to pressure the administration to help Chennault. On January 25, Congressman Mike Mansfield wrote to Truman, expressing his concern over the CAT affair. He worried that "because of the length of time it would take to process this matter through the courts, it might be possible that the Chinese Communists would be able to make off with these planes at Kowloon and thereby create a tense situation." The lawmaker urged the president to "do all in your power to see to it that these planes do not fall into the hands of the Chinese Communists."[74]

The Hong Kong authorities came under increasing pressure from all sides as the courts deliberated the various claims to the airplanes. Washington demanded that American property be protected. Beijing threatened to confiscate British property in Shanghai for every transport plane denied it. Officials in the colony did not want to alienate the Chinese government. On February 23, a local court ruled that the airplanes were the property of the PRC under the principle of sovereign immunity. American reaction was swift and angry. At a press conference on February 24, Secretary of State Acheson protested to authorities in Hong Kong and London. Senator William Knowland called the transfer of the aircraft to China "one of the greatest blows to the non-Communist world that has been delivered in that part of the world."[75]

While Washington increased pressures on the British, Beijing was no less active. On April 4, Premier Zhou Enlai blamed the Hong Kong government for the sabotage of seven planes and demanded the immediate transfer of the remaining aircraft to China. The Hong Kong authorities, Zhou charged, had impeded the planes from returning to China while never seriously taking measures to protect them. "Therefore the Hong Kong Government must be held fully and directly responsible for the present losses incurred by China."[76]

London finally yielded to American pressure. On May 10, the British government issued an Order-in-Council, which replaced the existing law with a new law that instructed Hong Kong officials to keep the aircraft in the colony pending an adjudication as to their ownership. The order ensured a long litigation in the Hong Kong courts with final right of appeal to the Privy Council in London. Beijing was furious with this decision. Vice-Foreign Minister Zhang Hanfu handed the British chargé d'affaires in Beijing, John Hutchison, a note branding the order "a demonstration of a most unfriendly attitude toward the Chinese People's Republic."[77]

In 1952, the Privy Council decided to hand over the planes to the Americans. The Chinese government lodged strong protests and retaliated by taking over the British trolley, gas, water, and banking companies in China. General Chennault's wife Anna later claimed that, in the general's view, the "brilliant capture-by-purchase" of the aircraft saved Taiwan because it had prevented the Chinese Communists from using them in an attack against the island.[78]

The whole incident underscored Britain's dilemma in East Asia. While desiring to improve relations with the PRC, London had also to accommodate Washington's tough policy toward Beijing. To preserve the more important Anglo-American alliance, the British often had to sacrifice their relations with the Chinese.

BEIJING'S CRITICISM OF BRITAIN
AND HOSTILITY TOWARD THE UNITED STATES

Beginning in late 1950, China's media increased its indictments of British domestic and foreign policies. One article in *Shijie zhishi*, published on January 1, 1951, described Britain as "the 49th state" of the United States, referring to London's political and economic reliance on Washington. The British people, the author claimed, understood better than anyone else that the threat to their survival came not from Communist countries but from America. Another article in the same journal published two weeks later said that the Marshall Plan and the North Atlantic Treaty Organization (NATO) had made the British dependent on the United States and deepened England's economic crisis.[79]

British colonial rule in Malaya, especially its treatment of Chinese nationals there, drew heavy fire from Beijing's commentators. On December 29, 1950, the PRC issued an official statement condemning British persecution of the Chinese in Malaya under its Emergency Law. Beijing also announced that an investigating team had been established by the Chinese People's Relief Committee for the Overseas Chinese Refugees in Malaya to look into the matter. A *Shijie zhishi* commentary portrayed the Malayan Emergency as resembling the Japanese handling of the Malayan people during World War II. It singled out the British confinement of Chinese Malayans in concentration camps as an example. The Chinese people, the writer asserted, would not tolerate such oppression of their compatriots in Malaya.[80]

Although China's attitude toward the British after late 1950 was characterized by increasing animosity, Beijing's policy toward America was marked by total antagonism. In an address celebrating the first anniversary of the founding of the PRC, Zhou Enlai referred to the United States as "the most dangerous enemy" of the Chinese people. Beijing was very angry at United States efforts to block its entry into the United Nations. Regarding the dispatch of the Seventh Fleet into the Taiwan Strait as "American occupation of Chinese territory," the Chinese leadership launched a nationwide anti-American campaign in the early 1950s.[81]

In March 1951, the Chinese government announced that it had exposed an American spy ring in Tianjin. Commenting on the incident, a *Shijie zhishi* editorial argued that, since their setback on mainland China in 1949, the American imperialists had started to undermine the Chinese government through fifth columns. To support its argument, the editorial cited statements by Roy Andrews and General Chennault in *The New York Herald*

Tribune and *Colliers,* which called for the overthrow of the Communist regime in China through sabotage, uprisings, and guerrilla warfare. The article cited Soviet suppression of counterrevolutionaries after the October Revolution to show the importance of maintaining high vigilance against imperialist subversion.[82]

Sino-American antagonism further intensified as a result of the Anglo-American initiative to draft a peace treaty with Japan. On December 4, 1950, Zhou Enlai said in a public statement that since the Chinese people had contributed to the defeat of Japanese imperialism, the PRC, as the sole representative of China, was fully entitled to be involved in the preparation, negotiation, and conclusion of the peace settlement with Japan. The PRC kept a close watch as John Foster Dulles drafted the Japanese peace treaty. Before Dulles's visit to Tokyo in January 1951, *Shijie zhishi* charged that the trip was aimed at turning Japan into a tool of American aggression in Korea, China, and Southeast Asia.[83]

In a telegram to Mao on May 6, 1952, Stalin notified the Chinese of the Soviet position on the Japanese peace treaty. The Soviet leader said that the preparation for the draft of the peace treaty should not be conducted by the American government alone but should involve the People's Republic of China, the Soviet Union, the United States, and Great Britain as well as all the other countries that had participated in the war against Japan; the treaty should be based on the Cairo Declaration, the Potsdam Declaration, and the Yalta Agreement; it should follow the principles of making Japan a peaceful, democratic country of independence, of limiting Japan's armed force to self-defense, of opposing the revival of Japanese militarism, and of developing Japan's peaceful economy without restrictions. Mao immediately responded to Stalin expressing agreement with the Soviet position.[84]

Upon obtaining a draft copy of the Japanese treaty, Zhou Enlai sent a note on May 22 to Soviet Ambassador N. V. Roshchin, charging that the document violated the legal requirements of the Potsdam Agreement. The central purpose of the new treaty, he pointed out, was nothing but "the revival of Japanese militarism in order to continue and expand [U.S.] aggression against the Asian countries."[85] In September, the Japanese Peace Treaty was signed in San Francisco. In a September 18 statement, Zhou Enlai declared the treaty "illegal and invalid." The Chinese government also organized mass demonstrations against the Japanese-American Security Pact.[86]

Dulles's handling of the Japanese Peace Treaty had not only infuriated the Chinese government but also strained U.S. relations with Britain. From the beginning, the two Western powers had experienced differences over which Chinese government was to be invited to attend the Japanese peace conference, with Washington in favor of Chiang Kai-shek and London supporting Beijing. Finally they reached a compromise in the form of the so-called "Dulles-Morrison understanding" of June 19, 1951, which included the following points: (1) no Chinese representatives would be invited to the coming peace conference to sign the multilateral peace treaty; (2) Tokyo's future attitudes toward China "must be determined by Japan itself in the exercise of the sovereign and independent status contemplated by the treaty."[87]

The Dulles-Morrison formula, however, did not really solve Anglo-American divergences over Japan's policy toward China. The British government preferred that Tokyo assume a position of equal distance from the contending Chinese governments. In a September 26, 1951, memorandum, Foreign Office analyst Robert Scott said that Britain wanted Japan to trade with both mainland China and Taiwan. In a meeting with Dulles on September 9, Morrison expressed the hope that "nothing would be done to crystallize the Japanese position toward China until after the Treaty of Peace came into force." It would be "seriously objectionable" to London, the British foreign minister warned, for Japan to recognize the Chiang regime as "having legitimacy and power to bind all China." If such a thing happened before the effective date of the peace treaty, Morrison contended, the British government would be vulnerable to the "charge of having been deceived by the United States."[88]

British officials, in fact, hoped that Japan would establish de facto relations with the PRC as London had done. Two considerations lay behind the British position. The first was political. The establishment of normal contacts between Japan and China was in line with the general British policy of "keeping a foot in China" and encouraging Sino-Soviet schism by maintaining Beijing's touch with the West. The second was economic. Before World War II, Japanese products had invaded British colonies and dominions, undermining English exports. After the war, London was afraid that Japan would again pose a threat to its position in the Southeast Asian market, a likely prospect given American efforts to establish a Japan-Southeast Asia trade link as a compensation for Tokyo's loss of the market in China.[89]

The Japanese themselves wanted to renew trade with China. Like the British, Japanese Prime Minister Yoshida Shigeru believed that the Chinese Communist government would eventually become another Tito regime, and he saw China as a valuable future market for Japanese products. Pressed by Japanese business interests, Yoshida was reluctant to conclude a treaty with Taiwan as demanded by the Americans. But Dulles was determined to commit Japan to Taiwan. He told Yoshida plainly that the United States was more powerful than Britain and could help Japan more in its economy and security. And since Japan had selected the course of cooperation with the West as shown in the conclusion of the peace treaty, Dulles went on, it was to its advantage to accept the position of the United States in regard to Taiwan. The Japanese finally yielded to American pressures. The result was the well-known "Yoshida letter" of December 24, 1951, which committed Japan to Chiang Kai-shek before the conclusion of the peace treaty between Japan and Taiwan in April 1952.[90]

The Yoshida letter reopened the Anglo-American crack plastered over by the Dulles-Morrison formula. London reacted angrily to the document. To placate British feelings, Dulles wrote to Prime Minister Churchill on January 17, 1952. While offering apologies for the "misunderstanding between our Governments," Dulles stressed the importance of maintaining a common Western position on the issue. "When we are divided," Dulles concluded, "neither of us gains, but only our enemies." Distrust, however, had been created between American and British officials. The high-handed treatment by which Dulles coerced the Japanese to sign the Yoshida letter marred his relationship with British Foreign Secretary Anthony Eden to the extent that the Englishman wrote Eisenhower in 1952 asking him not to appoint Dulles secretary of state in the event of a Republican election victory.[91]

The episode demonstrated that owing to its power and influence, Washington could usually carry the day when there was a difference in Anglo-American approaches in the Far East. The exclusion of the PRC from the formation of the Japanese Peace Treaty reinforced Beijing's suspicion of the hostile intention of the United States.

CONCLUSION

The outbreak of the Korean War had very negative effects on China's relations with the United States and Great Britain. The hostilities reinforced the Truman administration's determination to keep Taiwan from mainland China and to oppose the PRC's admission into the United Nations. Acheson contended that the question of Chinese representation in the international organization was related to the war in Korea and should not be treated on its own merit. To further shelve the issue, the United States proposed a moratorium in May 1951. Dulles was resolved to sever all political and economic relations between Japan and the PRC and commit Tokyo to Taipei. His handling of the Yoshida letter greatly strained Anglo-American relations.

Washington's pressure on London to block the PRC's entry into the United Nations and deny Beijing the aircraft in Hong Kong not only resulted in a total hostility between China and the United States but also caused lack of progress in Sino-British relations. To maintain Anglo-American unity, London often had to succumb to Washington's pressure in terms of China policy. This was especially the case with the question of Chinese representation in the United Nations and the Hong Kong aircraft incident. Britain's global weakness and its dependence on American economic assistance allowed the United States the luxury of ignoring its major ally's sensitivities and concerns.

Beijing was very unhappy with Britain's lack of "sincerity" in establishing diplomatic relations with China. The British mistreatment of Chinese nationals in Malaya provided a pretext for Beijing to vent its wrath against the British. Meanwhile, the Chinese leadership watched carefully and reacted indignantly to the close cooperation between America and Taiwan and the conclusion of the Japanese Peace Treaty. They perceived in the United States a sworn foe determined to isolate and overthrow the Chinese government. During the Korean fighting, the Chinese government kept up a continuous anti-American campaign as a means to mobilize the populace and to legitimize its authority.

6 Conclusion of the Korean War, 1952–1953

CHURCHILL, EDEN, AND CHINA

In October 1951, the Churchill government came to power in Britain. Out of London's strategic and economic needs as well as Churchill's personal inclination, the Conservative government attached great importance to Anglo-American solidarity. While continuing the basic Labor policies in the Far East, Churchill and his foreign secretary, Anthony Eden, appeared more cooperative with the Americans. They were less inclined to criticize U.S. policy and more willing to lend at least rhetorical support to Washington. As for the war in Korea, they were eager to see an early conclusion of the fighting.

Churchill adhered to the principle that Britain stood at the center of three interlocking circles: the "alliance of the English-speaking peoples," unity within the Commonwealth, and cooperation with Western Europe. Very much an Anglo-American supremacist, he regarded solidarity with the United States as the basis of postwar British foreign policy. In a meeting with John Foster Dulles in April 1954, the prime minister claimed that "only the English-speaking people counted" and that "together they could rule the world." President Eisenhower observed that Churchill "has developed an almost childlike faith that all of the answers are to be found merely in British-American partnership."[1]

Throughout his life, Churchill had been mostly concerned with European affairs and had little knowledge of the Far East. He once said: "I, of course, thought Europe was the most important place because I lived there. I never was much of a China man myself. I used to say to President Roosevelt that he preferred the Chinese empire to the British empire. I told him that China would be divided by war after World War II."[2] On another occasion, he admitted to Arthur Radford that "he had never been beyond Calcutta and that he did not really know the problems and solutions for the area."[3]

In fact, Churchill was so ethnocentric that he developed a strong contempt for non-Western civilizations. He once wrote Dwight D. Eisenhower, "In my view China is not important enough to be a cause of major hazards. More

113

people over here exaggerate the power and importance of China as a military factor. . . . I am old-fashioned enough to look to Steel as a rather decisive index of conventional military power, and of manufacturing and communication capacity."[4] In a discussion with Henry Luce concerning China in 1955, Churchill asserted that "I think your people have been remarkably patient" in the face of "all the abuse from those dirty dogs, and the threats, and your airmen in prison. And you could destroy them as a military power in ten days."[5]

Eden also subscribed to Churchill's principle of "three unities," but he had a different order of priorities. Although for Churchill Anglo-American unity always came first, followed by the Commonwealth and Western Europe, Eden placed the Commonwealth first and partnership with the United States last. Both statesmen were confronted with the fundamental problem of maintaining Britain's world power status with diminishing resources in a harsh and rapidly shifting international context.[6]

As far as China policy was concerned, Churchill and Eden adopted the basic approach of Attlee and Bevin. They shared with their Labor predecessors the assumption that the Chinese Communist government would last a long time, and, therefore, accommodation with it was preferable to a head-on confrontation over major issues. They believed that Chiang Kai-shek had no chance to return to China and that assistance to him would only increase tensions in East Asia.[7]

As for U.S. policy toward China, the Foreign Office believed that Washington "has been so preoccupied with domestic politics" that it failed to pay attention to the long-term aspects of its Far Eastern policy and "has attempted to solve each problem in isolation." Only a long-term settlement, British officials contended, including admission of the PRC to the United Nations and some compromise over Taiwan, offered hope of modifying Beijing's conviction that the West was hostile to it, and inducing it to adopt "responsible non-aggressive policy."[8]

Regarding the Sino-Soviet alliance, the Churchill government had the same conviction as Labor that the best way to wean China from the Soviet Union was to maintain Beijing's contact with the West. Churchill told American officials in early 1952 that China "was not permanently communist" and that "in a number of years . . . China would not take all its orders from Russia."[9]

Out of a desire to improve Anglo-American relations, however, the Churchill government sought at least the appearance of moving closer to Washington's hard-line policy toward China. This position was clearly demonstrated during Churchill's visit to Washington in January 1952.

During discussions with American officials, the prime minister went out of his way to praise the U.S. role as "leader" in the Far East and pledged that his government would "do its utmost to meet US views and requests in relation to that area." He commended the decision to intervene in Korea, arguing that it was a "turning point" in the Cold War and that Britain "was profoundly grateful to the United States for its action." He agreed with Acheson's contention that the ongoing stalemate at Panmunjom was the result of a Soviet plan to transfer the Korean problem to the United Nations where political issues could be raised.[10]

Churchill admitted that British diplomatic relations with the PRC were "essentially a fiction" because Beijing had not recognized Britain. He added that if he had been in power, he would have broken relations with China when the Chinese attacked the U.N. troops in Korea. But when he was back in office, the armistice negotiations had started, and he did not believe that such a British action would be desirable any longer because of its possible effect on the negotiations. Speaking of Taiwan, Churchill asserted that it would be "shameful" to abandon the Nationalists, who "had fought on our side" during World War II and since then. He personally, however, did not want to see Chiang Kai-shek's regime "recognized as the legitimate government of mainland China."[11]

During the talks, Truman raised the issue of British trade with China. He told Churchill that his military advisers had informed him that between November 1950 and December 1951, 167 British ships had engaged in trade with Communist ports in China. He asked for London's cooperation in stopping these activities.[12] Churchill responded that he would send the information home, and if the facts supported what Truman had said, he would see that it was stopped immediately. The prime minister added that his government, which had only been in office for about two months, had no responsibility in this matter, but it would, nevertheless, immediately assume responsibility.[13]

The two sides also discussed the problem of Sino-Soviet relations. In this regard, Acheson told Churchill and Eden basically what he had said to Attlee in Washington a year earlier. The secretary of state said that in January 1950, he had believed that it was possible "to play on Chinese-Russian differences with a view to fomenting a split between these two Communist powers." Now, however, he no longer held this view; "this being especially true since the Chinese intervention in the Korean war." Acheson stressed that "in the view of the United States we must proceed in our relations with China on the basis of specific situations. For example, what should we do in the case of a breach of the armistice? Our actions should be based on such concrete considerations and not on the tenuous and moot consideration of the responsibility of splitting China away from the USSR. We must act as we think best in specific cases even at the risk of pushing Communist China towards the Soviets."[14] It is interesting to observe that although in 1950 Attlee had argued with the Americans about the possibility of separating Beijing from Moscow, this time Churchill and Eden unenthusiastically accepted Acheson's views. Eden said that his government no longer believed that Titoism could be promoted in China or that policy should be based "on such a tenuous possibility."[15]

One reason for the Churchill government's eagerness to show solidarity with the United States in East Asia was that London hoped to elicit some American support for British policy in the Middle East. Britain faced serious problems in the area caused by a rising tide of Arabic nationalism. The Egyptian government had denounced the 1936 treaty with Britain that allowed the stationing of British troops along the Suez Canal until 1956, and early in 1952 the whole of the British strategic reserve was dispatched to Egypt to confront terrorism in the canal zone. In Iran, Prime Minister Mossadeq had nationalized the petroleum business and expelled the Anglo-Iranian oil company.[16]

In Washington, Churchill told Truman and Acheson that he knew that the Americans were bearing "a great burden" in the Far East and that London should not do something that would make the American task more difficult but should do its best to help Washington. The British in their turn, he continued, were "carrying a great burden in the Middle East." The Americans should adopt policies in the area which would help London. Churchill expressed the belief that if Britain and the United States worked together, "things would fall into place."[17]

It should be pointed out that, despite its rhetorical support for the American position in the Far East, the Churchill government, in reality, did not change British policy toward China. It continued to recognize Beijing and to reject the view that Chiang represented the authentic voice of China. As were the Labor ministers earlier, Churchill and Eden were unwilling to take risks in the Far East that might cause a world war. This mixture of public toughness and private cautiousness in British policy was clearly demonstrated in London's attitude toward the American proposal for a "Great Sanctions" statement against China in case the latter violated an armistice in Korea.

THE "GREATER SANCTIONS" STATEMENT

When Churchill came into office, a military stalemate existed in Korea and armistice negotiations were in progress between the United Nations Command (UNC) and the Communists. The major issues involved were the armistice demarcation line, arrangements for ensuring adherence to a cease-fire, and the repatriation of prisoners of war. The Communists argued at the beginning that the demarcation line should be the thirty-eighth parallel, the line of division before June 1950. The UNC deemed this unacceptable because U.N. forces occupied territory north of the parallel. Progress was gradually made in settling the disputes over the demarcation line and inspection arrangements, but the issues related to prisoners of war remained intractable and almost destroyed the prospects for a truce.

Like Labor officials before them, Churchill and Eden also opposed an escalation of the war, which, they feared, would pin down the United States in Asia and benefit the Soviet Union. Yet, in general, they were less obstructive with the Americans than the preceding government had been. Churchill took a personal interest in the Panmunjom negotiations. On November 16, 1951, he wrote to Eden, "No one knows what is going on in Korea or which side is benefiting in strength from the bombing and grimaces at Panmunjom. We must try to penetrate the American mind and purpose."[18]

The first serious discussion the Churchill government conducted with Washington regarding Korea concerned the American proposal for retaliatory measures against China in the event the latter violated an armistice. The State Department and the JCS had devoted much attention to the question because they believed that it was unlikely to resolve the issue of inspection arrangements at Panmunjom. Administration officials were considering such sanctions as a complete economic blockade of the Chinese coast; a U.N. naval blockade of China; military actions against China (including air bombardment of military targets and harassing amphibious raids) but short of land operations; a refusal to consider admitting the PRC into the United Nations; and British agreement to maintain at least its present level of force commitment in Korea pending clarification following an armistice. Deputy Under Secretary of State H. Freeman Matthews informed British Ambassador Oliver Franks of this "greater sanctions" plan on November 21, 1951.[19]

Acheson told Eden in Rome on November 28 that because adequate inspection arrangements were unlikely to be made at Panmunjom, the United States intended to make the Communists realize that they would provoke harsh measures if they violated the armistice. This "greater sanctions" warning, the secretary of state explained, could be issued either as an Anglo-American declaration, or as a U.S. statement supported by Britain. The United States, Acheson added, did not contemplate issuing the warning through the United Nations. Defense Secretary Lovett told Eden that "he should realize that if there was a violation of the truce, our country would be swept with great indignation and the people would want the administration to throw the book at the communists." Eden replied that he would consult Churchill but mentioned that British public opinion had also to be considered. As for the retaliatory measures envisaged against China, the foreign secretary said, from a personal point of view, that "the bombing beyond the Yalu would be less difficult for his government than the blockade."[20]

Churchill convened a meeting of defense ministers and the Chiefs of Staff on November 30. The participants argued that the Chinese and North Korean Communists would probably comply with an armistice agreement and that, if a warning statement was made, it should be confined to general terms. Soviet ports would have to be excluded, rendering such a blockade ineffective. Worse, a naval blockade would be highly dangerous and capable of triggering a global war. Bombardment north of the Yalu would be less risky. Churchill revealed his attitude, saying "that Russia would start World War III when she wanted to; she certainly would not do so merely to honour her pledge to China. He was, therefore, not unduly worried about bombing targets in Manchuria. As regards a war with China he considered that China was not a country against which one declared war; rather a country against which war was waged."[21]

On December 3, Eden told Acheson that London approved the "greater sanctions" statement but added that it should be adopted by as many as possible of the countries contributing forces to the UNC in Korea and be made "in very general terms." Regarding a naval blockade of China and bombardment north of the Yalu, the Admiralty did not expect that a sea blockade would be effective, except over years rather than months; excluding the Soviet ports would make a blockade futile, and including them would risk a world war. The Chiefs of Staff had doubts about the efficacy of bombing north of the Yalu, but it was less dangerous than a blockade.[22] It was obvious that although the British supported the "greater sanctions" statement, they were reluctant to be bound to specific courses of action against China if the statement's provisions came into force.

The "greater sanctions" statement was largely a psychological measure designed to deter the Communists from breaching the armistice agreement.

In reality, the United States did not possess the resources to carry it out. The Americans realized that the U.S. Air Force was incapable of inflicting lasting damage on China, particularly if the Soviet Union provided fighter support; any expansion of the war in Asia would risk precipitating a third world war.[23] The "greater sanctions" idea, nonetheless, anticipated Eisenhower's later practice of employing bluffs to pressure the Communists.

THE PRISONERS OF WAR ISSUE

The prisoners of war (POW) issue was the most thorny one during the armistice negotiations. What had from the outset appeared a simple matter became entangled in politics and ideology. In theory, the question was covered by the Geneva Convention of 1949, which called for immediate and compulsory repatriation. Designed to prevent a recurrence of the situation after World War II, when the Soviet Union kept captive large numbers of German and Japanese prisoners of war as forced labor for its postwar reconstruction, the Geneva agreement did not provide for prisoners who had no intention of being repatriated. Although neither Pyongyang nor Beijing were signatories, both declared their willingness to abide by the Geneva code in North Korea in July 1950 and China two years later.

The United States was an original signatory, but did not ratify the convention. Even so, very early in the Korean War, Washington, along with the Seoul government, announced that it would adhere to the Geneva Accords. As the U.N. forces began to capture large numbers of prisoners, however, and as many of them indicated their unwillingness to be repatriated, the United States began to reconsider its position. President Truman took a moralistic approach toward the issue: because America had made a moral commitment to save South Korea from the Communists, the United States must not permit Chinese and North Korean POWs to be repatriated against their will. "To agree to forced repatriation," Truman once said, "would be unthinkable. It would be repugnant to the fundamental moral and humanitarian principles which underlie our action in Korea."[24]

Aside from this consideration, there were other political motivations for insisting on voluntary repatriation. For one thing, American officials wanted to exploit the propaganda advantages in publicizing the many Communist prisoners refusing repatriation, a demonstration of the illegitimacy of the regimes in Beijing and Pyongyang. For another, the granting of freedom to these POWs might encourage further defections from enemy ranks and act as a deterrent to future Communist aggression. Last, any attempt to return Chinese anti-Communists would be seized upon by the Republicans as a potent campaign issue in a presidential election year. The Republicans could ask no better confirmation of McCarthy's indictment that the Democrats were "soft on Communism."[25]

The British had private reservations about the evolution of American POW policy. They were anxious to secure both a quick conclusion of the war and the release of their own prisoners currently in Communist hands. A Foreign Office memo dated on January 29, 1952, observed that the Americans "with help from the Chinese Nationalists" had enjoyed "some success in re-indoctrinating Chinese PWs in their charge." These people would join Chiang's army. The longer the talks dragged on over this issue, the longer British prisoners would be held by the Communists. London had "no interest at all" in seeing KMT forces expand "at the expense of additional suffering to British and Commonwealth prisoners."[26] The British doubted the benefits of such a transfer to these Chinese POWs themselves. They wondered whether it might not be a case of leaping from "the Communist frying pan into the Nationalist fire."[27]

The British were also suspicious of the procedure for ascertaining the wishes of prisoners. They were uneasy with the U.S. practice of using KMT agents to implement "reindoctrination" in the camps. In March 1952, Foreign Office official Robert Scott observed that although one could sympathize with Washington's determination to uphold voluntary repatriation, the point might be reached eventually where the Americans would have to consider an element of forcible repatriation. This might be acceptable to the Communists and speed the negotiations.[28]

Eden shared these sentiments, but he and Churchill took care not to allow these internal disagreements to undermine Anglo-American relations. To them, it was more important to preserve unity with the Americans. With Washington clearly committed to voluntary repatriation in early 1952, London was reluctant to jeopardize relations by breaking ranks.[29]

The camp riots on Koje Island on May 8, 1952, however, disturbed Eden. The incident revealed unmistakably that the management of the camps had been poor and inept. The foreign secretary informed the State Department that he was greatly upset with the mutiny and the aftermath. From there, he went on to elaborate his grievances on a range of issues involving the POWs. For example, the report of the international committee of the Red Cross and in news accounts challenged the validity of procedures for canvasing POWs about their preferences with respect to repatriation; the British public found it difficult to understand how within ten days 170,000 prisoners could be satisfactorily interrogated "individually and in reasonably privacy." He recommended that a second screening be conducted, adding that although the British government abided by the principle of voluntary repatriation, public opinion must be satisfied on the screening process.[30]

In the summer of 1952, the United States began to put more pressure on China by bombing targets on the Yalu River. On June 23, American planes assaulted the four most vital dams and power complexes in North Korea for the first time. One of these was the huge Supung Dam on the Yalu, which provided about 90 percent of North Korea's total electrical power and about 10 percent of the power for northeast China. The attack on Supung was the largest single air strike of the Korean War and involved more than five hundred U.S. planes. It caused a blackout all over North Korea for fifteen days.[31]

The bombardment strained U.S. relations with its allies, especially Britain. Washington was supposed to inform London before it undertook any such operation. When the first raids were taking place, Acheson happened to be in London where he was criticized by British politicians. In the House of Commons, Eden openly pleaded for "no more surprises."[32] The assault undermined London's trust in Washington's credibility and leadership and revived the fear that the U.S. military was playing too great a role in shaping policy. As a result, the British government insisted on sending a deputy chief of staff to General Mark Clark's headquarters.[33] Britain's reaction to the bombing of the Yalu power facilities showed clearly the disruptive effect on Anglo-American relations of a failure to share information and the damage that such a failure could cause to the image of a solid Western bloc.

But Allied criticism did not prevent Clark from continuing his escalation of the air war as a means of forcing a quick military conclusion to the fighting in Korea. In the next several months, U.S. aircraft stepped up their assaults on North Korean targets, even attacking one oil refinery near the Soviet border.[34]

In late 1952, the British and Canadians showed growing weariness with the war and impatience with the POW issue. Many British officials were annoyed at Washington's insistence on voluntary repatriation, which, they believed, both contradicted the Geneva Convention on prisoners of war and unnecessarily postponed a cease-fire.[35]

British and Canadian differences with the Americans over the settlement of the Korean War were further exacerbated in the fall of 1952 when London and Ottawa reacted favorably to an Indian resolution in the United Nations that suggested the establishment of an international commission to decide the fate of nonrepatriates over an unspecified period. Earlier in October, Washington had gained the support of twenty other countries for its proposal to reaffirm the principle of voluntary repatriation in the United Nations. But this support quickly crumbled when the Indian resolution was introduced. Britain and Canada saw the proposal as a way to break the deadlock on the POW issue. But the Americans were determined to block it. Acheson exerted great pressure on the British and Canadian delegates. The State Department tried to convince London that its support was crucial not only for the sake of the American administration but also for the benefit of the U.K. government. The new president, Acheson warned, would be advised by people who intended to expand the war into China. If London failed to support the U.S. resolution, it would forsake its chance of constraining the next administration from adopting this harsh policy. Furthermore, Acheson said, Anglo-American differences over the issue "would bring grave disillusionment in the United States regarding collective security, which would not be confined to Korea but would extend to NATO and other arrangements . . . of the same sort."[36]

In the end, the Canadians were prepared to yield to Washington's pressure, but the British remained unconvinced and uncooperative. With Truman's approval, Acheson was ready to proceed in the United Nations without Britain in a U.S.-led effort to defeat the Indian proposal. This turned out to be unnecessary, however, when on November 24 the Soviet Union publicly condemned the Indian resolution, which led New Delhi to compromise and accept the U.S. suggestion of a three-month time limit for the detention of nonrepatriates.[37]

It is obvious that in the closing months of the Truman administration great differences existed between Britain and the United States over the settlement of the Korean War. If the Soviet Union had not intervened to kill the Indian resolution and if Acheson had carried out his plans, even more serious damage would have been done to Anglo-American relations in the Far East.

PEACE WITH HONOR

In January 1953, Eisenhower became the thirty-fourth president of the United States.[38] His first foreign policy priority was the termination of the fighting in Korea. It has been generally accepted that the Korean question was an important factor in Eisenhower's victory in the 1952 election. During the campaign, the Republican candidate had promised to go to Korea if elected, with the implication that he would find a way to end the war. After winning the election, the president-elect made his trip in December 1952.[39]

Once in office, Eisenhower found himself in the dilemma that had bedeviled Truman: the Chinese Communists had to be persuaded to stop the hostilities on terms acceptable to the West, and the administration had to find an instrument of pressure that did not hurt the United States more than it damaged the Communists. Eisenhower was tired of the war's diversion and drain on American resources. His political credibility depended on securing an honorable conclusion of the war. The new executive resorted to a strategy of strength and psychological warfare designed to bring the fighting to a close. In this regard, Eisenhower and Dulles took several measures to pressure the Communists to make concessions at the armistice negotiations as well as prevent Beijing's intervention in Indochina.

The first act was Eisenhower's decision to launch a U.N. offensive in the spring of 1953, employing a strengthened South Korean army and American reinforcement. In May, Mark Clark, the head of the U.N. Command, was authorized to strengthen Syngman Rhee's troops to twenty divisions.[40]

The second measure was the decision to "unleash" Chiang Kai-shek: the United States would withdraw the orders of the Seventh Fleet to neutralize the Taiwan Strait. Largely a symbolic gesture, the decision pleased the China lobby, but administration officials realized that Chiang was, in the words of Vice-President Richard Nixon, "a liability rather than an asset." The public unleashing was followed by private instructions demanding restraint. U.S. advisers were told not to engage in "precipitate action" that might cause an expanded war with China.[41] At an NSC meeting on April 8, 1953, Secretary of State Dulles recommended that the United States suspend delivery of jet bombers to the Chinese Nationalists until Washington could "secure very quickly a commitment from Chiang Kai-shek that he would not use these aircraft recklessly and in a fashion to embarass United States policy."[42]

The third measure to coerce the Communists was the nuclear threat. Unlike Truman and Acheson, Eisenhower and Dulles had a very different view of the potential political value of atomic weapons.[43] The Republican administration found the atomic bomb useful in both military and economic terms. From the military point of view, it had the advantage of regaining the initiative that had been lost in Korea: from now on, America would deal with the enemy on terrain and with weapons of its own selection rather than theirs. From the economic perspective, dependence on nuclear deterrence could reduce the cost of conventional force expenditures. Thus, the president publicly declared that "atomic weapons have virtually achieved conventional status within our armed service."[44]

Shortly after assuming office, the Republican administration began to study the use of tactical nuclear weapons. There was disagreement among Eisenhower's advisers regarding the advantages of such weapons. The military tended to be cautious. General Omar Bradley, chairman of the Joint Chiefs of Staff, advised circumspection because of possible allied reactions.[45] Army Chief of Staff General J. Lawton Collins was very suspicious about the value of employing tactical atomic weapons in Korea. "The Communists," he argued, "are dug into positions in depth over a front of one hundred fifty miles," and American tests had shown that "men can be very close to the explosion and not be hurt if they are well dug in."[46]

The president's own thoughts on the issue were unclear. On the one hand, he told his NSC aides that the United States "have got to consider the atomic bomb as simply another weapon in our arsenal."[47] But, on the other hand, he recognized that America should take the fears of its allies into consideration. He said at an NSC meeting on March 31, 1953, that "we could not blind ourselves to the effects of such a move on our allies, which would be very serious since they feel that they will be the battleground in an atomic war between the United States and the Soviet Union."[48] Furthermore, the president was aware of the danger of Soviet retaliation. Always "in the back of his mind" was the likelihood of "attacks by the Soviet Air Force on the almost defensive population centers of Japan."[49]

But if Eisenhower and his lieutenants could not agree upon the advantages of the actual employment of nuclear weapons, they were not at all unwilling to give the impression that such weapons might be used to break the deadlock in Korea.[50] In fact, as early as December 1952, when Eisenhower returned from Korea, he stated in a news conference that the United States faced an enemy "whom we cannot hope to impress by words, however eloquent, but only by deeds—executed under circumstances of our own choosing."[51]

Secretary of State Dulles was even more eager to talk about American nuclear superiority. He was anxious to please the Republican right and avoid the political controversy that had beset Acheson. This made it imperative to look tough on China. He told Emmet John Hughes, Eisenhower's assistant, in April 1953, "I don't think we can get much out of a Korean settlement until we have shown—before all Asia—our clear superiority by giving the Chinese one hell of a licking."[52]

On May 21, Dulles told Indian Prime Minister Nehru that "if the armistice negotiations collapsed, the United States would probably make a stronger rather than a lesser military exertion, and that this might well extend the area of conflict." According to his notes of the conversation, Dulles believed that Nehru would relay the message to Beijing.[53]

In sum, the Eisenhower administration was intent on bringing the inconclusive and costly war in Korea to a close. To achieve this aim, Eisenhower and Dulles were prepared to introduce new harsh measures against the Communists, including nuclear threats. They recognized that a vigorous policy in Korea enjoyed strong domestic support.

BRITAIN AND THE ARMISTICE

London was concerned about the danger of an American expansion of the war in Korea. Churchill had welcomed the succession of Eisenhower to the White House and hoped to revive the wartime Atlantic partnership with the new president. But he was suspicious of the Republican right and McCarthyism and felt uncomfortable with the hawkish and irresponsible Secretary of State Dulles.[54]

The first British complaint about the new Republican administration in the Far East concerned Washington's decision to unleash Chiang Kai-shek. Eden was offended by Eisenhower's failure to consult London in the first major act of his administration.[55] The foreign secretary told U.S. officials that the British government regretted the action, which would cause "unfortunate political repercussions particularly in the United Nations." Furthermore, Eden said, the change of the orders would not "carry with it compensating military advantages" or "help in any way towards a solution of the Korean conflict."[56] Churchill also conveyed to Eisenhower his concern about the American action.[57]

On March 5, 1953, Dulles told Eden that if South Korea's territory could be expanded to the waist of the peninsula, that would place "some 85% of the population of Korea . . . and the industrial complex above the 38th parallel" within the control of Seoul and bolster the morale of Rhee's army. Dulles added that he had no idea of the military cost of such an operation. Eden "seemed to agree with" Dulles's general line but warned that Britain must be "consulted" before any major action was taken.[58]

Between April and June, owing to Eden's absence for major surgery, Churchill assumed a principal responsibility for handling Korean affairs.

Spurred by his aspiration to improve East-West relations, the prime minister showed much interest in an early settlement of the Korean War. The peace overtures by Stalin's successors encouraged Churchill. On April 15, he notified Parliament of the agreement reached at Panmunjom for the exchange of sick and wounded prisoners.[59]

At this time, the British leader had second thoughts on the wisdom of issuing the "greater sanctions" statement, prepared fifteen months earlier, because such an announcement could be counterproductive in Korea when Moscow had started a peace campaign to reduce world tensions. On May 14, British Counselor Frank Tomlinson confirmed with U. Alexis Johnson, the deputy assistant secretary of state for Far Eastern affairs, Churchill's decision to "withdraw" his agreement to the "greater sanctions" statement. The American official found this communication "seriously disturbing."[60]

When the Eisenhower administration appeared uncompromising on the POW issue in mid-May, Churchill spoke in Parliament, criticizing the lack of progress in the truce negotiations at Panmunjom and urging the United States to meet with the Soviets face to face. He said that Stalin's death had apparently caused "a change of attitude . . . in the Soviet Union," and he called for a "conference on the highest levels . . . between the leading powers without delay."[61] On June 2, the British leader sent a personal letter to Molotov, the new Soviet foreign minister, recalling their cooperation during World War II and hoping that they could work together again to reduce world tension. The prime minister went on to say that it would "help if this Panmunjom prisoners-of-war business were got out of the way."[62]

It is clear that Britain was anxious to conclude the Korean fighting. The changes in Soviet foreign policy after Stalin's death encouraged Churchill, who had been strongly interested in securing an East-West détente while he was in office. He feared that U.S. intransigence at the armistice talks in Korea would jeopardize whatever chances existed for world peace. Together with other Western countries, his government exerted pressure on Washington to moderate its position at Panmunjom.

CHINA AND THE ARMISTICE

China watched closely the 1952 presidential election in the United States. Some officials were concerned about the candidacy of Eisenhower because he was from the military. Du Ping, director of the Political Department of the CPV, told Peng Dehuai in 1952 that "according to a radio broadcast,

Eisenhower plans to run for the presidency. If this military general becomes the president, it is likely that the Korean War will be expanded. We'd better prepare our troops for this." Peng agreed with this analysis, but added that "a military commander will not necessarily be war-like because he knows better than other people the cost of war. On the surface, war is about steel and iron, but in fact, it involves such things as politics, military, finance, materials and manpower." Without complete confidence in victory, Peng went on, a commander would not make hasty decisions to start war. Therefore, he concluded, "it is hard to say if Eisenhower will escalate the war. But, of course, it is very necessary for us to be prepared. Preparedness averts peril."[63] Noting Eisenhower's campaign promise that if he were elected, he would end the Korean War, Chinese analysts began to examine the possibilities for limiting hostilities in Korea.[64]

While waiting for opportunities to restart the armistice negotiations, which had been in recess since October 8, 1952, when the Communists rejected the U.N.'s package proposal about nonforcible repatriation, the Chinese leadership did not relax their vigilance or slow preparations for new military threats from the United States. Throughout the summer and fall of 1952, the war had remained stalemated at the front. Both sides were well entrenched in their positions. Given this situation, China's leaders estimated that, because the enemy could not advance at the front, it might attempt another Inchon-like landing at the CPV's rear. On November 23, 1952, Peng Dehuai, now in Beijing taking charge of the daily function of the CCP's Central Military Commission, sent a telegram to the CPV Command, instructing them to begin antilanding preparations immediately in case the enemy should launch an operation on the CPV's flanks the next spring.[65]

Beijing was very apprehensive about Eisenhower's visit to Korea in early December. On December 2, the CPV Command received a circular from the Central Military Commission, which pointed out that the president-elect had just begun his trip to Korea in the company of new Secretary of Defense Charles E. Wilson, Chairman of the Joint Chiefs of Staff Bradley, and Commander of the Seventh Fleet Admiral Radford. The document asked the CPV to pay attention to this development.[66]

In early December, Mao met Acting Commander of the CPV Deng Hua in Beijing. Mao reiterated the party's anticipation of a possible enemy landing on the western coast of the Korean peninsula, mentioning four reasons for his concern: (1) the American forces had suffered heavy losses in Korea, but these damages had not reached the extent that would force Washington to stop the war; (2) Eisenhower had arrived in Korea with new military plans; (3) the United Nations had recently endorsed the Indian resolution on nonforcible repatriation for POWs, which embodied America's ideas on the issue, and would encourage Washington to initiate new military ventures; and (4) the CPV were well entrenched along the front and it was very unlikely that the enemy would start a new offensive there. The U.N. forces were more likely to attempt landing operations to the rear of the CPV. Therefore, the Chinese leader asked Deng Hua to base the CPV's future planning on this calculation.[67]

On December 11, Mao sent four armies (the First, Sixteenth, Twenty-first and Fifty-fourth armies) into Korea to guard against the possible landing by the Americans.[68] Four days later, Deng Hua returned to Korea and informed the other members of the CPV Command of his meeting with Mao.[69] On December 20, Mao sent a formal instruction to the CPV Command that contended that, according to various indications, serious possibilities existed that the enemy might land about seven divisions behind the CPV's front, especially in the area between the Yalu and Chongchon rivers on the west coast of the Korean peninsula. The directive ordered the CPV to make all necessary preparations to defeat any landing ventures by the enemy.[70]

The Chinese leadership took Eisenhower's unleashing of Chiang seriously. The Central Military Commission dispatched a memorandum to the CPV Command, warning them that the United States had withdrawn the order to neutralize the Taiwan Strait in an attempt to encourage the KMT to attack the mainland.[71] On February 7, 1953, Mao officially responded to Eisenhower's threat by declaring at the Fourth Session of the first National Committee of the Chinese People's Political Consultative Conference:

First, [we] must intensify the struggle to resist the U.S. and aid Korea. Because American imperialism persists in holding Chinese and Korean prisoners-of-war and undermining the cease-fire negotiations and, moreover, is vainly attempting to expand its war of aggression against Korea, the struggle to resist the U.S. and aid Korea must continue to be intensified. We desire peace, but as long as American imperialism does not discard its barbaric and unreasonable demands and its plots to expand its aggression, the resolution of the Chinese people can only be to continue to fight together with the Korean people to the end. This is not because we like war; we would like to stop the war immediately and wait to resolve the remaining problems in the future, but American imperialism doesn't want to do things this way. If that's the case, that's all right; we'll continue to fight.[72]

On February 22, General Clark proposed an exchange of sick and wounded prisoners. Mao analyzed the gesture, saying that the series of measures taken by Eisenhower since his assumption of office reflected his attempt to extricate himself from the difficulties in Korea left by Truman; the American proposal might be a prelude to its change of policy at Panmunjom.[73]

China immediately started consultations with North Korea and the Soviet Union on how to react to Washington's move.[74] It is possible that Zhou discussed the Korean situation with the new Soviet leadership in Moscow between March 8 and 17 when he was there for Stalin's funeral. A series of Chinese-Soviet-North Korean diplomatic initiatives followed.

On March 15, Georgi Malenkov argued before the Supreme Soviet that "at present there is no disputed or unsettled question that could not be settled peacefully on the basis of mutual agreement between the countries concerned."[75] On March 28, Kim Il Sung and Peng Dehuai responded to Clark, accepting his offer to exchange sick and wounded POWs. But they went a step further; this exchange should lead to a solution of the whole POW issue and an armistice "for which people throughout the world are longing."[76]

Two days later, Zhou Enlai announced an even greater surprise. In a conciliatory statement over Beijing Radio, the Chinese foreign minister declared, "Both parties to the negotiations should undertake to repatriate immediately after the cessation of hostilities all those prisoners of war in their custody who insisted upon repatriation, and to hand over the remaining POWs to a neutral state so as to ensure a just solution to the question of their repatriation."[77] This was an important compromise on the part of the Communists because for the first time they had given up their insistence on strict compliance with the Geneva Convention and the automatic repatriation of all POWs at the conclusion of war. On March 31, Kim Il Sung endorsed Zhou's suggestion. The next day, Soviet Foreign Minister Molotov voiced support for the Chinese and North Korean position.[78]

On April 11, the agreement on the exchange of sick and wounded was signed. Two weeks later on April 26, the armistice negotiations resumed. At first, the Chinese still insisted that the nonrepatriates had not made a free choice without "intimidation." They demanded that the POWS be sent to a neutral country, there to be provided with "explanations" by their side seeking to persuade them to return home.[79]

On May 7, the Communists made further concessions. They agreed that POWs would not be transferred to neutral countries to receive their "explanations"; that the period for persuasion should be four months instead of six;

that a five-country Neutral Nations Repatriation Committee be created including Czechoslovakia, India, Poland, Sweden, and Switzerland; and that the fate of the remaining POWs after this time would be settled at the political conference as provided in the armistice agreement.[80]

On May 13, the U.S. negotiators made a counterproposal, which stated that Korean nonrepatriates under U.N. Command control should not be transferred to the repatriation commission but should be freed in South Korea as soon as the armistice agreement was signed. The Communists considered this suggestion unacceptable.[81]

Washington's stiff position was a product of Rhee's intransigence and congressional pressures.[82] But America's allies were very unhappy with this development. As noted before, Churchill criticized the U.S. delegates at Panmunjom for dragging their feet. The Canadian government believed that the Communist proposal of May 7 had already gone "a long way" to meet the Western demands and that Beijing and Pyongyang had made "an important concession in no longer insisting that the prisoners who do not wish to be returned home should be physically removed from Korea."[83] Owing to Allied pressures, the Eisenhower administration had to modify its position at the negotiations. After some further bargaining, the POW issue was solved on June 8. With this major hurdle removed, the armistice was signed on July 27.

What caused the Communists to make concessions on the POW issue? Eisenhower and Dulles believed that it had been the American nuclear threat that forced the Chinese and North Koreans to modify their positions. Eisenhower later told his special assistant, Sherman Adams, that the reason for the final conclusion of the armistice was the menace of a nuclear war.[84] Dulles made a similar argument at the Bermuda Conference in December 1953, where he remarked in the presence of British and French officials that "it was their [the Communists'] knowledge of the U.S. willingness to use force that brought an end to hostilities."[85]

But, as Rosemary Foot has argued, the American leaders exaggerated the effect of their nuclear threats. In fact, the major Communist concessions were made before Washington had communicated such threats. Furthermore, it is doubtful whether Nehru ever passed Dulles's message of May 21 to the Chinese. The Indian prime minister himself denied it.[86] There is no evidence in available Chinese sources to show that Beijing ever received Dulles's warning through Nehru. Throughout late 1952 and early 1953, the Chinese Communists were more concerned with an American landing operation than a U.S. nuclear attack.

Until further Chinese records or any North Korean documents are opened, it will be difficult to make a precise judgment of the efficacy of the American nuclear threats against China during the conclusion of the Korean War. It seems more plausible to argue that the general cost of the war, even without the danger of nuclear escalation, was more decisive in determining China's willingness to make concessions at the armistice talks.

The hostilities had been an enormous drain on China's economy. To finance the war, the Chinese government had resorted to such mobilization measures as high taxes, confiscation of private enterprises, withholding of wages, intensive issuing of bonds and voluntary contribution drives, and the implementation of the "Three-Anti" and "Five-Anti" campaigns. In fact, high agricultural taxes had caused complaints from people like Liang Shuming, a leader of the Democratic League, who called for a "benevolent policy" toward the peasants. Mao criticized this kind of sentiment at the Twenty-fourth Session of the Central People's Government Council on September 13, 1953.[87] According to one source, in 1951, the Chinese government allocated 41.6 percent of its total expenditure to defense and 25.6 percent to economic development.[88] Furthermore, Beijing had decided to begin its First Five-Year Plan in 1953, and money and resources were needed to carry it out.

Changes in the Soviet Union also played a role in influencing Beijing's policy. As McGeorge Bundy recalls, a Chinese of high professional standing told him that Zhou Enlai credited Stalin's death with making the armistice possible.[89] Even early in late 1952, the Soviet leadership had begun to increase emphasis on domestic development. Some delegates at the Nineteenth Party Congress in October had called for the termination of the arms race and the strengthening of the Soviet economy. The death of Stalin led his successors to display more flexibility in adapting to new opportunities in international affairs.[90]

The American leaders' categorical contention that their action caused the Communists to change their behavior shows a common misperception in international relations, namely the tendency to exaggerate one's own input into the other's decision and to overlook other influences. When the Communists acted in accord with Washington's desires, Eisenhower and Dulles overestimated the extent to which they played a central role in the Communist policy. Such thinking can meet pyschological needs. To use Jervis's words, it "gratifies the ego."[91]

CONCLUSION

There were basic continuities in the policies of the British Labor and Conservative governments in the Far East. Both Attlee and Churchill recognized the PRC and sought to limit the fighting in Korea. But, owing to economic and geopolitical needs as well as personal sentiment, Churchill attached greater importance than Attlee to Anglo-American solidarity. As a result, his government tried to be less obstructive toward U.S. policy with respect to China. This was demonstrated in London's reception of the "greater sanctions" statement in 1952.

There were limits, however, to this British willingness to cooperate with the Americans in the Far East. When Washington showed a tendency to escalate the war in Korea or appeared too intransigent at the armistice talks, London did not hesitate to attempt to moderate American behavior. This was clearly the case in June 1952 when U.S. planes bombed Communist power installations on the Yalu River and in May 1953 when the American negotiators refused to compromise on the POW issue. Furthermore, Anglo-American relations in the Far East during 1952 and 1953 were sometimes marked by a lack of prior consultations and communication. For instance, when the United States attacked the North Korean dams in May 1952, it came as a surprise to the British.

The Truman administration had been frustrated by the protracted armistice negotiations and stalemate over the POW issue. Beginning in mid-1952, Washington showed an increasing willingness to expand the war as a way to force a speedy military conclusion of the fighting. The administration's tendency to provoke the Communists into an offensive and its uncompromising position on the question of nonrepatriates greatly strained U.S. relations with the allies, especially the British. Determined to end the war, the Eisenhower administration initiated a series of tough measures against the Communists, including threatening the use of nuclear weapons. But it could not totally ignore the pressure of the allies to moderate its position on the POW issue.

Beijing's leaders were wary of the election of Eisenhower and took his visit to Korea and his decision to unleash Chiang seriously. Throughout late 1952 and early 1953, they were preoccupied with the prevention of an American amphibious attack on the Korean peninsula. Although the role of the U.S. nuclear threats could not be excluded, it was primarily for economic and political reasons that the Chinese leadership decided to modify its position on the POW issue and sign the armistice agreement.

7 Settlement of the Indochina Crisis, 1954

During the period between 1945 and 1949, when both Mao Zedong and Ho Chi Minh were preoccupied with their respective domestic struggles for power, contact between the Chinese and Vietnamese Communist parties was limited and difficult because they were physically separated by the presence of the KMT troops in southern China. This was a period when Ho was being careful not to antagonize Chiang Kai-shek for fear of being confronted with a hostile rear. Influenced by Stalin's thinking, Ho did not expect the CCP to win national power in China in the near future.[1]

After the establishment of the PRC in October 1949, Ho Chi Minh sent representatives to Beijing to seek China's assistance in his struggle against the French. At the time, Mao was visiting the Soviet Union. Liu Shaoqi, secretary-general of the CCP Central Committee and vice-chairman of the Central People's Government, was in charge of the party's daily activities. While maintaining close consultation with Mao in Moscow, Liu was responsible for the actual handling of Beijing's Indochina policy during this period. In early January 1950, Liu informed Luo Guibo, director of the General Office of the CCP Central Military Commission, that the party had decided to send him to Vietnam as a "liaison representative" to establish communications with Ho's party. Liu asked Luo to investigate conditions in Vietnam and report his findings to Beijing so that the party could make decisions regarding assistance to Ho. Before Luo's departure to Vietnam on January 16, Liu asked Yang Shangkun, director of the General Office of the CCP Central Committee, to arrange a meeting between Luo and Ho's envoys in Beijing. In addition to supervising the selection of the members of Luo's team— including a staff, a telegraph operator, secretaries, and guards—Liu also wrote a letter of introduction for Ho.[2]

Eager to win legitimacy and international recognition, the Democratic Republic of Vietnam (DRV) on January 15, 1950, telegraphed Beijing, requesting establishment of diplomatic relations. Mao Zedong sent a cable from the Soviet Union to Liu Shaoqi asking him to convey immediately to Ho China's agreement to establish official ties with the DRV. In the same telegram, Mao also instructed the Chinese Foreign Ministry to forward Ho's request for establishing diplomatic relations to the Soviet Union and Eastern European countries.[3] China became the first country in the world to recognize the DRV. Stalin followed suit on January 30. Then Communist countries in Eastern Europe and North Korea did the same.

The French were angry at the action of the Soviet Union and the PRC. Paris blamed Moscow for violating international law: "Vietnam is part of the French Union, and it is to the government of Bao Dai that France has just transferred the sovereignty she possessed in this Union." Until then, France had vacillated in following the British example in recognizing the PRC. Any idea of this sort was now completely dropped.[4]

In late January, Ho made a secret visit to Beijing. Informing Mao of Ho's arrival, Liu Shaoqi reported that the party had formed a committee composed of Zhu De, vice-chairman of the Central People's Government and general commander of the PLA, Nie Rongzhen, acting chief of staff of the PLA, Li Weihan, director of the CCP United Front Department, and Liao Chengzhi, vice-chairman of the Overseas Chinese Affairs Commission under the Central People's Government, to deal with the issues raised by Ho.[5] Mao and Zhou Enlai sent Liu a telegram from Moscow asking him to pass their best regards to the Vietnamese leader. They congratulated Ho on the DRV's joining the "big anti-imperialist and democratic family headed by the Soviet Union" and wished Ho an early success in unifying his country.[6]

According to Hoang Van Hoan, the first Vietnamese ambassador to the PRC (who later defected to Beijing after the Sino-Vietnamese conflicts of 1978–79), Liu Shaoqi told Ho that he expected France to postpone recognition of the PRC as a result of Beijing's solidarity with the Vietminh (the short form for the League for the Independence of Vietnam, founded by Ho in 1941). China would not be afraid, Liu continued, because when China became stronger later, the French would have to recognize it. The Chinese government asked Soviet Ambassador Roshchin to convey to the Kremlin Beijing's suggestion that the Soviet Union invite Ho to visit Moscow and talk to Stalin directly. Ho made his trip to the Soviet Union in February.[7]

In April, the DRV asked the PRC to send military experts to Vietnam to act as advisers at the Vietminh Army headquarters and at the division level and as commanders at regimental and battalion levels. The CCP responded that it would dispatch advisers but not commanders. On April 17, the CCP Central Military Commission ordered the formation of the Chinese Military

Advisory Group (CMAG), including advisers capable of assisting the Vietminh Army headquarters, three divisions, and an officers' training school. The military experts would be selected from the PLA's Second, Third, and Fourth Field Armies. In late July, the CMAG was formally established at Nanning, Guangxi Province, with General Wei Guoqing as chairman and Mei Jiasheng and Deng Yifan as deputy chairmen. The mission included seventy-nine advisers and some other assistants.[8]

In August, Luo Guibo became the head of a Chinese mission of political and administrative advisers to Vietnam. In a telegram to Luo, Liu Shaoqi instructed him not to impose his ideas on the Vietnamese. Given the fact that the contact between the Chinese and Vietnamese parties had just been established and "there is still considerable lack of understanding," Liu asked Luo to be patient in dealing with Vietminh cadres and not to take offense if they refused to adopt his suggestions.[9]

China's decision to assist the DRV in the early 1950s was motivated by a blend of geopolitical, ideological, and historical factors. First, Indochina was one of the three fronts (others were Korea and Taiwan) that the CCP perceived as vulnerable to foreign intervention. The Chinese leaders were concerned not only with possible international hostility from Indochina but also with remnant Nationalist troops in Vietnam. After the Communist occupation of Guangxi in December 1949, some of Chiang Kai-shek's units fled to northern Vietnam while others escaped into the mountains in Guangxi. After the outbreak of the Korean War, these remaining Nationalist troops, both in Vietnam and in the Guangxi mountains, began to harass the new government in Guangxi. Mao was very apprehensive about this situation. Throughout 1950 and early 1951, he paid much attention to the elimination of these remnant Chiang followers.[10] Viewed in this context, the defeat of the French troops in northern Vietnam would greatly strengthen China's border.

Second, the international obligation to assist a fellow Communist party made the CCP unwilling to turn down the requests from Ho. When Liu Shaoqi visited the Soviet Union in July 1949, Stalin said to him that the center of world revolution had moved from Europe to the Soviet Union and would shift to China later. With this eastward movement of the focus of world revolution, the Soviet leader expected China to play a major role in promoting revolution in the East.[11]

Furthermore, Ho Chi Minh and many Chinese Communist leaders had forged close ties in revolutionary struggles in the past. Sharing identical beliefs and values, they had gone through common hardships and ordeals. Ho met such CCP leaders as Zhou Enlai, Wang Ruofei, and Li Fuchun in

Paris in the early 1920s. Around late 1924 and early 1925, the Communist International sent Ho from Moscow to Guangzhou (Canton) to assist Mikhail Borodin, the Comintern representative to the new Chinese revolutionary government. At Guangzhou, Ho also engaged in anticolonial activities, running a "special political training class" for Vietnamese youth. He invited Liu Shaoqi, Zhou Enlai, Li Fuchun, and Peng Pai to speak before his class. Well-versed in Chinese, Ho later translated Mao's work, "On the Protracted War," from Chinese into French.[12]

Mao told the CMAG on June 30, 1950, that it was a "glorious international task" to be advisers to the Vietminh. The Chinese people had won liberation, but the Vietnamese were still suffering under the oppression of French colonialism. Their cause of liberation deserved China's sympathy and support. Ho and many other Vietnamese had participated in China's revolutionary struggle in the past. Some of them had shed their blood. Now, China ought to assist their fight against the French.[13]

Finally, Beijing's involvement in Indochina should be viewed in terms of China's traditional relations with neighboring countries. Historically speaking, Chinese emperors considered Vietnam within the orbit of China's influence and kept that country within the tributary system. They did not hesitate to send troops into Vietnam to restore peace and order if the authority of an existing tributary ruler there was endangered by either domestic uprisings or foreign invasions. For instance, between 1788 and 1790, Qing Emperor Qianlong dispatched an expeditionary force to Vietnam to restore the Lê King, who had been overthrown by a domestic rebellion.[14] About one century later, the Qing government again intervened in Vietnam in 1884–85 to resist a French invasion.

In June 1950, Ho Chi Minh decided to launch a border campaign. Originally, the Vietminh Army planned to employ the four crack regiments that had been undergoing training and organization in China since April 1950 to attack Lao Kay and Cao Bang, two important French outposts located on the RC4 (Route Coloniale 4), parallel to the border with China. After considering logistic difficulties, it modified its plan by concentrating on Cao Bang. In addition to asking China to provide supplies and send the military advisory group to Vietnam as soon as possible, Ho also requested the dispatch of a senior Chinese military adviser to coordinate the entire border operation.[15]

After reaching the Vietminh Army headquarters at Guang Nguyen on August 12, the CMAG immediately dispatched its members to the Vietnamese 304th, 308th, and 312th Divisions. Later in the year, it also sent advisers to the 316th Division and the 351st Engineering and Artillery Division (also called the Heavy Division).[16] Upon Ho's request, the CCP Central Committee selected General Chen Geng, commander of the Yunnan Military Region, as its representative to the Vietminh. At the same time, General Li Tianyou, deputy commander of the Guangxi Military Region, was appointed as the head of a logistic committee responsible for the preparation and transportation of food, ammunition, and medical supplies to Vietnam. Two special field hospitals were set up to treat wounded Vietminh soldiers.[17]

In Vietnam, Chen directed the campaign to clear the Sino-Vietnamese border of French troops. He skillfully employed Vietminh forces in mobile warfare and defeated the French in northern Vietnam. France had to jettison a string of bases along the frontier and concede Vietminh control over the entire Viet Bac region, thus giving Ho easy access to his source of supplies in China. After the conclusion of the border campaign, Mao sent a telegram to Chen congratulating him on his success.[18]

Highly commending Chen on his military leadership, Ho said that the border campaign achieved a greater victory than he had expected and called it "a triumph of proletarian internationalism." Vo Nguyen Giap, commander of the Vietminh Army, claimed that the campaign thwarted the French plan to close the Vietnamese border and to isolate the Vietminh; it had military as well as political and economic significance. "The victory shows," the Vietminh general continued, "Mao's military thought was very applicable to Vietnam." Ho asked Chen to stay in Vietnam to direct the next military operation. But Chen received new orders from Beijing and left Vietnam in early November 1950.[19] (On June 8, the next year, Chen was appointed deputy commander of the Chinese People's Volunteers and went to Korea in August). After Chen's departure, the Chinese military advisory group remained in Vietnam. It assisted Ho in the Northwest campaign of 1952 and the siege of Dien Bien Phu in 1954.[20]

Although the Soviet Union recognized the DRV on January 30, 1950, no evidence suggests that Stalin furnished any direct aid to the Vietminh before 1955. Ho Chi Minh attended the Soviet state banquet in honor of Mao on February 16, 1950, during which the Vietminh leader said to Stalin— "jokingly," according to Wu Xiuquan—that the Soviet Union might sign a treaty with the DRV along the same lines as that signed with the Chinese. But Stalin did not do that.[21] In Hoang Van Hoan's account, Stalin told Ho that assisting the Vietminh was primarily Chinese business.[22] Until 1954, China bore full responsibility for guiding and supporting the Vietnamese revolution. According to one account, by 1952 approximately seven thousand Chinese advisers and troops were in Vietnam. Between 1949 and 1954 Beijing trained about forty thousand Vietnamese soldiers.[23] In the estimate of another study, by early 1954, China's aid to Ho had increased from about three hundred to five hundred tons per month in 1951 to more than four thousand tons per month. The supplies were principally Chinese products.[24]

Although displaying solidarity with Ho's cause, China publicly tried to appear moderate and cautious in its relationship with the Western powers. This was demonstrated by the diplomatic distance Beijing maintained with Vietnam in the early 1950s. Hoang Van Hoan presented his credentials to the Chinese government as the DRV's representative on April 28, 1951, but the Chinese media did not report it until October 10, 1952. China did not dispatch an official envoy to the DRV until September 1954 when the Geneva Accords were concluded; and it was only then that Hoang Van Hoan acquired the title of ambassador.[25]

Zhou Enlai and the Geneva Conference

After the conclusion of the Korean War, Beijing put increasing stress on the doctrine of "peaceful coexistence": to use diplomatic means to improve China's international standing. Zhou Enlai first mentioned the "Five Principles of Peaceful Coexistence"—mutual respect for territorial integrity and sovereignty, nonaggression, noninterference in each other's internal affairs, equality and mutual benefit, and peaceful coexistence—during a meeting with an Indian delegation in December 1953. Beijing contended that the Five Principles were applicable not only to Sino-Indian relations but also to international affairs in general. During the break between sessions of the Geneva Conference, Zhou visited New Delhi and Rangoon in June, and the Five Principles of Peaceful Coexistence were officially embodied in the ensuing Sino-Indian and Sino-Burmese agreements.[26]

During late 1953 and early 1954, the Communist world launched a peace initiative. On September 28, 1953, the Soviet Union sent a proposal to the United States, France, and Britain, calling for a five-power conference, including China, to examine ways to reduce international tensions. About ten days later, Zhou Enlai issued a statement supporting the Soviet suggestion. On November 26, Ho Chi Minh told the Swedish newspaper *Expressen* that he was prepared to negotiate with the French on the Indochina conflict. On January 9, 1954, Zhou made another pronouncement, declaring that the urgent international problems in Asia had developed to a stage where they must be examined and solved through consultation among the big powers that were involved.[27]

On January 25, Soviet Foreign Minister Molotov proposed at the Berlin Conference that a five-power international conference be held to deal with the tensions in Asia. Despite initial U.S. opposition, the British and French were eager to see a solution of the disputes in the region. The conference finally endorsed the plan to convene an international meeting to restore peace in Korea and Indochina.[28]

Beijing attached great importance to the conference. In March, the Chinese government prepared a "Preliminary Paper on the Estimation of and Preparation for the Geneva Conference," which said that China should take advantage of the differences between the United States, France, and Britain over the Indochina issue and try to reach agreements, even temporary ones. The goal, according to the document, was to avoid a fruitless conference.[29]

To coordinate Chinese-Soviet-North Vietnamese policies at Geneva as well as to overcome Beijing's inexperience in international meetings, the Chinese government had close consultations with the governments of the Soviet Union and the DRV before the conference opened. In March, a Sino-Vietnamese preparatory meeting was held in Beijing. According to Shi Zhe, who was then political adviser to the Chinese delegation to the Geneva Conference, Zhou Enlai made three visits to the Soviet Union in April. During his first trip, Zhou held discussions with Nikita Khrushchev and Molotov. The Soviet foreign minister related to the Chinese his evaluation of the likely process and outcome of the conference.[30]

After the first visit, Zhou returned to Beijing to report on his trip to the Chinese leadership. Several days later he went to Moscow again to hold further talks with Soviet officials regarding conference strategy as well as the composition of the Chinese and Soviet delegations. Molotov informed Zhou how the Soviet Union had selected its delegation, which totaled more than 120 people, including experts with various specialties. As a result, the Chinese delegation also contained people with diverse areas of expertise.[31]

According to Wang Bingnan, who was secretary-general of the Chinese delegation, Zhou Enlai entrusted him to select the Chinese participants and establish rules of conduct for the delegation. Together with his colleagues, Wang worked "day and night making all kinds of preparations." Huang Hua was appointed spokesman for the Chinese delegation. To ensure that Huang would be able to handle different questions that were likely to arise at the conference, a mock press meeting was held to test the appropriateness of Huang's answers.[32]

On April 19, the Chinese delegation was announced, with Zhou Enlai as chief representative and Deputy Foreign Ministers Zhang Wentian, Wang Jiaxiang, and Li Kenong as representatives. The party leadership gave the delegation the following instructions: (1) to exercise active diplomacy at Geneva to break the U.S. policy of isolation and embargo toward China and to reduce world tensions; (2) to try to conclude agreements so as to set a precedent for solving international problems through big-power consultations.[33]

Zhou made his third visit to Moscow when he was leading the Chinese delegation on the way to Geneva. To familiarize the Chinese delegation with the usual proceedings of an international meeting, Molotov asked Andrei Gromyko, the deputy Soviet foreign minister, to talk to the Chinese about Soviet experiences in international gatherings. After that, the Chinese and Soviet delegations left Moscow for Geneva separately. Zhou's airport arrival at Geneva on April 14 was a media sensation.[34]

The Korean session of the Geneva Conference did not produce any agreement largely because the contending sides had divergent views regarding the role of the United Nations in the political settlement of the Korean dispute. The South Koreans, backed by the United States, insisted on using the international organization to supervise the postwar election in Korea. China rejected U.N. authority over collective security in Korea, stressing the international role of neutral countries. To the Chinese, the United Nations was not an impartial force because it had been used by the United States to condemn China as an "aggressor" in Korea.[35]

It was during the Indochina session that Zhou Enlai found more opportunities to prove himself a skillful diplomat. China's basic approach to the Indochina issue was to prevent the internationalization of this conflict as had happened in Korea. Both internal and external reasons were behind this position. Domestically, China needed to concentrate on its plan to rehabilitate the economy, a process that had been disrupted and postponed by Beijing's participation in the Korean War. According to Khrushchev, Zhou Enlai told him in Moscow before the Geneva Conference that China could not meet Ho Chi Minh's demands to send Chinese troops to Vietnam. The Chinese premier claimed: "We've already lost too many men in Korea—that war cost us dearly. We're in no condition to get involved in another war at this time."[36]

Internationally, the Chinese leadership was apprehensive about the possibility of American intervention in Indochina. Beijing believed that Washington, determined to torpedo the Geneva Conference, was looking for opportunities to move into Southeast Asia.[37] During the Geneva Conference, the Chinese media repeatedly condemned "the U.S. plot of organizing a Southeast Asian military bloc" to "use Asians to fight Asians." A *Shijie zhishi* editorial of May 20 contended that "the ruling clique in the United States is carrying out a policy of establishing new colonial authority in Asia" to replace the old imperial powers such as Britain, France, and the Netherlands. Another editorial in the same journal published two weeks later asserted that the plan to create a military organization in Southeast Asia was part of America's general policy of establishing a new colonial empire, which resembled the "Greater East Asian Coprosperity Sphere" advocated by Japan during World War II.[38]

Furthermore, a moderate policy in Indochina was in line with Beijing's new diplomatic emphasis on peaceful coexistence. The Geneva Conference provided China a good opportunity to enhance its international prestige and increase influence among the neutral nations in Asia by playing the part of peacemaker. Beijing insistently claimed that it was speaking for all Asia.

With the strategy of avoiding an extension of the Indochina conflict and denying the United States the chance to intervene, Zhou Enlai engaged in active diplomacy, bringing into play an unexpected flexibility. His approach was to win over the majority of the participants, including France, and to isolate the United States. His job was made easier by the Vietminh victory at Dien Bien Phu, which made the French all the more eager to extricate themselves from Indochina. As Wang Bingnan recalled, when the news of Dien Bien Phu came, "we spread it to each other. We were very much encouraged and felt more confident in solving the Indochina issue."[39]

In response to what China perceived as the U.S. strategy of "using Asians to fight Asians," Zhou employed his Five Principles of Peaceful Coexistence. At the third plenary session on Indochina on May 12, Zhou stated:

Asian countries must mutually respect each other's independence and sovereignty and not interfere in each other's internal affairs; they must solve their disputes through peaceful negotiation and not through threats and military force; they must establish normal economic and cultural relations on the basis of equality and mutual benefit and disallow discrimination and limitation. Only in this way can the Asian countries avoid the neo-colonialist exploitation of the unprecedented catastrophe of Asians fighting Asians and achieve peace and security.[40]

King Chen has summarized Zhou's three contributions to the conclusion of the Geneva Accord on Indochina: (1) persuading North Vietnam to withdraw its troops from Laos and Cambodia; (2) obtaining Ho Chi Minh's consent to proceed with the general peace plan at Geneva, and (3) solving the issue of the composition of the international supervisory commission.[41] Recent Chinese sources throw new light on Zhou's contributions to the conference, especially his role in persuading the North Vietnamese to accept the seventeenth parallel as the demarcation line.

On June 16, Pierre Mendès-France was elected premier in France. During the election campaign, he had promised that he would secure a settlement of the Indochina dispute by July 20 or resign. In Shi Zhe's account, the Chinese initially were not sure of Mendès-France's intentions regarding Indochina. Zhou decided to visit the new French leader. On June 23, the two leaders met in Berne, Switzerland. From this discussion, Zhou realized that France was very tired of the Vietnam War and domestic antiwar sentiment was high. The French government was anxious to withdraw from Indochina, but it wanted to do so "gracefully in appearance." In this way, Mendès-France hoped to consolidate his power at home.[42]

According to American documents, during his talk with Mendès-France, Zhou spoke most of the time. The French side detected "a considerable advance over Zhou's previous position." By acknowledging the presence of two governments in the territory of Vietnam, the Chinese premier for the first time "recognized the valid existence of the [South] Vietnamese government." Mendès-France told Zhou that negotiations with the Vietminh had been "at a practical standstill for the past week or ten days," and that he wanted the Chinese leader to talk to the head of the Hanoi delegation to speed things up. Zhou agreed to intervene with the Vietminh and asked them to make progress in negotiations.[43]

Zhou Enlai saw an opportunity in the French distress to reach agreement at Geneva. Shi Zhe asserts that after the meeting with the French prime minister, Zhou reported his findings on the French situation to Pham Van Dong, head of the Vietminh delegation to the Geneva Conference. He asked the Vietminh leader not to "haggle over" (*jijiao*) the sixteenth or seventeenth parallel. Giving Mendès-France a way to save face would be a small price to pay for his withdrawal of the French troops, Zhou went on. "After French withdrawal, the whole of Vietnam will be yours."[44] Clearly, Zhou considered the acceptance of the seventeenth parallel as a temporary tactical concession on the part of the Vietminh. In his view, when the French troops were no longer in Vietnam, the Vietminh would be able to unify the country.

From July 3 to 5, Zhou met with Ho Chi Minh in Liuzhou, a city near the Sino-Vietnamese border. He persuaded the Vietminh leader to accept the idea of compromising on the issue of the demarcation line to end the war. On July 10, on his way back to Geneva, Zhou stopped in Moscow to confer with the Soviet leaders, who shared China's view that it was time to conclude a deal at Geneva while Mendès-France was still in office. The United States was putting pressure on the French leader, the Soviets believed; if the Vietminh insisted on Mendès-France's accepting "unacceptable" demands, the Americans would take advantage of this, the prowar faction within France would gain the upper hand and the Mendès-France government would collapse. This would be detrimental both to the solution of the Indochina conflict and the welfare of the DRV.[45]

The Geneva Accords of 1954 reflected the moderating influences of the Chinese and Soviet delegations. Vietnam was to be divided temporarily along the seventeenth parallel to allow the regrouping of military forces from both sides. The country was to be neutralized, and neither side was to enter a military alliance. Elections were to be held in July 1956 under the supervision of an international commission composed of Canadian, Indian, and Polish representatives. The accords also made cease-fire arrangements for Laos and Cambodia. Vietminh forces were to leave Laos and Cambodia and French forces to vacate all three.[46]

The Vietminh accepted the solution reluctantly. As Wang Bingnan admitted, "some people in the Vietminh hoped to unify the whole of Vietnam at one stroke."[47] Ho Chi Minh must have realized that without Chinese and Soviet assistance, he could not have defeated the French and achieved the position he then had. He could not afford to resist the pressure of his two Communist allies. But the Vietminh leader, no doubt, had every reason to believe, as did Zhou Enlai and Molotov, that all of Vietnam would be his in two years.

To the surprise and disappointment of the three Communist countries, Ngo Dinh Diem consolidated his regime in South Vietnam with the help of the United States. When the time came for the national election on reunification in accordance with the Geneva Accords, Saigon refused to participate on the ground that a free vote was impossible in North Vietnam. Furthermore, Diem claimed that his government was not bound by the Geneva Accords because it had not signed them.

According to Western journalists, Zhou Enlai was very upset with this development. In August 1971, when James Reston of *The New York Times* asked Zhou if he was willing to mediate the conflict between the United States and North Vietnam, the Chinese premier answered, "We don't want to be a mediator in any way. We were very badly taken in during the first Geneva Conference." On another occasion, Zhou told Harrison Salisbury of *The New York Times* that "never again" would he "put pressure" on Hanoi to accept an international solution of the war modeled on the Geneva

Conference of 1954. He had been "personally responsible for urging the Vietnamese to go along with the agreement. He would not be party to any similar effort in the future."[48]

SINO-SOVIET RELATIONS AT THE GENEVA CONFERENCE

The Soviet Union had its own reasons to moderate the Vietminh demands. Aside from having limited interests in Southeast Asia, Moscow wanted to encourage France to reject the European Defense Community (EDC). Mendès-France was a bitter opponent of the EDC, and his continuation in office would reduce the likelihood that the French would approve the EDC. To the Soviet leadership, the opportunity to undermine the plan for German rearmament was clearly more important than the perpetuation of a Communist war in Indochina.[49] During the Geneva Conference, Eden found Molotov very willing to "get moving" on Indochina.[50]

At Geneva, the Soviet Union was eager not only to achieve a settlement in Indochina but also to reduce tensions in China's relations with the West, especially with the United States. The Kremlin was obviously very uneasy about the intense hostility between the United States and China. Another military conflict between Beijing and Washington like the Korean War would only divert Moscow's attention and resources from its own priorities, such as domestic development. As early as the Berlin Conference, Moscow had urged Washington to recognize the PRC. Molotov told Dulles that U.S. policy toward China "was bankrupt" and "would never succeed in overthrowing [the] Chinese Communists. They were proud people who demanded [a] rightful place." The Soviet foreign minister expressed the hope "with apparent sincerity" that his proposal for a five-power conference "would be an acceptable opening for better relations between [the] US and China."[51]

At Geneva, the Soviets again urged the United States to improve relations with Beijing. During a meeting with American representative Walter Bedell Smith on May 22, Molotov said that "China was only five years old and she also needed time to devote her attention and resources to her problems." When Smith claimed that "there was a line beyond which compromise could not go . . . we would not abandon our principles" in dealing with China, Molotov replied that he understood and stressed again that "China was a very young country."[52] Molotov's remarks were interesting in that they betrayed Soviet perceptions of China's foreign policy. By describing China as "young," Molotov must have meant that Beijing was inexperienced and rash in international politics and that when China grew older, it would become more restrained. Therefore, the United States should be patient with China.

The Soviet foreign minister also showed familiarity with the issues in Sino-American relations. When Smith raised the question of detained American citizens and air force personnel in China, Molotov responded by mentioning Chinese students in the United States who were unable to return to China. He said that he saw no reason why a matter of this sort could not be very readily resolved. Molotov's knowledge of Sino-American grievances may reflect the constant exchange of views and consultations between China and the Soviet Union before and during the Geneva Conference.[53]

At Geneva, the Soviet Union not only intervened in Sino-American relations but also facilitated the improvement of the Sino-British relationship. As Shi Zhe recalls, Zhou first met with Eden at the residence of the Soviet delegation. Molotov invited the Chinese and British representatives to a party at his quarters to encourage a Sino-British dialogue.[54] The British told the Americans later that Molotov "raised no question of substance but seemed interested rather in encouraging cordiality between his guests."[55]

Although recent Chinese memoirs and official histories generally stress the unity and cooperation between the Soviet Union and China regarding the Geneva Conference, there are indications that Moscow was more moderate and cautious than Beijing. According to Shi Zhe, during a preparatory meeting in Moscow before the Geneva Conference, Molotov cautioned the Chinese not to entertain "unrealistic illusions" in Geneva because imperialist countries had "unshakable interests." The proper line, the Soviet foreign minister argued, was to be flexible, striving for the best and adjusting policy to the development of the conference and the international situation as a whole.[56]

Obviously, the Soviets did not have as high an expectation in Geneva as the Chinese did, not to mention the Vietminh. Khrushchev said in his memoirs that "we gasped with surprise and pleasure" when "we were informed of" the French proposal of the seventeenth parallel as the demarcation line. "We hadn't expected anything like this," Khrushchev continued, "the seventeenth parallel was the absolute maximum we would have claimed ourselves." At Geneva, Molotov himself acknowledged to Eden that the Soviet Union had differences with its allies. He claimed that "it would be wrong to believe that [the] Soviet Union controls China."[57]

The British had an explanation for Mosocw's eagerness to conclude peace in Korea and Indochina. According to this theory, the Soviet Union was now a "'satisfied power,' anxious for stability and repose, and, therefore, likely to be apprehensive about the activities of unsatisfied adventurers like

Chou En-lai."[58] At Geneva, Eden said to Molotov jokingly that the Soviet Union and Britain were playing the role of "inside left and inside right" respectively. The Soviet foreign minister liked the idea very much.[59]

At Geneva, Eden's principal private secretary Evelyn Shuckburgh observed: "Molotov is more afraid of a world war and atomic bombs than Chou En-lai, partly because Russia is more open to attack, partly because she is more of a satisfied power and has a lot to lose, and partly because he (Molotov) is a wiser and calmer man. One has a feeling that the Chinese are in a reckless and self-assertive mood." Before coming to Geneva, Shuckburgh had wanted "to get close to Chou, and try to detach him from Molotov." But as it had turned out, the British were "more in the mood of getting close to Molotov, to help him control Chou."[60]

SINO-BRITISH RAPPROCHEMENT

The Geneva Conference marked an improvement in Sino-British relations. Zhou and Eden exchanged visits several times in the course of the negotiations, during which they discussed bilateral relations. At their June 2 meeting, the British foreign secretary raised the question of the Chinese treatment of Humphrey Trevelyan, the British chargé in Beijing. He asked that Trevelyan be given the usual diplomatic courtesies and privileges and be allowed to meet appropriate Chinese officials. The Chinese replied that they would take care of these matters.[61] It was at Geneva that diplomatic relations were established between Britain and China at the level of chargé d'affaires. Beijing recognized Trevelyan's status as British chargé and agreed to send a Chinese chargé to London. Before that time, the Chinese government had only recognized Trevelyan as the "head of the British delegation for negotiations of the establishment of diplomatic relations."[62]

Zhou and Eden's assistants also exchanged regular visits. Many of the controversial issues between the two countries, such as the treatment of British firms in China, exit permits for British businesspeople and the release of British prisoners, were dealt with at this level of talks. It was agreed that a trade delegation from the China National Export and Import Corporation would visit London and that a return visit by British companies to China would follow.[63]

These lower-level meetings, like the Zhou-Eden discussions, were often characterized by relaxation and cordiality. Trevelyan informed the

Americans that in general his relations with the members of the Chinese delegation had been "pleasant and friendly," and he "[got] along best" with Huan Xiang, Qiao Guanhua, and Gong Peng. The British diplomat also criticized American press reports that the British diplomats were laughed at in the streets of China as being "not in accord with facts." He said that he personally had never encountered any slight or mockery by Chinese in Beijing.[64]

At Geneva, Zhou Enlai also had contact with the representatives of the British Labor Party. At a meeting with Harold Wilson, former Labor president of the Board of Trade, they discussed the possibilities of developing Sino-British trade. One result was the visit to China later in the year by Clement Attlee and other leaders of the Labor party. As Morgan Phillips, secretary of the British delegation, recalled, Zhou spent a lot of time "discussing the new constitution of China and the problem of Formosa." To meet the British visitors, Zhou and a number of ministers and officials came to the British mission in Beijing for the first time. Aneuran Bevan delivered a speech to the Chinese People's Consultative Committee.[65]

Writing in *Shijie zhishi* on August 20, Ji Chaoding, secretary-general of the Chinese International Trade Promotion Committee, called for the expansion of trade between Britain and China. After noting the recent increase in Sino-British trade, the author argued that continuation of this trend would not only help fulfill China's First Five-Year Plan but also help alleviate the British economic recession.[66]

Optimism in Sino-British relations was evident in China's media during this time. A September 5 *Shijie zhishi* article forecast hopeful future ties between London and Beijing. The author attributed the lack of progress in the Sino-British relationship since 1950 to the pressures of the U.S. government, especially during the Korean War. The absence of normal relations had inflicted great damage on the Chinese and English people as well as the cause of world peace. During the Geneva Conference, the article continued, Sino-British relations had improved as a result of the efforts of the two countries' statesmen. But it was just a beginning, and further opportunities existed to develop the relationship, most notably trade. The American economic embargo against China had undermined British overseas commerce and deepened its domestic economic difficulties. "Today," the author concluded, "it was only the United States that showed anger, fear and apprehension" about the improvement in Sino-British relations.[67] Obviously, the author was trying to sow discord between London and Washington.

DULLES'S SNUB OF CHINA

The Eisenhower administration inherited the principles of Indochina policy bequeathed by Truman and Acheson. The architects of the "New Look" foreign policy saw Ho Chi Minh as a tool of international communism and believed that the loss of Indochina would produce a "domino" effect throughout the rest of the region with serious damage to the political, economic, and strategic interests of the United States. Therefore, they were resolved to prevent the fall of Indochina.

In April 1954, when the French position in Indochina began to crumble, Dulles asked the British to join a "United Action," a coalition including the United States, Britain, France, Australia, New Zealand, the Philippines, Thailand, and the Associated States to guarantee the security of Southeast Asia. But London objected to intervening before the Geneva Conference. Churchill and Eden did not share the American "domino" theory regarding Indochina. They feared that outside military interference would dash any hope of a negotiated settlement at Geneva and provoke a war with China. They did not want to involve Britain in a conflict in which they had more to lose but little to gain. Furthermore, Britain's Commonwealth allies in Asia would have opposed an expansion of the war in Indochina.[68]

Dulles viewed the Geneva Conference, as Gary R. Hess observes, "as a 'holding action'—a necessary step to assure French participation in the EDC while rebuilding their position in Indochina."[69] As for Chinese participation, the secretary of state refused to accept Beijing as one of the "Five Big Powers." At the Berlin Conference early in the year, despite Dulles's vigorous efforts to prevent it, America's allies prevailed in inviting China to the Geneva Conference. After an agreement had been reached at Berlin to convene the Geneva conference, Dulles claimed, "We maintain our refusal to give it [China] any position of preferment, or to contribute to the enhancement of its authority and prestige."[70] In fact, the Berlin communiqué had included a caveat, which stated that "neither the invitation to, nor the holding of" the Geneva Conference "shall be deemed to imply diplomatic recognition in any case where it has not already been accorded."[71]

The Eisenhower administration was under political attack for participating in an international meeting at which Beijing, rather than Taipei, was represented. Right-wing members of Congress and the China lobby drew an analogy between Yalta and Geneva. In this connection, the experience of Arthur Dean, special ambassador to Korea and chief U.S. delegate in the

Panmunjom talks, must have alerted Eisenhower and Dulles to the strong domestic sentiment against "appeasement" of communism.

In an interview published in the *Providence Journal* on January 3, 1954, Dean called for a review of U.S. policy toward China, resurrecting the old idea that America could drive a wedge between China and the Soviet Union by improving relations with Beijing.[72] Senator Herman Welker spoke in Congress on January 14, charging that Dean "offers the view which has long been held by pro-Red China apologists in the State Department." The current U.S. policy, the senator from Idaho claimed, "is a real policy because it refuses to offer a bribe to the slave rulers of China" and "because it refuses even to discuss the possibility of United Nations membership for a bloody aggressor whose policies have brought murderous ruin and destruction to millions." Welker closed his remarks by linking Dean to such reputedly Communist entities as the Institute of Pacific Affairs.[73]

Throughout the conference, Dulles remained sensitive to indications of congressional and public criticism of the administration's conduct at Geneva. His behavior there must have pleased his political detractors. The secretary of state contended that he would not meet Zhou Enlai "unless our automobiles collide." He refused to shake hands with the Chinese premier when the latter approached him at Geneva.[74]

On July 13, when Mendès-France asked Dulles to return to Geneva for the conference's final sessions, Dulles declined, contending that "the memories of Yalta in the United States were very fresh." "The US Government," he went on, "cannot be associated with a settlement which would be portrayed in the US as a second Yalta." The fact that the president and he had agreed to the conference "has been a political liability."[75]

The Geneva Conference provided the administration an opportunity to observe the operation of the Sino-Soviet alliance at close range. There are indications that American analysts perceived the differences between the two Communist powers about Indochina. U.S. journalists speculated at the time that the Soviets viewed "with significant discomfiture" China's efforts to "strike [an] independent role" at Geneva.[76]

To Dulles, Moscow appeared to have taken a position more moderate than Beijing's. The Soviets "might exert an influence on Communist China to desist," the secretary of state told French Foreign Minister Georges Bidault on April 21, 1954, "because they feared that the Chinese might drag them into a general war." Bidault shared this view, for he also argued that "the Soviet Union is afraid of China and the possibility that China might drag Russia into something against her will."[77]

Eden also detected Russian uneasiness about China's independent role in Geneva. During a dinner with Eden on May 20, Molotov said he had read in the newspapers that Britain and the United States were having differences and that he did not believe it. Eden answered that he was right not to do so because allies often had "to argue their respective points of view." Molotov continued, "'That is right, we have to do that amongst ourselves, too.'. . . China was very much her own master in these matters."[78]

On June 26, Senator Knowland sent Dulles some intelligence information from Beijing regarding tensions in Sino-Soviet relations. According to this source, when American military intervention in Indochina "seemed to be a reality," Beijing asked Zhou to secure a Soviet commitment if the United States attacked China. After consultations with Moscow, Molotov replied that both the Soviet Union and China "are not adequately prepared for war on a large scale" and that Moscow would retaliate immediately if "the United States attacks China with atomic or hydrogen bombs." In the event of a conventional assault, the Soviet Union "will aid China with all the available weapons, industrial products, materials and technical skills. It is to the advantage of China that Soviet Russia should temporarily stand aside." Beijing's reaction, the document asserted, "is mild resentment." The Chinese thought that "the Russian comrades are somewhat selfish."[79]

Knowland's intelligence material must have reinforced Dulles's conviction that high pressure on China represented the best strategy to promote divisions in the Sino-Soviet relationship. Viewed in this context, Dulles's refusal to acknowledge China's "big power" status and his cold-shouldering of Zhou Enlai at Geneva assume meanings that go beyond the surface appearances. His hostility toward China not only represented a keen sensitivity to domestic sentiments but also underscored a calculated intention to drive a wedge between Beijing and Moscow.[80]

Despite Dulles's antagonism toward China, the Geneva Conference did result in one limited contact between China and the United States: Sino-American negotiations about American prisoners in China and Chinese students in the United States. At Geneva, the United States asked Trevelyan to approach China on the issue of detained American citizens in China. Seeing this as an opportunity to open a channel of contact with the United States, Zhou Enlai responded that China would not discuss the issue with anyone but high-level American officials because both China and the United States had representatives in Geneva, and there was no reason to use intermediaries. At a special press conference on May 26, Huang Hua, spokesman of the Chinese delegation, announced that China was prepared to discuss with the United States the question of American prisoners in China. Huang also criticized the U.S. government for preventing Chinese students in America from returning to China.[81]

Securing the release of Americans proved more important than political isolation, and the U.S. government agreed to negotiate with the Chinese at Geneva. To minimize domestic reactions, Dulles instructed Bedell Smith to make a statement at Geneva stressing that these talks should not be construed as the opening step toward diplomatic recognition of China.[82] Between June 5 and 21, four official meetings were held at Geneva with China represented by Wang Bingnan and the United States by U. Alexis Johnson. Although the two sides did exchange information about people to be repatriated, Beijing failed to obtain any response to suggestions of wider discussions and substantial changes in Sino-American relations. Although these negotiations did not produce any agreement, they did pave the way for the Sino-American ambassadorial talks to begin in August 1955.[83]

CONCLUSION

Despite American opposition and delaying tactics, the Geneva Conference was a diplomatic triumph for China. For the first time, Beijing's diplomacy became the focus of attention in an international meeting. China's leaders clearly perceived their role in global rather than in regional terms. Their pride and confidence were best expressed by the *Renmin ribao* (People's Daily) editorial of July 22, 1954:

> For the first time as one of the Big Powers, the People's Republic of China joined the other major powers in negotiations on vital international problems and made a contribution of its own that won the acclaim of wide sections of world opinion. The international status of the People's Republic of China as one of the big world powers has gained universal recognition. Its international prestige has been greatly enhanced. The Chinese people take the greatest joy and pride in the efforts and achievements of their delegation at Geneva.[84]

Alone of the great powers, Beijing identified itself as a member of the Afro-Asian camp of newly independent nations. The Chinese leadership perceived China as the champion of the Afro-Asian cause against the oppression and exploitation of the West. It was within this context that China had played the major part in fashioning a new set of principles for world politics—the Five Principles of Peaceful Coexistence. This emphasis on Afro-Asian solidarity would culminate in the Bandung Conference of 1955.

Zhou Enlai played an important role in the Geneva Conference. He excelled in playing British and French realism off against the rigidity and inflexibility of American Cold War policies. His diplomacy epitomized the "United Front" strategy, which has been a distinct feature in the PRC's foreign policy: to unite with all possible forces to isolate China's most dangerous enemy. Zhou's performance at Geneva suggests that he was a shrewd practitioner of diplomacy of the possible.

Although Moscow appeared more moderate than Beijing regarding Indochina, the two countries shared a common desire to end the war in the region. On the whole, their relations during the period were marked by close consultations and cooperation. Together, they exerted restraining influences on the Vietminh. In this instance, their national self-interests surpassed ideological obligations to support the struggle of a fellow Communist party.

Sino-British relations improved during the Geneva Conference with the establishment of diplomatic relations at the level of chargés d'affaires and the increase of trade. To Beijing, however, major obstacles still prevented the complete normalization of relations between China and the United Kingdom. China's leaders still complained about London's continuing support of the KMT representative in the United Nations.

To Washington, the Geneva Accords represented a major advance of communism in Indochina. The United States did not sign the accords. In the wake of the Geneva Conference, the Eisenhower administration took a series of measures to contain the further expansion of communism in the area. It increased its aid to the Saigon regime, thus replacing France as the major Western intervenor in Vietnam. It also promoted the creation of the Southeast Asia Treaty Organization (SEATO) as a means to bolster the non-Communist countries in the region.

8 First Offshore-Island Crisis, 1954–1955

THE PRC AND THE OFFSHORE ISLANDS, 1949–1954

After the Korean armistice of July 1953 and the Geneva settlement of the Indochina issue, tensions in East Asia diminished temporarily. China began to refocus its attention on Taiwan. American security arrangements in Asia after the Korean truce irritated the Chinese leadership. On August 7, 1953, the United States and South Korea concluded a mutual defense treaty. One year later, on September 8, 1954, Washington signed a protocol creating SEATO. The negotiations between Washington and Taipei regarding the formation of a mutual defense treaty further angered Beijing's leaders, who feared that such a treaty would permanently divide Taiwan from China. To prevent such a separation and to show China's determination to reunify the country, Beijing initiated the first Taiwan Strait crisis of 1954–55.

After occupying Fujian Province in October 1949, the PLA immediately attempted an amphibious attack against Quemoy. The Twenty-eighth Army of the Tenth Corps of the Third Field Army was responsible for the assault. But because of hasty preparations, lack of air and naval support, as well as an intelligence failure (underestimation of the KMT strength on the island), the operation failed, with a loss of 7,200 PLA soldiers and boatmen.[1]

China's leaders did not abandon plans for further action, however. Mao Zedong instructed Ye Fei, commander of the Tenth Corps, stationed in Fujian after the liberation, to prepare for another attack on Quemoy. Only the outbreak of the war in Korea disrupted Mao's designs regarding Quemoy and other offshore islands. In November 1950, Mao ordered Ye to put aside the preparations for taking Quemoy.[2] Obviously, the presence of the Seventh Fleet in the Taiwan Strait made the Chinese leader cautious, and the war in Korea distracted his attention from the offshore islands.

In the summer of 1952, when the military situation in Korea became more favorable for the Chinese and North Korean forces, the Chinese leadership again turned its attention to the occupation of the offshore islands off the coast of Fujian and Zhejiang provinces. Chen Yi, commander of the East

China Military Region, asked his chief of staff, Zhang Aiping, to start preparations for liberating the offshore islands. Soon Mao approved a proposal by Peng Dehuai to authorize Zhang to take charge of the Fujian-Zhejiang military operation.[3]

According to the Central Military Commission, the strategy for liberating the offshore island was to "take small islands first, one island at a time, and from north to south." In line with this principle, the Tachen Islands, located off the Zhejiang coast at the northern end of the Nationalist-held offshore island chain, were selected as the initial target for the PLA's campaign. This incremental approach, China's military planners calculated, also would provide on-the-spot training in amphibious operations for the PLA, preparing the soldiers for later assault on the more heavily fortified islands of Quemoy and Matsu.[4]

After the conclusion of the Korean War in July 1953, China's leaders began to place increasing stress on peaceful coexistence in their foreign policy in order to secure the tranquil external environment necessary for China's domestic development. In this context, the existing policy of liberating the offshore islands "from small to large, one island at a time, and from north to south" was no longer considered appropriate. Beijing consequently modified the plan in 1954 by limiting the goal only to the liberation of the Tachens. In the new plan, the shelling of Quemoy would have two functions: to divert Chiang's attention from the Tachens and to show China's determination to reunify Taiwan. The second purpose was more important.[5]

Thus, between 1949 and 1954, Beijing's offshore island policy underwent a transformation from a purely military operation to a scheme that was closely integrated with China's general foreign policy. The attack on Quemoy was no longer just a military matter but a calculated political maneuver designed to test American intentions in the area, to aggravate Washington's differences with Taipei over the offshore islands, and to intensify U.S. disputes with allied and neutral Asian governments that were against Washington's commitment to Chiang Kai-shek. Although Beijing's fears about Taiwan's future were justified, its actions in the Taiwan Strait generated an unintended consequence. Instead of preventing the conclusion of a security treaty between Washington and Taipei, the Quemoy shelling facilitated the realization of such a pact. The bombardment provided an excuse to Chiang's supporters in the United States to push for a treaty with Taiwan.

THE ORIGINS OF THE MUTUAL DEFENSE TREATY

During a discussion with Dulles on March 19, 1953, Wellington Koo, the Nationalist ambassador in Washington, first broached the subject of a mutual defense treaty. Referring to U.S. security arrangements with Australia, New Zealand, the Philippines, and Japan, Koo asked the U.S. government to conclude a similar pact with Taiwan. Dulles welcomed the idea in principle, saying that "he himself had given a great deal of thought to the idea of the conclusion of a general pact of mutual security for Asia." About a bilateral treaty with Taiwan, though, Dulles had reservations. If the treaty only covered the defense of Taiwan and the Pescadores, he explained, how would it affect the offshore islands still controlled by the KMT? If these islands were included in the treaty and were subsequently attacked by the Communists, or if Taiwan launched attacks against the mainland from the islands and provoked a Communist retaliation, the United States would be "obliged" to assist Taiwan. This entailed a responsibility that the United States was not ready to assume at the moment. If the offshore islands were excluded, Dulles continued, such exclusion would "impair the prestige of the Nationalist government." Dulles concluded that he did not know "what would be the best way out of it."[6] Dulles's clear reluctance to include the offshore islands in a security treaty with Taiwan would later become the most difficult issue in the treaty negotiations.

There was no mention of the treaty in subsequent discussions between Koo and State Department officials. But the signing of the U.S.-South Korean Security Treaty in October 1953 rekindled Taiwan's interest in obtaining a similar pact. Nationalist officials brought the matter to Vice-President Richard Nixon's attention when he visited the island in November. On December 18, Chiang gave American ambassador Karl Rankin a draft security pact based on the Australia-New Zealand-United States Alliance (ANZUS) and U.S. treaties with the Philippines and South Korea. Rankin telegraphed the document to the State Department the next day. The draft committed the United States to the defense of the offshore islands. The key article stipulated that each party would regard an attack in the Pacific area on either party "in territories which are now or may hereafter be under its control" as an attack on both parties.[7]

Taiwan's proposal immediately won the endorsement of Arthur Radford, chairman of the Joint Chiefs of Staff. The State Department Bureau of Far Eastern Affairs was also eager to go ahead with treaty negotiations with

Taiwan. In a memorandum to Dulles, Walter Robertson, assistant secretary of state for Far Eastern affairs, pointed to the advantages of establishing a security treaty with Taiwan: it would improve the morale of the KMT; give the Chiang regime "a similar status in our system of alliances in the Pacific to Japan, Korea, [the] Philippines, and the ANZUS countries;" offset Taiwan's misgivings about the Geneva Conference; and "make clear to our allies and to the Communists our determination to stand back of" Chiang Kai-shek on Taiwan.[8]

Dulles responded that he was "impressed" by Robertson's arguments and that he had been convinced that "any concession to the Chinese Communists as to Formosa would be unthinkable because it would constitute a betrayal of several millions of our Chinese friends on Formosa who are strongly anti-Communist; and because it would deprive us of an indispensable link in our chain of strong positions off the Mainland of Asia from the Aleutians to the Philippines." Without Taiwan, Dulles claimed, the United States could not maintain its offshore island chain. On the other hand, Dulles pointed out that any announcement of the conclusion of a security treaty with Taiwan before the Geneva Conference "would not be palatable to the governments or the public of Great Britain and France. It might be construed as provocative and calculated to prejudice the chances for any agreement at Geneva." Therefore, the secretary of state concluded that "the study of the issue would have to be very carefully prepared." He preferred to postpone the resolution of the case until he could consider it further.[9]

During March 1954, military activity escalated in the Taiwan Strait. The PLA shelled Quemoy for the first time, although on a small scale, and there was fighting around the Tachens. The PRC probably started this March assault in reaction to the report of the treaty negotiations between Washington and Taipei.[10]

When Dulles returned from Geneva, Koo went to see him on May 19 to discuss the proposed treaty, which, the ambassador said, "was very close to the heart of his Government." Dulles replied that it was difficult for the United States to conclude a security treaty "with a country which is actually carrying on military operations." Although Washington did not wish to "hamper the operations" of Taiwan against the mainland, Dulles went on, it "is not prepared to assume treaty obligations the terms of which might bring about its direct involvement." Therefore, the secretary of state asserted, a genuine problem existed in formulating the language that would preserve Taiwan's freedom of action "without committing the United States to a possible course of action which might not then be in the best general interest."

A similar situation, Dulles told Koo, had existed in the negotiation of the U.S.-South Korean defense treaty, which was not concluded until after the Korean armistice. The situation in the Taiwan Strait was fluid and there were ongoing hostilities between Taiwan and the mainland which neither Washington nor Taipei wanted to stop. Given this situation, Dulles concluded that no modification of the current defense arrangements for Taiwan should be made, although the issue would continue to be reviewed in the light of shifting circumstances. Koo noticed that Dulles "spoke deliberately, apparently weighing every word he was saying."[11]

In Taiwan, Chiang Kai-shek kept urging visiting American officials to conclude a security treaty. He made the point in several discussions between May 13 and 24 with General James Van Fleet and Defense Secretary Charles Wilson. On May 28, the KMT leader raised the matter again during a meeting with Rankin, who observed that Chiang showed "great disappointment and disillusionment over what he understood to be [the] present US position." Chiang remarked that the "China mainland was lost due in large part to [the] withdrawal of US political and moral support."[12]

Throughout May, Beijing intensified its military operations in the strait, especially around the Tachens. There were both air and naval clashes, and PLA units occupied several small islands to the north of the Tachens.[13] It was very likely that this new flurry of fighting represented Beijing's reaction to the visit of Van Fleet and Wilson to Taiwan. This would become a pattern of Communist action throughout the later offshore island crises: whenever American officials came to Taiwan, Beijing would increase its military pressures in the strait to show its resolve and to discourage further cooperation between Taipei and Washington.

Chiang was eager to elicit an official U.S. commitment to the offshore islands, but Washington was wary of the consequences of such an action. During a meeting with his national security advisers on May 22, President Eisenhower "seriously questioned" any public pronouncement regarding a U.S. promise to defend the offshore islands "as too big a commitment of U.S. prestige and forces." It was agreed that no such public statement should be made. To show support for the KMT and to deter the Chinese Communists, the president suggested that ships of the Seventh Fleet visit the Tachens and other offshore islands held by Chiang. "This show of US strength," the chief executive contended, "would make our position clear."[14]

In Washington, Koo pursued the Americans for some official pledge to defend the offshore islands. During a talk with Dulles on July 1, the Nationalist ambassador asked "if the U.S. government could not make some official statement which would show its interest in the protection of the off-shore islands." Such a statement, Koo said, "would have psychological value." If the United States did not wish to include the offshore islands in its defense zone, Koo suggested, "at least a statement that the U.S. Navy would patrol the waters adjacent to the offshore islands would have a deterrent effect on the Chinese Communists." Dulles, however, remained unwilling to yield on this point. He told Koo that the vessels of the Seventh Fleet had already patrolled the area of the Tachens, and that "actions spoke louder than words."[15]

In August, the Bureau of Far Eastern Affairs again pressured Dulles for the treaty with Taiwan. Robertson argued that since the Geneva Conference, the Chinese Communists had "launched a violent propaganda campaign" to "liberate" Taiwan. The move was designed "to generate increasing international pressures for a negotiated change in the status of Formosa as a means of removing a serious cause of tension." Because the United States was intent on maintaining the current status of Taiwan, Robertson reasoned, Beijing's pressures only increased tensions. If this point were made clear to the world through the signing of the security treaty with Taiwan, it would "remove the basis for the pressures and undermine the effectiveness of the Communist propaganda campaign." Robertson asked Dulles for approval to start treaty negotiations with Taiwan.[16]

Other agencies within the State Department, however, had reservations about Robertson's plan. The Bureau of Near Eastern, South Asian, and African Affairs contended on August 27 that India's reaction had to be considered. Indian-American relations, it pointed out, had "slightly deteriorated" during the past five months, largely as a result of American collective security efforts in the general area. It was U.S. policy "to support the continuation in power in India of elements which are friendly to the United States, but the proposed treaty would further antagonize India and might drive it closer to Communist China." Furthermore, the bureau continued, "such a treaty would increase the misgivings of countries in the Near East which are skeptical of our policy with respect to Communist China and tend to share India's views on developments in Asia."[17]

Representatives of the Policy Planning Staff and the Bureau of European Affairs, as well as State Department counselor Douglas MacArthur II, all opposed commencing treaty negotiations "at this particular time." They preferred negotiating a treaty with Taiwan after the Manila Conference.[18] Before his departure for the Philippine capital on September 1, Dulles again decided to delay setting a date for treaty negotiations with Taiwan because of "the complexities of the offshore island problem."[19]

On September 3, the Chinese Communists launched a massive shelling of Quemoy. The timing was deliberate, for it coincided with Dulles's arrival in Manila for the meeting that was to establish SEATO. The action was intended to foreclose the possibility of extending SEATO's protection to Taiwan. The secretary of state had planned to visit Taiwan after the Manila Conference. Now in view of the crisis in the Taiwan Strait, he began to wonder if it was wise to make the trip and subject himself to certain KMT demands for U.S. participation in the defense of Quemoy. On the other hand, the secretary of state recognized that failing to visit Taiwan after having accepted Chiang's invitation would be interpreted as a "snub" to the Nationalists and might cause unwelcome political consequences in the United States. Dulles sought Bedell Smith's advice on the question. After consulting the president, Smith advised Dulles to visit Taiwan after leaving Manila but to make it a purely social call and to limit his stay there to several hours.[20]

The administration was divided on how to respond to the Communist bombardment. The majority of the JCS took a hard-line view. Admiral Radford, together with the chief of staff of the Air Force and the chief of Naval Operations, "regarded the retention of the offshore islands as of very great importance, and recommended the use of U.S. armed forces, if necessary, to prevent Communist seizure of these islands." General Ridgway, chief of staff of the Army, dissented, contending that the islands were not of sufficient military significance to warrant the commitment of American forces. Defense Secretary Charles Wilson worried that intervention would entangle the United States in the raging Chinese civil war. The defense of the offshore islands, he argued, "would come closer to war with China than if we had tried to save Dien Bien Phu."[21]

To Eisenhower and Dulles, the crisis was, in the words of the secretary of state, "a horrible dilemma." On the one hand, they recognized the psychological and political importance of the offshore islands, the loss of which "would have disastrous consequences" in Taiwan, Korea, Japan, and the Philippines. On the other hand, they were conscious that they would lack the support of their European allies as well as "a substantial part of the U.S. people" if they went to the defense of those islands at the risks of war with mainland China. Dulles acknowledged that "the British fear atomic war and would not consider the reasons for our action to be justified." The president said that "his letters from the farm areas . . . constantly say don't send our boys to war. It will be a big job to explain to the American people the importance of these islands to U.S. security."[22]

To solve the dilemma, Dulles suggested presenting the offshore islands question to the U.N. Security Council. The United States would seek an injunction against changing the status quo on the ground that the Communist action was a threat to world peace. In Dulles's view, such an option had several advantages. First, "it offered the possibility of avoiding going to war alone with the moral condemnation of the world or having the effect of the loss of the islands on the defense of Formosa." Second, it "could put a serious strain" on Sino-Soviet relations. If the Soviets vetoed the move, it would gravely undermine their "peace offensive" and then the United States "would win a measure of support from allies and world opinion now lacking." If the Soviets went along in the Security Council, the Chinese Communists could be expected to react adversely in defiance of the United Nations. In that case, Beijing would again become "an international outcast." Finally, the option could reap domestic benefits. Dulles contended that "if we act without Congress now we will not have anyone in the United States with us. On the other hand, if we act under the UN we will not have to act without Congressional authorization."[23] Eisenhower endorsed Dulles's plan.[24]

The administration also calculated that neither Beijing nor Taipei could be expected to accept the plan because it would represent an outside interference in an issue both of them regarded as domestic. Washington would try to persuade Chiang to go along in the anticipation that when the Communists rejected the proposal, Taiwan's acceptance would improve the Nationalist government's image. Moreover, the Soviet Union might veto the plan in the Security Council. In that event, the United States, Britain, and New Zealand would try to preserve the item on the agenda, hoping that its existence would deter Beijing's aggression.[25]

Since early 1953, Chiang had pushed persistently for a defense treaty with the United States. He wanted the Americans to help him defend both Taiwan and the offshore islands. His supporters within the administration, most notably Radford and Robertson, eagerly argued his case. Although recognizing the psychological importance of the offshore islands, Eisenhower and Dulles, preferring to maintain their operational flexibility, refused to commit the United States to their defense. Some State Department officials also remained sensitive to the reactions of the Allies and neutral countries. Therefore, before the onset of the Communist shelling of Quemoy in September 1954, Dulles repeatedly found excuses to postpone treaty negotiations. His success demonstrated the limited influence of pro-Chiang officials.

The Communist attack on Quemoy exacerbated Washington's dilemma over the offshore islands. Faced with the prospect of disgrace or war, Dulles proposed a U.N. scheme that would free the United States from these "horrible" alternatives. In his calculations, a U.N.-arranged cease-fire would preserve the offshore islands for Chiang and avoid a war between Washington and Beijing. Furthermore, the plan would serve his long-term strategy of straining Sino-Soviet relations.

ANGLO-AMERICAN DIFFERENCES OVER THE OFFSHORE ISLANDS

To implement his U.N. plan—code-named "Oracle"—Dulles knew that the United States needed the cooperation of its allies, especially Britain. If the British would go along with the scheme, he believed, "it might mark the beginning of our coming together on the Far East."[26] On September 17, Dulles informed Eden in London of his intention to take the matter to the United Nations.[27]

The British did not attach the same psychological and political significance to the offshore islands as the Americans did. The British Chiefs of Staff asserted that the islands were "indefensible and unessential to the defense of Formosa." The United States "should keep clear of any commitment to help defend" them, the British military argued. "The real defense of Formosa is the US 7th Fleet." If the American government became involved in war with China over the offshore islands, the Foreign Office contended, there would be no support in the United Kingdom.[28]

Fearful that the crisis might develop into a world war, the British pressured Washington to restrain Chiang Kai-shek, whom they considered a "palooka."[29] In a letter to Eisenhower, Churchill expressed U.K. apprehension that during the next few years, Washington might "through impulsiveness or lack of perspective, be drawn into a Chinese war." Eden wrote later in his memoirs that "no great power could seriously want to fight" about the offshore islands, which "could be a cause of war, just the same." In Eden's view, Chiang's occupation of the islands provided Beijing with "a constant grievance with which most of world opinion would sympathize." If the generalissimo were to withdraw from Quemoy and Matsu, Eden believed, "the Chinese Communist case against Chiang and the United States would be much weaker, politically and militarily." From the U.S. point of view, Eden concluded, Taiwan "would be stronger without the commitment of the off-shore islands."[30]

Despite the reservations of some officials,[31] the British government welcomed Oracle with the hope that it would lead to a wider settlement of the

Taiwan issue, including American recognition of the PRC and its admission into the United Nations. Because both London and Washington were reluctant to initiate the action in the United Nations, they decided to ask New Zealand, a current member of the Security Council, to introduce Oracle and agreed that London would sound out Beijing and Moscow before presenting the resolution.[32]

Differences soon emerged between Britain and the United States regarding the scope of Oracle and Washington's decision to proceed to conclude a defense treaty with Chiang Kai-shek. Eden believed that the American draft minute on the U.N. resolution, which emphasized that the United States, Great Britain, and New Zealand would make "every effort to limit the discussion of and action on New Zealand resolution in the United Nations to the hostilities around Quemoy" was "unduly restrictive." The foreign secretary had thought that the original purpose of the exercise "was that it looked toward a wider settlement." Now he feared that if the item were treated on the proposed restrictive basis, it would be viewed as merely another cold-war gambit rather than as a "cautious first step" toward a wider settlement. He, therefore, recommended that the draft minute be amended.[33]

But the Americans would not yield to British pressure. To maintain control of Oracle, Dulles told the British and New Zealand ambassadors in Washington on October 9 that "he had never intended to suggest that if this particular situation [the Quemoy fighting] were settled we would move right on from there to a general settlement of the Formosan problem . . . leading perhaps to recognition of Communist China and its admission to the UN." But, the secretary of state continued, the alternative to not pursuing Oracle would be "fraught with perilous possibilities."[34] Quite understandably, in the face of the threat of inaction and a dangerous outcome, London and Wellington consented to Washington's draft and its strict limitation of debate to the subject of fighting around Quemoy.[35]

Dulles's stiff position reflected both his intention to maintain pressure on the Chinese Communists as a way of stimulating Sino-Soviet differences and his sensitivity to domestic political reactions. During the crisis, the secretary of state told Chinese Nationalist Foreign Minister George Yeh that the Russians were "trying to match U.S. military power with an industrial base only one-third or one-fourth that of the U.S. Communist China was undoubtedly pressing the Soviet Union hard for more military and industrial assistance. . . . The whole Communist domain was overextended." Therefore, Dulles concluded that it was important "to keep the Communist regimes under economic and other pressures . . . which will lead to disintegration."[36]

Administration officials were aware that the Soviet Union was reluctant to provide support for the PRC's action in the Taiwan Strait. Ambassador Bohlen reported from Moscow that the Russians probably did not intend "to run [a] risk of involvement in [a] major war over Chinese claims to Formosa."[37] Allen Dulles of the CIA tended to regard recent Soviet expressions of support for the Chinese Communists "with a grain of salt."[38] The president himself was suspicious of the extent to which Moscow and Beijing agreed on the offshore island question. He told Press Secretary James Hagerty early in 1955, "I have a feeling that the Chinese Communists are acting on their own on this and that is considerably disturbing to the Russians."[39]

Throughout the crisis, Chiang's supporters in Congress clamored for a strong policy toward Beijing. Senators H. Alexander Smith and William Knowland called for American participation in the defense of the offshore islands. Senator William Jenner urged that the United States equip the Nationalist regime for an invasion of the mainland. Senator Joseph McCarthy demanded the administration to allow KMT troops to attack the "soft-belly" of mainland China.[40]

Pro-Chiang officials within the administration, such as Radford and Robertson, had agreed to Oracle only in the belief that the resolution, in the words of Radford, "has as its ultimate aim the creation of a situation which will lay the ground work for U.N. acceptance of U.S. or allied assistance to the Nationalist Chinese in holding the offshore islands."[41] In fact, Robertson and Rankin had already employed Oracle as a method of trying to push Dulles toward the conclusion of a defense treaty with Taipei.

On October 5, Rankin urged the State Department to inform Chiang of the New Zealand proposal. "Unless other offsetting steps are taken," the ambassador argued, it might be anticipated that the Nationalists would consider the resolution as "another Yalta by which free China, this time at British behest, is to be sold down [the] river" as a result of secret bargains made behind their back. A mutual security treaty, Rankin contended, could provide assurances to Taiwan as an example of "U.S. determination to help defend free China."[42] Robertson also urged upon Dulles the importance of an immediate conclusion of the security treaty with Chiang.[43]

Finally, Dulles decided to conduct the treaty discussions. He was persuaded to do so, however, not by Robertson and Rankin but by those who viewed the treaty as a way to control Chiang. Eisenhower and Dulles insisted that Chiang should assume a more passive posture and accept a truly defensive treaty.[44]

On October 12, Robertson and Walter P. McConaughy, director of the Office of Chinese Affairs, were sent to Taipei to confer with the Nationalists. Chiang objected vigorously to the proposed New Zealand move, contending that "harm rather than benefit would result from the resolution." He wanted Washington to prevent New Zealand from introducing the proposal; he urged the United States to sign a defense treaty with him that would cover the off-shore islands, and if these measures were not possible, he wanted the American government to announce that a treaty would be concluded in advance of the introduction of the New Zealand proposal.[45]

The British were afraid that the proposed treaty with Chiang would jeopardize the chances for Oracle's success. In a message to the British Embassy in Washington on October 15, the Foreign Office said that the cabinet believed that the treaty would alter "the nature of the [Oracle] operation and we cannot go ahead in the Security Council until we know the terms of the treaty with Chiang and its purpose." Washington's agreement to a treaty with Taipei, the message went on, "would be bound to leak and after it was known any action which we were to take in the Security Council over the coastal islands would look merely like a move to preserve them for the Nationalists." The Foreign Office insisted that it must know the nature of the treaty before it could support any move in the United Nations to secure a limited settlement. Furthermore, London could not approach Beijing and Moscow without giving them any indication of the treaty.[46]

After consultations with American officials, the British Embassy reported to London that the State Department was not yet clear about the "exact nature and scope" of the treaty and that it would probably follow closely the model of the Korean defense treaty, "purely defensive, of indefinite duration, with a one year termination clause. The geographical area to be covered will depend on conditions at the time when it is concluded and these in turn may be considerably influenced by the effect of proceedings in the Security Council if the New Zealand plan goes forward." The State Department hoped, the report continued, that the offshore islands might "achieve some special neutralised status by means of a UN resolution, in which case it would be much easier to exclude them from any new defense treaty." The Embassy concluded that this might be one of Dulles's motives in wanting to press forward in the United Nations.[47]

In a cable to the Foreign Office on October 18, British Ambassador Roger Makins suggested that Dulles believed the treaty would give formal protection to Taiwan and the Pescadores while U.N. action under the New Zealand resolution would cover the offshore islands.[48] These British communications rightly depicted Dulles's calculations on the way to defuse the crisis in the Taiwan Strait. He clearly saw a close connection between Oracle and the treaty. The two measures, in his view, would serve as a double-edged sword to cut the tangle in the Taiwan Strait and stabilize the situation there: Oracle would neutralize the offshore islands and the treaty would protect Taiwan.

To ensure the acceptability of Oracle to the Communists, the British believed that the Americans should emphasize the defensive provisions of the treaty. Dulles was unwilling to move in that direction at the moment, however, agreeing only that the British could cover this point in their private communications to Beijing and Moscow.[49]

On November 1, bombers from the mainland attacked the Tachens. The operation was related to the presence of the Nationalist foreign minister, George Yeh, in Washington to conclude negotiations for the defense treaty. During the meetings with State Department officials, Yeh sought to tie the United States as much as possible to Chiang's policy—both to the protection of Taiwan, the Pescadores, and the offshore islands, and to a possible future military adventure to recapture the mainland. The Americans, however, were prepared to commit themselves only to the defense of Taiwan and the Pescadores. To avoid being dragged into an unwanted war in the Taiwan Strait, U.S. negotiators asked Yeh to promise that Taiwan would not start an attack against the mainland without American concurrence. Washington wanted the pledge included in a formal protocol. After hard bargaining, Chiang agreed to these terms but insisted that this promise be included in a less-formal "exchange of notes." Realizing that this assurance of prior consultation with the United States would arouse criticism from both the Nationalist legislature and the general public in Taiwan, Chiang's negotiator asked the Americans to keep the exchange of notes secret and separate the dates of the treaty signing and the exchange of notes in order to make the two appear as different issues.[50]

On December 2, the Mutual Defense Treaty between the United States and Taiwan was signed by Dulles and Yeh. (The exchange of notes was made public on January 14, 1955.) The treaty committed the United States to the defense of Taiwan, the Pescadores, and "such other territories as may be determined by mutual agreement." By purposely not mentioning the offshore islands in the text, the administration hoped to deter the mainland from attacking Chiang's positions there and at the same time to discourage Taiwan from using the islands as a stepping-stone to invade the mainland.[51]

Beijing reacted promptly to the treaty. *Renmin ribao* declared on December 5 that "The Chinese people's determination to liberate Taiwan is unalterable. The signing of the U.S.-Chiang Kai-shek 'mutual security treaty' is illegal and invalid and the American war clique must be responsible for all consequences that may arise from this illegal 'treaty'."[52]

At the same time, the Chinese media criticized the British for collaborating with Washington in interfering with Chinese internal affairs. The *Guangming ribao* said that London had shown "extreme unfriendliness to China." A long article in *Da gong bao* accused the British of asking the Chinese to ease tension in the Taiwan Strait in order to tie their hands while the Americans carried out their "evil designs in China" and of using small islands as a bait to induce the Chinese to give up their sovereign rights over Taiwan.[53]

On December 9, the East China Military Region submitted to the CCP Central Military Commission a battle plan for occupying Yijiangshan, an island located between the mainland and the Tachens. On December 11, Mao asked Peng Dehuai and Su Yu, deputy chief of staff, to consider carefully the timing for attacking Yijiangshan. He believed that it was not appropriate to launch the assault at the moment when the United States was conducting a naval maneuver in the Taiwan Strait.[54] Mao's comment clearly showed that he did not want a direct confrontation with the Americans in the Taiwan Strait. Throughout the Tachen campaign, Beijing emphasized the principle of not provoking the United States. Nie Fengzhi, the air force commander at the front, instructed his pilots not to engage American planes during the Yijiangshan battle. On January 10, 1955, PRC planes raided the Tachens, and eight days later, Communist troops took Yijiangshan.[55] Zhang Aiping initially planned to occupy the Tachens one week following the conclusion of the Yijiangshan battle. But Peng Dehuai ordered him to postpone the operation. Peng's intervention reflected Beijing's apprehension about U.S. reactions.[56]

After the Communist occupation of Yijiangshan, Washington quickly decided that the Nationalists should withdraw from the Tachens on the grounds that they were too far from Taiwan's airfields and not as defensible militarily as Quemoy and Matsu.[57] When the KMT troops on the Tachens began to evacuate to Taiwan with the help of the Seventh Fleet in early February, Zhang planned to attack them. Mao again intervened, instructing Peng not to assault the retreating Nationalist troops. Clearly with American reactions in mind, Mao asked Peng "not to be anxious to gain petty advantages." Accordingly, the minister of defense ordered Zhang in a telephone instruction not to interfere with the KMT withdrawal because an attack would have "consequence on international relations."[58] The PLA did not take the Tachens until after Chiang's troops had evacuated.

The administration viewed the Communist attack on Yijiangshan and the Tachens as an escalation of Beijing's aggression. To compensate for the damage to Taiwan's morale that could stem from evacuation, Dulles told Yeh that "under present conditions" the United States would assist in the defense of Quemoy. The secretary of state believed that "the announcement as to the protection of Quemoy would largely offset the adverse morale factor involved in a withdrawal from the Tachens."[59]

On January 19, Dulles informed the British ambassador of U.S. plans to give a provisional guarantee to defend Quemoy, explaining that this would require congressional authorization and requesting London's cooperation in implementing Oracle. American decisions to defend Quemoy alarmed Eden, who asked Makins to tell Dulles that Britain would agree to proceed with Oracle in the United Nations only if the United States dropped its commitment to guarantee Quemoy.[60] The British believed that to make the U.S. obligation to Quemoy and Matsu "stick," Washington "might be obliged to use atomic weapons." If the United States were to issue a public explanation of its position at this point, the British feared, "the decision would be irrevocable, and efforts to stabilize the situation in the United Nations would prove futile."[61]

The Eisenhower administration itself remained divided on the issue of defending Quemoy and Matsu. Although this time the president, Dulles, and Radford were prepared to commit the United States to the defense of these islands, other officials had strong reservations. Eisenhower's special assistant for National Security Affairs, Robert Cutler, argued that the American commitment ran the risk of war with Communist China. Treasury Secretary George Humphrey found it "very hard" to justify the proposal to retain the Quemoys, which "were set right down in the middle of a Chinese Communist harbor." Defense Secretary Charles Wilson believed that "it was foolish to fight a terrible war with Communist China simply in order to hold all these little islands." The United States, he continued, "should defend only Formosa and the Pescadores and let the others go."[62]

Partly because of internal disagreements and partly as a result of British pressure, Eisenhower and Dulles moderated their position on Quemoy. At an NSC meeting on January 21, Dulles said that, while working on the presidential address to Congress, he had come to the conclusion that it would be "best not to nail the flag to the mast by a detailed statement respecting our plans and intentions on evacuating or holding certain of these islands." The matter, the secretary of state concluded, could be handled by informing Chiang privately what the administration had in mind. Eisenhower stressed that the U.S. "ultimate objective" was to defend Taiwan and the Pescadores, and the other offshore islands were "incidental to this objective." He, therefore, proposed only a temporary inclusion of Quemoy and Matsu within the American defense perimeter.[63]

Subsequently, Dulles informed the British ambassador that the administration had agreed to make no public statement regarding its intentions with respect to Quemoy and Matsu. At the same time, the secretary of state pointed out that he "could not accept or give any commitment" with respect to the British contention that the offshore islands should "finally be allowed to pass to the control of the mainland government."[64]

On January 24, Eisenhower sent his message to Congress requesting permission to deploy armed forces if Taiwan were under attack. Four days later, the Senate, following the House of Representatives, passed the Formosa Resolution, which authorized the president to employ the armed forces of the United States for the protection of Taiwan, the Pescadores, and "related positions and territories of that area in friendly hands."[65]

On January 31, Herbert Hoover, Jr., acting secretary of state, asked Rankin to deliver a message to Chiang, which said that "under present circumstances," the president intended to assist in the defense of Quemoy and Matsu against armed attacks if he judged that such attacks were preliminary to an assault on Taiwan. The message emphasized that "an attack by the communists at this time on Quemoy and Matsu which seriously threatened their loss would be deemed by the President to be of this character."[66] While remarking that he understood that the United States would not mention Quemoy and Matsu in public statements, Chiang hoped that Washington might agree to some indication of the islands in Taiwan's pronouncements on the Tachen withdrawal. But Rankin gave him no encouragement in this respect. The KMT leader also expressed objection to the British Commonwealth proposal that Taiwan abandon all of the offshore islands in return for a cease-fire. He asked the United States to set Britain "straight on this point."[67]

While assuring Taiwan privately of the U.S. intention to protect Quemoy and Matsu, Washington also took measures on the diplomatic front. On January 28, New Zealand presented Oracle in the United Nations, proposing that the Security Council discuss the hostilities around the offshore islands. On February 3, Zhou Enlai responded to the Security Council, criticizing the New Zealand resolution as "an intervention in China's internal affairs, a cover-up for American aggression against China, and a direct violation of the basic principles of the U.N. Charter." The Chinese government, Zhou said, would not send delegates to participate in the discussion of the resolution.[68]

On February 4, the Soviet Union proposed a ten-nation conference to discuss the Taiwan issue, but the United States rejected the suggestion on the grounds that Taipei was not invited. On February 5, U.N. Secretary-General Dag Hammarskjöld asked the Swedish ambassador in Beijing to persuade the Chinese government to accept the New Zealand proposal. Zhou reiterated the Chinese position that the resolution was not acceptable because it was designed to put China's domestic matters in the international arena. The reason for the tensions in the Taiwan Strait, the Chinese premier argued, was U.S. policy in the region. If the world community wanted to reduce the tensions there, they should pressure the United States to change its policy. The Chinese government, he concluded, would not refuse to discuss solutions to the conflict in the area through diplomatic negotiations with the Americans.[69]

During this time, the differences between London and Washington over the offshore islands continued. In a meeting with Dulles on February 9, Makins conveyed an "oral communication" from the British government, which said that, although the evacuation of the Tachens appeared to be proceeding well, the position regarding the offshore islands "still gave cause for concern." If fighting should occur over Quemoy and Matsu, the message contended, "the great weight of opinion in the UK . . . would not support U.S. intervention in the offshore islands, which were regarded as a part of China."[70]

On February 10, Eisenhower sent a letter to Churchill which pointed out that "under existing conditions" he had given Taiwan "certain assurances with respect to the offshore islands."[71] In his reply, the British prime minister first requested explanations of the nature of the "assurances" and then went on to express the British view that, although the Nationalist government on Taiwan should not be "liquidated" by the Communists, the offshore islands were not "a just cause of war." A war to keep them for Chiang Kai-shek, Churchill asserted, "would not be defensible" in Britain.[72]

In an uncompromising response, Eisenhower refuted Churchill's arguments and referred to the Munich lesson to support the American position: "There comes a point where constantly giving in only encourages further belligerency. I think we must be careful not to pass that point in our dealings with Communist China. In such a case, further retreat becomes worse than a Munich because at Munich there were at least promises on the part of the aggressor to cease expansion and to keep the peace. In this case the Chinese Communists have promised nothing."[73] Eisenhower's remarks showed clearly the influence of his reading of history on his perceptions of the existing situation. But his analogy was flawed because the Munich incident involved the aggression of one country against another, and the offshore island crisis resulted from China's internal conflict; a person's memory of a previous crisis could lead him to make inappropriate comparisons to a current one. The president's memory of Munich led him to believe that the United States should stand firm against Beijing's provocations. Eisenhower's reasoning, however, did not convince the British. When Dulles and Eden met in late February in Thailand, they continued their debates over the proper course of action regarding the offshore islands.[74]

The controversy over U.S. commitments to the offshore islands greatly strained Anglo-American relations. London and Washington had different expectations of Oracle. The British hoped that the operation would lead to a wider settlement of the Taiwan issue, but the Americans wanted to limit the exercise to the fighting around the offshore islands. To Dulles, Oracle constituted a part of his intricate strategy for stabilizing the situation in the Taiwan Strait. The British were afraid that Washington's plan to protect the islands would further involve the United States in the Chinese civil war. London's persistent pressure, together with disagreements within the administration itself, prevented Eisenhower and Dulles from making public their intention to defend the offshore islands.

FROM NUCLEAR THREATS TO DEESCALATION

From the perspective of the Chinese, by mid-February they had achieved their immediate goals in the Taiwan Strait. Militarily they had liberated the Tachens and diplomatically they had riveted world attention on the Taiwan issue by shelling Quemoy. In fact, Beijing at this time was prepared to deescalate tensions in the Taiwan Strait by showing its willingness to negotiate with Washington. Zhou's remarks to the Swedish ambassador on February 5 demonstrated this intention. But the United States read Beijing's motives differently. Instead of viewing the mainland's occupation of the Tachens as the conclusion of its offshore island campaign, American officials believed that the action was a prelude to the occupation of Quemoy and Taiwan. During his trip to East Asia at the end of February, Dulles believed that the situation was more serious than he had thought. He was convinced that the Chinese Communists intended to take Taiwan by force and that the United States had reached the point where the "line of retreat nears its end."[75]

Upon his return to Washington on March 6, Dulles told the president that if the Communists "crushed" Chiang's troops on Quemoy and Matsu, the consequence would be "dangerously bad" not only on Taiwan but also in other parts of Asia. The two leaders agreed that the United States should help to defend the two coastal positions and concluded that "this would require the use of atomic missiles," by which they referred to tactical nuclear weapons. Eisenhower suggested that Dulles include in his proposed public speech on March 8 a paragraph indicating that the United States "would use atomic weapons as interchangeable with the conventional weapons."[76] On March 16, the president himself declared at a news conference that he could see no reason why nuclear weapons should not be used "just exactly as you would use a bullet or anything else."[77]

Like his previous threats to use nuclear weapons during the Korean War, Eisenhower's March 16 statement "was more a declaratory than an actual policy."[78] In a meeting with his top national security advisers on March 11, the president had said that the United States "should do every practical thing that could be done" to assist the Chinese Nationalists to defend themselves, but "if it was necessary later for the U.S. to intervene, it should do so with conventional weapons." Atomic weapons should be used as a last resort.[79]

Anglo-American disputes over the offshore islands continued unabated during March. On March 25, Eden wrote to Dulles warning that there was an "immediate and serious danger if we were to press ahead with Oracle." The introduction of the New Zealand resolution, the foreign secretary believed, would not focus "attention on our desire to have a ceasefire" but "on the difference between the United States, on the one hand, and other free nations, on the other, regarding the coastal islands."[80]

Obviously enraged, Dulles responded that "I rather expected the Soviets to veto the Resolution but I must confess I did not expect that you would. . . . Our purpose in seeking this further step in the Security Council," the secretary of state contended, "is to use that solemn forum to create and rally the forces of world opinion so that those forces will become a moral deterrent to the breach of the peace by anyone in the China area." Dulles also feared that at Bandung, the Chinese Communists "will get what they consider a green light for violence unless there are some counteracting opinions."[81]

In his reply on March 28, Eden said that he shared Dulles's worry about Bandung: "The Chinese will certainly do all they can to get the conference to give them its approval and we must try to stop this." But "if we initiate a debate in the Security Council," the foreign secretary went on, "the Asians will simply regard us as expressing Western views and as trying to forestall them at Bandung. I am sure that the effect on Nehru and U Nu for example would be bad."[82]

This exchange of correspondence suggests that Dulles was apprehensive about the prestige and influence China would gain from the coming Bandung Conference and wanted to tarnish Beijing's image before Asian and African countries by passing a United Nations injunction against the fighting in the Taiwan Strait. Eden, on the other hand, was afraid of alienating Asian and African opinions, especially those of India, through Western actions in the United Nations. He feared that Oracle would only create suspicion of the West among nonaligned countries.

Eisenhower wrote to Churchill on March 29, lamenting the increasing gap between British and American policies in the Far East: "Although we seem always to see eye to eye with you when we contemplate any European problem, our respective attitudes toward similar problems in the Orient are frequently so dissimilar as to be almost mutually antagonistic." The president called for more unity and effectiveness in Anglo-American policy against Communists everywhere.[83]

In late March, it became clear that the persistence of divisions within the administration and of differences between the United States and Britain was forcing Eisenhower and Dulles to change their attitudes toward the offshore islands. Administration officials began to discuss extensively the possibility of persuading Chiang Kai-shek to reduce his military presence on the offshore islands.[84] On April 4, Eisenhower and Dulles discussed the issue at length, deciding that the best solution was to persuade Chiang that the offshore islands should be considered as "outposts" rather than "citadels."[85]

Britain's lack of cooperation on Oracle frustrated Dulles's plan to use U.N. authority to protect the islands. During a meeting with the president at Augusta, Georgia, on April 17, the secretary of state unveiled a new scheme to solve the problem of Quemoy and Matsu. He told Eisenhower that it would be better for the United States to "encourage a clean break"—abandoning the islands. As a substitute, the United States and the Nationalists would institute a sea "interdiction" along China's coast to prevent the Communists from attacking Taiwan. Dulles also suggested stationing "atomic capabilities" on Taiwan.[86]

Initially, Eisenhower had doubts about Dulles's proposal but was finally persuaded by the secretary of state to proceed with the plan. The president insisted that Washington should not force Chiang into anything unacceptable to him. The Nationalists should determine whether to keep the islands or give them up. Eisenhower also asked whether Dulles considered mentioning the plan to the British. Dulles replied that he might "hint at it" but that he doubted the wisdom of pushing London on the matter at this stage, particularly when the British "were very sensitive to the domestic political situation." The two leaders seemed satisfied with their discussions. Dulles believed that his program "would immeasurably serve to consolidate world opinion." Eisenhower said that he shared this view.[87]

On April 20, Radford and Robertson, the two officials whom Chiang trusted the most, traveled to Taiwan to present the administration's new plan. But the Nationalist leader refused to accept the suggestion to abandon the offshore islands.[88] Thus, Dulles's evacuation and blockade scheme did not succeed.[89] In retrospect, although Dulles's interdiction scheme might have freed the United States from the precarious situation in the offshore islands, it would undoubtedly have led to further tensions in the Taiwan Strait and involved Washington in a costly and long-drawn-out operation in the region; Beijing would not have been likely to renounce the use of force against Taiwan. Moreover, instead of "consolidating" international opinion as Dulles had claimed, the operation would certainly have caused further ruptures in Anglo-American relations, for the British would unquestionably have opposed it.

The initiative to conclude the crisis finally came from Beijing. On April 23, Zhou Enlai declared at Bandung: "The Chinese people are friendly to the American people. The Chinese people do not want to have war with the United States of America. The Chinese government is willing to sit down and enter into negotiations with the United States Government to discuss the question of relaxing tensions in the Far East, and especially the question of relaxing tension in the Taiwan Strait."[90]

A number of reasons were behind Beijing's change of policy. First, by early 1955, China had achieved its goals in the offshore island campaign: the liberation of the Tachens and the shelling of Quemoy demonstrated to the world the risks and tensions that would confront any country that tried to divide Taiwan from the mainland. Then the Chinese leadership switched to peaceful means to get Washington to reduce its military presence in the Taiwan Strait. The Bandung Conference provided an ideal occasion for the Chinese government to announce its intentions to deescalate the crisis.

Second, the tensions in the Far East as a result of China's actions in the strait had aroused the anxieties and concerns of world opinion, particularly Asian opinion, which worried about the specter of Sino-American war. As

Wang Bingnan recalls, at Bandung, several Asian countries expressed to the Chinese delegation serious concern about the offshore island situation.[91] Therefore, a conciliatory approach would calm the fears of neutral countries and at the same time serve as a vehicle for the Chinese leadership to launch a broad anti-imperialist united international front of the underdeveloped countries by impressing them with Beijing's tactical flexibility and peaceful disposition.

Third, the Soviet Union played a role in pushing China toward a peaceful posture. At this time, the Soviet leadership was eagerly seeking improvement of relations with the West. When Chinese Defense Minister Peng Dehuai visited the Soviet Union in 1955, Khrushchev told him that at the moment the United States was still very powerful and, therefore, peaceful negotiations should be encouraged to solve international disputes. He hoped that China would disarm so as to cooperate with the Soviet Union on the political front. Agreeing with the Soviet leader's analysis of the world situation, Peng asserted that international tensions should be reduced and that China also needed a peaceful period to build up the economy, train and reform the army, and strengthen the defense industry as well as defense projects along the Chinese coast.[92]

Lastly, the role of U.S. nuclear threats has to be considered. Although, given available Chinese sources, the precise effects of those threats remain unclear (as in the Korean War), it can be argued that Mao's decision to launch China's nuclear weapons program in early 1955 was a response to Washington's atomic blackmail.[93] Furthermore, the apprehension of the Asian nations about the tensions in the Taiwan Strait stemmed from the possibility of U.S. use of nuclear weapons in the region.

The State Department reacted harshly to Zhou Enlai's proposal of April 23. It insisted that to obtain negotiations the PRC should take further steps (such as the prior release of detained Americans in China) to demonstrate its good intentions and that the Nationalists should participate in any discussion regarding the Taiwan issue. This was a condition unacceptable to Beijing. The U.S. response was poorly received both at home and abroad. Senator Walter George, chairman of the Senate Committee on Foreign Relations, urged that China's offer be accepted. Other Senate Democratic leaders endorsed his view. In Bandung, neutral countries thought that Washington did not want negotiations because of its nuclear superiority. On April 26, Dulles, who had been on vacation and had not seen his department's response, reversed its initial decision by stating that Zhou's proposal was being studied. The next day President Eisenhower also criticized the State

Department's initial approach as an "error in terminology" and claimed that the United States was interested in discussing a cease-fire as well as American prisoners in China.[94]

The British felt relieved at America's acceptance of Beijing's proposal.[95] In May, the British chargé in China, Humphrey Trevelyan, played the active role of a mediator in expediting the talks. On May 9, Trevelyan passed to Zhou an oral message from British Foreign Secretary Harold Macmillan, which said that London viewed Zhou's Bandung speech with great interest and was willing to forward any Chinese message to the United States.[96] On May 26, Zhou met Trevelyan and stated China's position on the proposed Sino-American talks: the subject should be the reduction of tensions in the Taiwan region, and the form could be either a multinational conference as suggested earlier by the Soviet Union or a Sino-American bilateral dialogue with the support of other countries, but under no circumstances should Taiwan be included. China was prepared to hold separate direct talks with the Nationalists. These would be two different kinds of talks: one international and the other internal.[97] On July 13, Washington responded through Britain that Sino-American negotiations at the ambassadorial level be held in Geneva. The negotiations started on August 1, 1955.

CONCLUSION

Between 1949 and 1954, Beijing transformed its offshore island policy from a solely military operation to a scheme closely linked with China's general foreign policy. In line with Mao's traditional practice of using military means to achieve political goals, the shelling of Quemoy in 1954 was primarily designed to demonstrate Beijing's refusal to accept a two-China outcome of the civil war. The Chinese leadership hoped that their pressures would demoralize the Nationalists and convince the United States that it should disengage from Taiwan. But the result was just the opposite. Instead of preventing the conclusion of the U.S.-Taiwan defense treaty, Beijing's action facilitated the creation of a formal and long-term American commitment to the defense of Taiwan.

When the Communists started shelling Quemoy, Washington faced a dilemma in the Taiwan Strait. Eisenhower and Dulles did not want to commit the United States to the protection of the offshore islands, but they also realized that the loss of the islands would greatly damage the morale of Chiang's forces on Taiwan. To resolve the problem, the administration took several interrelated measures. On the diplomatic front, Dulles initiated Oracle as a means of international pressure to force Beijing to stop the fighting around the offshore islands. On the military front, Washington signed the mutual defense treaty with Chiang to show U.S. resolve to protect Taiwan and the Pescadores and to prevent Chiang from launching military adventures against the mainland. When Eisenhower and Dulles perceived that the situation was deteriorating as a result of the Communist attack on the Tachens and occupation of Yijiangshan, they gave Chiang private guarantees to protect the offshore islands. They also resorted to nuclear threats to deter China. In April 1955, Dulles proposed to Chiang that if he would forsake Quemoy and Matsu, the United States would erect a naval blockade along the mainland's coast until the Communist government renounced its intention to use force against Taiwan. Chiang's intransigence, however, frustrated Dulles's plan.

In retrospect, the Eisenhower administration misunderstood Beijing's intentions during the crisis. Instead of regarding the occupation of the Tachens as the culmination of Mao's offshore island campaign, Washington took the Communist action as evidence of the mainland's further aggression against Quemoy and Taiwan. This highlighted the problems of Sino-American communications in crises and the adverse effects of misperceptions. It also demonstrated how one actor's sense of vulnerability during a confrontation could lead him to exaggerate the threats from the other side.

London was disturbed by Washington's reaction to the crisis in the Far East. The British made a clear distinction between Taiwan and the coastal islands. While agreeing with the Americans that Taiwan should be protected, they believed that the offshore islands belonged unquestionably to the mainland and did not deserve Western commitment. British officials believed that, if the United States recognized Beijing, admitted it to the United Nations, and forced Chiang to abandon the offshore islands, the PRC would be satisfied and the crisis would be defused in the Taiwan Strait. Accordingly, London accepted Oracle with the hope that it would lead to a broader solution of the Taiwan issue. Britain's pressure played a role in moderating Washington's behavior during the crisis. It was the British opposition, coupled with the divisions within the administration itself, that prevented Eisenhower and Dulles from announcing their private commitment to the defense of Quemoy and Matsu.

In dismissing Chiang as a "palooka," the British underestimated the calculation and scheming of the Nationalist leader, who was skillful in taking advantage of American domestic politics and involving Washington in his struggle with the Communists. Just as London had underrated Rhee's capacity for manipulation and obstruction during the final stages of the Korean War in early 1953, it now overlooked Chiang's tenacity and stubbornness during the offshore island crisis. By criticizing Washington as too accommodating to its small allies, London failed to appreciate the political difficulties confronting American officials when they were making decisions.

The internal dynamic of China's policy, together with the pressure of international opinion, influenced Beijing's decision to wind down the offshore island crisis in early 1955. The U.S. nuclear threats must also have played a role because in the middle of the crisis Mao decided to launch China's own atomic weapons program.

Both the Oracle operation, which tried to maintain the status quo in the Taiwan Strait, and the U.S.-Taiwan treaty, which protected Chiang on the island but prevented him from reconquering the mainland, in effect, promoted the goal of two Chinas. Both Beijing and Taipei opposed Oracle because they saw the operation as a Western attempt to sanctify the existence of two Chinas. Neither Mao nor Chiang wished to renounce the use of force in the Taiwan Strait. To both of them, the offshore islands were symbols of the unity of China and of their claims to each other's territory, which they were determined to "liberate" peacefully if possible, forcefully if necessary. This unanimity between the two Chinese leaders ensured the prolongation of a bitter civil war and created difficulties for Washington as it attempted to stabilize the situation in the Taiwan Strait. Mao viewed the U.S.-Taiwan treaty as an offense against the mainland. In fact, the pact was designed to releash rather than unleash Chiang. The Communist leader would find this out later during the second offshore island crisis in 1958.

9 *Second Offshore-Island Crisis, 1958*

"THE EAST WIND IS PREVAILING OVER THE WEST WIND"

The opening of the Sino-American ambassadorial talks in the summer of 1955 marked an easing of tensions in the Far East. In the next two years, the two sides held seventy-three meetings with meager results. During the negotiations, the Chinese played a more active role than the Americans, initiating a series of proposals with the hope of settling the basic issues between Beijing and Washington, especially the problem of Taiwan.

But the United States was not prepared to make any concessions on Taiwan and had no inclination to add to China's international position by recognizing the PRC. Washington continued its economic embargo against the PRC and refused to admit it into the United Nations. During this period, the administration's strategy was to play for time in which to form a world opinion that would oblige Beijing to accept the status quo in the Taiwan region and not alter it by force. Dulles hoped to apply the solution of Germany, Korea, and Vietnam to China.[1]

One reason for Dulles's inflexibility at the talks was Washington's evaluation of Taiwan's strategic importance. Both Eisenhower and Dulles viewed the island as geopolitically significant to the U.S. position in the Western Pacific. The president told Senator Knowland that Taiwan "is a part of a great island barrier we have erected in the Pacific against Communist advance. We are not going to let it be broken." Dulles believed that any concessions to the PRC with regard to Taiwan would be unthinkable because they would not only constitute a betrayal of an American ally, the Chiang regime on the island, but also deprive the United States of an indispensable link in the chain of strong positions off the mainland of Asia extending from the Aleutians to the Philippines. America could not hold its offshore chain without Taiwan.[2]

The second reason for the administration's unwillingness to compromise at Geneva lay in Dulles's consideration of domestic politics. Throughout the period, Chiang's supporters both inside and outside Congress all demanded

178

a harsh policy toward the PRC. On March 12, 1955, Congressman Walter Judd sent Eisenhower a copy of his statements in an NBC interview in which he criticized some writers who had cast doubts on U.S. policy toward China. These people, the legislator from Minnesota asserted, "could lead the Chinese Reds to start aggressive action in the belief we can be bluffed into backing down. It is not firmness by the United States, but persistent and irresponsible misrepresentation of our policy as one of vacillation and weakness that is endangering the peace."[3]

On June 8, 1955, William Bullitt, a staunch supporter of Chiang, wrote to Eisenhower: "In spite of our strong words, the tragedy of Indo-China is moving to a gruesome climax. Japan is drifting away from us. Only a little more appeasement is needed to hand the remainder of Asia to the Communists. We need only permit the Red Chinese Air Force to bomb Matsu and Quemoy with impunity. . . . On the other hand, if we tell the Russians . . . that as soon as any one of the islands is bombed we will knock out the Red airfields in the area, we shall stop the rot."[4]

The third motivation behind Dulles's rigidity at the negotiations was his desire to undermine the Sino-Soviet relationship by means of a high-pressure American policy toward China. "There are some people who suggest that, if we assist the Chinese Communists to wax strong, then they will eventually break with Soviet Russia," the secretary of state contended in San Francisco in June 1957. "No doubt there are basic power rivalries between Russia and China in Asia." But it was important to bear in mind that both countries adhered to an ideology antithetical to the interests of the United States. The Axis powers might well have fallen into disputes among themselves if they had triumphed in World War II, "but no one suggested that we should tolerate and even assist an Axis victory because in the end they would quarrel over the booty—of which we would be a part."[5]

While stalling at the ambassadorial talks, the administration continued to support Chiang with large sums of military aid. According to one American source, annual U.S. aid to Chiang was $260 million, almost two-thirds of the Nationalist budget.[6] The United States also constructed on Taiwan a huge air base capable of accommodating B-52s and introduced into the island Matador missiles with the capacity to deliver nuclear warheads. Although the administration had tried to persuade Chiang to evacuate Quemoy and Matsu after the first offshore island crisis, the Nationalist leader remained intransigent. As a result, Chiang's troops became firmly entrenched on the islands by increasing the number of soldiers and building permanent fortifications. Admiral Radford told Canadian officials in January 1956 that the garrisons on Quemoy and Matsu amounted to nearly one-third of Chiang's forces.[7]

By acquiescing to Chiang's deployment of so many of his troops to the islands, the United States had unwittingly committed itself to defending the islands as part of its pledge to defend Taiwan. Dulles expressed the administration's intention to protect Quemoy and Matsu at an NSC meeting in October 1957, noting that the "defense of all of the offshore-islands was now so complete and so integral a part of the defense of Taiwan, that it was not to be compared with the fluid situation of three years ago. . . . If there were an all-out attack on Quemoy or the Matsus, the United States should not sit to one side and permit the loss of these islands, because their loss would surely result in the loss of Taiwan and the Penghus [Pescadores]."[8]

The combination of a large contingent of KMT troops on the offshore islands threatening mainland ports, constant raids against the Communist regime, harassment of coastal shipping, and Chiang's propaganda operations constituted a sharp thorn in Beijing's side. Mao was eager to punish Chiang.

In 1956, as a result of Khrushchev's de-Stalinization campaign at the Soviet Twentieth Party Congress, riots broke out in Eastern Europe. Zhou Enlai's subsequent mediation efforts in Poland and Hungary in support of Soviet policy enhanced the PRC's status in the world Communist movement and promoted Beijing's self-confidence in international affairs. It led China's leaders to pay more attention to global issues and increased their desire to play an active part in confronting the United States.[9]

The Soviet military success in testing the world's first intercontinental ballistic missile (ICBM) on August 26, 1957, together with the parallel triumph of launching Sputnik on October 4 of the same year, greatly reinforced Mao's view that communism was superior to capitalism. On November 18, 1957, he told a group of Chinese students in Moscow that "the international situation has now reached a new turning point. . . . The East Wind is prevailing over the West Wind."[10] This new interpretation of the global balance of power and optimism in the strength of socialism would have important implications for Beijing's foreign policy. It signaled that Mao would be more willing to take risks in challenging the United States.

By 1958, Mao and Khrushchev had developed divergent perceptions of the world situation and prescriptions for global strategy. The post-Stalin Soviet leadership no longer believed that war between the socialist and capitalist systems was inevitable. Its new position held that it was possible for the socialist countries to prevail worldwide through peaceful competition. The increased strength of the Soviet Union, the weakening of capitalism, and the advent of atomic weapons made this new strategy both likely and necessary. Moscow believed that the real danger to world peace was nuclear confrontation between the two superpowers.[11] During his visit to Beijing July 31–August 3, 1958, Khrushchev persistently warned Mao of the menace of nuclear war to the world.[12]

But Mao found it difficult to accept the Soviet analysis of international affairs. He feared that détente with the United States would compromise his plans for recovering Taiwan. Convinced that a militant policy would better serve China's interests, the Chinese leader stressed that the Communist bloc should prepare for a vigorous challenge to the capitalist West.[13] As for nuclear weapons, Mao tended to dismiss the danger of atomic conflicts, still referring to America's nuclear power as a "paper tiger."[14] When the United States dispatched marines to Lebanon in July 1958, Mao expected Moscow to react forcefully. But Khrushchev's failure to send Soviet troops into the area to counter the American action incensed the Chinese leader, who proceeded to show the Soviet Union how Communists should deal with imperialists by shelling Quemoy.[15]

To a lesser extent, Mao's military initiative in the Taiwan Strait was also related to his domestic policy. In 1958, the CCP leader launched the Great Leap Forward, a radical plan for building socialism in China, which reflected the utopian fantasies of Maoism. Mao's fast growth and commune programs constituted a political challenge to Moscow because some Chinese statements implied, at least for a brief period in 1958, that China had now developed ahead of the Soviet Union in moving from socialism to communism. The Chinese leader had always believed in the spontaneous workings of the human will and the strength of the masses. He called upon the Chinese people to exert all their efforts to "surpass Britain and catch up with the United States." To promote this goal, he thought it necessary to break down the myth of American omnipotence by challenging the U.S. presence in the Taiwan Strait.[16]

In sum, it was the mixture of the foregoing factors—the intention to stop Chiang's harassment against the mainland, to show Beijing's defiance of the United States, to divert American attention from the Middle East, to contest the Soviet advocacy of détente with the West, as well as to mobilize the domestic population—that caused Mao to begin a new crisis in the Taiwan Strait in August 1958. China's Bandung-phase diplomacy, with its emphasis on "peaceful coexistence," gave way to a much more assertive policy toward the United States.

CONCENTRATING ON THE NATIONALISTS

On July 17, 1958, Defense Minister Peng Dehuai conveyed Mao's instructions to the General Staff that the PLA's air force and artillery units should deploy in Fujian as soon as possible. At a meeting held the next day, attended by the vice-chairmen of the Central Military Commission and the commanders of the air force and navy, Mao said that China's support for the Arab struggle against imperialist aggression should not be limited to moral encouragement but should include actions. The PLA should attack Quemoy and Matsu to divert U.S. attention from the Middle East. He then laid down the principle of employing superior artillery power to sever Chiang's supply lines to Quemoy and Matsu, thus blockading the two islands and rendering their position untenable. He asked the Fujian front to prepare for two to three months of fighting and ordered two air force divisions to occupy the air fields in Shantou and Liancheng. Mao expected that the shelling would exacerbate the tensions between Taipei and Washington over the range of American treaty commitments in the Taiwan area and would produce increased U.S. pressure on Chiang to abandon the offshore islands.[17] In forming this conclusion, the Chinese leader must have had in mind the Tachen experience in 1955 when Washington pressured the Nationalists to withdraw from the island, but he must also have ignored the fact that the United States stood firm to help defend Quemoy and Matsu at the time.

At another Central Military Commission meeting on the same day, Peng Dehuai emphasized that the artillery should play a major role in attacking Quemoy and Matsu and the air force should not engage enemy planes over the high seas. The air force should complete the occupation of the air fields in Fujian and East Guangdong before July 27, and the naval air force in Zhejiang should coordinate this deployment. The meeting made the preliminary decision to begin the bombardment on July 25.[18]

After the meeting, the Central Military Commission informed Ye Fei, political commissar of the Fuzhou Military Region, of its decisions by telephone. He, in turn, immediately convened a conference of local commanders, which decided to deploy thirty artillery battalions around Xiamen (Amoy) to attack Quemoy and three artillery battalions at Liancheng to assault Matsu. The artillery positions were to be protected by antiaircraft guns. Meanwhile, the Fuzhou Military Region Air Force Command was established under the direction of General Nie Fengzhi, who had been commander of the Chinese People's Volunteers' Air Force in Korea.

On July 19, the Fuzhou Military Region Front Command headed by Ye Fei moved from Fuzhou to Xiamen.[19]

To ensure the success of the bombardment, Mao later postponed the operation. On July 27, he ordered Peng to wait for the Nationalists to attack first before striking back. On the same day, Peng passed Mao's instruction to Ye.[20] In early August, the PLA air force established control over Fujian after battles with Nationalist planes.

On August 20, Mao summoned Ye to Beidaihe. At a meeting with Mao on the next afternoon, attended also by Peng Dehuai, Lin Biao, and Wang Shangrong, director of the War Department of the General Staff, Ye reported on the preparations for the offshore island campaign. Mao asked Ye whether it was possible to avoid hitting the Americans. Ye's answer was negative. Hearing that, Mao adjourned the meeting without saying anything more. In the evening, Wang Shangrong showed Ye a note written by Lin Biao to Mao which suggested that, in order to avoid attacking the Americans, Wang Bingnan, the Chinese ambassador in Poland, should inform U.S. diplomats in Warsaw of China's intentions to shell Quemoy and Matsu. Ye was surprised to read the note because he believed that to tell the Americans of China's plan was tantamount to informing the Nationalists. Wang told Ye that Mao had not reacted to Lin's suggestion. The meeting resumed the next day. Ignoring Lin's proposal, Mao decided to go ahead with the plan to attack Quemoy and Matsu. Mao also asked Ye to stay at Beidaihe to direct the fighting at the front through the telephone.[21]

Mao's conversations with Ye showed clearly the cautious and limited nature of his operation. Although willing to challenge the American presence in the Taiwan Strait, the Chinese leader was not prepared to provoke a direct confrontation with the United States. This was consistent with his behavior during the first offshore-island crisis.

THE U.S. RESPONSE

Even before the fighting broke out on August 23, U.S. policymakers had worried about the tensions in the Taiwan Strait. Because Chiang had placed so many of his troops on the offshore islands, Eisenhower and Dulles were keenly aware of the adverse effect the loss of these islands would have on Taiwan's morale as well as that of the rest of Asia. In a meeting with General Nathan Twining, chairman of the JCS, on August 11, the president said that there were good reasons for taking the view that the islands should be abandoned, but, because a great part of Chiang's forces were now deployed on the islands, their removal "would be a signal to all of Asia that there is no hope that can be held out against the Communists in China."[22]

During a discussion with the president on August 12, Secretary of State Dulles said that "if Quemoy and Matsu were lost, the Chinese Nationalists do not consider that they could hold Formosa. Morale would crumble and Chiang's control would be lost." Concurring that "the key point is an evaluation of morale," Eisenhower suggested that the secretary of state consider stating in a news conference that "the islands have now been so tightly integrated with Formosa that there is no possibility that an all-out attack could be conducted against them without bringing in the United States."[23]

When the shelling began on August 23, Washington's reaction was quick but equivocal in terms of U.S. commitment. On that day, Washington sent an implied warning to Beijing in a widely publicized letter from Dulles to Thomas Morgan, acting chairman of the House Committee on Foreign Affairs. The secretary of state pointed out that "over the last four years the ties between these islands and Formosa have been closer and their interdependence increased." Any attempt to conquer the islands, Dulles warned, would be "a threat to the peace of the area." But he did not spell out the exact nature of U.S. commitment. It would be up to the president, he wrote, to decide the "value of certain coastal positions" to Taiwan if the Communists did attack.[24]

Clearly, the U.S. strategy was ambiguity—to keep the enemy guessing.[25] To Eisenhower and Dulles, ambiguity had several benefits. First, it would confound Beijing's efforts to calculate the risks. Second, it would provide a way to restrain Chiang from reckless provocations by increasing his doubts about the reliability of American assistance. Finally, it would help minimize domestic criticism, which would certainly emerge if a clear public commitment were made.

Chiang Kai-shek, however, pressed for a clear and direct U.S. commitment to the offshore islands. In a meeting with American Ambassador Everett Drumright on August 24, the Nationalist leader urged Washington to issue some further public statement to clarify the situation.[26] Chiang also directed his ambassador in Washington, Hollington Tong, to press the Americans further. Meeting Acting Assistant Secretary of State for Far Eastern Affairs J. Graham Parsons on August 25, the ambassador first expressed appreciation for Dulles's letter to Congressman Morgan and then went on to stress that "something stronger was needed to deter the Communists from further aggressive moves against the offshore islands." What Taiwan wanted, Tong said explicitly, was a statement to the general effect that in the view of the United States any major attack on the islands would constitute a threat to the safety of Taiwan. Promising to consult with the United States before taking any retaliatory action against the mainland, Tong emphasized that the morale of the Nationalist troops on the offshore islands "would be seriously affected" if no retaliation were taken at the moment when they were under heavy and persistent assault from the Communists.[27]

While agreeing to convey Taiwan's request to Dulles, Parsons referred to the undesirability of a further U.S. declaration on the grounds that "too many statements within a short period" would lead the Communists to "discount our words" and that "it is more useful to demonstrate our intentions by action than by more words." But he did not tell Chiang's representative what specific action the administration contemplated against the Communists.[28] It is clear from this conversation that U.S. officials wanted to maintain maximum flexibility in dealing with the crisis in the Taiwan Strait. They were trying to balance between reassuring the Nationalists and deterring the Communists while retaining freedom of action.

In private discussions, administration officials pondered nuclear options. On August 25, the JCS advised the president that although political calculations might demand initial retaliatory actions against the Communists with conventional weapons, "we will require atomic strikes" to check the mainland's aggression "effectively and quickly." Eisenhower approved a cable to the commander in chief, Pacific (CINCPAC), instructing that initial operations would probably be only conventional but authorizing preparation "to use atomic weapons to extend deeper into Chinese Communist territory if necessary."[29] Two days later, the State Department's Far Eastern Bureau recommended to Dulles that early use of one or two low-yield nuclear weapons against Fujian air fields might be necessary and that further, more extensive attacks might also be needed.[30]

But in public, discussion of nuclear alternatives was more indirect and vague than it had been in the 1954–55 crisis. When asked at a news conference on August 27 about the discretion allowed local commanders for use of atomic weapons, Eisenhower reaffirmed that his personal approval was needed. Confining his remarks to the principle of general support to Taiwan, the president said that the U.S. government would not "desert" the commitment it had already made. The most explicit remark the chief executive was willing to make was his observation that Taiwan's deployment of one-third of its forces to the offshore islands "makes a closer interlocking between the defense systems of the islands with Formosa than was the case before that."[31]

The president's caution regarding the use of nuclear weapons in the Taiwan Strait reflected his sensitivity to the reaction of international, especially Asian, opinion. Eisenhower was well aware that the costs of using them in such a situation would very possibly surpass the prospective benefits.[32] Moreover, the American leader's circumspection may also have shown his cognizance of the existence of Soviet nuclear power. Eisenhower later wrote in his memoirs:

> In the stridency of Mao's public boasts and threats to seize Formosa by force, this new challenge resembled the earlier one of 1955. But the current situation included new dangers that seemed to make our position more difficult. . . . For one thing, the Soviets had used the intervening years to build up their nuclear striking force, which now included a more formidable arsenal of hydrogen weapons. I did not doubt our total superiority, but any large-scale conflict stimulated here was now less likely to remain limited to a conventional use of power.[33]

As a measure to reassure Chiang and to deter Mao, the United States sent both the *Essex* and four destroyers from the Sixth Fleet to reinforce the Seventh Fleet on August 27. At the same time, however, administration officials feared that Chiang intended to involve the United States in the hostilities while reserving his own naval forces. This was a shared sentiment at a combined meeting of Department of State, Defense, and CIA representatives at the Pentagon on August 28. Acting Secretary of State Christian Herter wondered whether Taiwan "might not be holding back naval forces in an effort to bring about a commitment of United States forces." Admiral Arleigh Burke, chief of the Naval Operations, believed that "something of this sort might well be involved." Acting Secretary of Defense Donald Quarles felt that it was necessary for the United States "to be very cautious about increasing our involvement."[34]

Admiral Burke remarked that the first step that should be taken was for the U.S. forces in the region to take over the defense of Taiwan so that the Nationalist troops could "engage more actively and fully in the resupply and defense of the islands." If Taiwan was then still unable to handle the situation by itself, he continued, the United States should provide naval and air escort for Nationalist convoys. American naval vessels would first proceed halfway to the islands, then all the way; U.S. planes would simply go all the way over the islands.[35]

As it turned out, the course the United States later followed was exactly the scenario Admiral Burke had articulated. So long as Chiang's troops could resist Communist assaults on their own, the Americans would play an indirect role, helping to strengthen the defense of Taiwan without being involved in the struggle over the coastal islands. When Beijing's attacks intensified, Washington increased its military supplies, including howitzers, Sabre jets, and, eventually, Sidewinder air-to-air missiles. The administration refused to consider carrying the war to the Chinese mainland, or even bombing the Fujian coast, as part of its effort to keep Quemoy and Matsu in Chiang's hands.

As the tension continued, the administration felt the need to allay Chiang's fears and to warn Beijing further. Dulles said at a meeting of State and Defense officials on September 3 that it was "essential" that the Chinese Communists not have the impression that the United States would fail to intervene, pointing out also "the serious effect" such a miscommunication would have on Taiwan's morale. He stressed that the U.S. objective was to "deter" a "massive assault" on the islands. As for the reactions of the Allies, the secretary of state believed that "as a general rule they will go along with a course of action that we propose to take if they are reasonably sure that we are in fact going to proceed with that course."[36]

After discussions with the president at the summer White House in Newport, Rhode Island, Dulles made an official statement on September 4, warning Beijing that Eisenhower "would not hesitate" to employ armed forces "in ensuring the defense of Formosa" if he considered such action necessary. The secretary of state also reiterated that "the securing and protecting of Quemoy and Matsu have become increasingly related to the defense of Taiwan" and contended that "military dispositions have been made by the United States so that a Presidential determination, if made, would be followed by action both timely and effective."[37] Like the vague threats embodied in Dulles's letter to Congressman Morgan on August 23, the secretary of state's Newport warning continued to be ambiguous. This reflected the administration's consistent effort to deter the Chinese Communists by generating uncertainty in their minds over the risks involved if they attempted to occupy Quemoy and Matsu.

Dulles's subtle but tough reaction must have played a role in moderating Beijing's policy. On September 4, the PLA stopped shelling the offshore islands for three days. At the same time, the Chinese government laid official claim to all waters and islands within twelve miles of its coast, but the United States declared that it would only respect a three-mile limit.[38] At the Supreme State Conference on September 5, Mao admitted that in planning the bombardment of the offshore islands, "I simply did not calculate that the world would become so disturbed and turbulent."[39] The next day, Zhou Enlai stated that the PRC was prepared to resume the ambassadorial talks with the Americans.[40] Beijing's willingness to reopen the negotiations indicated its readiness to take the first step toward defusing the crisis.

On September 7, U.S. ships began to convoy Nationalist vessels carrying supplies to Quemoy. Chinese Front Commander Ye Fei, who had returned to Xiamen in late August, requested Mao's instruction on how he should deal with the American fleet. Mao told him that he should shell Chiang's ships only, and, even if American ships opened fire first, he should not retaliate.[41] As it happened, when Communist guns assaulted the Nationalist vessels, the U.S. fleet did not join the battle. According to Ye's later account, he expected an American attack, but when that did not occur, he was "very surprised."[42] Clearly, by concentrating on the Nationalists only, Mao was testing how far the Americans were prepared to go in carrying out their treaty commitment to Taiwan. After the September 7 combat experience, Mao realized there was a limit in U.S. involvement in the Taiwan Strait and that Washington did not intend to wage war against China.

According to one recent Chinese study, Mao undertook a reevaluation of U.S. policy during this period. At the discussions of the Supreme State Conference on September 5 and 8 and in a meeting with provincial leaders on September 12, Mao pointed out that American policy toward China and the Soviet Union was mainly defensive, not offensive. The United States was primarily interested in dominating the Third World, the area between the socialist and capitalist camps. Thus, the offensive military threat to China posed by the U.S.-Taiwan security treaty, Mao continued, was no longer as serious or as immediate as had previously been thought. The treaty was basically defensive and constrictive, designed to restrain rather than unleash Chiang. The Chinese leader also reiterated Beijing's willingness to resolve the dispute with the United States through negotiations.[43]

Mao's analysis of the defensive nature of U.S. policy toward China represented an important change in his perceptions of Sino-American relations. Ever since the founding of the PRC, he had been obsessed with the danger of American military threats to China's security. On several occasions, he had believed that Washington intended to invade his country from the three fronts of Taiwan, Korea, and Indochina. Now his sense of China's vulnerability was no longer as keen as it had been. Mao's reassessment of

Washington's intentions demonstrated that images could be modified in the face of new information and situation.

In contrast to the crisis in 1954–55 when the administration was divided on whether the United States should defend Quemoy and Matsu, American officials were unanimous in 1958 on the wisdom of protecting the islands. Unlike the previous crisis, when Eisenhower had made crude threats by comparing a nuclear bomb to a bullet, Washington's nuclear threats against China this time were indirect and subtle. This indicated the administration's intention to keep the Communists guessing. It may also have reflected an awareness of the strength of the Soviet atomic arsenal. While making firm but subtle warnings to deter further Communist actions, Washington also took actual measures by increasing Chiang's capabilities to hold the islands and by reinforcing its own military strength in the region.

THE BRITISH REACTION

In 1958, Britain's basic attitudes toward the offshore islands remained the same as those in 1954–55. In a telegram to British diplomats in the Commonwealth capitals on August 28, 1958, the Commonwealth Relations Office said that London continued to stand by Eden's House of Commons statement of February 4, 1955, which contended that the United Kingdom recognized the legal right of the PRC to the islands but would deplore any attempt to seize them by force.[44]

British officials continued to disagree with the Americans over the psychological importance of the islands. Peter Dalton of the Foreign Office contended that it had been a "grave mistake" for Chiang to strengthen his garrison there, thus offering "such a hostage" to the mainland.[45] Viscount Hood, the British minister in Washington, told State Department officials on August 30 that London "would greatly deplore a war that developed from an effort to hold the offshore islands. Such hostilities would be most unpopular in the UK and it would be difficult for the Government to defend the United States on the issue."[46]

American officials believed that China was embarking on an adventurist policy. Warren Randolph Burgess, the U.S. representative to NATO, said in Paris on September 2 that, although U.S. intelligence did not expect an immediate PRC attack on the major offshore islands, recent events, coupled with other relevant developments, "suggested that the Communist Chinese

Government, with Russian approval, was starting a new expansionist policy." Beijing's success at Quemoy, the U.S. official continued, "would lead to further Communist Chinese aggression against Formosa and possibly elsewhere. The United States Government considered it best to meet force with force at the outset."[47]

American diplomats in London also stressed the "expansionist" nature of China's policy. In a meeting with Dalton on September 6, Francis Galbraith, the first secretary in the U.S. Embassy, repeated basically the same argument as that made by Burgess at the NATO Council meeting four days before. But Dalton did not agree with the American contention that the Chinese leaders were now "reckless." He asserted that "it was a confusion of the issues to label the Chinese attitude as 'aggressive' or 'expansionist.' . . . Their arrogant and defiant mood might lead them to become so but, for the present at least, they seemed to be playing the hand reasonably cautiously."[48]

Foreign Office official Con O'Neill also had reservations about the American argument that a failure on Washington's part to help defend the offshore islands if they were attacked would have a catastrophic effect on confidence throughout the Far East in U.S. readiness to support its allies. In a memorandum dated September 9, O'Neill said that the American contention was not "sound." He believed that no American obligation was involved in the offshore islands and that many countries, including U.S. allies, would welcome any solution of the issue that avoided war, even if it involved their abandonment by Chiang. Therefore, O'Neill contended that he did not understand why it should necessarily weaken the faith of U.S. allies in Washington's determination to act in cases where it had a definite commitment, including Taiwan.[49]

While disagreeing with the Americans over the importance of the offshore islands and over China's intentions, the British this time were even more unwilling to argue their case vigorously than they had been in 1954–55. Dalton told Galbraith on September 6 that, although London did not agree with Washington's view on the offshore islands and believed that it was wrong for Chiang to strengthen his fortifications there, "we did not, on the other hand, want to make too much of this in public." The British government, he went on, was "trying to pursue the somewhat difficult path of neither disowning the Americans (which, because of our close alliance with them and desire not to give comfort to our enemies, we did not wish to do) nor committing ourselves to their support (which . . . would be difficult to defend in this country). We were, therefore, concentrating on expressions of concern and efforts to reduce tension."[50]

Sir Frederick Hoyer Millar, permanent under secretary at the Foreign Office, told French ambassador Jean Chauvel on September 10 that "it seemed important that things should not develop in such a way as to allow the Chinese Communists to claim that they had scored a great victory since anything like this might have serious consequences on the Western position in the other countries in the Far East and lead to a break up of the present anti-Communist front" there. Accordingly, Millar continued, it seemed crucial that "we should be careful to refrain from anything like criticism of the American Government at the present time." The French diplomat agreed with Millar's analysis, saying that his government's position was "very similar" to that of London.[51]

Prime Minister Macmillan was eager to demonstrate solidarity with the Americans. He wrote to Eisenhower on September 3: "Although in the past we have taken rather a different view about the legal and practical considerations concerning the off-shore islands, my overriding concern is that our countries should not be divided or appear to be divided. . . . I feel that I may have to try to steer public opinion here at very short notice and, if the worst should happen, in critical circumstances." [52]

Students of this period have pointed out that London's reluctance to criticize U.S. policy in 1958 arose partly from the "serious breach" in Anglo-American relations that had happened over Suez and partly because of Macmillan's replacement of the truculent Eden. As Lord Beloff has observed, in the wake of Suez, there was a "general acceptance in the Conservative party of the fact that the dominance of the United States in world affairs could not be challenged and that the path of safety was at almost any cost to align British policy with that of the United States. Macmillan himself was the conscious agent of this revolution." From the moment of his succession to Eden as prime minister, Macmillan decided that he had to go to meet Eisenhower in person in order to restore the Anglo-American partnership that had been injured by Suez. His meeting with the American president in March 1957 at Bermuda, where they renewed their cooperation and friendship during World War II, revived the special relationship on a highly personal footing.[53]

The Lebanese crisis in early 1958 made Macmillan put an even higher premium on Western unity. He instructed the Foreign Office to refrain from criticizing Washington not only in public but also in private. On September 8, he asked his private secretary, Philip de Zulueta, to tell Dalton that he wished that Britain would not blame the Americans or "hark back . . . to the 1955 statements or make too much of the juridical position of the offshore islands or the mistake that had been made in letting the Nationalists put so many of their eggs into the Quemoy basket." The crucial thing now, Macmillan stressed, "was to stand by the Americans both in the interests of *interdependence* and in order not to give comfort and encouragement to our enemies and we should not appear even in private discussion to be sniping at the Americans over the rights and wrongs of the situation" (italics added).[54]

But Foreign Office officials had reservations about Macmillan's instruction. Dalton told de Zulueta that, although he agreed with the prime minister that the British government should not adopt a critical attitude toward the United States in public and that "our remarks to the press etc., should be so devised as to take the middle line avoiding on the one hand criticism and possible dissociation and on the other any formal commitment," he believed that it would be very difficult and undesirable if, when asked for an exchange of opinions by the United States, or Commonwealth and NATO countries, "we should simply take the line that the Americans were right and we must support them."[55]

There were several disadvantages for being less than honest with the Americans, Dalton continued. First, if Britain appeared to have abandoned its past position regarding the offshore islands, other interested countries would ask why. London was likely to be forced to discuss the matter in any case, and it might be "more embarrassing to appear to be covering up some change of front than to take a straightforward line." Second, Dalton pointed out, it would "carry more conviction if, while not appearing to be trying to paper over differences, we can explain why we are taking the public line that we are taking." Third, if London seemed to have discarded its long-held view, Dalton warned, the Americans might conclude that "they have us in their pocket and need not to bother about us further. . . . If the Americans get the impression that everyone really agrees with them, they will be the less likely to pay any great attention to seeking a solution this time." Therefore, Dalton concluded that "while sticking strictly to the line agreed for public consumption, we should exercise a certain flexibility in private discussion according to the circumstances."[56]

Sharing Dalton's view, Millar pointed out, "Our anxiety not to appear to be infringing the principles of 'interdependence' and our desire not to upset the Americans more than we can help ought not . . . to deter us from doing what we can to dissuade the Americans from pursuing a policy which we feel is bound to create grave difficulties for the Western Governments and put a very serious strain on Anglo-American relations."[57] De Zulueta himself was more inclined to agree with the Foreign Office's view. After talking with Macmillan further, he told Dalton that the prime minister accepted that "there must be certain nuances in our approach in this matter according to the circumstances." [58]

Labor party leader Hugh Gaitskell wrote to Macmillan on September 15, expressing concern about the U.S. consideration of using nuclear weapons in defense of Quemoy and suggesting that the prime minister visit Washington to dissuade the United States from engaging in war in the Far East.[59] In his reply to Gaitskell, Macmillan reaffirmed that "the immediate question is not the present or future status of the off-shore islands, it is whether a dispute of this nature should be settled by force. On that point we strongly support our American friend." [60]

British Foreign Secretary Selwyn Lloyd contended on September 19 that Britain's treatment of the Americans so far had been correct. "If we had tried to lecture them about the rights and wrongs of their policy," he believed, "the effect would only have been to make them extremely resentful and less liable to take our advice. Indeed . . . it would have changed the whole nature of our present relationship." [61]

While maintaining public solidarity with Washington, London was concerned by the continuation of the crisis and apprehensive about the possible use of atomic weapons by the United States. During his visit to the United States in September, Lloyd held several meetings with top American officials about the Quemoy crisis. He was anxious to know whether the administration intended to employ nuclear weapons against China.

In his discussion with Dulles on September 16, Lloyd inquired about the situation on the offshore islands and U.S. countermeasures in dealing with the crisis. The secretary of state told him that if the Communists maintained their heaviest fire, the Nationalists would be unable to use the beaches to get supplies through. In that case, the islands could only last twenty to thirty days. Because "in any case one would not want to stay there until the very end of the stores," Dulles continued," the answer was either evacuation or attack on the Communist gun positions." If effective action were to be taken to silence the mainland's batteries, Dulles asserted, "the Americans would have to do it themselves." Lloyd asked the form of American attack. Dulles replied that the United States would use air assault with conventional weapons first; if that did not work, "then with air bursts of nuclear weapons;" if that still "did not do the trick, with ground bursts of nuclear weapons, realizing the danger of radioactivity." Dulles believed that conventional attack would not stop the Communist batteries. Lloyd observed that Dulles's mind "was completely unmade up between evacuation and bombing of the gun positions." [62]

On September 21, Lloyd asked Eisenhower about the nature of U.S. military action with regard to the offshore islands. The president answered that Washington would proceed by stages, indicating the same sort of phases as Dulles had mentioned on September 16. The British foreign secretary returned to the topic several times and, finally, Eisenhower said very firmly that his own personal view was that "it was out of the question to use nuclear weapons for a purely local tactical counter-battery task." If such weapons were to be used, the president went on, that should be for "the big thing. . . . When you use nuclear weapons you cross a completely different line." In his opinion, "If there had to be a fight, the four imprisoned United States airmen were a much better issue. The American people understand about them but not about Quemoy and Matsu." (Eisenhower was referring to the U.S. pilots captured by the Chinese during the Korean War.) Lloyd felt "very much relieved" with Eisenhower's remarks about counter-battery action.[63]

These Anglo-American conversations showed clearly the difficult choices facing Eisenhower and Dulles in a possible limited war over Quemoy and Matsu. The American leaders grasped the adverse effects of using nuclear weapons in such a situation. Sensitive to domestic reactions, the president, in particular, insisted on the distinction between declaratory and actual policy. The discussions also revealed that while the British did not voice objection to the American contemplation of using nuclear weapons against China, they were very much concerned about such a prospect.

Accordingly, London tried to encourage diplomatic solutions to the Quemoy crisis. When the fighting broke out, the British had first thought of asking India to talk to the Chinese to restrain them but soon abandoned the idea on the grounds that in the current conditions of Sino-Indian relations, "this would be unlikely to lead to effective action."[64] London had also considered the possibility of communicating with Beijing directly but had concluded that this would be "useless," given Britain's strained relations with China.[65]

The British then suggested to the Americans the Soviet channel to defuse the crisis. In his discussion with Acting Secretary of State Herter on August 30, British Minister Hood inquired whether it would serve any useful purpose if London were to approach Moscow, pointing out the danger that China's attack on the offshore islands could develop into more widespread hostilities and urging the Soviets to "counsel Peiping to exercise restraint." The U.S. official answered that an approach focusing on opposition to the use of force by the Chinese Communists to achieve their goals "was all to the good." But he added that "it was important any approach should be made in such a way that the Russians would not receive the impression that the U.S. had inspired the approach."[66] But Lloyd soon dismissed the idea of approaching the Soviet Union as unwise. He told Dulles on September 16 that to go to the Russians "would be regarded as a sign of weakness. It would be thought that the Americans had asked us to go round to appeal to the Russians." Dulles agreed with this analysis.[67]

On September 19, Lloyd asked Dulles whether he had considered raising the level of the Sino-American talks. The British official believed that because the PRC seemed very eager to enhance their international status, it might be prepared to make more compromises in an agreement between Zhou Enlai and Dulles than it would between the ambassadors. The secretary of state replied that when Beijing had proposed the resumption of the talks, he had expected that it would demand them to be at a higher level; but it had not done so, and he was not certain that the level of the talks was really important.[68] Dulles later told British Ambassador Harold Caccia that he did not believe that the time had arrived to consider negotiations at a higher level.[69]

During his meeting with Eisenhower on September 21, Lloyd again raised the issue of high-level talks between China and the United States. He said that such an event "would be much easier for the allies of the United States." The president replied that the American public would not support his taking part in a meeting with the head of the Chinese government, but he did not exclude the possibility of a meeting at the foreign minister's level. Reminding Eisenhower of the Geneva Conference of 1954, the foreign secretary suggested that it might be possible to convene a meeting of the United States, Great Britain, the Soviet Union, and the PRC with, perhaps, the Indians present. Lloyd expressed the fear that the Warsaw negotiations might fail and the situation become worse. "If real hostilities were in prospect," he pointed out, "the United Kingdom and European public opinion would not understand United States failure to attempt a higher level meeting." Eisenhower "appeared to agree," saying that he realized that he had not secured U.S. public opinion behind him in the manner that he had over Lebanon. The president concluded that "a democratic Government could not go to war without the support of the bulk of its people."[70]

Despite his doubt about the desirability of approaching the Russians for a solution to the Quemoy crisis, Lloyd did so in a meeting with Soviet Foreign Minister Gromyko in New York on September 24. He reminded Gromyko of the "common interest" of the British and Soviet governments in "doing everything we could to bring about a reduction of tension" in the

Far East. Gromyko answered that "it was inconceivable that the Soviet Union should bring any kind of pressure to bear on its Chinese ally in this matter. China was fully entitled to insist on the withdrawal of the United States from Chinese territory and to adopt whatever means were necessary to restore its national unity." The Soviet official concluded that the "crisis was exclusively the fault of the Americans."[71]

The British support for U.S. policy during the Quemoy confrontation worsened Sino-British relations, which had already deteriorated since the Middle East crisis in the summer of 1958, when Beijing criticized London's backing of King Hussein's government in Jordan. During the Quemoy crisis, the Chinese media increased its censure of British policy. Apparently in defense of China's own twelve-mile territorial water principle, a September 3 *Renmin ribao* article attacked the British position in the Anglo-Icelandic dispute over territorial waters: "According to international law, each country has the right to decide the extent of its own territorial waters and therefore Iceland was perfectly entitled to extend its territorial waters to 12 miles. In future, Britain and the United States will be unable to prevent any countries from extending their territorial waters."[72]

On October 14, *Da gong bao* accused Britain of being "the accomplice of the U.S. aggressors."[73] Commenting on a speech by Foreign Secretary Lloyd in the House of Commons on October 30, which described the CCP-KMT conflict as a dispute between two Chinas and called for the abandonment of "the use of force," a November 3 *Renmin ribao* editorial charged Lloyd with "trying to help Dulles sell the 'two Chinas' plot." Since Dulles's scheme had come into the open, the article continued, the British had become anxious to take the lead in acting for the United States. Lloyd was creating a so-called "international climate of opinion" to impose on the PRC the "two Chinas" plot. The United Kingdom had diplomatic relations with China, the editorial concluded, yet its foreign secretary carried on hostile activities against the Chinese people and openly exalted the Chiang clique. "This is extremely unfriendly toward China and has aroused the indignation of the Chinese people."[74]

In sum, although the British had different perceptions from the Americans about Chinese Communist intentions in the 1958 Quemoy crisis and continued to nurse private reservations about U.S. policy in the region, they on the whole abstained from criticizing Washington's position and showed much more unity with the Eisenhower administration than they had done in the previous offshore island crisis. Although in 1954–55, London had opposed U.S. commitment to the defense of the offshore islands, no such efforts were made in 1958. Government statements in London often concentrated solely on the fact that China was using force to achieve its objectives. Prime Minister Macmillan, in particular, emphasized "interdependence" in Anglo-American relations. At a time of Middle East tensions when London prized American support, the Macmillan government in public moved as closely as possible to Washington's position in the Far East. The British, nonetheless, worried about the possibility of the U.S. use of nuclear weapons against China. To forestall such a development, they encouraged Washington to seek diplomatic resolutions to the crisis.

The Eisenhower administration, in general, appreciated London's cooperation during the second Quemoy crisis. On September 16, Dulles told Lloyd that both he and the president were "grateful" for the British support.[75] Although Britain's solidarity with the United States pleased the Americans, it infuriated the Chinese. Beijing's media flailed away at British policy during the crisis.

THE SOVIET INVOLVEMENT

Controversy still exists over whether China informed the Soviet Union in advance of shelling the offshore islands. Recent Chinese sources claim that Beijing notified the Soviet adviser in the General Staff Department of the Ministry of Defense before it launched its bombardment.[76] But the Soviets contended that they did not know China's plan before the attack.[77] As noted earlier, Dulles believed that the two Communist powers collaborated in initiating the offshore island crisis.[78]

The Soviet Union refrained from taking firm actions to support China until after the crisis had passed its most dangerous point.[79] In the first week of the crisis, the Soviets avoided threatening the United States. They exercised great restraint until the tension began to ease on September 6. Moreover, Moscow's initial warnings were not issued in the name of the Soviet government or made by top leaders whose official positions would have indicated a commitment on the part of the Kremlin. Before September 6, the most direct threat appeared in an article in *Pravda* on August 31, which warned Washington that a threat of an attack on China would be a threat to the Soviet Union and that, in that case, the Soviet people would give every kind of "moral and material aid" to the Chinese people. This threat, although muted, was the only major warning by Moscow before the United States declared its intention on September 4 to defend Quemoy.[80]

The American threat of the use of force and China's belligerency caused great anxiety in the Kremlin. On September 5, Soviet Foreign Minister Andrei Gromyko visited Beijing where Mao and Zhou told him that the shelling of the offshore islands was not intended to liberate Taiwan by force but was designed to punish the Nationalists and to prevent the United States from creating "two Chinas." The Chinese leaders assured the Soviet visitor that, if the bombardment should lead to further hostilities, China would assume the responsibility and would not involve the Soviet Union in them.[81]

According to M. S. Kapitsa, who accompanied Gromyko on his visit to China, Mao's remarks regarding possible nuclear war disturbed the Soviet foreign minister.[82] Gromyko himself later contended in his memoirs that Mao anticipated a U.S. attack on China at the time. If that should happen, the CCP leader proposed, Chinese troops would retreat from the border area and lure the Americans into the depths of the country where the Soviet Union should "give them everything" it possessed, namely, atomic weapons. Astounded, Gromyko said to Mao that "such a proposal would not meet with a positive response from us. I can say that definitely."[83] Although the Chinese government has claimed that Gromyko's account of his discussion with Mao in 1958 "does not agree with the facts," the Soviet diplomat's version is not totally incredible, given Mao's characteristic disregard of human cost in achieving his goals.[84]

Only after Gromyko had secured Mao's assurance that China would not invoke the Sino-Soviet alliance treaty in a Sino-American military showdown and only after Zhou Enlai had declared Beijing's readiness for the resumption of the talks on September 6 did Moscow step up its warnings against Washington. On September 7, Khrushchev wrote to Eisenhower officially announcing Soviet extended deterrence: "An attack on the Chinese People's Republic, which is a great friend, ally and neighbor of our country, is an attack on the Soviet Union."[85]

After Sino-American ambassadorial talks reopened on September 15, Khrushchev sent Eisenhower another letter on September 19, contending that neither the Soviet Union nor China would be intimidated by Washington's "atomic blackmail." "May no one doubt," he declared, "that we shall completely honor our commitments" to China.[86] The president dismissed Khrushchev's "false accusations" as "abusive and intemperate" the next day.[87] It is clear that the Soviet Union was very cautious in providing support to China. By the time Khrushchev went on record with a threat of nuclear retaliation, the United States had already modified its assessment of the situation, and the warning was no longer very relevant.

Later events showed that Khrushchev was unhappy with Beijing's offshore island policy in 1958. During his talk with Mao in Beijing on October 2, 1959, the Soviet leader complained that China's shelling of Quemoy "created difficulties" for the Soviet Union. He urged Mao to abandon the use of force against Taiwan.[88]

Both Eisenhower and Dulles believed that Moscow was behind Beijing's action in the Taiwan Strait. The president felt sure that "to disturb and divide the Free World, Khrushchev would never fail to suggest dark and dangerous possibilities whenever he had an excuse."[89] Secretary Dulles speculated on several occasions during the period that the two Communist powers were cooperating in testing the United States in the Far East. At a meeting with Eisenhower on August 12, Dulles argued that "maybe the Chinese Communists and the Soviets are together probing us, to see whether Soviet possession of ballistic missiles is softening our resolve anywhere. The loss of Formosa would . . . be a mortal blow to our position in the Far East."[90] In a joint meeting of the Departments of State and Defense on September 3, Dulles said, "This present activity is essentially a probing operation, probably agreed upon at the recent meeting between Khrushchev and Mao" in Beijing.[91] Talking with Canadian diplomats on September 9, the secretary of state further commented that China and the Soviet Union "had adopted a new posture of dangerous truculence. The most recent tension in the Far East seems to have been concerted between them."[92]

While Eisenhower and Dulles assumed that Khrushchev had instigated Mao to start the trouble in the Taiwan Strait, U.S. intelligence analysts were convinced that the USSR and the PRC had significant differences, which were exacerbated by the equivocal Soviet support for the Chinese during the Quemoy crisis.[93] In retrospect, the CIA seemed to have a better appreciation of the situation than the president and the secretary of state.

But the U.S. policymakers' misassessment of the Sino-Soviet relationship at the beginning of the Quemoy crisis did not mean that they no longer believed in the inherent contradictions between the two Communist powers. In fact, after Beijing had moderated its behavior, Eisenhower began to wonder in November 1958 whether "the Soviets were not really becoming concerned about Communist China as a possible threat to them in the future."[94] On January 14, 1959, Dulles told the Senate Foreign Relations Committee that "you could very well have a struggle between . . . Mao Tsetung and Khrushchev as to who would be the ideological leader of International Communism."[95]

In sum, Beijing's shelling of Quemoy in 1958 disturbed the Kremlin leadership, which was hesitant to provide timely support to China. It did issue warnings of retaliation against Washington only after the tension had passed its peak. But these warnings were made more for the record—to forestall possible Chinese Communist accusations that the Soviet Union had failed to provide fraternal support or to fulfill its obligations under the Sino-Soviet treaty—than to achieve real deterrence against the United States. Sino-Soviet strains created doubts about the alliance on both sides. The crisis revealed a major division in Sino-Soviet relations, resulting from divergent assessments of U.S. power as well as the strategy and tactics to be adopted in dealing with American opposition.

TOWARD A PACKAGE SOLUTION OF THE TAIWAN ISSUE

As the danger of hostilities with China receded, the Eisenhower administration began urging Chiang to reduce his troop strength on the offshore islands. Several reasons were behind Washington's action. First, U.S. officials believed that it was "a military liability" to station so many Nationalist soldiers on the islands because they were difficult to resupply and were directly under the mainland's guns.[96] Second, by inducing Chiang to remove his garrisons from the islands, the last physical link between the mainland and Taiwan, the United States hoped to eliminate a potential source of conflict between the two contending Chinese regimes and facilitate its scheme of two Chinas.[97]

Third, the withdrawal of Chiang's troops from the islands would help improve international opinion, which seemed to assume that the troops were deployed for offensive actions against the mainland rather than for the protection of the islands. Eisenhower acknowledged on September 29 that "he did not like to wage a fight on the ground of someone else's choosing, and this is the case in Quemoy and Matsu where we are at a great disadvantage in terms of world opinion."[98]

Under U.S. pressure, Chiang acknowledged on September 29 that the offshore islands had become a "shield" for the defense of Taiwan rather than a springboard for an attack on the mainland.[99] The next day, Dulles claimed at a press conference, "If there were a cease-fire in the area which seemed to be reasonably dependable, I think it would be foolish to keep these forces on these islands."[100] But Chiang immediately voiced his objections to reducing the island garrisons as the price for a cease-fire.[101]

Mao was apprehensive about these developments. According to He Di's study, the CCP leader considered the advantages and disadvantages of occupying Quemoy and Matsu in early October. While realizing the benefits of recovering the islands, such as the alleviation of Taiwan's threat to China's coastal shipping and economic construction, Mao was conscious of the long-term costs of such an action. In his view, if Chiang disengaged from the offshore islands, there would be no physical connections between the mainland and Taiwan. And this, in turn, would take the United States off the hook in the Taiwan Strait, allowing the administration to implement its two Chinas plan. After weighing the pros and cons, the Chinese leader decided to defer an invasion of the offshore islands and to leave them in Taiwan's possession.[102]

On October 6, Peng Dehuai announced the first "Message to Our Taiwan Compatriots," which declared a seven-day cease-fire and expressed hope for a peaceful solution among the Chinese in order to create one China. With the aim of stimulating differences between Taipei and Washington, Peng contended: "We all are Chinese. Of all choices, peace is the best . . . there is only one China, not two in the world. To this, you also agree, as proved by the documents issued by your leaders . . . The day will certainly come when the Americans will abandon you. Do you not believe it? . . . The clue is already there in the statement made by Dulles on September 30. Placed in such circumstances, do you not feel wary? In the final analysis, the American imperialists are our common enemy."[103]

The ensuing events demonstrated that Beijing's strategy of creating a rift between the Americans and the Nationalists worked. After China's announcement of its one-week cease-fire, the U.S. government halted convoying Nationalist supply operations. These developments disturbed Chiang. On October 7, George Yeh, who had just replaced Tong as the Nationalist ambassador in Washington, conveyed Taiwan's fears of Beijing's intentions to Robertson, asserting that the "psychological object" of the mainland's cease-fire would be to "soften American public opinion." The Communists, Yeh continued, "could see that U.S. public opinion did not support the administration's policy 100%," and they could also observe "a slight difference" between Washington and Taipei on the matter. Dulles's use of the word *foolish* in his press conference "hurt" Chiang's personal pride. The mainland's real aim behind its cease-fire offer, the ambassador believed, was to "build themselves up" and then to "renew their attacks." Robertson, however, did not agree with Yeh's analysis, saying that the Communist bombardment of Chiang's positions had been "far heavier" than the

Nationalist shelling of the mainland's positions. Therefore, it did not seem as though Beijing would need a cease-fire to resupply the position. Meanwhile, the U.S. official assured Yeh that if the mainland resumed firing, the United States would recommence convoying.[104]

In a second "Message to Our Taiwan Compatriots" on October 13, Peng declared that the PLA would extend the cease-fire for two more weeks and permit supplies, including food and military equipment, to reach Quemoy. This measure, Peng stressed, "was directed at the Americans" and was for the "righteous cause" of the Chinese nation. It was a "sacred mission" of the Chinese people, the defense minister concluded, to recover Taiwan, the Pescadores, Quemoy, and Matsu and to "unify the motherland." This was China's internal affair, and no foreigners had the right to interfere with it, nor did the United Nations.[105]

Beijing's psychological warfare constituted a new challenge to the Eisenhower administration. In a discussion with Yeh after the announcement of Peng's second message, Dulles acknowledged that the "big danger" in the Taiwan Strait was "political." "More and more countries of the free world," the secretary of state pointed out, "wanted to deal with the Chinese Communists because they represented power. People like to deal with power. We are having a difficult time holding our friends back who are attracted to this power." Washington could not "hold countries like Canada, Belgium and France indefinitely. Once one or two of them switched there would be an avalanche." Given Beijing's "political offensive," Dulles recognized the problem of preserving the Chiang government's "international status . . . without running the risk of arousing anti-American feelings in Taiwan especially in the light of current Communist appeals for Chinese unity against the United States." Accordingly, Dulles stressed to Yeh the necessity of clarifying the role of Taiwan: "We must keep alive the idea of a free China close to the Chinese mainland which would play an important role if the mainland became the scene of unrest. . . . The forces on Quemoy were no good whatsoever for this purpose."[106]

It was with this intention of clarifying the role of the Nationalist government that Dulles visited Chiang October 21–23. During their talks, the KMT leader refused to abandon Quemoy and Matsu, claiming that "so long as I live, I will not give them up."[107] The secretary of state was finally able to persuade the generalissimo to renounce the use of force in returning to the mainland. A joint communiqué issued on October 23 stated that "The Government of the Republic of China considers that the restoration of freedom to its people on the mainland is its sacred mission. It believes that the foundation of this mission resides in the hearts and minds of the Chinese people and that the principal means of successfully achieving its mission is the implementation of Dr. Sun Yat-sen's three people's principles and not the use of force." [108] This document was significant because it showed that for the first time Chiang had officially acknowledged the reality that he had no hope of recovering the mainland. It represented a diplomatic victory in Dulles's effort to win international support for American policy by moderating Chiang's position. The statement served to dissipate the impression around the world as well as in the United States that the Nationalist regime existed only for the day when it could launch an attack against the mainland. Eisenhower was satisfied with the outcome of Dulles's visit, referring to his trip as "useful" and "satisfactory." [109]

It is interesting to note the shift of congressional attitudes during the Quemoy crisis in 1958. Unlike the situation in 1954–55, when pro-Chiang lawmakers such as Smith, Knowland, and Jenner had called for more support for Taiwan against the mainland, this time, Democratic legislators were more vocal in voicing their objections to Chiang's cause. They feared that the KMT leader was bent on dragging the United States into a war over some obscure islands with no strategic significance on the doorstep of mainland China. Democratic Senator Theodore Green, chairman of the Senate Foreign Relations Committee, wrote Eisenhower on September 29, expressing "his deep concern that the course of events in the Far East may result in military involvement at the wrong time, in the wrong place, and on issues not of vital concern to our security."[110] Robertson told Yeh on October 29 that the Taiwan government "was losing support in this country especially among Democrats," and some Democratic leaders like William Fulbright "were hostile" to the Republic of China.[111]

On October 25, Peng issued a third "Message to Our Taiwan Compatriots." Aimed at widening the gap between Washington and Taipei, it reiterated the theme that "Chinese affairs should be handled by the Chinese people themselves and the Americans have no right to intervene." The message also declared that the PLA would shell the offshore islands on alternate days.[112] This gesture shows that Mao was ready to allow supplies to reach the offshore islands but was not prepared to relinquish his demonstration of discontent with a de facto cease-fire that only confirmed the status quo ante.

In an interview with Gerald Clark of the North American Newspaper Alliance on November 1, Chinese Foreign Minister Chen Yi made an important statement about Beijing's policy toward the Taiwan Strait crisis.

He asserted that the PRC was not interested in compromise solutions of the crisis and that the United States should withdraw its forces from the region. He stressed that Taiwan, the Pescadores, and the offshore islands must be "liberated as a whole" and rejected any suggestion that the present crisis could be resolved merely by an award of the offshore islands to Beijing or by the PRC's being admitted into the United Nations. He also brushed aside such proposals for a settlement of the crisis as demilitarization of the offshore islands or submission of the issue to the United Nations or the International Court of Justice. In an effort to justify Beijing's refusal to accept renunciation of force, Chen reiterated the mainland's position that whether or not force should be used in "liberating" Taiwan was an "internal matter" and that the PRC saw no need to "make a so-called guarantee to anyone." As for the continued shelling of Quemoy, the foreign minister claimed that the purpose was to "enlighten" Chiang with a "sense of national dignity," referring to the bombardment as "a kind of medicine to make him more clear-headed."[113]

It is now clear that Beijing had totally integrated its policy toward the offshore islands and Taiwan. The PRC wanted to settle the Taiwan issue in a package deal. The unusual outcome of the on-and-off cease-fire reflected Mao's intention of continuing to punish Chiang, on the one hand, and of permitting the Nationalists to survive on the offshore islands, on the other hand, so as to foil the U.S. scheme for creating two Chinas by forcing Chiang to disengage from the offshore islands.

CONCLUSION

The shelling of Quemoy served to crystallize China's policy toward the offshore islands. By 1958, the islands had become an integral part of the Taiwan reunification issue. At the beginning of the crisis, Mao had expected a replay of the Tachen experience—a Nationalist evacuation under U.S. pressure. But when Washington showed resolution by issuing warnings against Beijing and by convoying Chiang's supply ships to Quemoy, Mao realized that he had miscalculated. While realizing America's determination to help Chiang defend the offshore islands under attack, the Chinese Communist leader also became aware that Washington did not intend to invade China through Taiwan but desired to create two Chinas. When the administration began pressuring Chiang to withdraw from the offshore islands after the suspension of the fighting, Mao became apprehensive about the danger of Taiwan's separation from the mainland. Accordingly, he adjusted his policy by permitting the islands to remain temporarily in Chiang's hands.

Throughout the crisis, Mao was the prime mover of the mainland's policy. He wrote all of Peng's messages to the "Taiwan Compatriots." Sensitive to disagreements between Taipei and Washington over the offshore islands, he strove to exploit those differences by working at both ends of the U.S.-Taiwan alliance. To the Americans, he was firm but cautious. By shelling Quemoy, he signaled Washington that he was not satisfied with the American presence in the Taiwan Strait. But when the administration displayed resolve by convoying Taiwan's supply operations, he ordered Ye not to engage American vessels. Toward the Nationalists, he used both the stick and the carrot. He first launched a massive assault on Quemoy to force a Nationalist evacuation. Later, when he detected Washington's intention of inducing Chiang to withdraw from the offshore islands, he switched tactics by allowing Chiang's troops to stay on the islands. He began to stress the theme of one China and worked on Chiang's nationalistic sensitivities by dwelling on the U.S. intention of creating two Chinas. To Mao, the offshore island affair had become not just a military operation but a political and diplomatic game. Judging by the quarrels between Washington and Taipei over the role of the offshore islands in October, Mao's wedge strategy seems to have been effective. But his action also confirmed the American view that the PRC represented the most dangerous threat to peace in the Far East.

Aware of the need to stand firm before Communist challenges, the administration reacted to the crisis quickly, supporting Chiang in holding the islands under attack. While in public Washington's threat to use nuclear weapons against China was vague, U.S. officials in private discussed this possibility as a last resort. The concern with international and domestic opinion as well as an awareness of the Soviet atomic capabilities underscored Eisenhower's caution in contemplating nuclear options against China. When the crisis began to recede, the United States began pressuring Chiang to reduce his troops on the offshore islands as a step toward the stabilization of the situation and the ultimate separation of Taiwan from the mainland. But Chiang was unwilling to abandon the offshore islands. It was only with hard cajoling and pressure that Dulles was finally able to persuade Chiang to renounce the use of force against the mainland.

Although Eisenhower and Dulles initially viewed the Communist bombardment as a combined Sino-Soviet probe of U.S. resolution in the Far East, American intelligence specialists believed that the differences between

Beijing and Moscow were increasing as a result of the Soviets' lukewarm support for the PRC. After the Chinese Communists had backed down, the president and the secretary of state again emphasized the contradictions within the Communist bloc. The U.S. leaders carried their concept of driving a wedge between the Soviet Union and China consistently to the end of their terms in office.

Two other concepts persisted in the minds of top American policymakers throughout the two offshore island crises. One was the non-use of force. The Eisenhower administration persistently opposed Beijing's effort to change by force the status quo in the Taiwan Strait and unfailingly prevented Chiang from employing force against the mainland. The ultimate goal, as Mao had correctly suspected, was the creation of two Chinas. The second was credibility, which involved the American willingness to take firm action in support of allies under attack. In both crises, U.S. officials stressed the importance of standing resolute before Communist provocations with the fear that failing to do so would discourage U.S. allies in the region.

In 1958, the British moved much closer to the American position than they had done in 1954–55. Although during the previous crisis London had objected to Washington's commitment to the defense of the offshore islands, this time Whitehall refrained from criticizing U.S. policy. The Macmillan government provided maximum support to the United States despite adverse British public opinion and Labor opposition. Because of the Lebanese crisis in the summer of 1958, London's officials attached great importance to Anglo-American unanimity. The absence of Britain's restraining influence on U.S. policy indicated clearly the further decline in London's position as a world power.

While maintaining a public front of Atlantic solidarity, the British in private tried to encourage diplomatic solutions to the crisis as a way to forestall the possibility of a general war and the U.S. use of nuclear weapons against China. London's advocacy of high-level Sino-American negotiations represented a consistent strand in British thinking with regard to China throughout the 1950s. The British believed that by recognizing the PRC and admitting it to the United Nations, the West would satisfy Beijing, and, consequently, the situation in East Asia would become stable. From the Chinese perspective, however, the real cause of tensions in the Far East was the American prevention of China's attempt to reunify Taiwan. As long as that island remained separated from the mainland, no Western compromises would have likely satisfied Mao. That is why the Chinese government was so resistant to any suggestion of a "two Chinas" solution in British policy. In this respect, the

British clearly failed to understand the Chinese government's determination to recover Taiwan. Britain's cooperation with the United States angered Beijing, causing Sino-British relations to reach the lowest point since 1950.

The Quemoy crisis of 1958 was a major event in the worsening of Sino-Soviet relations. In Beijing's view, the Soviet Union was not prepared to provide China with the support it needed, even on an issue which the PRC considered fundamental to its national interests. From the Soviet perspective, the offshore island confrontation underscored the danger that the Chinese might involve the Soviet Union in possible conflicts with the United States that it wished to avoid. Moscow's behavior clearly demonstrated that its own interests and welfare came first. The Soviet lack of forthright assistance caused the PRC's bitterness, which subsequently added to the doctrinal dispute about the nature of imperialism and the ineluctability of war.

Conclusion

The purpose of this exercise in international history has been to avoid the tunnel vision so common in explorations of bilateral relationships by structuring the examination of Chinese, British, and American perceptions, policies, and interactions between 1949 and 1958 around the initiatives and responses of each of those countries to events that were inherently multilateral in character. Relations between the three countries during this period were dynamic and complex. The story was one of mutual stimulations and mutual constraints.

When the CCP came to power in 1949, it confronted a hostile international environment. Consolidating the new regime's security was one major goal of the PRC's foreign policy. Mao concluded an alliance treaty with the Soviet Union in early 1950, chiefly as a deterrent against what he perceived to be Washington's threat. Beijing provided advisers and materials to assist Ho Chi Minh in his struggle against the French, mainly as a way to secure the safety of China's southern border. It was also largely for security reasons that Mao sent his army to fight the Americans in Korea. To some extent, though, a sense of revolutionary obligation to help fellow Communists also shaped Mao's decisions to assist the Vietminh and the North Koreans in 1950.

When security interests conflicted with ideological considerations, the Chinese Communists generally gave priority to the former. This was clearly the case during the Geneva Conference in 1954 when the PRC stopped short of supporting the Vietminh's effort to unify Vietnam. Beijing's primary concern at the time was to deny Washington any excuse to intervene in Indochina.

The reunification of all China's territories represented another important objective of Beijing's foreign policy. Immediately after the establishment of the PRC, Mao set out to occupy Tibet and Taiwan. Although suspicious of Anglo-American interference, the Communists did not encounter any Western intervention in their occupation of Tibet. Their effort to recover Taiwan, however, was disrupted by the outbreak of the Korean War. After the Korean armistice in 1953 and the Geneva settlement of the Indochina issue in 1954, Mao resumed his effort to reunify Taiwan. His campaigns to bombard the offshore islands in 1954–55 and 1958 were designed to prevent the separation of Taiwan from the mainland by the Americans.

Two characteristics emerge from examining the PRC's policy between 1949 and 1958. The first is principle. This was clearly demonstrated by Beijing's insistence on one China. From the beginning, the PRC made clear that to establish diplomatic relations, a foreign government should first sever all relations with the Chiang regime and vote to expel the Nationalist representative from the United Nations. In this respect, Beijing found London's position ambiguous. Britain's reluctance to vote against Chiang's representative in the United Nations and its decision to open a consulate in Taipei alienated Beijing's leadership, resulting in lack of progress in the Sino-British negotiations for the establishment of diplomatic relations following London's recognition of the PRC in early 1950.

The second characteristic is a consistent effort to divide enemies in order to promote China's foreign policy goals. The CCP's acceptance of Britain's suggestions on trade was partly aimed at exploiting Anglo-American differences over this issue. During the Korean War, Zhou believed that China's participation would entrap the United States and undermine its plan to send troops to Western Europe, thus creating disputes between Washington and its European allies. At the Geneva Conference, Zhou Enlai tried to work with British Foreign Secretary Eden to isolate the Americans and to achieve a settlement in Indochina. During the Quemoy crisis of 1958, Mao's appeal to Chiang's nationalism was explicitly designed to stimulate disagreements between the Nationalist leader and the Americans over the offshore islands.

Britain and the United States reacted to the Chinese Communist victory in 1949 differently and adopted dissimilar approaches toward the People's Republic of China during the 1950s. Initially, London and Washington recognized that although the Chinese Communists were Marxists, they were a different brand from the Soviet variety. Both British and American officials shared the view that Chinese nationalism was a potential force that could be used against the Russians and that it was possible to promote a Sino-Soviet schism as a way to protect Western interests in East Asia. They agreed that recognition and trade would be useful tools to keep China in contact with the West.

But differences soon emerged. Eager to reach an accommodation with the Chinese Communists, the United Kingdom accorded recognition to the PRC shortly after its founding and quickly sent a representative to Beijing to start negotiations for the establishment of diplomatic relations. The United States, however, although desiring to avoid any commitment to protect the Chiang regime on Taiwan and not excluding an eventual reconciliation with the Communists, continued to recognize the Chinese Nationalist government and to support its membership in the United Nations. Disgusted by the failure of the Communists to adhere to what he regarded as their international obligations, increasingly worried about the Communist insurgency in Southeast Asia, beset by domestic pressure for a tougher stand, Secretary of State Acheson became less and less willing in late 1949 and early 1950 to make any overtures to the Communists.

The Korean War had a greater impact on U.S. policy toward China than on British policy. China's entry into the Korean fighting dashed any remaining hope of reconciliation between Beijing and Washington. After the Korean hostilities, the British and the Americans developed different perceptions of China's intentions in Asia. Washington no longer compartmentalized its views of Asia. U.S. decision makers considered the fighting in Korea part of a broader and coordinated campaign of expansion spearheaded by the Chinese Communists. Acheson believed that the PRC had embarked on an aggressive path in Asia with immediate goals in Korea, Indochina, Burma, Malaya, and the Philippines and with medium-range objectives in Hong Kong, Indonesia, Thailand, India, and Japan. Although still confident that inherent differences existed between China and the Soviet Union, American officials modified their estimate of the chances for promoting a Sino-Soviet split, relegating that possibility to a long-term prospect. For the moment, they believed, the United States had to concentrate on the containment of China. Accordingly, the Truman administration adopted a hostile stand against Beijing.

The British, however, did not share Acheson's analysis of the PRC's intentions. Foreign Secretary Bevin contended that Mao's aim for the time being was nothing more than the reunification of Taiwan. He asserted that maintaining China's contact with the West remained the best course to divide the Chinese and Soviet Communists and to serve Western interests. Therefore, London continued its moderate approach to the PRC.

Viewing the PRC as more dangerous and expansionist than the Soviet Union, Eisenhower and Dulles inherited the Truman administration's harsh policy toward Beijing. To the secretary of state, the best way to stimulate divisions in the Sino-Soviet partnership was to exert maximum pressure on the PRC; when Moscow could not meet Beijing's needs, problems would arise. Thus, the Republican administration executed a policy of political isolation, economic embargo, military encirclement, and nuclear harassment against the Chinese Communists.

British officials remained convinced that China's external ambitions were limited and that internal construction and economic growth were the top priorities of the regime. Anti-Western rhetoric should be considered, they thought, in the light of the domestic function it served rather than as a manifestation of overseas aggression. The British felt uneasy with Dulles's high-pressure posture regarding China, which they feared, apart from giving Beijing a grievance it could exploit to gain international sympathy, might lead the United States into an unnecessary war in the Far East. They consistently sought to accommodate the PRC by attempting to integrate it into the world community of nations.

Throughout the period under study, Britain and the United States each tried to steer the other toward policies it favored. On the whole, the British made more concessions to the Americans' demands than the other way around. Examples include Washington's pressure on London to support the passing of the United Nations resolution condemning the PRC as an aggressor in Korea in early 1951; Britain's acceptance of the U.S. moratorium on Chinese representation in the United Nations; and the American success in preventing Beijing from obtaining aircraft in Hong Kong.

London's reliance on Washington to contain the Soviet Union in Europe and its need for American economic assistance explain this British willingness to yield to U.S. demands. After all, the United Kingdom was a weakened power after World War II and its strategic priorities were in Europe and the Middle East, not in the Far East where the Americans bore the major responsibility. To the British, therefore, Anglo-American solidarity was far more important than Sino-British relations. London could not afford to jeopardize its cooperation with Washington in Western Europe by disagreements in the Far East.

American influence, however, was not always successful. London was able to obtain Washington's acceptance of its need to depart from the U.S. position on certain issues. For instance, Britain recognized the PRC in early 1950 despite the Truman administration's disapproval. Later, the British secured American acknowledgment of the desirability of their trading with China in nonstrategic goods.

Furthermore, when British officials perceived that Washington was on the verge of war in the Far East, they did not hesitate to bring pressure to bear on the Americans, even at the risk of straining Anglo-American relations. Three episodes demonstrate this clearly. The first occurred in December 1950 when Prime Minister Attlee made an urgent trip to Washington to warn U.S. officials of the danger of expanding the fighting in Korea. The second took place in the spring of 1953 when American intransigence on the POW issue appeared to torpedo the chance for an armistice in Korea, and the Churchill government appealed to the Americans to moderate their position. The last came during the 1954–55 Quemoy crisis when the U.S. decision to defend the offshore islands alarmed the British, who feared that the American commitment would involve the United States in a possible nuclear war against mainland China. In all three instances, British pressure played some constraining role in modifying Washington's positions.

There were a number of reasons for the differences in Anglo-American policies toward China between 1949 and 1958. First, American China policy was subject to greater domestic constraints than British policy. This was the era of McCarthyism in the United States, and the China question was a sensitive and explosive issue in American politics. The pro-Chiang China lobby objected to any move toward conciliation between the United States and the PRC. Acheson had suffered considerable criticism for his handling of China, and Dulles was determined not to alienate Chiang's supporters. In Britain, there was nothing like the American China lobby. If there was a China interest group, it was the business community, which supported recognition of Beijing in the hope that this would enable them to continue their activities in China.

Second, British policy was shaped by immediate and concrete concerns, whereas U.S. decision makers were inclined to view China within a wider strategic framework. The United Kingdom had a larger commercial stake in China and desired to preserve Hong Kong's status and prosperity. London recognized the PRC with a view to strengthening and solidifying its economic presence there.

American interests in Asia in the post–World War II period, as Phillip Darby has observed, were "externally derived. . . . The United States was not so much pulled in by interests or events in Asia . . . as pushed to become involved by its understanding of the global conflict with the Soviet Union."[1] To U.S. officials, Cold War conflicts with the Russians provided a prism through which to view events in the Far East. This fixation with the Soviet role often led the Americans to give short shrift to indigenous concerns. A good illustration of this preoccupation with the Russians was the Truman administration's surprise and distress at China's entry into the Korean War. U.S. officials had been so preoccupied with possible Soviet reactions that they failed to appreciate the effects of their march to the Yalu River on the Chinese.

Third, London and Washington were subject to different constraints from their respective partners. To maintain the unity of the British Commonwealth, the British government paid great attention to India's attitude toward China. The Indians saw in the Chinese revolution the counterpart of their own triumphant struggle for independence. New Delhi's government favored recognition of the PRC, supported its admission to the United Nations, and opposed the U.S. decision to send the Seventh Fleet into the Taiwan Strait during the Korean War. The Indians also showed reluctance to provide strong support to the Tibetans. All these sentiments influenced British policy.

Washington's ally, Chiang, was a shrewd exploiter of U.S. politics. He was intent on involving the United States in his struggle with the Communists. American policymakers often found their work complicated by the ruthless manipulation of the Nationalist leader. This was clearly the case in his reluctance to abandon the offshore islands during the 1950s. Although Washington often distrusted Nehru's policy and regarded Indian officials as unreliable, London constantly overlooked the tenacity and scheming of Chiang and underestimated the political difficulties confronting U.S. officials in making decisions.

Fourth, the British had a long tradition of relying on diplomacy and compromise to achieve their foreign policy goals. "It was a policy," in the words of Paul Kennedy, "predicated upon the assumption that, provided national interests were not too deleteriously affected, the peaceful settlement of disputes was much more to Britain's advantage than recourse to war."[2] Thus, throughout the period, London consistently sought diplomatic solutions to the disputes in the Far East. During his visit to Washington in December 1950, Attlee urged the Americans to negotiate with the Chinese Communists. At Geneva in 1954, the British played the role of mediator in facilitating the negotiations between the PRC and the United States over the issues of American prisoners in China and Chinese students in the United States. Later, London also helped to bring about the opening of Sino-American ambassadorial talks. During the second Quemoy crisis, British Foreign Secretary Lloyd suggested that Washington and Beijing hold high-level talks to solve their problems.

In contrast, U. S. policy displayed a tendency toward overdependence on the use of military power and nuclear deterrence at the expense of diplomatic initiatives. Moreover, American policymakers developed a hypersensitivity regarding their "credibility," with the fear that if they appeared soft and irresolute before Communist challenges, their allies in Asia would have doubts about Washington's commitment.

The British were constantly apprehensive about U.S. reliance on nuclear threats against China. Truman's unintentional remarks about nuclear retaliation against Beijing triggered Attlee's 1950 trip to Washington. In 1958, when Eisenhower assured Lloyd that he would not use atomic weapons over the offshore islands, the British foreign secretary felt much relieved.

This contrast between the British emphasis on diplomacy and American stress on deterrence, however, reflected the different status of British and U.S. strengths after World War II. London was now a second-class power that relied on Washington to maintain its influence. It had fewer choices available. The United States, however, was the premier economic and military power in the world.

Finally, disparate Anglo-American temperaments also accounted for dissimilarities in China policies. The British were more pragmatic and matter-of-fact. They were more detached in examining China. The Americans, however, were prone to be idealistic and emotional regarding China. The U.S. experience in the Far East in the nineteenth century had created a myth among the Americans about their relations with China. They tended to believe that they had protected the Chinese from the predatory aggression of other powers and that they had an obligation to help China toward liberal democracy and modernization. They viewed their role in China as disinterested and selfless. Therefore, they felt that they deserved the gratitude of the Chinese people. When they later encountered Chinese antagonism, they felt upset, perplexed, and "betrayed."[3] This sentiment colored American attitude toward China and was partly responsible for the heated domestic debate about "Who lost China?"

The British believed that American reasoning with respect to China "is ruled far more by sentiment than by logic."[4] They were inclined to view the Americans as inexperienced and impatient in international politics and in need of the wise counsel of a more mature and sophisticated, if somewhat exhausted, Britain. Bevin told Nehru in early 1951 that "the United States is a young country and the Administration was too apt to take unreflecting plunges. We had made it our business to try to restrain them."[5] Of course, there was a limit in how far the British could control the Americans.

In retrospect, miscalculations and misunderstandings characterize the behavior of policymakers in all three countries. The Chinese Communists' misuse of the "lessons" of the Russian Revolution, their distrust of U.S. motives, and their anxiety to expel Western influence from China led them to overestimate the threat from the United States. In the late 1940s and the early 1950s, the CCP leaders expected an American invasion to overthrow their government. But, in fact, during the period, the United States had no intentions of doing this. The party's knowledge of American policy formation was limited. As Allen Whiting has perceptively pointed out, the Chinese Communists "ignored the pluralistic political process in the West and failed to differentiate between the true locus of power in Washington and the confusion of voices on both sides of the Pacific Ocean."[6] They often confused MacArthur's statements with the administration's policy. According to Michael Schaller's 1989 study, ultimately all of MacArthur's actions, ranging from his advocacy of employing Chiang's forces against the mainland to his demand for nuclear weapons for use if the Russians attacked Japan, had domestic political roots.[7] The general had presidential ambitions and wanted to show that the Democratic administration was soft on communism, but the Chinese failed to understand this.

During both of the offshore island crises, Mao misjudged U.S. reactions. Instead of forestalling the conclusion of the U.S.-Taiwan security treaty, his shelling of Quemoy in 1954 facilitated the realization of a formal and long-term U.S. commitment to the defense of Taiwan. During the second Quemoy crisis, Washington's determination to help Chiang defend the island dashed Mao's hope that the United States would pressure the Nationalists to evacuate the offshore islands.

Miscalculations abounded in U.S. policy. Lack of proper communication channels contributed to Washington's misreading of Beijing's intentions. For example, during the first Quemoy crisis, rather than regarding the occupation of the Tachens as the conclusion of the Communist offshore island campaign, U.S. policymakers interpreted the move as a preliminary step toward the invasion of Quemoy and Taiwan. The administration went on to threaten the PRC with nuclear retaliation, thus escalating the tensions in the Taiwan Strait.

The British failed to understand the importance and sensitivity of the Taiwan issue in the PRC's foreign policy. London's officials believed that by admitting Beijing into the international community of nations, the West would satisfy the Chinese leadership and stabilize the situation in the Far East. From Beijing's view, nonetheless, the root of tensions in East Asia was Washington's resistance to China's efforts to recover Taiwan. The Chinese government resisted any suggestions of a "two China" solution in British policy. Because of London's failure to vote against the Nationalist representatives in the United Nations, the PRC refused to establish diplomatic relations with the United Kingdom at the ambassadorial level.

This examination of Anglo-American responses to China points to the limitations of the so-called "special relationship" between the two Western powers. During World War II, there had been little meeting of minds between Washington and London regarding the Far East. This situation continued after 1945. Even when Soviet behavior pushed Britain and the United States closer together during the Cold War, they remained divided in their approaches toward the Far East. In the words of Christopher Thorne, they were only "allies of a kind."[8]

Notes

Introduction

1. For general treatments of Sino-American relations during the period, see J. H. Kalicki, *The Pattern of Sino-American Crises: Political-Military Interactions in the 1950s;* Dorothy Borg and Waldo Heinrichs, eds., *Uncertain Years: Chinese-American Relations 1947–1950;* Kenneth S. Chern, *Dilemma in China;* William W. Stueck, Jr., *The Road to Confrontation: American Policy Toward China and Korea, 1947–1950;* Nancy Bernkopf Tucker, *Patterns in the Dust: Chinese-American Relations and the Recognition Controversy, 1949–1950;* Leonard A. Kusnitz, *Public Opinion and Foreign Policy: America's China Policy, 1949–1979;* Thomas E. Stolper, *China, Taiwan, and the Offshore Islands: Together with an Implication for Outer Mongolia and Sino-Soviet Relations;* June M. Grasso, *Truman's Two-China Policy, 1948–1950;* Harry Harding and Yuan Ming, eds., *Sino-American Relations, 1945–1955: A Joint Reassessment of a Critical Decade;* Shu Guang Zhang, *Deterrence and Strategic Culture: Chinese-American Confrontations, 1949–1958.*

For discussions of Sino-British relations, see Evan Luard, *Britain and China;* Brian E. Porter, *Britain and the Rise of Communist China: A Study of British Attitudes, 1945–1954;* Robert Boardman, *Britain and the People's Republic of China, 1949–1974;* James Tuck-Hong Tang, *Britain's Encounter with Revolutionary China, 1949–54;* Ritchie Ovendale, "Britain, the United States, and the Recognition of Communist China," 139–58; David C. Wolf, "'To Secure a Convenience': Britain Recognizes China—1950," 299–326.

For the CCP's policy toward Western economic and cultural interests in China at the founding of the PRC, see Beverley Hooper, *China Stands Up: Ending the Western Presence, 1948–1950;* Wenguang Shao, *China, Britain, and Businessmen: Political and Commercial Relations, 1949–57;* Aron Shai, "Imperialism Imprisoned: The Closure of British Firms in the People's Republic of China," 88–109.

2. Edwin W. Martin, *Divided Counsel: The Anglo-American Response to Communist Victory in China.* Based on secondary materials, Roderick MacFarquhar's "The China Problem in Anglo-American Relations" is a sketchy comparison of Anglo-American approaches to the PRC during the Cold War. It is included in Wm. Roger Louis and Hedley Bull, eds., *The "Special Relationship": Anglo-American Relations since 1945,* 311–19; Rosemary Foot, "The Search for a *Modus Vivendi:* Anglo-American Relations and China Policy in the Eisenhower Era" is a recent treatment comparing London and Washington policies toward Beijing during 1953 and 1960. It contains a detailed discussion of Anglo-American responses to the first offshore island crisis but is weak on the second offshore island crisis. It is included in Warren I. Cohen and Akira Iriye, eds., *The Great Powers in East Asia, 1953–1960,* 143–63.

3. For a recent survey of post-1945 Anglo-American relations, see Louis and Bull, *"Special Relationship."*

4. David Allan Mayers, *Cracking the Monolith: U.S. Policy Against the Sino-Soviet Alliance, 1949–1955;* John Lewis Gaddis, *The Long Peace: Inquiries into the History of the Cold War,* 147–94; idem, "The Unexpected John Foster Dulles," 47–77; Gordon H. Chang,

Friends and Enemies: The United States, China and the Soviet Union, 1948–1972.

5. Sally Marks, "The World According to Washington," 265–82.

6. For timely reports on recent Chinese materials, see Michael H. Hunt and Odd Arne Westad, "The Chinese Communist Party and International Affairs: A Field Report on New Historical Sources and Old Research Problems," 258–72; Steven M. Goldstein and He Di, "New Chinese Sources on the History of the Cold War," 4–6; David Shambaugh, "New Sources and Research Opportunities in the Study of China's Foreign Relations and National Security," 24–27.

7. Robert Jervis, "Hypotheses on Misperception," 454–79; idem, *Perception and Misperception in International Politics.*

8. Specifically, I intend to test the explanations of alliance formation advanced by Stephen M. Walt, whose theories have challenged and refined the conventional interpretations of alliances. See Walt, *The Origins of Alliances;* idem., "Testing Theories of Alliance Formation: The Case of Southwest Asia," 275–316.

1 PERCEPTION AND ALLIANCE: THE CCP'S FOREIGN POLICY IN 1949

1. Edgar Snow, *Red Star over China,* 141–42, 147–48; Mao Zedong, "On the People's Democratic Dictatorship," June 30, 1949, *Selected Works of Mao Tse-tung,* 4:413.

2. Jin Chongji, ed., *Zhou Enlai zhuan, 1898–1949* (A biography of Zhou Enlai, 1898–1949), 24, 35–36, 55–57; Percy Jucheng Fang and Lucy Guinong J. Fang, *Zhou Enlai: A Profile,* 15–17, 200n; Dick Wilson, *Zhou Enlai: A Biography,* 37–39.

3. For brief descriptions of these leaders' backgrounds, consult Donald W. Klein and Anne B. Clark, eds., *Biographical Dictionary of Chinese Communism, 1921–1965;* Tang, *Britain's Encounter,* 19–23; for Ren Bishi, Chen Yun, and Kang Sheng's activities in the Comintern in the 1930s, see Zhonggong Huanggang xianweihui, ed., *Huiyi Chen Tanqiu* (Reminiscences of Chen Tanqiu), 112–13, 118–19; for Zhang Wentian's background, see Zhang Peisen, ed., *Zhang Wentian yanjiu wenji* (Collection of studies on Zhang Wentian).

4. Renmin chubanshe, ed., *Huiyi Chen Yi* (Reminiscences of Chen Yi), 9; Chen Yun, "Zai Shenyang gongren daibiao dahui shang de jianghua" (Speech before the Conference of Shenyang Workers' Representatives), January 5, 1949, in *Chen Yun wenxuan, 1926–1949* (Selected works of Chen Yun, 1926–1949), 279.

5. Mao, "The Present Situation and Our Task," December 25, 1947, in *Selected Works of Mao Tse-tung,* 4:158, 163; Chen Yun, "Fadong nongmin shi jianli Dongbei genjudi de guanjian" (Mobilization of the peasants is the key to the establishment of the northeast base area), July 13, 1946, in *Chen Yun wenxuan, 1926–1949,* 238; Zhu De, "Muqian xingshi he jundui jianshe wenti" (The current situation and military buildup), May 14, 1948, in *Zhu De xuanji* (Selected works of Zhu De), 229–30.

6. Mao, "Greet the New High Tide of the Chinese Revolution," February 1, 1947, in *Selected Works of Mao Tse-tung,* 4:123; Zhou Enlai, "Quanguo dafangong, da dao Chiang Jieshi" (Waging a nationwide counteroffensive and overthrowing Chiang Kai-shek), September 28, 1947, in *Zhou Enlai xuanji* (Selected works of Zhou Enlai), 1:281; Zhou, "Huifu shengchan, jianshe Zhongguo" (Restoring production and building China), July 23, 1949, in ibid., 1:360.

7. Mao, "The Present Situation and Our Task," in *Selected Works of Mao Tse-tung,* 4:172–73.

8. Stuart R. Schram, ed., *Quotations from Chairman Mao Tse-tung,* 41; Mao, "Talk with the American Correspondent Anna Louise Strong," August 1946, in *Selected Works of Mao Tse-tung,* 4:100.

9. Mao, "'Friendship' or Aggression?" August 30, 1949, in *Selected Works of Mao Tse-tung,* 4:447–49.

10. In recent years, the study of the Marshall Mission has become a cottage industry in the field of Sino-American relations. Drawing on newly available materials, Chinese scholars point out that the CCP placed real hope in the prospect of achieving peace in China during the early stage of Marshall's mediation, but after the outbreak of fighting between the Communists and the Nationalists in March 1946 and with subsequent American support of Chiang Kai-shek, Mao and his comrades became entirely disillusioned with the Americans. For Chinese discussions of the Marshall Mission and its impact on the CCP's policy toward the United States, see Niu Jun, *Cong Heerli dao Maxieer: Meiguo tiaochu guogong maodun shimuo* (From Hurley to Marshall: A history of the American mediation of the KMT-CCP contradictions); Tu Chuande, *Meiguo teshi zai Zhongguo, 1945. 12–1947. 1* (U.S. special envoy in China, December 1945–January 1947); He Di, "The Evolution of the Chinese Communist Party's Policy towards the United States, 1944–1949," 31–50; Zhang Baijia, "KangRi zhanzheng jiesu qianhou Zhongguo gongchandang dui Meiguo zhengce de yanbian" (The evolution of the Chinese Communist party's policy toward the United States around the conclusion of the Anti-Japanese War), 40–48.

11. Mao, "Talk with Anna Louise Strong," in *Selected Works of Mao Tse-tung,* 4:99.

12. Mao, "Cast Away Illusions, Prepare for Struggle," August 14, 1949, in ibid., 4:428; Han Nianlong, ed., *Dangdai Zhongguo waijiao* (Contemporary Chinese diplomacy), 4. American scholar Steven M. Goldstein discusses this point briefly in his "Chinese Communist Policy toward the United States: Opportunities and Constraints, 1944–1950," in Borg and Heinrichs, *Uncertain Years,* 266, 269.

13. Zhou Enlai, "Guanyu heping tanpan wenti de baogao" (The report on the peace negotiations), April 17, 1949, in *Zhou Enlai xuanji,* 1:323. For balanced treatments of the American intervention in the October Revolution, see Betty M. Unterberger, *America's Siberian Expedition, 1918–1920;* John Lewis Gaddis, *Russia, the Soviet Union, and the United States: An Interpretive History,* 72–82.

14. Zhou, "Guanyu heping tanpan de baogao," in *Zhou Enlai xuanji,* 323.

15. Mao, "Why It Is Necessary to Discuss the White Paper," August 28, 1949, in *Selected Works of Mao Tse-tung,* 4:445; Mao, "On the People's Democratic Dictatorship," in ibid., 4:417.

16. Mao, "On the People's Democratic Dictatorship," in ibid., 4:414; Mao, "The Present Situation and Our Task," in ibid., 4:172.

17. Bough memorandum, enclosed in Heathcote-Smith to Lamb, December 2, 1948, Foreign Office Records, FO371/75779, F124/1016/10, Public Record Office, London; see also Steve Yut-sang Tsang, *Democracy Shelved: Great Britain, China, and Attempts at Constitutional Reforms in Hong Kong, 1945–1952.*

18. For Peng's statements, see Colonial Political Intelligence Service, March 1951, Colonial Office Records, CO537/6798, Public Record Office, London; see also Tang, *Britain's Encounter,* 186. For the CCP's activities in Hong Kong during the civil war, see Zhonggong Guangdong shengwei dangshi yanjiu weiyuanhui, ed., *Huiyi Fang Fang* (Reminiscences of Fang Fang).

19. Jin, *Zhou Enlai zhuan,* 715.

20. Zhonggong zhongyang wenxian yanjiushi, ed., *Zhou Enlai nianpu, 1898–1949* (A chronicle of Zhou Enlai's life, 1898–1949), 789.

21. General Ye Fei, Commander of the Tenth Corps of the Third Field Army of the PLA, which was responsible for crossing the Yangtse River when the *Amethyst* incident occurred, admitted recently in his memoirs that it was a Communist army commander on the spot who issued the order to fire first on the *Amethyst. Ye Fei, Ye Fei huiyilu* (Memoirs of Ye Fei), 538–43; for Western accounts of the incident, see Lawrence Earl, *Yangtse Incident: The Story of HMS Amethyst;* Malcolm H. Murfett, *Hostage on the Yangtze: Britain, China, and the Amethyst Crisis of 1949.*

22. Nanjing to Foreign Office, April 27, 1949, FO371/75889, F5023.

23. For Mao's public statement, see "On the Outrages by British Warships—Statement by

the Spokesman of the General Headquarters of the Chinese People's Liberation Army,"
April 30, 1949, in *Selected Works of Mao Tse-tung,* 4:401–3; for his private remarks, see Mao's
telegram to the PLA General Front Committee, April 28, 1949, published in *Dangde wenxian*
(Party documents), 4 (1989): 43.

24. Zhonggong zhongyang wenxian yanjiushi, *Zhou Enlai nianpu,* 824–25.

25. Mao, "On Policy," December 25, 1940, in *Selected Works of Mao Tse-tung,* 2:444;
A. Doak Barnett, *China and the Major Powers in East Asia,* 163, 254.

26. Zhang Wentian, "KangRi minzu tongyi zhanxian zhong de 'zuo'qing weixian" (The
danger of the 'leftist' tendency in the National United Front against Japan), August 10, 1940,
in *Zhang Wentian xuanji* (Selected works of Zhang Wentian), 276.

27. Zhonggong zhongyang wenxian yanjiushi, *Zhou Enlai nianpu,* 799–800.

28. On traditional Chinese practice in handling foreign powers, see John K. Fairbank, ed.,
The Chinese World Order: Traditional China's Foreign Relations; Earl Swisher, ed., *China's
Management of the American Barbarians: A Study of Sino-American Relations, 1841–1861,
with Documents.*

29. For Zhou's comments, see Zhou, "Gongchan guoji he Zhongguo gongchandang" (The
Comintern and the Chinese Communist party), July 14–15, 1960, in *Zhou Enlai xuanji,* 2:311;
Zhou, "Guanyu dang de 'Liuda' de yanjiu" (A study of the Sixth Convention of the Chinese
Communist party), March 3–4, 1944, in ibid, 1:178–79; for Molotov's remarks to Hurley, see
U.S. Department of State, *United States Relations with China, with Special Reference to the
Period 1944–1949,* 72.

30. For the Comintern's activities in China during the 1920s, see Robert C. North, *Moscow
and Chinese Communists,* 92–97; Conrad Brandt, *Stalin's Failure in China, 1924–1927;*
C. Martin Wilbur and Julie Lien-ying How, *Missionaries of Revolution: Soviet Advisers and
Nationalist China, 1920–1927.* For an explanation of the eclipse of Comintern influence in
China after 1927, see Charles B. McLane, *Soviet Policy and the Chinese Communists,
1931–1946,* 5–13; Zhou, "Gongchan guoji he Zhongguo gongchandang," in *Zhou Enlai xuanji,*
2:305–7.

31. For a recent account on how Chiang Kai-shek shrewdly used diplomatic manipulations
to win Soviet support for China's war effort, see John W. Garver, *Chinese-Soviet Relations,
1937–1945: The Diplomacy of Chinese Nationalism.*

32. For Chuikov's activities in China, see his memoirs, Zhu Kefu (Vasilii Chuikov), *Zai
Hua shiming* (Mission to China).

33. Yang Kuisong, "Kangzhan shiqi Gongchan guoji, Sulian, yu Zhongguo gongchandang
guanxi zhongde jige wenti" (Several issues in the relationship between the Comintern, the
Soviet Union, and the CCP during the War of Resistance against Japan), 132–49.

34. John Gittings, *Survey of the Sino-Soviet Dispute: A Commentary and Extracts from the
Recent Polemics, 1963–1967,* 8–10.

35. Niu Jun, *Cong Heerli dao Maxieer,* 123–24.

36. Ibid., 125.

37. Nie Rongzhen, *Nie Rongzhen huiyilu* (Memoirs of Nie Rongzhen), 734; Zhang Wenjin,
"Zhou Enlai yu Maxieer shiHua" (Zhou Enlai and the Marshall Mission in China), in "Zhou
Enlai yanjiu xueshu taolunhui lunwenji" bianjizu, ed., *Zhou Enlai yanjiu xueshu taolunhui lun-
wenji* (Proceedings of the conference on the study of Zhou Enlai), 259–72.

38. Mao, "The Present Situation and Our Task," in *Selected Works of Mao Tse-tung,*
4:158–59.

39. Shi Zhe, "Peitong Maozhuxi fangSu" (Accompanying Chairman Mao to visit the Soviet
Union), 6; Nie, *Nie Rongzhen huiyilu,* 678.

40. Li Yinqiao, "Zaishuo Jiang Qing xiangma de wangshi" (Recalling Jiangqing's story of
taming the horse), 40–51.

41. Shi, "Peitong Maozhuxi fangSu," 6.

42. Ibid., 6–8 (Shi Zhe was the interpreter for the Mao-Mikoyan talk); Zhonggong zhongyang wenxian yanjiushi, *Zhou Enlai nianpu*, 810–11.

43. Shi, "Peitong Maozhuxi fangSu," 6–8.

44. Mao, "On the People's Democratic Dictatorship," in *Selected Works of Mao Tse-tung*, 4:415.

45. Peter Van Ness, *Revolution and Chinese Foreign Policy: Peking's Support for Wars of National Liberation*, 11.

46. Robert R. Simmons, *The Strained Alliance: Peking, Pyongyang, Moscow and the Politics of the Korean Civil War*, 61.

47. Tang Tsou, *America's Failure in China, 1941–50*, 505.

48. Mayers, *Cracking the Monolith*, 48.

49. Liu Shaoqi, "The Victory of Marxism-Leninism in China," September 14, 1959, in *Collected Works of Liu Shaoqi, 1958–1967*, 47.

50. Mao, "Statement on the Present Situation," January 14, 1949 in *Selected Works of Mao Tse-tung*, 4:316.

51. Mao, "On the People's Democratic Dictatorship," in ibid., 4:415, 417.

52. Mao, "Speech at the Tenth Plenum of the Eighth Central Committee," September 24, 1962, in Stuart R. Schram, ed., *Chairman Mao Talks to the People: Talks and Letters, 1956–1971*, 191.

53. Zhou, "Women de waijiao fangzhen he renwu" (Our diplomatic principles and tasks), April 30, 1952, in *Zhou Enlai xuanji*, 2:86–87.

54. Mao, "Cast Away Illusions, Prepare for Struggle," in *Selected Works of Mao Tse-tung*, 4:425–31.

55. Shi Zhe, "Zhongxin genggeng, guangming leiluo: Huiyi Wang Jiaxiang tongzhi" (Whole-hearted loyalty and total honesty: Reminiscences of Comrade Wang Jiaxiang), 85–86; Shi, "Peitong Maozhuxi fangSu," 5–20; Nie, *Nie Rongzhen huiyilu*, 734; Wu Xiuquan, *Wangshi cangsang: Wu Xiuquan huiyilu* (The vicissitudes of my life: Memoirs of Wu Xiuquan), 181. According to a recent Russian account, during his visit in Moscow Liu Shaoqi asked Stalin to support a CCP attack on Taiwan with Soviet air force units and submarines, but Stalin declined for fear of a confrontation with the United States. (See Sergei N. Goncharov, "Stalin's Dialogue with Mao Zedong," 53.) But Shi Zhe contends that Liu did not ask Stalin for direct Soviet participation in the CCP's plan to occupy Taiwan. (See Li Haiwen, "A Distortion of History: An Interview with Shi Zhe about Kovalev's Recollections," 59–64.)

56. Shi, "Peitong Maozhuxi fangSu," 9.

57. Deng Liqun, "Xinjiang heping jiefang qianhou: ZhongSu guanxi zhi yiye" (Around the peaceful liberation of Xinjiang: One page in the history of Sino-Soviet relations), 143–50; Zhu Yuanshi, "Liu Shaoqi 1949 nian mimi fangSu" (Liu Shaoqi's secret visit to the Soviet Union in 1949), 74–89.

58. Zhu, "Liu Shaoqi 1949 nian mimi fangSu;" Shi, "Peitong Maozhuxi fangSu," 11; Bo Yibo, *Ruogan zhongda juece yu shijian de huigu* (Recollections of certain important decisions and events), 1:37–38.

59. Mao to the CCP Central Committee, January 3, 1950, *Jianguo yilai Mao Zedong wengao* (Mao Zedong's manuscripts after the founding of the PRC) (1987) 1:213.

60. According to Mao's interpreter Shi Zhe's recollection, when Stalin asked Mao what he had in mind in visiting Moscow, the Chinese party chairman, instead of giving a straightforward answer, said he wanted "something that should not only appear nice but taste delicious." Later it was Chinese Ambassador to the Soviet Union Wang Jiaxiang who found out Mao's real intention and hinted to Soviet Foreign Minister Andrei Vyshinsky that Mao wanted to sign a Sino-Soviet alliance treaty. See Shi, "Peitong Maozhuxi fangSu," 10; see also Wu, *Wangshi cangsang*, 182. For a Soviet description of the Mao-Stalin talks, see N. Fedorenko, "The Stalin-Mao Summit in Moscow," 134–48.

61. For a description of the Sino-Soviet bargain over the stipulations of the treaty, see Wu, *Wangshi cangsang,* 183–87.

62. For Zhou's statements, see *Renmin ribao* (People's daily), February 14, 1950; see also Wu, *Wangshi cangsang,* 186.

63. Walt, *Origins of Alliances,* 5.

64. Ibid.

65. Jin, *Zhou Enlai zhuan,* 742.

66. Han, *Dangdai Zhongguo waijiao,* 3; Zheng Weizhi, "Independence Is the Basic Canon—An Analysis of the Principles of China's Foreign Policy," 16–17.

67. Mao, "Report to the Second Plenary Session of the Seventh Central Committee of the Communist Party of China," March 5, 1949, in *Selected Works of Mao Tse-tung,* 4:370.

68. Zhou, "Women de waijiao fangzhen he renwu," in *Zhou Enlai xuanji,* 2:87.

69. Zhou, "Guanyu heping tanpan de baogao," in ibid., 1:321–22.

70. Mao, "Report to the Second Plenary Session," in *Selected Works of Mao Tse-tung,* 4:371.

2   PERCEPTION AND RECOGNITION: ANGLO-AMERICAN POLICIES IN 1949

1. D. C. Watt, "Britain and the Cold War in the Far East, 1945–58," 91; Tang, *Britain's Encounter,* 8–9.

2. Avi Shlaim, Peter Jones, and Keith Sainsbury, *British Foreign Secretaries Since 1945,* 28.

3. Raymond Smith and John Zametica, "The Cold Warrior: Clement Attlee Reconsidered, 1945–7," 237–52. See also Kenneth O. Morgan, *Labour People: Leaders and Lieutenants, Hardie to Kinnock,* 138–39; Henry Pelling, *The Labour Government, 1945–51,* 35; Tang, *Britain's Encounter,* 9.

4. Alan Bullock, *Ernest Bevin: Foreign Secretary, 1945–1951,* 103; Frank Roberts, "Ernest Bevin as Foreign Secretary," 23; for the Cadogan quote, see David Dilks, ed., *The Diaries of Sir Alexander Cadogan, 1938–1945,* 776; Tang, *Britain's Encounter,* 9–10.

5. Shlaim, Jones, Sainsbury, *British Foreign Secretaries,* 36.

6. Wolf, "'To Secure a Convenience,'" 301.

7. Porter, *Britain and the Rise of Communist China,* 14–21.

8. For Seymour's statement, see Christopher G. Thorne, *Allies of a Kind: The United States, Britain and the War Against Japan, 1941–1945,* 320; Porter, *Britain and the Rise of Communist China,* 20–21.

9. Research Department minutes, February 3, 1949, Foreign Office records, FO371/75745, F4062, Public Record Office, Kew, U.K.

10. Bevin to cabinet, "The Situation in China," March 4, 1949, Cabinet records, CAB129/32, C.P. (49) 39, app., "Chinese Communists," Public Record Office, Kew, U.K.

11. P. D. Coates memo, April 1949, FO371/75749, F5826.

12. Cabinet minute, December 13, 1948, CAB128/13, C.M. 80 (48); FO371/75814, F12843/1023/10; Bevin to Cabinet, "Recognition of the Chinese Communist Government," October 24, 1949, CAB129, C.P. (49)214. Hugh Dalton said in his diary on September 2, 1950, that Bevin never believed "that China is a Russian satellite," quoted in Bullock, *Ernest Bevin,* 1803.

13. Nicholls to M. E. Denning, February 9, 1950, FO371/83314, FC10338/50.

14. Nicholls to Bevin, February 17, 1950, FO371/83315, FC10338/60.

15. For Bateman quote, see Denning minute, February 2, 1950, FO371/83314, FC10338/39.

16. For detailed discussions of these departments' contributions to the formation of Britain's China policy, see Tang, *Britain's Encounter,* 38–42.

17. Bevin to Cabinet, "Recent Developments in the Civil War in China," December 9, 1948, CAB129/31, C.P. (48)299.

18. Ibid.

19. Ibid.

20. Ibid.

21. Ibid. Britain informed the State Department of this document in January 1949. See *Foreign Relations of the United States* (hereafter *FRUS*), *1949*, IX, 2–11.

22. For detailed treatments of British consultation with Commonwealth countries, France, Netherlands and so on, see Tang, *Britain's Encounter*, 58–62.

23. Robert L. Messer, "Roosevelt, Truman, and China: An Overview," 68.

24. Quoted in Richard Lawrence Miller, *Truman: The Rise to Power*, 348.

25. Alonzo L. Hamby, "The Mind and Character of Harry S. Truman," 25.

26. Margaret Truman, *Letters from Father: The Truman Family's Personal Correspondence*, 33.

27. George Mowry contended that of all presidents from Warren Harding to John Kennedy, Harding and Truman used history most inexactly. Mowry, "The Uses of History by Recent Presidents," 6–7, 14–16. William Pemberton has also discussed Truman's tendency to misuse history in his *Harry S. Truman: Fair Dealer and Cold Warrior*, 7–8.

28. Messer, "Roosevelt, Truman, and China," 75; for Truman's statements, see Truman memorandum for Secretary of Commerce Wallace, January 25, 1946, President's Secretary's Files, box 173, Truman Library; for Truman's intervention in China policy, see Warren I. Cohen, "Acheson, His Advisers, and China, 1949–1950," 13–52; Tucker, *Patterns in the Dust*, 174.

29. Cohen, "Acheson," 16–17.

30. Ibid., 17–18.

31. For Rusk's background, see Thomas J. Schoenbaum, *Waging Peace and War: Dean Rusk in the Truman, Kennedy and Johnson Years*, chaps. 1–3; Warren I. Cohen, *Dean Rusk*, 1–5.

32. For a description of Davies's influence on Kennan on China matters, see David Allan Mayers, *George Kennan and the Dilemma of U.S. Foreign Policy*, 170–80; Cohen, "Acheson," 20.

33. Mayers, *Dilemma of U.S. Foreign Policy*, 161–62; Kennan Naval War College speech, October 11, 1948, quoted in Gaddis, *Long Peace*, 161.

34. Davies's words are quoted in *Long Peace*, 163; see also Cohen, "Acheson," 20–21.

35. PPS39, September 7, 1948, *FRUS, 1948*, VIII, 148; NSC34/2, February 28, 1949, *FRUS, 1949*, IX, 492–95; NSC41, *FRUS, 1949*, IX, 826–34.

36. Memo of Acheson-Bevin talk, April 4, 1949, *FRUS, 1949*, VII, 1138–41.

37. Memo of Acheson-Dewey telephone conversation, April 10, 1949, Acheson Papers, box 65, Truman Library.

38. Acheson's Press Club speech, January 12, 1950, *State Department Bulletin* 22 (January 23, 1950): 114–15.

39. Nicholls to Bevin, February 17, 1950, FO371/83315, FC10338/60.

40. American writers tend to miss the mark when they cite the small sum of Soviet economic aid to imply that Mao was not satisfied with the treaty. For example, Adam B. Ulam called Stalin "incredibly stingy" in providing only a loan of $300 million to Mao. Joseph Nogee and Robert Donaldson referred to it as "a miserly sum," and David Mayers described it as "niggardly assistance." Adam B. Ulam, *Expansion and Coexistence: Soviet Foreign Policy, 1917–1973*, 495; Joseph L. Nogee and Robert H. Donaldson, *Soviet Foreign Policy since World War II*, 95; Mayers, *Cracking the Monolith*, 67.

41. Gascoigne to Scarlett, December 28, 1949, FO371/83313, FC10338/6; Scarlett to Gascoigne, January 30, 1950, FO371/83313, FC10338/6.

42. Sprouse memo of conversation, January 6, 1949, *FRUS, 1949*, IX, 6.

43. British Embassy to State Department, March 19, 1949, ibid., IX, 12.

44. Stuart to Acheson, April 29, May 3, May 4, 1949, ibid., IX, 12–16.

45. Acheson to certain Diplomatic and Consular Officers, May 6, 1949, ibid., IX, 17; Acheson to Stuart, May 13, 1949, ibid., IX, 21–23.

46. Douglas to Acheson, June 29, 1949, *FRUS, 1949,* IX, 47–48.

47. Douglas to Acheson, August 17, 1949, ibid., IX, 57–61.

48. MacDonald to Strang, August 19, 1949; MacDonald to Strang, August 22, 1949, enclosing Gimson letter to MacDonald, August 15, 1949, FO371/75814, F13405/1023/10.

49. Strang to MacDonald, September 2, 1949, FO371/75814, F13405/1023/10G.

50. Acheson memo of conversation, September 13, 1949, ibid., IX, 81–85.

51. Douglas to Acheson, August 26, 1949, ibid., IX, 68–69.

52. Chief of Staff Committee Joint Planning Staff report, "Current U.K. Policy in China and Hong Kong," September 14, 1949, Defense Department records, DEFE 6/10, J.P. (49) 97.

53. For the British note, see ibid., IX, 103; for American reaction, see Web to Douglas, October 7, 1949, ibid., IX, 109; for Truman's quote, see Acheson memo of the meeting with the president, October 17, 1949, Acheson Papers, box 64, Truman Library.

54. MacDonald to Bevin, November 4, 1949, FO371/75819, F16589/1023/10; Sprouse memo of conversation, November 8, 1949, *FRUS, 1949,* IX, 184–87.

55. Franklin minute, November 16, 1949, FO371/75821, F17052/1023/10; Douglas to Acheson, November 16, 1949, *FRUS, 1949,* IX, 193; British Embassy to State Department, November 28, 1949, ibid., IX, 200–201.

56. Ogburn memo, November 2, 1949, ibid., IX, 160–62.

57. Perkins memo, November 5, 1949, ibid., IX, 168–70.

58. Sprouse memo of conversation, November 10, 1949, ibid., IX, 188; British Embassy to State Department, November 28, 1949, ibid., IX, 201; according to a recent Chinese study, Ward and his aides were accused of committing "espionage" because the Communists wanted to find a way to close the case although the party did not have direct evidence to prove its spy charge against Ward. Shi Yinhong, "Dulumen dui xinZhongguo de zhengce: Cong dishi dao zhanzheng de lishi huigu" (A historical review of Truman's policy toward the New China: From hostility to war) (Ph.D. diss., Nanjing University, 1987), 61–62.

There is reason to believe that the CCP felt embarrassed by the Ward impasse. In a speech on November 28, 1948, Chen Yun, the head of the Shenyang Military Control Commission, referred indirectly to the case as diplomatic "trouble" *(Luanzi);* see Chen Yun, "Jieshou Shenyang de jingyan" (The lessons of taking over Shenyang), November 28, 1948, in *Chen Yun wenxaun, 1926–1949,* 273.

59. Quoted in Tsou, *America's Failure,* 509.

60. Bevin to Acheson, December 16, 1949, *FRUS, 1949,* IX, 224–26.

61. Boardman, *Britain and the People's Republic of China,* 24.

62. On the China myth, see Michael H. Hunt, *The Making of a Special Relationship: The United States and China to 1914;* David McLean, "American Nationalism, the China Myth, and the Truman Doctrine: The Question of Accommodation with Peking, 1949–50," 25–42.

3 CONTROVERSY OVER TIBET, 1949–1950

1. For Zhu's statement, see Nanjing to Foreign Office, November 2, 1949, FO371/76413, F16413; Mao, "Don't Attack on All Fronts," June 6, 1950, in *Selected Works of Mao Tse-tung,* 5:33–36.

2. For the Panchen Lama's message, see "Panchen Lama on 'Tibetan Independence,'" 10. For the Kashag's letter to Mao, see FO371/76317; Donovan to Acheson, November 21, 1949, *FRUS, 1949,* IX, 1081.

3. Mao to the CCP Central Committee, January 2, 1950, *Jianguo yilai Mao Zedong wengao,* 1:208–9.

4. Han Huaizhi and Tan Jingjiao, eds., *Dangdai Zhongguo jundui de junshi gongzuo* (The military work of the contemporary Chinese army), 1:206–7.

5. Mao to the CCP Central Committee, Deng, Liu, and others, January 10, 1950, *Jianguo yilai Mao Zedong wengao*, 1:226–27.

6. Hunan renmin chubanshe, ed., *Huainian He Long tongzhi* (In memory of Comrade He Long), 262–74; Han and Tan, *Dangdai Zhongguo jundui de junshi gongzuo*, 1:206–10.

7. Melvyn C. Goldstein, *A History of Modern Tibet, 1913–1951: The Demise of the Lamaist State*, 612.

8. Han and Tan, *Dangdai Zhongguo jundui de junshi gongzuo*, 1:205. See also acting U.K. high commissioner in India to Commonwealth Relations Office, July 25, 1949, FO371/76316.

9. Kashag to Foreign Office, December 3, 1949, FO371/76314; Kashag to Acheson, December 3, 1949, *FRUS, 1949*, IX, 1087–88; BBC monitoring, January 29, 1950, FO371/84452.

10. For British interest in Tibet during the nineteenth and early twentieth centuries, see Alastair Lamb, *Britain and Chinese Central Asia: The Road to Lhasa, 1767 to 1905*, especially chaps. 3–10; Eden to Soong, August 5, 1943, FO371/93001.

11. Foreign Office proposal, December 16, 1948, FO371/76319.

12. Foreign Office to Treasury, January 1949, FO371/76319.

13. Commonwealth Relations Office to U.K. high commissioner in India, November 26, 1949, FO371/76314; Foreign Office to Beijing, February 22, 1950, FO371/84452.

14. Commonwealth Relations Office to U.K. high commissioner in India, November 26, 1949, FO371/76314.

15. Hutchison to Foreign Office, November 2, 1949, FO371/76314, F16413.

16. Henderson to Acheson, December 2, 1949, *FRUS, 1949*, IX, 1087; Sir G. Falconer (Katmandu) to Foreign Office, October 31, 1950, FO371/84452.

17. Draft telegram from Commonwealth Relations Office to U.K. high commissioner in India, December, 1949, FO371/76314; Henderson to Acheson, December 1, 1949, *FRUS, 1949*, IX, 1086; Taylor minute, January 26, 1950, FO371/84456; Bevin's second response was cited in a telegram, U.K. high commissioner in India to Commonwealth Relations Office, January 5, 1950, FO371/84461; Franks to Foreign Office, December 22, 1949, FO371/76317.

18. Donovan to Hull, July 2, 1942; Hull to Roosevelt, July 3, 1942; Roosevelt to the Dalai Lama, July 3, 1942, *FRUS, 1942: China*, 624–25.

19. Sprouse memo of telephone conversation, July 12, 1948, *FRUS, 1948*, VII, 759–60; Chinese Embassy to State Department, July 15, 1948, ibid., 761–62; Sprouse memo of conversation, July 16, 1948, ibid., 762–63.

20. For Henderson's background, see Loy W. Henderson, *A Question of Trust: The Origins of US-Soviet Diplomatic Relations;* Daniel Yergin, *Shattered Peace: The Origins of the Cold War and the National Security State*, 25–26; Hugh De Santis, *The Diplomacy of Silence: The American Foreign Service, the Soviet Union, and the Cold War, 1933–1947*, 30, 34, 36–37; H. W. Brands, *Inside the Cold War: Loy Henderson and the Rise of the American Empire, 1918–1961;* Henderson to Acheson, October 31, 1950, *FRUS, 1950*, VI, 549.

21. Ruth Bacon memorandum, April 12, 1949, *FRUS, 1949*, IX, 1065–71.

22. Indian trade agent in Gyantse to political officer in Sikkim, September 15, 1949, FO371/76315; officer in charge of Indian Mission in Lhasa to political officer in Sikkim, November 14, 1949, FO371/76315, F19050.

23. U.K. high commissioner in India to Commonwealth Relations Office, November 8, 1949, FO371/76314; Franks to Foreign Office, December 29, 1949, FO371/76317.

24. Acheson to Henderson, January 12, 1950, *FRUS, 1950*, VI, 275–76.

25. Henderson to Acheson, January 20, 1950, ibid., VI, 285–86.

26. Franks to Foreign Office, December 22, 1949, FO371/76317.

27. Henderson to Acheson, January 20, 1950, *FRUS, 1950*, VI, 283–85.

28. Acheson to Henderson, March 1, 1950, ibid., VI, 314–15.

29. Henderson to Acheson, March 8, 1950, ibid., VI, 317–18.

30. The State Department received this information from the law firm that represented the Tibetan trade mission in the United States; see Acheson to Henderson, April 19, 1950, ibid., VI, 330–31.

31. Henderson to Acheson, June 9, 1950, ibid., VI, 361–62.

32. Acheson to U.S. Embassy in Britain, June 16, 1950, ibid., VI, 364–65; Douglas to Acheson, June 20, 1950, ibid., VI, 365–66; Foreign Office to Washington, June 15, 1950, FO371/84469.

33. Henderson to Acheson, July 15, 1950, *FRUS, 1950,* VI, 376–78.

34. Acheson to Henderson, July 22, 1950, ibid., VI, 386–87.

35. Quoted in Goldstein, *History of Modern Tibet,* 669.

36. Henderson to Acheson, August 7, 1950, *FRUS, 1950,* VI, 424–26.

37. Goldstein, *History of Modern Tibet,* 675–76.

38. Ibid., 677–78; Henderson to Acheson, October 26, 1950, *FRUS, 1950,* VI, 540–41.

39. Goldstein, *History of Modern Tibet,* 678.

40. Acheson to Henderson, October 27, 1950, *FRUS, 1950,* VI, 545.

41. Henderson to Acheson, November 3, 1950, ibid., VI, 550–51.

42. Goldstein, *History of Modern Tibet,* 707–8.

43. Sir G. Jebb (United Kingdom's U.N. delegation in New York) to Foreign Office, November 13, 1950, FO371/84454.

44. Foreign Office to Jebb, November 10, 1950; Commonwealth Relations Office to U.K. high commissioner in India, November 11, 1950; Jebb to Foreign Office, November 14, 1950, FO371/84454.

45. In a report to the Foreign Office, Sir Gladwyn said, "We do not know for certain what prompted El Salvador but we suspect that Castro must have had a long conversation with Dr. Tingfu Tsiang," the Chinese Nationalist representative to the United Nations. See Jebb to Foreign Office, November 17, 1950, FO371/84454.

46. Acheson summarized the November 24 General Committee debate in his telegram to Henderson on November 28; see Acheson to Henderson, November 28, 1950, *FRUS, 1950,* VI, 583; Jebb to Foreign Office, November 24, 1950, FO371/84455; see also Goldstein, *History of Modern Tibet,* 729–36.

47. For a text of the second Tibetan appeal to the United Nations, see FO371/84455.

48. Henderson to Acheson, December 18, 1950, *FRUS, 1950,* VI, 603.

49. Henderson to Acheson, December 30, 1950, ibid., VI, 612.

50. Aide-Mémoire, State Department to British Embassy, December 30, 1950, ibid., VI, 612–13; Acheson to Henderson, January 6, 1951, ibid., VI, 618; R. H. Scott minute, January 10, 1951, FO371/93002.

51. Acheson to Embassy in India, January 6, 1951, *FRUS, 1950,* VI, 618.

52. Henderson to Acheson, January 12, 1951, *FRUS, 1951,* VII, 1506–8.

53. "Panchen Lama on 'Tibetan Independence,'" 11; Ngapoi Ngawang Jigmi, "On the 1959 Armed Rebellion," 25–29.

54. Han and Tan, *Dangdai Zhongguo jundui de junshi gongzuo,* 1:216; Han Xia, "Xizang xiandai gemingshi yanjiu gaishu" (A bibliographical survey of modern Tibetan revolutionary history), 73–79.

4 OUTBREAK OF THE KOREAN WAR, 1950

1. Allen S. Whiting, *China Crosses the Yalu: The Decision to Enter the Korean War.* Based on new Chinese materials and interviews, Hao Yufan and Zhai Zhihai, "China's Decision to Enter the Korean War: History Revisited," 94–115, is an article that also stresses the security considerations in China's decision to enter the Korean War. For another study that

emphasizes Mao's initial intention to drive the United States out of the Korean peninsula, see Jian Chen, "China's Changing Aims during the Korean War, 1950–1951," 8–41.

2. For recent Chinese memoirs and recollections, see Peng Dehuai (commander of the Chinese People's Volunteers), *Peng Dehuai zishu* (The autobiographical notes of Peng Dehuai); for the English version, see Peng Dehuai, *Memoirs of a Chinese Marshal: The Autobiographical Notes of Peng Dehuai;* Nie Rongzhen (acting chief of staff of the PLA), *Nie Rongzhen huiyilu;* Xu Xiangqian (chief of staff of the PLA), *Lishi de huigu* (Historical recollections); Yang Dezhi (commander of the Nineteenth Corps and, later, commander of the Chinese People's Volunteers), *Weile heping* (For the sake of peace); Du Ping (director of the General Political Department of the Chinese People's Volunteers), *Zai zhiyuanjun zongbu* (At the headquarters of the Chinese People's Volunteers); Chai Chengwen (Chinese chargé d'affaires in Korea in 1950) and Zhao Yongtian, *Banmendian tanpan* (Panmunjom negotiations); Hong Xuezhi (deputy commander of the Chinese People's Volunteers), *KangMei yuanChao zhanzheng huiyi* (Recollections of the War to Resist America and Aid Korea); Luo Yinwen, "Qiushi chuangxin: Denghua jiangjun ersanshi" (Seeking truth and creating: Reflections about General Deng Hua), 60–65.

For party and military history of the Korean War, see Yao Xu, "Peng Dehuai dui kangMei yuanChao zhanzheng zhihui shang de gongxian" (Peng Dehuai's contribution in commanding the War to Resist America and Aid Korea), 1–10; Hu Guangzheng, "Yingming de juece weida de chengguo: Lun kangMei yuanChao zhanzheng de chubing canzhan juece" (Wise decision and great result: On the decision of entering the War to Resist America and Aid Korea), 33–38; Bao Mingjong and Hu Guangzheng, "Qiantan Mao Zedong junshi sixiang zai kangMei yuanChao zhanzheng zhong de yunyong he fazhan de jige wenti" (A preliminary inquiry into the application and development of Mao Zedong military thought during the War to Resist America and Aid Korea), 32–41; Qi Dexue, "Guanyu kangMei yuanChao zhanzheng zhanlue mubiao de tantao" (A discussion of the strategic goal of the War to Resist America and Aid Korea), 64–67; Zhang Xi, "Peng Dehuai shouming shuaishi kangMei yuanChao de qianqian houhou" (Before and after Peng Dehuai's appointment to command the CPV in the War to Resist America and Aid Korea), 111–59.

Ye Yumeng, *Heixue: Chubing Chaoxian jishi* (Black snow: A record of China's entry into Korea), is a journalistic narrative of China's road to the Korean War. As an army correspondent, the author claims that, when writing this book, he interviewed people involved in the war and sought the assistance of war history researchers at the Academy of Military Science and the National Defense University in locating materials. It should be pointed out, however, that the volume contains some errors. For instance, the author writes that when Zhou Enlai visited the Soviet Union in October 1950 he met Stalin in Moscow. But according to Chai Chengwen's recollections, Zhou had talks with the Soviet leader in southern Russia. Nikita Khrushchev confirmed this point in his own memoirs.

Western scholars have begun to notice and use these new Chinese sources. For example, Jonathan Pollack, "The Korean War and the Sino-American Relations," 213–37; Mark A. Ryan, *Chinese Attitudes Toward Nuclear Weapons: China and the United States During the Korean War;* Thomas J. Christensen, "Threats, Assurances, and the Last Chance for Peace: The Lessons of Mao's Korean War Telegrams," 122–54; Michael H. Hunt, "Beijing and the Korean Crisis, June 1950-June 1951," 453–78. Russell Spurr, *Enter the Dragon: China's Undeclared War against the U.S. in Korea, 1950–51,* is another work on the Chinese perspective by a Western journalist that draws upon the author's interviews and research in China. The book portrays a reckless Mao and contrasts his rashness with the behavior of the cautious Peng Dehuai. This finding, as previously pointed out, has some problems. It ignores other sources such as the memoirs of Peng Dehuai and Nie Rongzhen, which show that, far from being indiscreet and hasty, Mao was actually engaged in difficult and uneasy deliberations before deciding to send Chinese troops into Korea. For criticism of Spurr's book, see Rosemary Foot, "How Far to Push the Americans," 9–11.

3. Whiting, *China Crosses the Yalu*, 53–58.

4. Chai and Zhao, *Banmendian tanpan*, 34–37.

5. Ibid., 37–38.

6. Ibid., 39–40.

7. Ibid., 41–46.

8. Ibid., 33; Nie, *Nie Rongzhen huiyilu*, 738; Luo, "Qiushi chuangxin," 63; John Hutchison, the British chargé d'affaires in Beijing, reported on July 26 that there were rumors of the dispatch of Chinese arms to the Chinese-Korean border. Beijing to Foreign Office, July 26, 1950, FO371/84093, FK1022/247.

9. Nie, *Nie Rongzhen huiyilu*, 738.

10. Luo, "Qiushi chuangxin," 63.

11. Chai and Zhao, *Banmendian tanpan*, 77–78.

12. Ibid., 77–79.

13. Kavaldin M. Panikkar, *In Two Chinas: Memoirs of a Diplomat*, 108; Han, *Dangdai Zhongguo waijiao*, 37.

14. Nie, *Nie Rongzhen huiyilu*, 739.

15. Ibid.; Yao, "Peng Dehuai dui kangMei yuanChao," 1–10.

16. Quoted in Han, *Dangdai Zhongguo waijiao*, 37–38.

17. Zhou, "KangMei yuanChao baowei heping" (Resist America, aid Korea, and defend Peace), *Zhou Enlai xuanji* 2:51–53.

18. Hao and Zhai, "China's Decision to Enter the Korean War," 106.

19. Ibid.

20. Mark Mancall, *China at the Center: 300 Years of Foreign Policy*, 145.

21. John K. Fairbank, Edwin O. Reischauer, and Albert M. Craig, *East Asia: Tradition and Transformation*, 204, 397.

22. Zhou, "KangMei yuanChao baowei heping," 51–53.

23. Chai and Zhao, *Banmendian tanpan*, 39–40; for further discussions of the CCP-North Korean relationship during the Chinese civil war, see Bruce Cumings, *The Origins of the Korean War: The Roaring of the Cataract, 1947–1950*, 350–64.

24. Escott Reid to Lester B. Pearson, September 26 1950, vol. 10, War in Korea File, Department of External Affairs, Ottawa, Canada. I thank Professor William Stueck for sharing this document with me.

25. Han, *Dangdai Zhongguo waijiao*, 37–38.

26. Nie, *Nie Rongzhen huiyilu*, 740; Chai Chengwen also recalls Lin's hesitation about joining the war. When Chai was in Beijing in September 1950 reporting on the Korean situation, Lin once asked him if it were possible that China did not intervene and let Kim Il Sung "go to mountains to wage guerrilla warfare." See Chai and Zhao, *Banmendian tanpan*, 78.

27. Chang Lifu and Ji Yeli, "Zai xibei junzhengweiyuanhui yinian" (One year at the Northwest Military and Administrative Committee), *Renmin ribao*, October 27, 1988; Peng, *Peng Dehuai zishu*, 257.

28. Ibid., 257–58.

29. Xinghuo liaoyuan bianjibu, ed., *Jiefangjun jianglinzhuan* (Biographies of Liberation Army generals), 3:508; Yao, "Peng Dehuai dui kangMei yuanChao," 1–10.

30. Xinghuo liaoyuan bianjibu, ed., *Jiefangjun jianglinzhuan*, 3:509; for Zhou's trip to the Soviet Union, see Chai and Zhao, *Banmendian tanpan*, 83; Shi Zhe, *Zai Lishi juren shenbian: Shi Zhe huiyilu* (At the side of historical giants: She Zhe memoirs), 495–503.

31. Mao to Stalin, October 2, 1950, *Jianguo yilai Mao Zedong wengao*, 1:539–41.

32. Mao to Peng, October 23, 1950, ibid., 1:588–89.

33. Central Committee's telegram to Peng, December 4, 1950, quoted in Qi Dexue, "Guanyu kangMei yuanChao zhanzheng," 65.

34. For Zhou's first statement, see Zhou, "KangMei yuanChao baowei heping," 53; for his

second remark, see Zhou, "Women de waijiao fangzhen he renwu" (Our diplomatic principles and tasks), April 30, 1952, in *Zhou Enlai xuanji,* 2:89.

35. Chai and Zhao, *Banmendian tanpan,* 83; Hong, *KangMei yuanChao zhanzheng huiyi,* 24–27; Zhang, "Peng Dehuai shouming shuaishi," 147–51. In his memoirs, Khrushchev also mentioned Zhou's visit to Stalin; see Nikita Khrushchev, *Khrushchev Remembers: The Last Testament,* 371; idem, *Khrushchev Remembers: The Glasnost Tapes,* 147.

36. Chai and Zhao, *Banmendian tanpan,* 83; Hong, *KangMei yuanChao zhanzheng huiyi,* 26.

37. After the founding of the PRC, Xu Xiangqian was appointed chief of staff of the PLA, but because of poor health, he had to recuperate Qingdao. Therefore, Vice-chief of Staff Nie Rongzhen became the acting chief during 1949 and 1951. For Xu's account of his 1951 trip to Moscow, see Xu, *Lishi de huigu,* 799–805.

38. Ibid.

39. Yao, "Peng Dehuai dui kangMei yuanChao," 1–10. According to Khrushchev, the Soviet ambassador was "not a professional soldier" and had no "basic military training." Khrushchev, *Last Testament,* 370.

40. Peng, *Peng Dehuai zishu,* 261; Nie, *Nie Rongzhen huiyilu,* 744–45. For General Wu's activities at the United Nations, see Wu Xiuquan, *Zai waijiaobu banian de jingli, 1950, 1–1958, 10* (Eight-year experience at the Foreign Ministry, January 1950–October 1958), 35–71.

41. Yao, "Peng Dehuai dui kangMei yuanChao," 1–10.

42. Burton I. Kaufman, *The Korean War: Challenges in Crisis, Credibility, and Command,* 1.

43. Kirk to Acheson, June 25, 1950, *FRUS, 1950,* VII, 139; intelligence estimate by State Department Office of Intelligence Research, June 25, 1950, ibid., 149; CIA intelligence memorandum, no. 300, June 28, 1950, Truman Papers, President's Secretary's Files, box 250, Truman Library. The historian Bruce Cumings argues that the Korean War was basically a civil war; see Cumings, *The Origins of the Korean War: Liberation and the Emergence of Separate Regimes, 1945–1947.*

44. Harry S. Truman, *Memoirs: Years of Trial and Hope,* 333. Dwight Eisenhower wrote in his diary on June 30, 1950, "I believe we'll have a dozen Koreas soon if we don't take a firm stand." Diary entry, June 30, 1950, Robert H. Ferrell, ed., *The Eisenhower Diaries,* 175.

45. William W. Stueck, Jr., *Road to Confrontation: American Policy toward China and Korea, 1947–1950*; Charles M. Dobbs, *The Unwanted Symbol: American Foreign Policy, the Cold War, and Korea, 1945–1950.*

46. On this point, see Stephen Pelz, "U.S. Decisions on Korean Policy, 1943–1950: Some Hypotheses," 93–132.

47. For a full text of NSC 68, see *FRUS, 1950,* I, 237–92. For a comprehensive analysis of the relationship between the Korean War and NSC 68, see John Lewis Gaddis, *Strategies of Containment: A Critical Appraisal of Post-War American National Security Policy,* chap. 4.

48. Minutes of Bohlen meeting with British and French representatives, Paris, August 4, 1950, *FRUS, 1950,* VI, 420.

49. According to John Muccio, the American ambassador in South Korea, the rivalry between MacArthur's two aides, Generals Courtney Whitney and Charles Willoughby, prevented the general from receiving the intelligence he needed; John Muccio Oral History, p. 71, Truman Library. For standard accounts of the Truman-MacArthur feud, see John W. Spanier, *The Truman-MacArthur Controversy and the Korean War;* Richard H. Rovere and Arthur M. Schlesinger, Jr., *The MacArthur Controversy and American Foreign Policy;* Michael Schaller, *Douglas MacArthur: The Far Eastern General.*

50. "U.S. Courses of Action in Korea," draft memorandum prepared in the Department of Defense, July 31, 1950, *FRUS, 1950,* VII, 502–3.

51. Johnson to Allison, September 26, 1950, Marshall to Truman, September 27, 1950, ibid., VII, 781–82, 792–93; Kaufman, *Korean War,* 85–86.

52. Marshall to MacArthur, September 29, 1950, *FRUS, 1950*, VII, 826.

53. Tokyo to Foreign Office, October 3, 1950, FO371/84099, FK1022/373.

54. Truman, *Memoirs: Years of Trial and Hope*, 462–63.

55. Kaufman, *Korean War*, 88.

56. Spanier, *Truman-MacArthur Controversy*, 120; Mayers, *Cracking the Monolith*, 91.

57. Substance of statements made at Wake Island Conference on October 15, 1950, *FRUS, 1950*, VII, 948–60.

58. Foreign Office minute, June 26, 1950, FO371/84058, FK1015/62; chief of staff (50) minutes, 101st meeting, July 3, 1950, DEFE 4. On British initial reaction to the Korean War, see M. L. Dockrill, "The Foreign Office, Anglo-American Relations and the Korean War, June 1950–June 1951," 459–76.

59. Attlee to Truman, July 6, 1950, *FRUS, 1950*, VII, 314–15. After reading a draft of Truman's June 27 speech, the British Cabinet found the phrase "centrally directed Communist Imperialism" "ham-fisted." It was agreed to urge Washington to omit it. See Alan Bullock, *Ernest Bevin*, 791.

60. Acheson to Douglas, July 10, 1950, ibid., 347–52.

61. Bevin to Acheson, July 15, 1950, *FRUS, 1950*, VII, 395–99.

62. Ibid., 462–63.

63. On the British idea of a demilitarized zone, see Peter N. Farrar, "Britain's Proposal for a Buffer Zone South of the Yalu in November 1950: Was It a Neglected Opportunity to End the Fighting in Korea?" 327–51; Peter Lowe, *The Origins of the Korean War*, 199.

64. Menon to Bevin, November 21, 1950, FO800/462, FE/50/42.

65. Before he left for Washington, Attlee had talks with René Pleven, the French prime minister, who, aside from fearing use of the nuclear bomb, worried that the Americans intended to get the United Nations to declare China an aggressor and to use this as a justification to bomb targets in Manchuria. Furthermore, Pleven was concerned with Beijing's support of Ho Chi Minh in Indochina and was under strong domestic pressure to negotiate with the Chinese. Bullock, *Ernest Bevin*, 821–22.

66. U.S. delegation minutes of the first meeting between Truman and Attlee, December 4, 1950, *FRUS, 1950*, VII, 1361–74.

67. U.S. delegation minutes of the second meeting between Truman and Attlee, December 5, 1950, ibid., 1397–1403.

68. Ibid.

69. Kennan to Bohlen, December 5, 1950, Kennan Papers, box 29, 2-A, 1950, Mudd Library, Princeton University.

70. On this point, see Rosemary Foot, "Anglo-American Relations in the Korean Crisis: The British Effort to Avert an Expanded War, December 1950–January 1951," 43–57; William Stueck, "The Limits of Influence: British Policy and American Expansion of the War in Korea," 65–95.

71. Smith to State Department, May 23, 1954, *FRUS, 1952–54*, XVI, 895–99.

72. Boardman, *Britain and the People's Republic of China*, 54.

73. Quoted in Pollack, "Korean War and Sino-American Relations," 231.

5 EFFECTS OF THE KOREAN WAR, 1950–1952

1. NSC37, "The Strategic Importance of Formosa," December 1, 1948, *FRUS, 1949*, IX, 261–62.

2. Lovett to Truman, January 14, 1949, ibid., 265–66.

3. Bishop (chief of the State Department Division of Northeast Asian Affairs) memorandum of conversation with MacArthur, February 16, 1949, ibid., VII, 656–57.

4. CIA, "Review of the World Situation," December 1948, President's Secretary's File, Truman Papers, Truman Library.

5. NSC37, "The Strategic Importance of Formosa," December 1, 1948, *FRUS, 1949,* IX, 261–62.

6. NSC37/3, "The Strategic Importance of Formosa," February 11, 1949, ibid., 284–86.

7. Acheson statement at NSC meeting, March 1, 1949, ibid., 295.

8. Acheson to Stuart, February 14, 1949, ibid., 287–88; Merchant Oral History, p. 31, Truman Library.

9. Stuart to Acheson, March 23, 1949, *FRUS, 1949,* IX, 302–3; Edgar (consul at Taipei) to Acheson, May 4, 1949, ibid., 324–26.

10. Acheson statement at NSC meeting, March 1, 1949, ibid., 296.

11. Souers (executive secretary of NSC) to NSC, April 4, 1949, ibid., 307–8.

12. NSC37/9, "Possible United States Military Action toward Taiwan Not Involving Major Military Force," December 27, 1949, ibid., 460–61.

13. Sprouse memorandum of conversation between Merchant and Graves (British counselor), December 6, 1949, ibid., 435–37.

14. *Public Papers of the Presidents: Harry S. Truman, 1950* (1965), 11–12; Acheson, "Crisis in Asia—An Examination of U.S. Policy," *Department of State Bulletin* 22 (January 23, 1950): 111–18.

15. Acheson memorandum of meeting with Knowland and Smith, January 5, 1950, *FRUS, 1950,* VI, 263.

16. Acheson news conference, January 5, 1950, *Department of State Bulletin* 22 (January 16, 1950): 81.

17. Dulles memorandum, May 18, 1950, *FRUS, 1950,* I, 314–16.

18. NSC37/10, "Immediate United States Courses of Action with Respect to Formosa," August 3, 1950, *FRUS, 1950,* VI, 413–14.

19. Douglas to Acheson, May 25, 1949, *FRUS, 1949,* IX, 341–43.

20. Minutes of a meeting by representatives of France, the United Kingdom, and the United States in Paris, August 4, 1950, *FRUS, 1950,* VI, 421; Annex A to the telegram from Tamsui to Foreign Office, February 1, 1956, FO371/120912, FC1043/17.

21. Freeman (assistant chief of the Division of Chinese Affairs) memorandum of conversation between Dening and Butterworth, September 9, 1949, *FRUS, 1949,* IX, 388–90.

22. Ibid.

23. British Embassy to State Department, December 6, 1949, ibid., 437–38; Acheson memorandum of conversation, December 8, 1950, ibid., 442–43.

24. Bevin to Acheson, July 7, 1950, *FRUS, 1950,* VII, 329–31.

25. Acheson to Douglas, July 10, 1950, ibid., 347–52.

26. Younger to Bevin, July 11, 1950, FO371/94091.

27. Douglas to Acheson, July 24, 1950, *FRUS, 1950,* VI, 388–90.

28. Acheson to Douglas, July 28, 1950, ibid., 346–48.

29. Douglas to Acheson, July 29, 1950, ibid., 398–99.

30. Allison memorandum of conversation, October 23, 1950, ibid., 534; see also Wang Jisi, "The Origins of America's 'Two China' Policy," 201–2.

31. Dulles to Acheson, November 15, 1950, *FRUS, 1950,* VI, 572–73; Wang, "America's 'Two China' Policy," 202–3.

32. Chen Xiaolu, "China's Policy towards the United States, 1949–1955," 186.

33. Zhonggong zhongyang wenxian yanjiushi, *Zhou Enlai nianpu,* 833.

34. Xiao Jingguang, *Xiao Jingguang huiyilu* (Memoirs of Xiao Jingguang) (1988), 2:1–2.

35. Ibid., 7–8.

36. Yao Xu, *Cong Yalujiang dao Banmendian* (From the Yalu River to Panmunjom), 2.

37. Xiao, *Xiao Jingguang huiyilu* 2:26.

38. Junshi kexueyuan junshi lishi yanjiubu, ed., *Zhongguo renmin zhiyuanjun KangMei yuanChao zhanshi* (A war history of the Chinese People's Volunteers' War to Resist American and Aid Korea) (internal circulation), app. 5, 10.

39. Xiao, *Xiao Jingguang huiyilu* 2:50.

40. Shanghai renmin chubanshe, ed., *Yidai mingjiang: Huiyi Su Yu tongzhi* (A famous general: Reminiscences of Comrade Su Yu), 473–74.

41. Xiao, *Xiao Jingguang huiyilu* 2:29.

42. Han, *Dangdai Zhongguo waijiao*, 12–13; Beijing to Foreign Office, February 14, 1950, FO371/83285, FC1022/215.

43. Han, *Dangdai Zhongguo waijiao*, 12–13.

44. For Mao's remarks, see Mao, "On Coalition Government," April 24, 1945, *Selected Works of Mao Tse-tung*, 3:256. Before Dong's departure for San Francisco, the party Central Committee gave him the following instructions: "to win foreign friends, to improve the party's international position, and to try to stay and work in the United States." See "Dong Biwu nianpu" bianjizu, ed., *Dong Biwu nianpu* (A chronicle of Dong Biwu's life), 224. For an account of the CCP's attitudes toward the United Nations, see Byron S. Weng, "Communist China's Changing Attitudes Toward the United Nations," 677–704.

45. Han, *Dangdai Zhongguo waijiao*, 15; Clubb to Acheson, January 20, 1950, *FRUS, 1950*, II, 200.

46. Mao to Zhou, January 7, 1950, *Jianguo yilai Mao Zedong wengao*, 1:219–20.

47. The British representative to the Security Council, Sir Alexander Cadogan, told Trygve Lie that he suspected that the Soviet boycott "was based on a calculated policy" of isolating China from the international community. Lie concurred with this view. Trygve Lie, *In the Cause of Peace: Seven Years with the United Nations*, 258.

48. Mao to Liu, January 13, 1950, *Jianguo yilai Mao Zedong wengao*, 1:235–36.

49. Foreign Office to Hutchison, February 2, 1950, FO371/83283, FC1022/175.

50. In a message to the British Embassy in Cairo, the Foreign Office said that Bevin had "decided to make a serious effort to resolve the deadlock in the Security Council" on the issue of Chinese representation. Foreign Office to Cairo, March 8, 1950, FO371/88504, UP213/63.

51. *Department of State Bulletin* (January 16, 1950), 105.

52. Gross (Deputy U.S. representative at the United Nations) to Acheson, March 11, 1950, *FRUS, 1950*, II, 239.

53. Ross memorandum of conversation with Trygve Lie, February 25, 1950, ibid., II, 228; for Lie's lobbying, see James Barros, *Trygve Lie and the Cold War: The UN Secretary-General Pursues Peace, 1946–1953*, 217–38.

54. Beijing to Foreign Office, May, 1950, FO371/88417, UP123/48; FO371/88418, UP123/63.

55. Boardman, *Britain and the People's Republic of China*, 52.

56. Acheson to Austin, July 3, 1950, *FRUS, 1950*, VII, 247.

57. Douglas (American ambassador in Britain) to Acheson, July 8, 1950, ibid., 331.

58. Acheson to Bevin, July 10, 1950, ibid., 349–50.

59. Douglas to Acheson, July 11, 1950, ibid., 361; Kirk to Acheson, July 11, 1950, ibid., 360.

60. Acheson to Franks, August 4, 1950, ibid., II, 258–59.

61. Bevin to Franks, August 11, 1950, ibid., 259–62.

62. Ibid.

63. Gaddis, *Strategies of Containment: A Critical Appraisal of Postwar American National Security Policy*, 143.

64. Zhou's letter is quoted in Austin to Acheson, August 26, 1950, *FRUS, 1950*, VII, 267.

65. Acheson to acting secretary of state, September 19, 1950, ibid., 301–2; Tang,, *Britain's Encounter*, 138.

66. Delhi to Commonwealth Relations Office, September 23, 1950, FO371/88425, UP123/211; Tang, *Britain's Encounter,* 138–39.

67. Acheson to Morrison, May 25, 1951, *FRUS, 1951,* II, 247–48.

68. Austin to Acheson, May 25, 1951, ibid., 249–50; Bacon (special assistant in the Bureau of Far Eastern Affairs) to Clubb (director of the Office of Chinese Affairs), June 7, 1951, ibid., 255. Anti-British sentiment was increasing at the time, partly because London was widely suspected of having caused General MacArthur's removal in April and partly because it had continued trade with China. Furthermore, MacArthur's dismissal and Aneurin Bevan's resignation from the British cabinet had made possible a greater degree of Anglo–American unity in international affairs. On this point, see Porter, *Britain and the Rise of Communist China,* 63–64.

69. For accounts of the episode, see William M. Leary, Jr., "Aircraft and Anti-Communists: CAT in Action, 1949–52," 654–69; idem, *Perilous Mission: Civil Air Transport and CIA Covert Operations in Asia,* 91–99; Tang, *Britain's Encounter,* 187–90.

70. Leary, *Perilous Mission,* 91–99.

71. In his memoirs, Grantham described Donovan's attitude as "bullying." See Alexander Grantham, *Via Ports: From Hong Kong to Hong Kong,* 162.

72. Ringwalt Oral History, pp. 38–41, Truman Library; Tang, *Britain's Encounter,* 188.

73. Chennault to Clifford, January 14, 1950, Clifford Papers, box 2, the "China" folder, Truman Library.

74. Wang Shijie diary entry, January 23, 1963, quoted in Tao Yinghui, "Wang Shijie yu Lianghang an zhenxiang," in *Zhuanji wenxue* (Biographical literature) 335 (April 1990): 14–17. (Wang claimed in his diary that he was dismissed by Chiang Kai-shek from his position in December 1953 as a "scapegoat" for not having solved the aircraft issue as satisfactorily as Chiang had expected); Mansfield to Truman, January 25, 1950, Truman Papers, President's Secretary's Files, box 173, Truman Library.

75. Knowland's statement is quoted in Leary, *Perilous Mission,* 97.

76. *New York Times,* April 4, 1950.

77. *New York Times,* May 20, 1950; Han, *Dangdai Zhongguo waijiao,* 13.

78. Han, *Dangdai Zhongguo waijiao,* 20–21; Anna Chennault, *A Thousand Springs: The Biography of a Marriage,* 235–36.

79. Hu Qian, "Yingguo yinxiang" (Impressions of Britain), *Shijie zhishi* (January 1, 1951): 28–29; idem, "Zhimindihua de Yingguo" (Colonialized Britain), ibid. (January 13, 1951), 21–22.

80. Dai Qing, "Yingdi zenyang yapo Malaiya huaqiao" (How British imperialism oppressed overseas Chinese in Malaya) *Shijie zhishi* (April 14, 1951): 12–13; for backgrounds of the Malayan Emergency, see Richard L. Clutterbuck, *The Long, Long War: Counterinsurgency in Malaya and Vietnam;* Anthony Short, *The Communist Insurrection in Malaya, 1948–1960.*

81. Zhou, "Wei gonggu he fazhan renmin de shengli er fendou" (Struggle for the consolidation and development of people's victory), September 30, 1950, in *Zhou Enlai xuanji,* 2:36.

82. "Fensui Meidiguozhuyi jiandie de zuie huodong" (Smashing the evil activities of American imperialist spies), *Shijie zhishi* (March 3, 1951): 2.

83. For Zhou Enlai's statement, see Han, *Dangdai Zhongguo waijiao,* 194–95; "Fensui Dulesi cedong dandu duiRi gouhe de yingmou" (Smashing Dulles's plot to conclude an exclusive peace treaty with Japan), *Shijie zhishi* (January 27, 1951): 3.

84. Mao to Stalin, May 6, 1952, *Jianguo yilai Mao Zedong wengao,* 2:274.

85. Cited in Ronald C. Keith, *The Diplomacy of Zhou Enlai,* 51.

86. Han, *Dangdai Zhongguo waijiao,* 195.

87. Notes of conversation between Dulles and George Yeh (Chinese Nationalist foreign minister), November 19, 1952, Koo Papers, box 187, Columbia University; Draft Joint Statement of the U.K. and U.S. Governments, "Chinese Participation and Formosa," June 19, 1951, *FRUS, 1951,* VI (pt. 1), 1134; see also Howard B. Schonberger, *Aftermath of War: Americans and the Remaking of Japan, 1945–1952,* 270–71.

88. Scott memorandum, September 26, 1951, FO371/92603; Dulles memorandum of conversation with Morrison, September 9, 1951, *FRUS, 1951*, VI (pt. 1), 1343–44.

89. For detailed treatments of this issue, see Michael Schaller, "Securing the Great Crescent: Occupied Japan and the Origins of Containment in Southeast Asia," 392–414; Andrew J. Rotter, *The Path to Vietnam: Origins of the American Commitment to Southeast Asia.*

90. Notes of conversation between Dulles and Yeh, November 19, 1952, Koo Papers, box 187, Columbia University; see also Chihiro Hosoya, "Japan, China, the United States, and the United Kingdom, 1951–2: The Case of the 'Yoshida Letter,'" 247–59; Schonberger, *Aftermath of War,* 273–78.

91. Dulles to Churchill, January 17, 1952, Dulles Papers, box 58, "Churchill" folder, Mudd Library, Princeton University; Dwight D. Eisenhower, *The White House Years: Mandate for Change, 1953–1956,* 142; Michael A. Guhin, *John Foster Dulles: A Statesman and His Time,* 264. In his discussion with George Yeh on November 19, 1952, Dulles also related British dislike of him as secretary of state; see notes of conversation between Dulles and Yeh, November 19, 1952, Koo Papers, box 187, Columbia University.

6   CONCLUSION OF THE KOREAN WAR, 1952–1953

1. Dulles to Eisenhower, April 12, 1954, Dulles Papers, White House Memoranda Series, box 1, Eisenhower Library; Eisenhower diary entry, January 6, 1953, Ferrell, ed., *Eisenhower Diaries,* 222–23.

2. Lodge (U.S. representative at the United Nations) memorandum of conversation, June 26, 1954, *FRUS, 1952–54,* VI, pt. 1, 1110.

3. Radford to U.S. consulate at Geneva, April 27, 1954, ibid., 1031.

4. Churchill to Eisenhower, December 7, 1954, Whitman File, International Series, box 17, "Churchill, July–December, 1954 (4)" folder, Eisenhower Library; see also *FRUS, 1952–54,* VI, pt. 1, 1056.

5. Notes of conversation with Churchill, April 14–17, 1955, Syracuse, Sicily, Whitman File, Administration Series, box 25, "Clare Boothe Luce (1)" folder, Eisenhower Library.

6. For a profile of Eden as Churchill's foreign secretary, see Shlaim, Jones, Sainsbury, *British Foreign Secretaries,* 81–109; Anthony Adamthwaite, "Introduction: The Foreign Office and Policy-Making," 13.

7. Negotiating paper, "Divergence of U.S. and British Policies Respecting China," January 5, 1952, Truman Papers, President's Secretary's Files, box 116, central file, Churchill-Truman meeting, Truman Library; Eden's authorized biographer Robert Rhodes James writes that although Eden had reservations about the Labor government's swift recognition of the PRC, "he was a realist." Robert Rhodes James, *Anthony Eden,* 333.

8. Gifford (U.S. ambassador in Britain) to State Department, December 29, 1951, *FRUS, 1952–54,* VI, pt. 1, 725.

9. Bradley notes of a dinner meeting, January 5, 1952, ibid., 740.

10. Truman-Churchill talks, January 8, 1952, President's Secretary's File, box 116, Truman Library; see also U.S. delegation minutes of the third formal meeting between Truman and Churchill, January 8, 1952, *FRUS, 1952–54,* VI, pt. 1, 784.

11. Ibid.

12. Acheson memorandum of a dinner meeting, January 5, 1952, ibid., 734.

13. Acheson memorandum of a dinner meeting, January 6, 1952, ibid., 743.

14. Ibid., 743–44; U.S. delegation minutes of the third formal meeting between Truman and Churchill, January 8, 1952, ibid., 782–85.

15. Ibid.

16. Adamthwaite, "Foreign Office and Policy-Making," 3.

17. Acheson memorandum of a dinner meeting, January 5, 1952, Bradley notes of the same meeting, ibid., 735, 741.

18. Quoted in Peter Lowe, "The Settlement of the Korean War," 209.

19. Johnson to Matthews, November 21, 1951, *FRUS, 1951*, VII, pt. 1, 1154–56.

20. Barnes (deputy director of the Executive Secretariat for the State Department) memorandum of conversation, November 28, 1951, ibid., 1189–93.

21. Quoted in Lowe, "Settlement of the Korean War," 210.

22. British Embassy to State Department, December 3, 1951, *FRUS, 1951*, VII, pt. 1, 1221–23.

23. Callum MacDonald, *Korea: The War Before Vietnam*, 131–33.

24. *Public Papers of the Presidents: Harry S. Truman, 1952–1953*, 321.

25. Kaufman, *Korean War*, 239–40; Barton J. Bernstein, "The Struggle over the Korean War Armistice: Prisoners of Repatriation?" 280.

26. Foreign Office minute, January 29, 1952, FO371/99561, FK1071/52, quoted in MacDonald, *Korea*, 144.

27. Lord Reading minute, May 8, 1952, FO371/99572, FK1071/228, quoted in MacDonald, *Korea*, 144–45.

28. Quoted in Lowe, "Settlement of the Korean War," 215–16.

29. MacDonald, *Korea*, 145; Lowe, "Settlement of the Korean War," 214.

30. Ibid., 217.

31. Rosemary Foot, *The Wrong War: American Policy and the Dimensions of the Korean Conflict, 1950–1953*, 178; Jon Halliday and Bruce Cumings, eds., *Korea: The Unknown War*, 187–88.

32. Halliday and Cumings, *Korea*, 187–88; Kaufman, *Korean War*, 277–78.

33. Foot, *Wrong War*, 179.

34. Kaufman, *Korean War*, 278.

35. Ibid., 277.

36. Foot, *Wrong War*, 185–86; Dean Acheson, *Present at the Creation: My Years in the State Department*, 701–3.

37. Bernstein, "Struggle over the Korean War Armistice," 304; Foot, *Wrong War*, 186.

38. During the 1950s and 1960s, Eisenhower was generally perceived as a naive, inactive, and disinterested president who left most foreign policy issues to his associates. In the 1970s and 1980s, however, largely owing to the availability of new documents, historians have come to modify their low regard of the president. The revisionist literature portrays Eisenhower as an effective leader who knew how to delegate power while maintaining ultimate control. His leadership style has been termed a "hidden-hand" presidency. See, for example, Fred I. Greenstein, *The Hidden-Hand Presidency: Eisenhower as Leader;* Richard Melanson and David Allan Mayers, eds., *Reevaluating Eisenhower: American Foreign Policy in the Fifties;* for historiographical surveys of the revisionist literature, see Vincent DeSantis, "Eisenhower Revisionism," 190–207; Gary Reichard, "Eisenhower as President: The Changing View," 265–81; Mary McAuliffe, "Commentary: Eisenhower, the President," 625–32; Arthur M. Schlesinger, Jr., "The Ike Age Revisited," 1–11; Robert Burk, "Eisenhower Revisionism Revisited: Reflections on Eisenhower Scholarship," 196–209; Stephen G. Rabe, "Eisenhower Revisionism: A Decade of Scholarship," 97–115.

39. Kaufman, *Korean War*, 292–93.

40. Foot, *Wrong War*, 221–23; MacDonald, *Korea*, 177.

41. MacDonald, *Korea*, 177.

42. Memorandum of discussion at the 139th meeting of the NSC, April 8, 1954, *FRUS, 1952–54*, XIV, pt. 1, 181.

43. Gaddis, *Long Peace*, 123–24.

44. For Eisenhower's statement, see his address to the United Nations, December 8, 1953, *Public Papers of the Presidents: Dwight D. Eisenhower*, 815.

45. Memorandum of discussion at the 131st meeting of the NSC, February 11, 1953, *FRUS, 1952–54,* XV, pt. 1, 769–70.

46. Memorandum of the substance of discussion at a State Department-Joint Chiefs of Staff meeting, March 27, 1953, ibid., 817.

47. Memorandum of discussion at the 143d meeting of the NSC, May 6, 1953, ibid., 977.

48. Memorandum of discussion at a special meeting of the NSC, March 31, 1953, ibid., 827.

49. Memorandum of discussion at the 145th meeting of the NSC, May 20, 1953, ibid., 1065.

50. Gaddis, *Long Peace,* 125–26.

51. *New York Times,* December 15, 1952.

52. Emmet John Hughes, *The Ordeal of Power: A Political Memoir of the Eisenhower Years,* 105.

53. Dulles memorandum of conversation, May 21, 1953, *FRUS, 1952–54,* XV, pt. 1, 1068.

54. MacDonald, *Korea,* 179–80; Kaufman, *Korean War,* 313–14.

55. MacDonald, *Korea,* 180.

56. Eden's statement was enclosed in Allison's memorandum to Eisenhower, February 2, 1953, *FRUS, 1952–54,* XIV, 136.

57. Eisenhower to Churchill, February 2, 1953, Whitman File, International Series, box 16, the "President-Churchill, January 20, 1953–May 28, 1953 (6)" folder, Eisenhower Library.

58. Dulles to Eisenhower, March 6, 1953, *FRUS, 1952–54,* XV, pt. 1, 806.

59. Lowe, "Settlement of the Korean War," 223.

60. Johnson memorandum of conversation, May 4, 1953, *FRUS, 1952–54,* XV, pt. 1, 968–69.

61. Kaufman, *Korean War,* 315–16.

62. Lowe, "Settlement of the Korean War," 225.

63. Du, *Zai zhiyuanjun zongbu,* 579.

64. Nie, *Nie Rongzhen huiyilu,* 765.

65. Du, *Zai zhiyuanjun zongbu,* 559.

66. Yang, *Weile heping,* 173. At this time, General Yang was the second deputy commander of the CPV.

67. Ibid., 177.

68. Junshi kexueyuan junshi lishi yanjiubu, *Zhongguo renmin zhiyuanjun,* app. 5, 44.

69. Yang, *Weile heping,* 177.

70. Junshi kexueyuan junshi lishi yanjiubu, *Zhongguo renmin zhiyuanjun,* app. 5, 44; Du, *Zai zhiyuanjun zongbu,* 559–60.

71. Yang, *Weile heping,* 189.

72. *Renmin ribao,* February 8, 1953.

73. Han, *Dangdai Zhongguo waijiao,* 49

74. Ibid.

75. Quoted in Simmons, *Strained Alliance,* 233.

76. Chai and Zhao, *Banmendian tanpan,* 258; Joseph C. Goulden, *Korea: The Untold Story of the War,* 630.

77. Chai and Zhao, *Banmendian tanpan,* 258.

78. Ibid., 258–59.

79. MacDonald, *Korea,* 184.

80. Clark to the Joint Chiefs of Staff, May 7, 1953, *FRUS, 1952–54,* XV, pt. 1, 979–81.

81. Chai and Zhao, *Banmendian tanpan,* 260.

82. Rosemary Foot, *A Substitute for Victory: The Politics of Peace Making at the Korean Armistice Talks,* 170–71. Sherman Adams wrote, "Resentment against Rhee for his stubborn refusal to participate in the truce proceedings ran so high behind the scenes in Washington that Eisenhower had to remind the Republican legislative leaders that our enemy in Korea was still the Reds not Rhee." Sherman Adams, *Firsthand Report: The Inside Story of the Eisenhower Administration,* 99.

83. Denis Stairs, *The Diplomacy of Constraint: Canada, the Korean War, and the United States,* 276–77.

84. Foot, *Substitute for Victory,* 177.

85. Second restricted tripartite meeting of the heads of government, Bermuda, December 7, 1953, *FRUS, 1952–54,* V, 1811–13.

86. Foot, *Substitute for Victory,* 177–81; Sarvepalli Gopal, *Jawaharlal Nehru: A Biography,* 2:148. Roger Dingman's study of nuclear diplomacy during the Korean War has shown that "nuclear weapons were not easily usable tools of statecraft that produced predictable results." Roger Dingman, "Atomic Diplomacy During the Korean War," 50–91.

87. The "Three-Anti" campaign focused on the corruption, waste, and bureaucracy of officials. The "Five-Anti" movement was directed at tax evasion, bribery, fraud, embezzlement of state assets, and theft of economic secrets. For Mao's criticism of Liang's thinking, see Mao, "Speech on the Victory in Resisting U.S. and Aiding Korea Movement," September 12, 1953, in *Selected Works of Mao Tse-tung,* 5:115–20.

88. Chen Xiaolu, "China's Policy towards the United States," 239.

89. McGeorge Bundy, *Danger and Survival: Choices about the Bomb in the First Fifty Years,* 241.

90. Nogee and Donaldson, *Soviet Foreign Policy since World War II,* 105.

91. Jervis, *Perception and Misperception in International Politics,* 348.

7 SETTLEMENT OF THE INDOCHINA CRISIS, 1954

1. William J. Duiker, *Vietnam: Nation in Revolution,* 43–44.

2. Luo Guibo, "Shaoqi tongzhi paiwo chushi Yuenan" (Comrade Shaoqi sent me to Vietnam), 233–42.

3. Mao to Liu, January 17, 1950, in *Jianguo yilai Mao Zedong wengao,* 1:238.

4. Jacques Dalloz, *The War in Indo-China, 1945–54,* 129.

5. Luo, "Shaoqi tongzhi paiwo chushi Yuenan," 235–36.

6. Mao and Zhou to Liu, February 1, 1950, in *Jianguo yilai Mao Zedong wengao,* 1:254.

7. Hoang Van Hoan, *Canghai yisu: Hoang Van Hoan geming huiyilu* (A drop in the ocean: Hoang Van Hoan's revolutionary reminiscences), 255–56. For evidence of Ho's visit to the Soviet Union in February 1950, see Wu, *Zai waijiaobu banian de jingli,* 13.

8. Han and Tan, *Dangdai Zhongguo jundui de junshi gongzuo,* 1:518–20.

9. Luo, "Shaoqi tongzhi paiwo chushi Yuenan," 238.

10. In late 1950 and early 1951, Mao sent many telegrams to PLA commanders in South China asking them to step up their campaigns of bandit elimination. These telegrams are included in *Jianguo yilai Mao Zedong wengao,* vols. 1, 2.

11. Shi, "Peitong Maozhuxi fangSu," 10.

12. Jean Lacouture, *Ho Chi Minh: A Political Biography,* 46; David Halberstan, *Ho,* 44; Luo, "Shaoqi tongzhi paiwo chushi Yuenan," 236; *Renmin ribao,* May 19, 1990.

13. Han and Tan, *Dangdai Zhongguo jundui de junshi gongzuo,* 1:519.

14. For the episode of Qianlong's intervention in Vietnam during 1788 and 1790, see Truong Buu Lam, "Intervention versus Tribute in Sino-Vietnamese Relations, 1788–1790," in Fairbank, *Chinese World Order,* 165–79.

15. Han and Tan, *Dangdai Zhongguo jundui de junshi gongzuo,* 1:522.

16. Ibid., 520.

17. Ibid., 522.

18. Ibid., 526.

19. Mu Xin, ed., *Ji Chen Geng jiangjun* (Commemorating General Chen Geng), 248–49; Hoang, *Canghai yisu,* 273–74.

20. Han and Tan, *Dangdai Zhongguo jundui de junshi gongzuo*, 1:527–34.
21. Wu, *Zai waijiaobu banian de jingli*, 13.
22. Hoang, *Canghai yisu*, 259.
23. Robert S. Ross, *The Indochina Tangle: China's Vietnam Policy, 1975–1979*, 18.
24. King C. Chen, *Vietnam and China, 1938–1954*, 276.
25. Melvin Gurtov, *The First Vietnam Crisis: Chinese Communist Strategy and United States Involvements, 1953–1954*, 9; Ross, *Indochina Tangle*, 19.
26. Han, *Dangdai Zhongguo waijiao*, 80–81.
27. Ibid., 56.
28. For the text of the Berlin communiqué, see State Department Press Release, February 19, 1954, *FRUS, 1952–54*, XVI, 415.
29. Han, *Dangdai Zhongguo waijiao*, 64–65.
30. Shi Zhe participated in Zhou's three visits to the Soviet Union. See Shi Zhe, "Rineiwa huiyi sanyi" (Random recollections of the Geneva Conference), 37–44. Khrushchev wrote in his memoirs that before the Geneva Conference the Soviet Union, China and North Vietnam held a preparatory meeting in Moscow "to work out the position" they would take at Geneva. China was represented by Zhou Enlai, Vietnam by President Ho Chi Minh and Prime Minister Pham Van Dong. Khrushchev, *Last Testament*, 481.
31. Shi, "Rineiwa huiyi sanyi," 38. Zhou even included two master cooks in the Chinese delegation so that at Geneva he could hold Chinese banquets to "make friends." See Wang Bingnan, *ZhongMei huitan jiunian huigu* (Recollections of the nine years of the Sino-American talks), 7.
32. Ibid., 5–7.
33. Ibid., 6.
34. Shi, "Rineiwa huiyi sanyi," 38.
35. Han, *Dangdai Zhongguo waijiao*, 51–52; Keith, *Diplomacy of Zhou Enlai*, 61.
36. Khrushchev, *Last Testament*, 482. China's desire to focus on domestic reconstruction was also noted by Western observers in China. British chargé in Beijing Humphrey Trevelyan told the American delegation at Geneva on May 14 that "the Chinese Communist regime is not interested in pushing forward externally for the time being but wishes to concentrate on internal developments." See memorandum of conversation with Trevelyan, by Edwin Martin (advisor to the U.S. delegation to the Geneva Conference), May 14, 1954, *FRUS, 1952–54*, XVI, 804.
37. Han, *Dangdai Zhongguo waijiao*, 67; Wang, *ZhongMei huitan jiunian huigu*, 11. Kuo-kang Shao has argued that a key element in Zhou Enlai's diplomacy in Indochina during the 1954–55 period was his effort to "neutralize" the area. Kuo-kang Shao, "Zhou Enlai's Diplomacy and the Neutralization of Indo-China, 1954–55," 483–504.
38. "Shixian Yazhou heping he anquan de genben daolu" (The basic route to the realization of peace and security in Asia) *Shijie zhishi* (May 20, 1954): 3; "Yazhou renmin de yuanwang shi juedui burong hushi de" (The aspiration of the Asian people cannot absolutely be ignored), ibid. (June 5, 1954): 3.
39. Han, *Dangdai Zhongguo waijiao*, 65–66; Wang, *ZhongMei huitan jiunian huigu*, 12.
40. Zhou, "Zai Rineiwa huiyi shang guanyu Yindu-Zhina wenti de fayan" (Speech on the Indochina question at the Geneva Conference), May 12, 1954, in *Zhou Enlai waijiao wenxuan* (Selected works of Zhou Enlai on diplomacy), 70.
41. Chen, *Vietnam and China*, 309.
42. Shi, "Rineiwa huiyi sanyi," 42.
43. Dillon (U.S. ambassador to France) to State Department, June 24, 1954, *FRUS, 1952–54*, XVI, 1240–41.
44. Shi, "Rineiwa huiyi sanyi," 43.
45. Han, *Dangdai Zhongguo waijiao*, 66–67.
46. For a complete text of the Geneva Accords, see Chen, *Vietnam and China*, app. 4, 375–405.

47. Wang, *ZhongMei huitan jiuian huigu*, 13.

48. For Zhou's statement to Reston, see Seymour Topping, *Journey Between Two Chinas*, 152; for Zhou's remarks to Salisbury, see Harrison E. Salisbury, *To Peking and Beyond: A Report on the New Asia*, 225–26. In 1979, the Vietnamese government issued a white paper on Sino-Vietnamese relations, on which it charged that "the Chinese leaders betrayed the revolutionary struggle of the peoples of Viet Nam, Laos and Kampuchea." See Ministry of Foreign Affairs of the Socialist Republic of Viet Nam, *The Truth about Vietnam-China Relations over the Last Thirty Years*, 23. In his memoirs, Wang refuted the Vietnamese charge as "a vicious, untruthful attack and slander." Wang, *ZhongMei huitan jiunian huigu*, 12.

49. David J. Dallin, *Soviet Foreign Policy after Stalin*, 153; Nogee and Donaldson, *Soviet Foreign Policy since World War II*, 111.

50. Smith to State Department, May 21, 1954, *FRUS, 1952–54*, XVI, 875.

51. Dulles to State Department, January 30, 1954, ibid., XIV, pt. 1, 353–54.

52. Smith to State Department, May 21, 1954, ibid., XVI, 898.

53. Ibid., 898–99. According to Shi Zhe, the Chinese, Soviet, and Vietminh delegations maintained frequent consultations during the Geneva Conference. The Soviet delegation stayed in a Soviet-owned house in Geneva in which most important Sino-Soviet discussions were conducted. Every couple of days, Zhou would go to Molotov's place to talk. When the Soviet Foreign Minister returned Zhou's visits, they never discussed important issues at the villa the Chinese delegation rented for fear that the building might have been bugged. Shi, "Rineiwa huiyi sanyi," 39.

54. Ibid., 41.

55. Dulles to State Department, May 1, 1954, *FRUS, 1952–54*, XVI, 648.

56. Shi, "Rineiwa huiyi sanyi," 37–38.

57. Khrushchev, *Last Testament*, 482–83; Smith to State Department, May 21, 1954, *FRUS, 1952–54*, XVI, 875.

58. Shuckburgh diary entry, May 5, 1954, Evelyn Shuckburgh, *Descent to Suez: Diaries 1951–56*, 193.

59. Ibid.

60. Shuckburgh diary entry, May 9, 1954, ibid., 198.

61. Smith to State Department, June 2, 1954, *FRUS, 1952–54*, XVI, 1011.

62. Humphrey Trevelyan, *Living with the Communists*, 83. Eden disclosed in his memoirs that at a dinner he held for Zhou at Geneva, when he "twitted" the Chinese Foreign Minister about not sending a representative to London, Zhou immediately expressed a willingness to do so. The Chinese clearly left a favorable impression on his host because Eden wrote: "Chou is poised and firm in negotiation. He works for the fine point, even by the standard of his country." Anthony Eden, *Full Circle*, 138.

63. Trevelyan, *Living with the Communists*, 82–83. During his negotiations with the Chinese at Geneva, Trevelyan also inquired on behalf of the United States the condition of detained Americans in China. Smith to State Department, May 17, 1954, *FRUS, 1952–54*, XIV, pt. 1, 417–18.

64. Martin memorandum of conversation with Trevelyan, May 14, 1954, *FRUS, 1952–54*, XVI, 803–6.

65. Morgan Phillips, *East Meets West*, 42; Trevelyan, *Living with the Communists*, 118–19.

66. Ji Chaoding, "Kuozhan ZhongYing maoyi de juda kenengxing" (The great opportunity in expanding Sino-British trade), *Shijie zhishi* (August 20, 1954): 5–6.

67. Su Chao, "Zhanwang ZhongYing guanxi" (Forecasting Sino-British relations), *Shijie zhishi* (September 5, 1954): 10–12.

68. For British attitudes toward Indochina, see Geoffrey Warner, "Britain and the Crisis over Dien Bien Phu, April 1954: The Failure of United Action," and "From Geneva to Malina: British Policy toward Indochina and SEATO, May–September, 1954," 55–77, 149–67.

69. Gary Hess, "Redefining the American Position in Southeast Asia: The United States and the Geneva and Malina Conferences," 126.

70. Dulles to State Department, February 18, 1954, *FRUS, 1952–54*, XVI, 17.

71. State Department Press Release, February 19, 1954, ibid., 415.

72. Mayers, *Cracking the Monolith*, 130.

73. *Congressional Record*, January 14, 1954, 250–51.

74. For Dulles's statement, see C. L. Sulzberger, *A Long Row of Candles*, 1003. In his memoirs, Wang Bingnan denied that Dulles refused to shake hands with Zhou Enlai. Wang, *ZhongMei huitan jiunian huigu*, 21–22.

75. Johnson memorandum of conversation, July 13, 1954, *FRUS, 1952–54*, XVI, 1352.

76. Johnson to State Department, June 2, 1954, ibid., 1251.

77. Godley (First Secretary of U.S. Embassy in France) to State Department, April 21, 1954, ibid., XIII, 1334.

78. Eden, *Full Circle*, 136.

79. Dulles to Knowland, June 30, 1954, Dulles Papers, box 79, "China, 1954" folder, Mudd Library, Princeton University.

80. For detailed treatments of Dulles's "wedge" strategy, see Gaddis, *Long Peace*, 147–94; Mayers, *Cracking the Monolith;* Chang, *Friends and Enemies*.

81. Wang, *ZhongMei huitan jiunian huigu*, 23–24; U. Alexis Johnson, *The Right Hand of Power*, 233–34.

82. Hagerty diary, June 3, 1954, *FRUS, 1952–54*, XIV, 442.

83. For documentation on these negotiations, see *FRUS, 1952–54*, XIV, pt. 1, 414–15, 416–21, 427, 434–43, 462–80, 501–5.

84. *Renmin ribao*, July 22, 1954.

8 First Offshore-Island Crisis, 1954–1955

1. Xiao Feng, "Nanwang de jiaohui" (Unforgettable teaching), 299–301. As acting commander of the Twenty-eighth Army, Xiao Feng directed the landing operation on Quemoy. See also Ye Fei, *Ye Fei huiyilu*, 597–609.

2. Ye Fei, *Ye Fei huiyilu*, 612–14.

3. Nie Fengzhi, Wang De, Wu Zaowen, and Hu Shihong, eds., *Sanjun huige zhan Donghai* (A campaign by the three armed services in the East China Sea), 38.

4. Ibid., 26; He Di, "The Evolution of the People's Republic of China's Policy toward the Offshore Islands," 222–45.

5. Ibid.

6. Allison memorandum of conversation between Dulles and Koo, March 19, 1953, *FRUS, 1952–54*, XIV, pt. 1, 158. See also notes of conversation with Dulles, March 19, 1953, Koo Papers, box 187, Columbia University.

7. Rankin to State Department, December 19, 1953, *FRUS, 1952–54*, XIV, pt. 1, 343.

8. Robertson (assistant secretary of state for Far Eastern affairs) to Dulles, February 25, 1954, ibid., 367–68.

9. Ibid., 369.

10. Stolper, *China, Taiwan, and the Offshore Islands*, 23–24.

11. McConaughy (director of the Office of Chinese Affairs) memorandum of conversation between Dulles and Koo, May 19, 1954, *FRUS, 1952–54*, XIV, pt. 1, 422–25; notes of conversation with Dulles, May 19, 1954, Koo Papers, box 191, Columbia University.

12. Rankin to the State Department, May 29, 1954, *FRUS, 1952–54*, XIV, pt. 1, 437–38.

13. Nie, *Sanjun huige zhan Donghai*, 2–3.

14. Cutler (special assistant to the president for National Security Affairs) memorandum of conversation, May 22, 1954, *FRUS, 1952–54*, XIV, pt. 1, 428–29.

15. McConaughy memorandum of conversation, July 1, 1954, ibid., 486–88.

16. Robertson to Dulles, August 25, 1954, ibid., 548–50.

17. Jernegan (assistant secretary of state for Near Eastern, South Asian, and African Affairs) to Robertson, August 27, 1954, ibid., 551.

18. MacArthur to Harold Waddell (Bureau of Far Eastern Affairs), August 27, 1954; Bowie (director of Policy Planning Staff) to Robertson, August 27, 1954; and Merchant (assistant secretary of state for European Affairs) to Robertson, August 27, 1954, ibid., 552–53.

19. Smith (acting secretary of state) to Robertson, September 1, 1954, ibid., 555.

20. Dulles to Smith, September 5, 1954, Smith memorandum of telephone conversation with Eisenhower, September 6, 1954, Smith to U.S. Embassy in the Philippines, September 6, 1954, ibid., 572–74; Eisenhower-Smith telephone conversation, September 6, 1954, Whitman File, DDE Diaries, box 7, "phone calls, June–December, 1954 (2)" folder. Smith also related the decision to Sir R. Scott, British ambassador, September 7, 1954, FO371/11023.

21. Anderson (acting defense secretary) to Eisenhower, September 3, 1954, *FRUS, 1952–54,* XIV, pt. 1, 556–57; memorandum of discussion at the 213th meeting of NSC, September 9, 1954, ibid., 586.

22. Memorandum of discussion at the 214th meeting of the NSC, September 12, 1954, ibid., 619.

23. Ibid., 619–21; Dulles memorandum, September 12, 1954, ibid., 612.

24. Memorandum of discussion at the 214th meeting of the NSC, September 12, 1954, ibid., 619–20.

25. Nancy Bernkopf Tucker, "Cold War Contacts: America and China, 1952–1956," 251.

26. Memorandum of discussion at the 214th meeting of NSC, September 12, 1954, *FRUS, 1952–54,* XIV, pt. 1, 619–20.

27. Foreign Office to New York, September 18, 1954, FO371/110231; Dulles to Eisenhower, September 18, 1954, *FRUS, 1952–54,* V, 1227–28.

28. Foreign Office minute, September 16, 1954, FO371/110231, FC1024/8G.

29. Gruenther (supreme commander of Allied Powers Europe) to Eisenhower, February 8, 1955, Whitman File, Administration Series, box 16, "Gruenther, 1955 (4)" folder, Eisenhower Library.

30. Eisenhower, *Mandate for Change,* 609; Eden, *Full Circle,* 343–44.

31. Sir Pierson Dixon, head of the British delegation to the United Nations, pointed out the difficulties that would confront countries recognizing the PRC "in arguing that the latter lacks the right to extend its control over territory which is unquestionably Chinese and virtually part of [the] Chinese mainland." New York to Foreign Office, September 23, 1954, FO371/110231, FC1042/12A. The British chargé in Beijing, Trevelyan, also worried that London's participation in Oracle would "harden the Chinese attitude toward us." Trevelyan to Foreign Office, December 12, 1954, FO371/110241, FC1042/249G.

32. Foreign Office to New York, September 28, 1954, FO371/110231, FC1042/12A; Dulles to State Department, September 28, 1954, *FRUS, 1952–54,* XIV, pt. 1, 664.

33. Bond (deputy director of the Office of United Nations Political and Security Affairs) memorandum of conversation, October 8, 1954, *FRUS, 1952–54,* XIV, pt. 1, 710–13.

34. Bond memorandum of conversation, October 9, 1954, ibid., 716–20. Dulles told the Nationalist foreign minister, George Yeh, later that Oracle "was especially designed to preclude the raising of any question of the status of Formosa or that of the mainland or that of the admission of Red China into the United Nations." Notes of conversation between Dulles and Yeh, November 2, 1954, Koo Papers, box 191, Columbia University.

35. Bond memorandum of conversation, October 10, 1954, *FRUS, 1952–54,* XIV, pt. 1, 724–28.

36. McConaughy memorandum of conversation between Dulles and Yeh, February 10, 1955, *FRUS, 1955–57,* II, 258.

37. Bohlen to State Department, October 2, 1954, *FRUS, 1952–54,* XIV, pt. 1, 674.

38. Minutes of the NSC meeting, October 6, 1954, ibid., 690.

39. Hagerty diary, February 3, 1955, *FRUS, 1955–57,* 203. For more discussions on America's wedge policy toward China and the Soviet Union during the Quemoy crisis in 1954–55, see Gaddis, *Long Peace,* 184–85; Mayers, *Cracking the Monolith,* 140–41; Chang, *Friends and Enemies,* 128–31.

40. For the activities of the pro-Chiang Congressmen during the crisis, see Harry Harding, "The Domestic Sources of Foreign Policy: The Quemoy Crisis of 1954–1955 and 1958" (Paper, Stanford University, 1970), 4–5.

41. Radford memorandum, October 29, 1954, *FRUS, 1952–54,* XIV, pt. 1, 817–19; Rosemary Foot, "Search for a *Modus Vivendi,*" 152–53.

42. Rankin to State Department, October 5, 1954, *FRUS, 1952–54,* XIV, pt. 1, 682–83.

43. Robertson to Dulles, October 7, 1954, ibid., 706–7.

44. Dulles memorandum to Robertson, October 8, 1954, ibid., 709. Nancy Bernkopf Tucker, "A House Divided: The United States, the Department of State, and China," 48.

45. McConaughy memorandum of conversation, October 13, 1954, *FRUS, 1952–54,* XIV, pt. 1, 728–53.

46. Foreign Office to Washington, October 15, 1954, FO371/110234, FC1042/68G.

47. Washington to Foreign Office, October 15, 1954, FO371/110234, FC1042/72.

48. Makins to Foreign Office, October 18, 1954, FO371/110235, FC1042/84G.

49. Merchant memorandum of conversation, November 5, 1954, *FRUS, 1952–54, XIV,* pt. 1, 866.

50. Notes of conversation between Dulles and Yeh, November 2, 1954, Koo Papers, box 191, Columbia University. See also Su Ge, "'A Horrible Dilemma': The Making of the U.S.-Taiwan Mutual Defense Treaty, 1948–1954" (Ph.D. diss., Brigham Young University, 1987), 354–55; Stolper, *China, Taiwan, and the Offshore Islands,* 50–52.

51. For the text of the treaty, see U.S. Department of State, *American Foreign Policy, 1950–1955: Basic Documents,* 945–47; Gaddis, *Long Peace,* 135.

52. *Renmin ribao,* December 5, 1954.

53. The *Guangming ribao* comment is quoted in Trevelyan to Foreign Office, December 8, 1954, FO371/110241, FC1042/237; *Da gong bao,* December 7, 1954.

54. Mao to Peng and Su, December 11, 1954, *Jianguo yilai Mao Zedong wengao,* 4:627.

55. Soviet military advisers in China were involved in the planning for the attack on Yijiangshan. Owing to divergent military backgrounds, they sometimes differed with Chinese commanders, who viewed the Soviet experts as dogmatic. For instance, drawing on their past experiences, the Soviets suggested that the PLA sail at night and launch the landing on Yijiangshan at dawn. But Zhang Aiping did not adopt this recommendation. Taking into consideration the topography of the island and the PLA's lack of experience in coordinated warfare, as well as the fact that the mainland now enjoyed naval and air control over the island, the Chinese general decided it was better to carry out the operation during the day. His plan proved successful. Nie, *Sanjun huige zhan Donghai,* 45–57.

56. Ibid.

57. Memorandum of telephone conversation between Eisenhower and Dulles, January 18, 1955, *FRUS, 1955–57,* II, 37–38; Dulles memorandum of conversation with the president, January 19, 1955, ibid., 41–43.

58. Mao to Peng, February 2, 1955, *Jianguo yilai Mao Zedong wengao,* 5:23; Peng's instruction to Zhang is quoted in Nie, *Sanjun huige zhan Donghai,* 57.

59. Memorandum of conversation between Dulles and Yeh, January 19, 1955, *FRUS, 1955–57,* II, 46–50; notes of conversation between Dulles and Yeh, January 19, 1955, Koo Papers, box 195, Columbia University.

60. Memorandum of conversation between Dulles and Makins, January 19, 1955, *FRUS, 1955–57,* II, 44–46; Foot, "Search for a *Modus Vivendi,*" 154.

61. Memorandum of discussion at the 233d meeting of the NSC, January 21, 1955, *FRUS, 1955–57,* II, 90–91.

62. Memorandum of discussion at the 232d meeting of the NSC, January 20, 1955, ibid., 69–82.

63. Memorandum of discussion at the 233d meeting of the NSC, January 21, 1955, ibid., 89–96.

64. Memorandum of conversation between Dulles and Makins, January 21, 1955, ibid., 96–99.

65. For the Formosa Resolution, see Public Law 4, ibid., 162–63.

66. Hoover (acting secretary of state) to Rankin, January 31, 1955, ibid., 182–84.

67. Rankin to State Department, February 2, 1955, ibid., 193–95.

68. Han, *Dangdai Zhongguo waijiao,* 75.

69. Zhou Enlai, "Fandui Lianheguo ganshe Zhongguo neizheng" (Opposing the United Nations' intervention in China's internal affairs), February 5, 1955, in Zhou, *Zhou Enlai waijiao wenxuan,* 106–8; Han, *Dangdai Zhongguo waijiao,* 75. Dulles was very unhappy with Hammarskjöld's communications with Zhou Enlai. He said to Makins that this exchange of correspondence was "extremely dangerous" because it might be "misunderstood" in Beijing. Memorandum of conversation between Dulles and Makins, February 9, 1955, *FRUS, 1955–57,* II, 246–47.

70. Memorandum of conversation between Dulles and Makins, February 9, 1955, ibid., 243–47.

71. Eisenhower to Churchill, February 10, 1955, ibid., 259–61.

72. Churchill to Eisenhower, undated, ibid., 270–73.

73. Dulles to the Embassy in the United Kingdom, February 18, 1955, ibid., 292–95.

74. Dulles to State Department, February, 25, 1955, ibid., 307–10.

75. Ibid.

76. Dulles memorandum of conversation with the president, March 6, 1955, ibid., 336–37; for Dulles's radio and television address on March 8, 1955, see *Department of State Bulletin,* March 21, 1955, 459–64.

77. Eisenhower news conference, March 16, 1955, *Public Papers of the Presidents: Dwight D. Eisenhower, 1955,* 332. Eisenhower later wrote in his memoirs that "I hoped this answer would have some effect in persuading the Chinese Communists of the strength of our determination." Eisenhower, *Mandate for Change,* 477.

78. Gaddis, *Long Peace,* 137.

79. Cutler memorandum of Eisenhower meeting with Dulles and other advisers, March 11, 1955, *FRUS, 1955–57,* II, 355–60.

80. Eden to Dulles, March 25, 1955, ibid., 397–98.

81. Dulles to Eden, March 26, 1955, ibid., 404–5.

82. Eden to Dulles, March 28, 1955, ibid., 416–17.

83. Eisenhower to Churchill, March 29, 1955, ibid., 418–22.

84. Hoover memorandum of Eisenhower's meeting with advisers, April 1, 1955, ibid., 439–41; Dulles memorandum of conversation with Eisenhower, April 4, 1955, ibid., 444–45; Eisenhower to Dulles, April 5, 1955, ibid., 445–50.

85. Dulles memorandum of conversation with the president, April 4, 1955, ibid., 444–45.

86. Memorandum of conversation between Eisenhower and Dulles, April 17, 1955, ibid., 491–93.

87. Ibid.

88. Robertson to Dulles, April 25, 1955, ibid., 510–17.

89. When Chiang remained firm, the president sympathized. Eisenhower later wrote in his memoirs: "Despite my disappointment, I could not help reflecting that if I had been in his position, I might well have made the same decision." Eisenhower, *Mandate for Change,* 481–82.

90. Han, *Dangdai Zhongguo waijiao,* 77–78.

91. Wang, *ZhongMei huitan jiunian huigu,* 44.

92. Liu Xiao, *Chushi Sulian banian* (Eight years as ambassador to the Soviet Union), 9–13. Thomas Stolper has said that the "discrepancy between China's conflict with the United States and Russia's hopes for détente grew larger as the United States and the USSR moved toward the [Geneva] summit. The discrepancy may have produced some pressure on Peking to lessen the conflict." Stolper, *China, Taiwan, and the Offshore Islands,* 101.

93. John Wilson Lewis and Xue Litai, *China Builds the Bomb,* 35–39.

94. Kalicki, *Pattern of Sino-American Crises,* 164; Stolper, *China, Taiwan, and the Offshore Islands,* 106; Tucker, "Cold War Contacts: America and China," 255.

95. Foot, "Search for a *Modus Vivendi,*" 158.

96. Han, *Dangdai Zhongguo waijiao,* 97–98.

97. Ibid., 99.

9 SECOND OFFSHORE-ISLAND CRISIS, 1958

1. Dulles memorandum of conversation with the president, August 5, 1955, Dulles Papers, White House Memorandum Series, box 3, "meetings with the president, 1955 (3)" folder, Eisenhower Library; Stolper, *China, Taiwan and the Offshore Islands,* 115.

2. For Eisenhower's remarks to Knowland, see Robert H. Ferrell, ed., *The Diary of James C. Hagerty: Eisenhower in Mid-Course, 1954–55,* 173. For Dulles's statement, see McConaughy memorandum, February 27, 1954, *FRUS, 1952–54,* XIV, pt. 1, 369.

3. Judd to Eisenhower, March 12, 1955, Dulles Papers, White House Memoranda Series, "White House correspondence, General 1955 (4)" folder, Eisenhower Library.

4. Quoted in Will Brownell and Richard Billings, *So Close to Greatness: A Biography of William C. Bullitt,* 320.

5. Dulles San Francisco speech, June 28, 1957, *Department of State Bulletin* (July 15, 1957): 94; Gaddis, *Long Peace,* 186; Qiang Zhai, "Dulles, Wedge, and the Sino-American Ambassadorial Talks, 1955–1957," 29–44.

6. Jonathan Howe, *Multicrises: Sea Power and Global Politics in the Missile Age,* 167.

7. C. T. Crowe (Foreign Office) to Sir Hubert Graves (Washington), January 9, 1956, FO371/120912, FC1043/1. Eisenhower suspected that Chiang's main purpose in concentrating large numbers of troops on the offshore islands was to ensure U.S. participation in their defense. Howe, *Multicrises,* 173.

8. Memorandum of discussion at the 338th meeting of the NSC, October 2, 1957, *FRUS, 1955–57,* III, 617.

9. For Zhou's activities in Poland and Hungary in early 1957, see Liu, *Chushi Sulian banian,* 33–39. During his visit in Moscow in January 1957, Zhou Enlai sent a message to Tito proposing that China and Yugoslavia cosponsor an international conference of Communist parties to coordinate their activities. But the Yugoslav leader did not support this proposal. Wu, *Zai waijiaobu banian de jingli,* 101–2.

10. Liu, *Chushi Sulian banian,* 57; Kalicki, *Pattern of Sino-American Crises,* 167.

11. Nogee and Donaldson, *Soviet Foreign Policy since World War II,* 120; Chang, *Friends and Enemies,* 205–6.

12. For revelations about the Mao-Khrushchev talk in the summer of 1958, see Fei Delin (Nikola T. Fedorenko), "Heluxiaofu fangwen Beijing" (Khrushchev visits Beijing), in *Shijieshi yanjiu dongtai* (Developments in world history studies) 25 (July 1989): 36–41, 48. This is an excerpt of Fedorenko's memoirs in Chinese translation. Fedorenko was Soviet deputy foreign minister between 1955 and 1958. He accompanied Khrushchev on his visit to China July 31–August 3, 1958.

13. Barnett, *China and the Major Powers in East Asia,* 33–34; Chang, *Friends and Enemies,* 206.

14. Fei Delin, "Heluxiaofu fangwen Beijing," 37.

15. Wang, *ZhongMei huitan jiunian huigu,* 69; Roderick MacFarquhar, "The China Problem in Anglo-American Relations" in Louis and Bull, *"Special Relationship,"* 315.

16. For the Great Leap Forward, see Jonathan Spence, *The Search for Modern China,* 574–83.

17. Han and Tan, *Dangdai Zhongguo jundui de junshi gongzuo,* 1:385–87; He, "Evolution of the People's Republic of China's Policy," 234.

18. Han and Tan, *Dangdai Zhongguo jundui de junshi gongzuo*, 1:387.

19. Ibid., 387–88; Ye, *Ye Fei huiyilu*, 650.

20. Han and Tan, *Dangdai Zhongguo jundui de junshi gongzuo*, 1:390; Ye, *Ye Fei huiyilu*, 650–51.

21. Ye, *Ye Fei huiyilu*, 655.

22. Goodpaster memorandum of conversation with the president, August 11, 1958, Whitman File, DDE Diaries, box 33, "August 1958 staff notes (2)" folder, Eisenhower Library.

23. Goodpaster memorandum of conversation with the president, August 12, 1958, Whitman File, DDE Diaries, box 21, "August 1958, staff notes (2)" folder, Eisenhower Library.

24. For Dulles's statement, see *Department of State Bulletin*, September 8, 1958, 379. Eisenhower later wrote in his memoirs that the letter was intentionally "well-publicized." Eisenhower, *Waging Peace*, 296.

25. The day before the bombardment commenced, White House Press Secretary James Hagerty said: "The Chinese Communists have been trying to find out for years what we might do if they tried to take Matsu and Quemoy on the way to Formosa. As far as I'm concerned, they can keep on guessing." Quoted in Kalicki, *Pattern of Sino-American Crises*, 206.

26. Memorandum of conversation between Tong and Parsons, August 25, 1958, 793.00/8-2558, box 3924, RG59, National Archives, Washington, D.C. (hereafter referred to as NA).

27. Ibid.

28. Ibid.

29. Richard K. Betts, *Nuclear Blackmail and Nuclear Balance*, 68.

30. Ibid.

31. *New York Times*, August 28, 1958.

32. Gaddis, *Long Peace*, 141–45.

33. Eisenhower, *Waging Peace*, 293.

34. Memorandum of conversation between State and Defense Departments officials, August 28, 1958, 793.00/8-2858, box 3924, RG59, NA.

35. Ibid.

36. Memorandum of conversation between State and Defense Department officials, September 3, 1958, 793.00/9-358, box 3924, RG59, NA.

37. *New York Times*, September 5, 1958.

38. Han and Tan, *Dangdai Zhongguo jundui de junshi gongzuo*, 1:400; Kalicki, *Pattern of Sino-American Crises*, 193.

39. Quoted in Allen S. Whiting, "Quemoy 1958," 265.

40. Kalicki, *Pattern of Sino-American Crises*, 193.

41. Ye, *Ye Fei huiyilu*, 659–60.

42. Ibid., 661–62.

43. He, "Evolution of the People's Republic of China's Policy," 236–37; Han, *Dangdai Zhongguo waijiao*, 106.

44. Commonwealth Relations Office to Ottawa, August 28, 1958, FO371/133525, FCN1193/61(a).

45. Dalton minute, "Situation in the Formosa Strait," September 8, 1958, FO371/133525, FCN1193/42A.

46. Memorandum of conversation between Hood and Herter, August 30, 1958, 793.00/8-3058, box 3924, RG59, NA.

47. Cheetham (U.K. permanent delegation to NATO) to Foreign Office, September 2, 1958, FO371/133525, FCN1193/42.

48. Dalton minute, "Situation in the Formosa Strait," September 8, 1958, FO371/133525, FCN1193/42A.

49. O'Neill minute, September 9, 1958, FO371/133529, FCN1193/165.

50. Ibid.

51. Millar minute, September 10, 1958, FO371/133528, FCN1193/140.

52. Harold Macmillan, *Riding the Storm, 1956–1959,* 545.

53. Foot, "Search for a *Modus Vivendi*," 160; Lord Beloff, "The Crisis and its Consequences for the British Conservative Party," 333; Alistair Horne, *Harold Macmillan: Volume II, 1956–1986,* 23–27.

54. Dalton minute, "Situation in the Formosa Strait," September 9, 1958, FO371/133529, FCN1193/173.

55. Ibid.

56. Ibid.

57. Millar minute, September 9, 1958, FO371/133529, FCN1193/165.

58. Dalton minute, "Situation in the Formosa Strait," September 9, 1958, FO371/133529, FCN1193/173.

59. Gaitskell to Macmillan, September 15, 1958, FO371/133530, FCN1193/204.

60. Macmillan to Gaitskell, September 16, 1958, FO371/133530, FCN1193/204; Macmillan, *Riding the Storm,* 553–54.

61. Lloyd to Foreign Office, September 19, 1958, FO371/133531, FCN1193/249.

62. Lloyd to Foreign Office, September 17, 1958, FO371/133530, FCN1193/217.

63. Lloyd to Foreign Office, September 22, 1958, FO371/133532, FCN1193/250.

64. Commonwealth Relations Office to Ottawa, September 3, 1958, FO371/133525, FCN1193/68.

65. Memorandum of conversation between Hood and Herter, August 30, 1958, 793.00/8–3058, box 3924, RG59, NA; Dalton minute, "Situation in the Formosa Strait," September 1, 1958, FO371/133535, FCN1193/326.

66. Memorandum of conversation between Hood and Herter, August 30, 1958, 793.00/8–3058, box 3924, RG59, NA.

67. Lloyd to Foreign Office, September 17, 1958, FO371/133530, FCN1193/217.

68. Lloyd to Foreign Office, September 19, 1958, FO371/133531, FCN1193/242.

69. Caccia to Foreign Office, September 23, 1958, FO371/133532, FCN1193/264.

70. Lloyd to Foreign Office, September 22, 1958, FO371/133532, FCN1193–250.

71. Lloyd to Foreign Office, September 24, 1958, FO371/133532, FCN1193/278.

72. *Renmin ribao,* September 3, 1958.

73. *Da gong bao,* October 14, 1958.

74. *Renmin ribao,* November 3, 1958.

75. Dixon to Foreign Office, September 17, 1958, FO371/133530, FCN1193/217.

76. Liu, *Chushi Sulian banian,* 72; Han, *Dangdai Zhongguo waijiao,* 115.

77. Soviet Vice-Foreign Minister M. S. Kapista later wrote that the Chinese did not fully inform Khrushchev of their intentions toward the offshore islands when Khrushchev visited Beijing just before the crisis. Kapista, *The CPR: Two Decades—Two Politics,* 194. Fedorenko made no mentioning of the offshore islands in his recollection of the Khrushchev-Mao talks in Beijing between July 31 and August 3, 1958.

78. On October 4, 1958, the Soviet chargé in China, Antonov, told his British counterpart in Beijing that the Soviet Union "had no previous knowledge that the Chinese would open the bombardment on Quemoy." It was a "pity," the Soviet diplomat said, that the United States did not believe this. Beijing to Foreign Office, October 4, 1958, FO371/133536, FCN1193/404.

79. Alice Hsieh, *Communist China's Strategy in the Nuclear Era,* 124; John Thomas, "The Limits of Alliance: The Quemoy Crisis of 1958," 131.

80. Ibid., 133–34.

81. Han, *Dangdai Zhongguo waijiao,* 115.

82. Kapitsa, *CPR: Two Decades—Two Politics,* 194.

83. Andrei Gromyko, *Memoirs,* 251–52.

84. For the Chinese government's statement, see *Renmin ribao* (overseas ed.), March 1, 1988. Gordon H. Chang tends to dismiss the credibility of Gromyko's account. Chang, *Friends and Enemies*, 190.

85. Quoted in Kalicki, *Pattern of Sino-American Crises*, 194–95.

86. Ibid., 195.

87. Ibid.

88. Han, *Dangdai Zhongguo waijiao*, 115–16. The Chinese later accused Khrushchev of "asking China to agree to the U.S. scheme of creating 'two Chinas'" at the time of his trip to Beijing in the fall of 1959. See "Statement of the Spokesman of the Chinese Government," September 1, 1963, *Beijing Review*, September 6, 1963, 7–16.

89. Eisenhower, *Waging Peace*, 293.

90. Goodpaster memorandum of conversation with the president, August 14, 1958, Whitman File, Dwight D. Eisenhower (DDE) Diaries, box 21, the "August 1958, staff notes (2)" folder, Eisenhower Library.

91. Memorandum of conversation between State and Defense Department officials, September 3, 1958, 793.00/9-358, box 3924, RG59, NA.

92. Memorandum of conversation between Dulles and Canadian Ambassador Robertson, September 9, 1958, 793.00/9-958, box 3924, RG59, NA.

93. On the CIA analysis, see Chang, *Friends and Enemies*, 187; Gaddis, *Long Peace*, 186–87.

94. Gray memorandum of Eisenhower meeting with U.S. delegation to Geneva technical military conference on surprise attack. November 5, 1958, Whitman Files, DDE Diaries, box 23, "Staff notes, November 1958" folder, Eisenhower Library.

95. Quoted in Gaddis, *Long Peace*, 187.

96. Record of State Department meeting, October 8, 1958, 793.00/10-858, box 3926, RG59, NA.

97. He, "Evolution of the People's Republic of China's Policy," 239.

98. Goodpaster memorandum of conversation with the president, September 29, 1958, Whitman File, DDE Diaries, box 22, the "Staff notes, September 1958" folder, Eisenhower Library; Record of Defense and State Departments meeting, October 10, 1958, 793.00/10-1058, box 3926, RG59, NA.

99. Kalicki, *Pattern of Sino-American Crises*, 196.

100. Ibid., 197.

101. Ibid., 198.

102. He, "Evolution of the People's Republic of China's Policy," 240.

103. Han and Tan, *Dangdai Zhongguo jundui de junshi gongzuo*, 1:411–12.

104. Memorandum of conversation between Yeh and Robertson, October 7, 1958, RG59, 793.00/10-758, box 3926, NA.

105. Han and Tan, *Dangdai Zhongguo jundui de junshi gongzuo*, 1:413–14.

106. Memorandum of conversation between Dulles and Yeh, October 13, 1958, RG59, 793.00/10-1358, box 3926, NA.

107. Han and Tan, *Dangdai Zhongguo jundui de junshi gongzuo*, 1:415.

108. Kalicki, *Pattern of Sino-American Crises*, 200. After returning to Washington, Dulles told Eisenhower on October 24 that "there was some considerable difficulty in getting the 'non-force' declaration" from Chiang. Dulles memorandum of conversation with Eisenhower, October 24, 1958, Dulles Papers, White House memorandums, box 7, "Meetings with president, July–December 1958" folder, Eisenhower Library.

109. Dulles memorandum of conversation with Eisenhower, October 24, 1958, Dulles Papers; Eisenhower, *Waging Peace*, 303–4.

110. Harding, "Domestic Sources of Foreign Policy," 25; Chang, *Friends and Enemies*, 186.

111. Memorandum of conversation between Robertson and Yeh, October 29, 1958, RG59, 793.00/10-2958, box 3927, NA.

112. Han and Tan, *Dangdai Zhongguo jundui de junshi gongzuo*, 1:416.

113. *New York Times*, November 2, 1958; "Interview with Chinese Communist Foreign Minister on Taiwan Strait Crisis," November 12, 1958, RG59, 793.00/11–1258, box 3927, NA.

CONCLUSION

1. Phillip Darby, *Three Faces of Imperialism: British and American Approaches to Asia and Africa, 1870–1970*, 143–44.

2. Paul Kennedy, *Strategy and Diplomacy, 1870–1945*, 19.

3. Hunt, *Making of a Special Relationship*; McLean, "American Nationalism," 25–42.

4. John Colville, *The Fringes of Power: 10 Downing Street Diaries, 1939–1955*, 693.

5. Quoted in M. L. Dockrill, "The Foreign Office, Anglo-American Relations and the Korean War," 475.

6. Whiting, *China Crosses the Yalu*, 169.

7. Schaller, *Douglas MacArthur*, 231.

8. Thorne, *Allies of a Kind*.

Bibliography

CHINESE-LANGUAGE SOURCES

Published Documents, Memoirs, Diaries, Books, and Articles

Bao Mingrong 鮑明榮 and Hu Guangzheng 胡光正. "Qiantan Mao Zedong junshi sixiang zai kangMei yuanChao zhanzheng zhong de yunyong he fazhan de jige wenti" 淺談毛澤東軍事思想在抗美援朝戰爭中的運用和發展的幾個問題 (A preliminary inquiry into the application and development of Mao Zedong military thought during the War to Resist America and Aid Korea). *Dangshi yanjiu* 黨史研究 (Study of party history) 6 (1983): 32–41.

Bo Yibo 薄一波. *Ruogan zhongda juece yu shijian de huigu* 若干重大決策與事件的回顧 (Recollections of certain important decisions and events). Vol. 1. Beijing: Zhonggong zhongyang dangxiao chubanshe, 1991.

Chai Chengwen 柴成文 and Zhao Yongtian 趙勇田. *Banmendian tanpan* 板門店談判 (Panmunjom negotiations). Beijing: Jiefangjun chubanshe, 1989.

———. *KangMei yuanCho jishi* 抗美援朝紀實 (A record of the War to Resist America and Aid Korea). Beijing: Zhonggong dangshi ziliao chubanshe, 1987.

Chang Lifu 常黎夫 and Ji Yeli 姬也力. "Zai xibei junzhengweiyuanhui yinian" 在西北軍政委員會一年 (One year at the Northwest Military and Administrative Committee) in *Renmin ribao* 人民日報 (People's Daily), October 27, 1988.

Chen Geng 陳賡. *Chen Geng riji* 陳賡日記 (Chen Geng diaries). 2 vols. Beijing: Jiefangjun chubanshe, 1984.

Chen Yun 陳雲. *Chen Yun wenxuan, 1926–1949* 陳雲文選, 1926–1949 (Selected works of Chen Yun, 1926–1949). Beijing: Renmin chubanshe, 1984.

———. *Chen Yun wenxuan, 1949–1956* 陳雲文選, 1949–1956 (Selected works of Chen Yun, 1949–1956). Beijing: Renmin chubanshe, 1984.

Chen Zaidao 陳再道. *Chen Zaidao huiyilu* 陳再道回憶錄 (Memoirs of Chen Zaidao). 2 vols. Beijing: Jiefangjun chubanshe, 1988–1991.

Cheng Hua 程華. *Zhou Enlai he tade mishu* 周恩來和他的秘書 (Zhou Enlai and his secretaries). Beijing: Zhongguo guangbo dianshi chubanshe, 1992.

249

Cheng Zihua 程子華. *Cheng Zihua huiyilu* 程子華回憶錄 (Memoirs of Cheng Zihua). Beijing: Jiefangjun chubanshe, 1987.

Dai Qing 戴菁. "Yingdi zenyang yapo Malaiya huaqiao" 英帝怎樣壓迫馬來亞華僑 (How British imperialism oppressed overseas Chinese in Malaya). *Shijie zhishi* 世界知識 (World knowledge) (April 14, 1951), 12–13.

"Dangdai Zhongguo renwu zhuanji" congshu bianjizu "當代中國人物傳記" 叢書編輯組, ed. *Chen Yi Zhuan* 陳毅傳 (A biography of Chen Yi). Beijing: Dangdai Zhongguo chubanshe, 1991.

Deng Liqun 鄧力群. "Xinjiang heping jiefang qianhou: ZhongSu guanxi zhi yiye" 新疆和平解放前後: 中蘇關係之一頁 (Around the peaceful liberation of Xinjiang: One page in the history of Sino-Soviet relations). *Jindaishi yanjiu* 近代史研究 (Study of modern history) 5 (1989): 143–50.

Deng Xiaoping 鄧小平. *Deng Xiaoping wenxuan, 1938–1965* 鄧小平文選, 1938–1965 (Selected works of Deng Xiaoping, 1938–1965). Beijing: Renmin chubanshe, 1989.

──────. *Deng Xiaoping wenxuan, 1975–1982* 鄧小平文選, 1975–1982 (Selected works of Deng Xiaoping, 1975–1982). Beijing: Renmin chubanshe, 1982.

"Dong Biwu nianpu" bianjizu "董必武年譜" 編輯組, ed. *Dong Biwu nianpu* 董必武年譜 (A chronicle of Dong Biwu's life). Beijing: Zhongyang wenxian chubanshe, 1991.

Du Ping 杜平. *Zai zhiyuanjun zongbu* 在志願軍總部 (At the headquarters of the Chinese People's Volunteers). Beijing: Jiefangjun chubanshe, 1989.

Fei Delin 費德林 (Nikola T. Fedorenko). "Heluxiaofu fangwen Beijing" 赫魯曉夫訪問北京 (Khrushchev visits Beijing). *Shijieshi yanjiu dongtai* 世界史研究動態 (Developments in world history studies) 125 (July 1989): 36–41, 48.

"Fensui Dulesi cedong dandu duiRi gouhe de yingmou" 粉碎杜勒斯策動單獨對日勾和的陰謀 (Smashing Dulles's plot to conclude an exclusive peace treaty with Japan). *Shijie zhishi* (January 27, 1951), 3.

"Fensui Meidiguozhuyi jiandie de zuie huodong" 粉碎美帝國主義間諜的罪惡活動 (Smashing the evil activities of American imperialist spies). *Shijie zhishi* (March 3, 1951), 2.

Fujian renmin chubanshe 福建人民出版社, ed. *Huainian Li Zhimin jiangjun* 懷念李志民將軍 (In memory of general Li Zhimin). Fuzhou: Fujian renmin chubanshe, 1988.

Geng Biao 耿飇. *Geng Biao huiyilu* 耿飇回憶錄 (Memoirs of Geng Biao). Beijing: Jiefangjun chubanshe, 1991.

Han Huaizhi 韓懷智 and Tan Jingjiao 譚旌樵, eds. *Dangdai Zhongguo jundui de junshi gongzuo* 當代中國軍隊的軍事工作 (The military work of the contemporary Chinese army). 2 vols. Beijing: Zhongguo shehui kexue chubanshe, 1989.

Han Nianlong 韓念龍, ed. *Dangdai Zhongguo waijiao* 當代中國外交 (Contemporary Chinese diplomacy). Beijing: Zhongguo shehui kexue chubanshe, 1987.

Han Xia 韓俠. "Xizang xiandai gemingshi yanjiu gaishu" 西藏現代革命史研究概述 (A bibliographical survey of modern Tibetan revolutionary history). *Zhonggong dangshi yanjiu* 中共黨史研究 (Study of Chinese Communist party history). 1 (1990): 73–79.

He Changgong 何長工. *He Changgong huiyilu* 何長工回憶錄 (Memoirs of He Changgong). Beijing: Jiefangjun chubanshe, 1987.

He Jinxiu 何靜修 et al., eds. *Mianhuai Liu Shaoqi* 緬懷劉少奇 (Remembering Liu Shaoqi). Beijing: Zhongyang wenxian chubanshe, 1988.

He Long 賀龍. *He Long junshi wenxuan* 賀龍軍事文選 (Selected military works of He Long). Beijing: Jiefangjun chubanshe, 1989.

He Yanhong 何延虹. "Qingyi shensihai: ji Zhou Enlai yu Hu Zhiming de jiaowang" 情誼深似海: 記周恩來與胡志明的交往 (Friendship as deep as the sea: Zhou Enlai's associations with Ho Chi Minh). *Renwu* 人物 (Biographical sketches) 4 (1991): 5–12.

Hoang Van Hoan 黃文歡. *Canghai yisu: Hoang Van Hoan geming huiyilu* 滄海一粟: 黃文歡革命回憶錄 (A drop in the ocean: Hoang Van Hoan's revolutionary reminiscences). Beijing: Jiefangjun chubanshe, 1987.

Hong Xuezhi 洪學智. *KangMei yuanChao zhanzheng huiyi* 抗美援朝戰爭回憶 (Recollections of the War to Resist America and Aid Korea). Beijing: Jiefangjun wenyi chubanshe, 1990.

Hu Guangzheng 胡光正. "Yingming de juece weida de chengguo: Lun kangMei yuanChao zhanzheng de chubing canzhan juece" 英明的決策, 偉大的成果: 論抗美援朝戰爭的出兵參戰決策 (Wise decision and great result: On the decision of entering the War to Resist America and Aid Korea). *Dangshi yanjiu* 1 (1983): 33–38.

Hu Qian 胡其安. "Yingguo yinxiang" 英國印象 (Impressions of Britain). *Shijie zhishi* (January 1, 1951), 28–29.

———. "Zhimindihua de Yingguo" 殖民地化的英國 (Colonialized Britain). *Shijie zhishi* (January 13, 1951), 21–22.

Huang Zheng 黃錚. *Hu Zhiming yu Zhongguo* 胡志明與中國 (Ho Chi Minh and China). Beijing: Jiefangjun chubanshe, 1987.

Hunan renmin chubanshe 湖南人民出版社, ed. *Huainian He Long tongzhi* 懷念賀龍同志 (In memory of Comrade He Long). Changsha: Hunan renmin chubanshe, 1979.

Ji Chaoding 冀朝鼎. "Kuozhan Zhong Ying maoyi de juda kenengxing" 擴展中英貿易的巨大可能性 (The great opportunity in expanding Sino-British trade). *Shijie zhishi* (August 20, 1954), 5–6.

Jiang Hua 江華. *Zhuiyi yu sikao: Jiang Hua huiyilu* 追憶與思考: 江華回憶錄 (Recollections and reflections: Memoirs of Jiang Hua). Hangzhou: Zhejiang renmin chubanshe, 1991.

Jin Chongji 金冲及, ed. *Zhou Enlai zhuan, 1898–1949* 周恩來傳, 1898–1949 (A biography of Zhou Enlai, 1898–1949). Beijing: Renmin chubanshe, 1989.

Jin Ye 金冶, ed. *Huiyi Tan Zhenlin* 回憶譚震林 (Reminiscences of Tan Zhenlin). Hangzhou: Zhejiang renmin chubanshe, 1992.

Junshi kexueyuan junshi lishi yanjiubu 軍事科學院軍事歷史研究部, ed. *Zhongguo renmin zhiyuanjun kangMei yuanCao zhanshi* 中國人民志願軍抗美援朝戰史 (A war history of the Chinese People's Volunteers' War to Resist America and Aid Korea). Beijing: Junshi kexue chubanshe, 1988.

Junshi kexueyuan "Ye Jianying zhuan" bianxiezu 軍事科學院 "葉劍英傳" 編寫組, ed. *Ye Jianying zhuanlüe* 葉劍英傳略 (A brief biography of Ye Jianying). Beijing: Junshi kexue chubanshe, 1987.

Li Yinqiao 李銀橋. "Zaishuo Jiang Qing xiangma de wangshi" 再說江青降馬的往事 (Recalling Jiang Qing's story of taming the horse). *Zhuanji wenxue* 傳記文學 (Biographical literature) 332 (January 1990): 40–51.

Liu Shaoqi 劉少奇. *Liu Shaoqi xuanji* 劉少奇選集 (Selected works of Liu Shaoqi). Beijing: Renmin chubanshe, 1984.

Liu Xiao 劉曉. *Chushi Sulian banian* 出使蘇聯八年 (Eight years as ambassador to the Soviet Union). Beijing: Dangshi ziliao chubanshe, 1986.

Liu Zhen 劉震. *Liu Zhen huiyilu* 劉震回憶錄 (Memoirs of Liu Zhen). Beijing: Jiefangjun chubanshe, 1990.

Lu Dingyi 陸定一. *Lu Dingyi wenji* 陸定一文集 (Selected works of Lu Dingyi). Beijing: Renmin chubanshe, 1992.

Lü Xingdou 呂星斗, ed. *Liu Shaoqi he tade shiye* 劉少奇和他的事業 (Liu Shaoqi and his careers). Beijing: Zhonggong dangshi chubanshe, 1991.

Lü Zhengchao 呂正操. *Lü Zhengchao huiyilu* 呂正操回憶錄 (Memoirs of Lü Zhengchao). Beijing: Jiefangjun chubanshe, 1987.

Luo Guibo 羅貴波. "Shaoqi tongzhi paiwo chushi Yuenan" 少奇同志派我出使越南 (Comrade Shaoqi sent me to Vietnam). In He Jin xiu et al., *Mianhuai Liu Shaoqi*, 233–42.

Luo Meiling 駱美玲. "KangMei YuanChao zhong zhengqu jianli guoji tongyi zhanxian de douzheng" 抗美援朝中建立國際統一戰綫的鬥爭 (The struggle to establish an international united front during the War to Resist America and Aid Korea). *Hubei daxue xuebao* 湖北大學學報 (Journal of Hubei University) 5 (1991): 115–20.

Luo Yinwen 羅印文. "Qiushi chuangxin: Denghua jiangjun ersanshi" 求實創新: 鄧華

將軍二三事 (Seeking truth and creating: Reflections about General Deng Hua). *Renwu* 3 (1985): 60–65.

Mao Zedong 毛澤東. *Jianguo yilai Mao Zedong wengao* 建國以來毛澤東文稿 (Mao Zedong's manuscripts after the founding of the PRC). 6 vols. Beijing: Zhongyang wenxian chubanshe, 1987–92.

———. *Mao Zedong junshi wenxuan* 毛澤東軍事文選 (Selected military works of Mao Zedong). Beijing: Zhanshi chubanshe, 1981.

———. *Mao Zedong xuanji* 毛澤東選集 (Selected works of Mao Zedong). 5 vols. Beijing: Remnin chubanshe, 1960–77.

Mu Xin 穆欣. *Chen Geng dajiang* 陳賡大將 (General Chen Geng). Beijing: Xinhua chubanshe, 1985.

———, ed. *Ji Chen Geng jiangjun* 記陳賡將軍 (Commemorating General Chen Geng). Changsha: Hunan renmin chubanshe, 1984.

Nie Fengzhi 聶風智, Wang De 王德, Wu Zaowen 吳早文, and Hu Shihong 胡士弘, eds. *Sanjun huige zhan Donghai* 三軍揮戈戰東海 (A campaign by the three armed services in the East China Sea). Beijing: Jiefangjun chubanshe, 1985.

Nie Rongzhen 聶榮臻. *Nie Rongzhen huiyilu* 聶榮臻回憶錄 (Memoirs of Nie Rongzhen). Beijing: Jiefangjun chubanshe, 1986.

Niu Jun 牛軍. *Cong Heerli dao Maxieer: Meiguo tiaochu guogong maodun shimuo* 從赫爾利到馬歇爾：美國調處國共矛盾始末 (From Hurley to Marshall: A history of the American mediation of the KMT-CCP contradictions). Fuzhou: Fujian renmin chubanshe, 1988.

———. *Cong Yanan zouxiang shijie: Zhongguo gongchandang duiwai guanxi de qiyuan* 從延安走向世界：中國共產黨對外關係的起源 (From Yanan to the world: The origins of Chinese Communist foreign relations). Fuzhou: Fujian renmin chubanshe, 1992.

Pei Jianzhang 裴堅章, ed. *XinZhongguo waijiao fengyun* 新中國外交風雲 (Events of New China's diplomacy). 2 vols. Beijing: Shijie zhishi chubanshe, 1990–91.

———, ed. *Huainian Chen Yi* 懷念陳毅 (In memory of Chen Yi). Beijing: Shijie zhishi chubanshe, 1991.

———, ed. *Yanjiu Zhou Enlai: Waijiao sixiang he shijian* 研究周恩來：外交思想和實踐 (Studying Zhou Enlai: His diplomatic thought and practice). Beijing: Shijie zhishi chubanshe, 1989.

Peng Dehuai 彭德懷 *Peng Dehuai junshi wenxun* 彭德懷軍事文選 (Selected military works of Peng Dehuai). Beijing: Zhongyang wenxian chubanshe, 1988.

———. *Peng Dehuai zishu* 彭德懷自述 (The autobiographical notes of Peng Dehuai). Beijing: Renmin chubanshe, 1981.

Qi Dexue 齊德學. "Guanyu kangMei yuanChao zhanzheng zhanlue mubiao de tantao" 關於抗美援朝戰爭戰略目標的探討 (A Discussion of the strategical goal of the War to Resist America and Aid Korea). *Zhonggong dangshi yanjiu* 6 (1989): 64–67.

――――. "Zhou Enlai zhidao kangMei yuanChao zhanzheng de zhongda gongxian" 周恩來指導抗美援朝戰爭的重大貢獻 (Zhou Enlai's contribution in the direction of the War to Resist America and Aid Korea). *Junshi lishi* 軍事歷史 (Military history) 1 (1992): 3–7.

Renmin chubanshe 人民出版社, ed. *Huiyi Chen Yi* 回憶陳毅 (Reminiscences of Chen Yi). Beijing: Renmin chubanshe, 1980.

Shanghai renmin chubanshe 上海人民出版社, ed. *Yidai mingjiang: Huiyi Su Yu tongzhi* 一代名將: 回憶粟裕同志 (A famous general: reminiscences of Comrade Su Yu). Shanghai: Shanghai renmin chubanshe, 1986.

"Shixian Yazhou heping he anquan de genben daolu" 實現亞洲和平和安全的根本道路 (The basic route to the realization of peace and security in Asia). *Shijie zhishi* (May 20, 1954), 3.

Shi Zhu 師哲. "Mao Zedong zai Xibaipo huijian Migaoyang" 毛澤東在西柏坡會見米高揚 (Mao Zedong met Mikoyan at Xibaipo). *Dangde wenxian* 黨的文獻 (Party documents) 6 (1991): 34–41.

――――. "Peitong Maozhuxi fangSu" 陪同毛主席訪蘇 (Accompanying Chairman Mao to visit the Soviet Union). *Renwu* (Biographical sketches) (1988): 5–21.

――――. "Rineiwa huiyi sanyi" 日內瓦會議散憶 (Random recollections of the Geneva Conference). *Renwu* 1 (1991): 37–44.

――――. *Zai lishi juren shenbian: Shi Zhe huiyilu* 在歷史巨人身邊: 師哲回憶錄 (At the side of historical giants: Shi Zhe memoirs). Beijing: Zhongyang wenxian chubanshe, 1991.

――――. "Zhongxin genggeng, guangming leiluo: Huiyi Wang Jiaxiang tongzhi" 忠心耿耿, 光明磊落: 回憶王稼祥同志 (Whole-hearted loyalty and total honesty: Reminiscences of Comrade Wang Jiaxiang), in "Wang Jiaxiang xuanji" bianjizu, ed., *Huiyi Wang Jiaxiang*, 85–86.

Song Zhongfu 宋仲福. "Jianguo chuqi dang he guojia dui waizi zai Hua qiye de zhengce" 建國初期黨和國家對外資在華企業的政策 (The policy of the party and the government toward foreign enterprises in China during the early years of the PRC). *Zhonggong dangshi yanjiu* 4 (1990): 39–46.

Su Chao 蘇潮. "Zhanwang ZhongYing guanxi" 展望中英關係 (Forecasting Sino-British relations). *Shijie zhishi* (September 5, 1954), 10–12.

Su Yu 粟裕. *Su Yu zhanzheng huiyilu* 粟裕戰爭回憶錄 (War memoirs of Su Yu). Beijing: Jiefangjun chubanshe, 1988.

Tao Yinghui 陶英惠. "Wang Shijie yu lianghang an zhenxiang" 王世杰與兩航案真相

(Wang Shijie and the truth about the incident of the two airlines). *Zhuangji wenxue* 335 (April 1990): 14–17.

Tu Chuande 屠傳德. *Meiguo teshi zai Zhongguo, 1945. 12–1947. 1* 美國特使在中國, *1945, 12–1947, 1* (U.S. special envoy in China, December 1945–January 1947). Shanghai: Fudan daxue chubanshe, 1988.

Wang Bingnan 王炳南. *ZhongMei huitan jiunian huigu* 中美會談九年回顧 (Recollections of the nine years of the Sino-American talks). Beijing: Shijie zhishi chubanshe, 1985.

Wang Jiaxiang 王稼祥. *Wang Jiaxiang xuanji* 王稼祥選集 (Selected works of Wang Jiaxiang). Beijing: Renmin chubanshe, 1989.

"Wang Jiaxiang xuanji" bianjizu "王稼祥選集" 編輯組, ed. *Huiyi Wang Jiaxiang* 回憶王稼祥 (Reminiscences of Wang Jiaxiang). Beijing: Renmin chubanshe, 1985.

Wang Shoudao 王首道. *Wang Shoudao huiyilu* 王首道回憶錄 (Memoirs of Wang Shoudao). Beijing: Jiefangjun chubanshe, 1987.

Wu Xiuquan 伍修權. *Huiyi yu huainian* 回憶與懷念 (Recollections and memories). Beijing: Zhonggong zhongyang dangxiao chubanshe, 1991.

———. *Wangshi cangsang* 往事滄桑 (The vicissitudes of my life). Shanghai: Shanghai wenji chubanshe, 1986.

———. *Zai waijiaobu banian de jingli, 1950, 1–1958, 10* 在外交部八年的經歷, *1950, 1–1958, 10* (Eight-year experience at the Foreign Ministry, January 1950–October 1958). Beijing: Shijie zhishi chubanshe, 1983.

Xiang Qing 向青. "Guanyu Sidalin quanzu jiefang dajun guojiang zhi wojian" 關於斯大林勸阻解放大軍過江之我見 (My views on the issue of whether Stalin asked the Liberation Army not to cross the Yangtse River). *Dangde wenxian* 6 (1989): 64–66.

Xiao Feng 肖鋒. "Nanwang de jiaohui" 難忘的教誨 (Unforgettable teaching), in Shanghai renmin chubanshe, ed. *Yidai mingjiang*, 299–301.

Xiao Jingguang 肖勁光. *Xiao Jingguang huiyilu* 肖勁光回憶錄 (Memoirs of Xiao Jingguang). 2 vols. Beijing: Jiefangjun chubanshe, 1988–89.

Xie Fang 解方. "Guanyu Chaoxian Kaicheng tingzhan tanpan de huiyi." 關於朝鮮開城談判的回憶 (Reminiscences of the Korean armistice negotiations at Kaisong). *Zhonggong dangshi ziliao* 中共黨史資料 (Materials on Chinese Communist party history) 32 (1989): 24–39.

Xinghuo liaoyuan bianjibu 星火燎原編輯部, ed. *Jiefangjun jianglinzhuan* 解放軍將領傳 (Biographies of Liberation Army generals). Vol. 3. Beijing: Jiefangjun chubanshe, 1986.

Xu Peilan 胥佩蘭 and Zheng Pengfei 鄭鵬飛. *Chen Geng jiangjun zhuan* 陳賡將軍傳 (A biography of General Chen Geng). Beijing: Jiefangjun chubanshe, 1988.

Xu Shiyou 許世友. *Xu Shiyou huiyilu* 許世友回憶錄 (Memoirs of Xu Shiyou). Beijing: Jiefangjun chubanshe, 1986.

Xu Xiangqian 徐向前. *Lishi de huigu* 歷史的回顧 (Historical recollections). Beijing: Jiefangjun chubanshe, 1987.

Xu Yan 徐焰. *Diyici Jiaoliang: KangMei yuanChao de lishi huigu he fansi* 第一次較量: 抗美援朝戰爭的歷史回顧與反思 (A historical review and analysis of the War to Resist America and Aid Korea). Beijing: Zhongguo guangbo dianshi chubanshe, 1990.

"Yazhou renmin de yuanwang shi juedui burong hushi de" 亞洲人民的願望是絕對不容忽視的 (The aspiration of the Asian people cannot absolutely be ignored). *Shijie zhishi* (June 5, 1954), 3.

Yang Chengwu 楊成武. *Yang Chengwu huiyilu* 楊成武回憶錄 (Memoirs of Yang Chengwu). 2 vols. Beijing: Jiefangjun chubanshe, 1987.

Yang Dezhi 楊得志. *Weile Heping* 為了和平 (For the sake of peace). Beijing: Changzheng chubanshe, 1987.

Yang Kuisong 楊奎松. "Kangzhan shiqi Gongchan guoji, Sulian, yu Zhongguo gongchandang guanxi zhongde jige wenti" 抗戰時期共產國際, 蘇聯, 與中國共產黨關係中的幾個問題 (Several issues in the relationship between the Comintern, the Soviet Union, and the CCP during the War of Resistance Against Japan). *Dangshi yanjiu* (Study of party history) 6 (1987): 132–49.

Yao Xu 姚旭. *Cong Yalujiang dao Banmendian* 從鴨綠江到板門店 (From the Yalu River to Panmunjom). Beijing: Renmin chubanshe, 1985.

——. "Peng Dehuai dui kangMei yuanChao zanzheng zhihui shang de gongxian" 彭德懷對抗美援朝戰爭指揮上的貢獻 (Peng Dehuai's contribution in commanding the War to Resist America and Aid Korea). *Dangshi yanjiu ziliao* 黨史研究資料 (Sources for the study of party history) 1 (1982): 1–10.

Ye Fei 葉飛. *Ye Fei huiyilu* 葉飛回憶錄 (Memoirs of Ye Fei). Beijing: Jiefangjun chubanshe, 1988.

Ye Yumeng 葉雨蒙. *Chubing Chaoxian: KangMei yuanChao lishi jishi* 出兵朝鮮: 抗美援朝歷史紀實 (Dispatching troops to Korea: A factual account of the War to Resist America and Aid Korea). Beijing: Shiyue wenyi chubanshe, 1990.

——. *Heixue: Chubing Chaoxian jishi* 黑雪: 出兵朝鮮紀實 (Black snow: A record of China's entry into Korea). Beijing: Zuojia chubanshe, 1989.

Yu Zhan 余湛 and Zhang Guangyou 張光祐. "Guanyu Sidalin cengfou quanzu wo guo Changjiang de tantao" 關於斯大林曾否勸阻我過長江的探討 (On the debate of whether Stalin ever asked us not to cross the Yangtse River). *Dangde wenxian* 1 (1989): 56–58.

Zeng Sheng 曾生. *Zeng Sheng huiyilu* 曾生回憶錄 (Memoirs of Zeng Sheng). Beijing: Jiefangjun chubanshe, 1991.

Zhang Baijia 章百家. "KangRi zhanzheng jiesu qianhou Zhongguo gongchandang dui Meiguo zhengce de yanbian" 抗日戰爭結束前後中國共產黨對美政策的演變 (The evolution of the Chinese Communist party's policy toward the United States around the conclusion of the Anti-Japanese War). *Zhongong dangshi yanjiu* (Study of Chinese Communist party history) 1 (1991): 40–48.

Zhang Peisen 張培森, ed. *Zhang Wentian yanjiu wenji* 張聞天研究文集 (Collection of studies on Zhang Wentian). Beijing: Zhonggong dangshi ziliao chubanshe, 1990.

Zhang Wentian 張聞天. *Zhang Wentian xuanji* 張聞天選集 (Selected works of Zhang Wentian). Beijing: Renmin chubanshe, 1989.

Zhang Xi 張希. "Peng Dehuai shouming shuaishi kangMei yuanChao de qianqian houhou" 彭德懷受命率師抗美援朝的前前後後 (Before and after Peng Dehuai's appointment to command the CPV in the War to Resist America and Aid Korea). *Zhonggong dangshi ziliao* (Materials on Chinese Communist party history) 31 (1989): 111–59.

Zhang Zongxun 張宗遜. *Zhang Zongxun huiyilu* 張宗遜回憶錄 (Memoirs of Zhang Zongxun). Beijing: Jiefangjun chubanshe, 1990.

Zheng Xiaoguo 鄭曉國. "'Yibiandao' waijiao fangzhen de chanshen he zhuanbian" "一邊倒" 外交方針的產生和轉變 (The origins and evolution of the policy of "leaning to one side"). *Zhonggong dangshi yanjiu* 1 (1991): 49–56.

———. "'ZhongSu youhao tongmeng huzhu tiaoyue' qianding de qianqian houhou" "中蘇友好同盟互助條約" 簽訂的前前後後 (Events surrounding the conclusion of the "Sino-Soviet Treaty of Friendship, Alliance, and Mutual Assistance"). *Shijieshi yanjiu dongtai* 161 (July 1992): 31–38.

Zhonggong Guangdong shengwei dangshi yanjiu weiyuanhui 中共廣東省委黨史研究委員會, ed. *Huiyi Fang Fang* 回憶方方 (Reminiscences of Fang Fang). Hong Kong: Sanlian shudian, 1986.

Zhonggong Huanggang xianweihui 中共黃岡縣委會, ed. *Huiyi Chen Tanqiu* 回憶陳潭秋 (Reminiscences of Chen Tanqiu). Wuhan: Hubei renmin chubanshe, 1981.

Zhonggong zhongyang wenxian yanjiushi 中共中央文獻研究室, ed. *Zhou Enlai nianpu, 1898–1949* 周恩來年譜, 1898–1949 (A chronicle of Zhou Enlai's life: 1898–1949). Beijing: Zhongyang wenxian chubanshe, 1989.

———, ed. *Bujin de sinian* 不盡的思念 (Endless memories). Beijing: Zhongyang wenxian chubanshe, 1991.

Zhongguo junshi guwentuan lishi bianxiezu 中國軍事顧問團歷史編寫組, ed. *Zhongguo junshi guwentuan yuanYue kangFa douzheng shishi* 中國軍事顧問團援越抗法鬥爭史實 (Historical facts about the role of the Chinese Military Advisory Group in the struggle to Aid Vietnam and Resist France). Beijing: Jiefangjun chubanshe, 1990.

Zhou Enlai 周恩來. *Zhou Enlai shuxin xuanji* 周恩來書信選集 (Selected letters of Zhou Enlai). Beijing: Zhongyang wenxian chubanshe, 1988.

———. *Zhou Enlai waijiao wenxuan* 周恩來外交文選 (Selected works of Zhou Enlai on diplomacy). Beijing: Zhongyang wenxian chubanshe, 1990.

———. *Zhou Enlai xuanji* 周恩來選集 (Selected works of Zhou Enlai). 2 vols. Beijing: Renmin chubanshe, 1980–84.

"Zhou Enlai yanjiu xueshu taolunhui lunwenji" bianjizu "周恩來研究學術討論會論文集" 編輯組, ed. *Zhou Enlai yanjiu xueshu taolunhui lunwenji* 周恩來研究學術討論會論文集 (Proceedings of the conference on the study of Zhou Enlai). Beijing: Zhongyang wenxian chubanshe, 1988.

Zhou Jun 周軍. "XinZhongguo chuqi renmin jiefangjun weineng suixing Taiwan zhanyi jihua yuanyin chutan" 新中國初期人民解放軍未能遂行台灣戰役計劃原因初探 (Preliminary inquiries into the reasons for the failure of the People's Liberation Army's plan to occupy Taiwan during the early years of the New China). *Zhonggong dangshi yanjiu* 1 (1991): 67–74.

Zhu De 朱德. *Zhu De xuanji* 朱德選集 (Selected works of Zhu De). Beijing: Renmin chubanshe, 1983.

Zhu Kefu 朱可夫 (Vasilii Chuikov). *Zai Hua shiming* 在華使命 (Mission to China). Beijing: Xinhua chubanshe, 1983. Originally published in Russian in the Soviet journal, *New World* 11/12 (1979).

Zhu Lin 朱霖. *Dashi furen huiyilu: Xiongyali, Yinni, Faguo, Meiguo* 大使夫人回憶錄: 匈牙利, 印尼, 法國, 美國 (Memoirs of an ambassador's wife: Hungary, Indonesia, France, and the United States). Beijing: Shijie zhishi chubanshe, 1991. (Zhu Lin is the wife of Huang Zhen, who was the PRC's ambassador to Hungary, Indonesia, France, and the United States.)

Zhu Yuanshi 朱元石. "Liu Shaoqi 1949 nian mimi fangSu" 劉少奇一九四九年秘密訪蘇 (Liu Shaoqi's secret visit to the Soviet Union in 1949). *Dangde wenxian* 3 (1991): 74–89.

Zhu Zhongli 朱仲麗. *Liming yu wanxia: Wang Jiaxiang wenxue zhuanji* 黎明與晚霞: 王稼祥文學傳記 (Dawn and dusk: A literary biography of Wang Jiaxiang). Beijing: Jiefangjun chubanshe, 1986. (Zhu Zhongli is the wife of Wang Jiaxiang.)

Zi Zhongyun 資中筠. *Meiguo duiHua zhengce de yuanqi he fazhan, 1945–1950* 美國對華政策的緣起和發展, 1945–1950 (The origins and development of U.S. policy toward China, 1945–1950). Chongqing: Chongqing chubanshe, 1987.

Zi Zhongyun 資中筠 and He Di 何迪, eds. *MeiTai guanxi sishinian, 1949–1989* 美台關係四十年, 1949–1989 (Forty years of American-Taiwan relations, 1949–1989). Beijing: Renmin chubanshe, 1991.

Newspapers and Periodicals (1949–1958)

Jiefang ribao 解放日報 (Liberation Daily)
Renmin ribao 人民日報 (People's Daily)
Da gong bao 大公報 (Impartial Daily)
Hong qi 紅旗 (Red Flag)
Shijie zhishi 世界知識 (World Knowledge)

Unpublished Papers

Wang Jianwei 王建偉. "XinZhongguo chengli qianhou Meiguo duihua zhengce jiexi" 新中國成立前後美國對華政策解析 (An analysis of America's China Policy at the time of the founding of the PRC). Master's thesis, Fudan University, 1985.
Shi Yinhong 時殷弘. "Dulumen dui xinZhongguo de zhengce: Cong dishi dao zhanzheng de lishi huigu" 杜魯門對新中國的政策: 從敵視到戰爭的歷史回顧 (A historical review of Truman's policy toward the New China: From hostility to war). Ph.D. diss., Nanjing University, 1987.

ENGLISH-LANGUAGE SOURCES

Archival Collections

Acheson, Dean. Papers. Harry S. Truman Library, Independence, Missouri.
Clifford, Clark M. Papers. Harry S. Truman Library.
Dulles, John Foster. Papers. Dwight D. Eisenhower Library, Abilene, Kansas.
_____. Papers. Seeley Mudd Library, Princeton University, Princeton, N.J.
Eisenhower, Dwight D. Papers. Whitman Files. Dwight D. Eisenhower Library.
Great Britain. Cabinet Records. Public Record Office, London.
_____. Colonial Office Records. Public Record Office, London.
_____. Ministry of Defense Records. Public Record Office, London.
_____. Foreign Office Records. Public Record Office, London.
_____. Prime Minister's Office Records. Public Record Office, London.
Hagerty, James. Papers. Dwight D. Eisenhower Library.
Herter, Christian. Papers. Dwight D. Eisenhower Library.
Kennan, George F. Papers. Seeley Mudd Library, Princeton University.
Koo, Wellington. Papers. Butler Library, Columbia University, New York.

Sumner, John. Papers. Harry S. Truman Library.

Truman, Harry S. Papers. Harry S. Truman Library.

U.S. Department of State. Decimal Files. Record Group 59. Diplomatic Branch. National Archives, Washington, D.C.

Oral History

Butterworth, W. Walton. Harry S. Truman Library.

Clubb, O. Edmund. Harry S. Truman Library.

Judd, Walter. Harry S. Truman Library; Dwight D. Eisenhower Library.

Merchant, Livingston. Harry S. Truman Library.

Muccio, John. Harry S. Truman Library.

Ringwalt, Arthur R. Harry S. Truman Library.

Robertson, Walter S. Mudd Library, Princeton University.

Smith, H. Alexander. Mudd Library, Princeton University.

Published Documents, Memoirs, Books, and Articles

Acheson, Dean. *Present at the Creation: My Years in the State Department.* New York: Norton, 1969.

Adams, Sherman. *Firsthand Report: The Inside Story of the Eisenhower Administration.* New York: Harper & Brothers, 1961.

Adamthwaite, Anthony. "Britain and the World, 1945–9: The View from the Foreign Office." *International Affairs* 61 (Spring 1985): 223–35.

———. "Introduction: The Foreign Office and Policy-Making." In John W. Young, ed., *The Foreign Policy of Churchill's Peacetime Administration*, 1–28.

Aldrich, Richard J. *British Intelligence, Strategy and the Cold War, 1945–51.* London: Routledge, 1992.

Alexander, Charles C. *Holding the Line: The Eisenhower Era, 1952–1961.* Bloomington: Indiana University Press, 1975.

Allison, Graham T. *Essence of Decision: Explaining the Cuban Missile Crisis.* Boston: Little, Brown, 1971.

Ambrose, Stephen E. *Eisenhower: The President.* New York: Simon and Schuster, 1984.

———. *Eisenhower: Soldier, General of the Army, President-Elect, 1890–1952.* New York: Simon and Schuster, 1983.

Anderson, Terry H. *The United States, Great Britain, and the Cold War, 1944–1947.* Columbia: University of Missouri Press, 1981.

Attlee, Clement. *Twilight of Empire: Memoirs of Prime Minister Clement Attlee.* New York: Barnes, 1962.

Bachrack, Stanley D. *The Committee of One Million: "China Lobby" Politics, 1953–1971.* New York: Columbia University Press, 1976.

Barnett, A. Doak. *China and the Major Powers in East Asia.* Washington, D.C.: Brookings Institute, 1977.

Barros, James. *Trygve Lie and the Cold War: The UN Secretary-General Pursues Peace, 1946–1953.* Dekalb: Northern Illinois University Press, 1989.

Beloff, Lord. "The Crisis and Its Consequences for the British Conservative Party." In Louis and Owen, eds., *Suez 1956,* 319–34.

Bernstein, Barton J. "The Struggle over the Korean War Armistice: Prisoners of Repatriation?" In Cumings, ed., *Child of Conflict,* 261–307.

_____, ed. *Politics and Policies of the Truman Administration.* Chicago: Quadrangle Books, 1970.

Betts, Richard K. *Nuclear Blackmail and Nuclear Balance.* Washington, D.C.: Brookings Institute, 1987.

Blum, Robert. *Drawing the Line: The Origin of the American Containment Policy in East Asia.* New York: Norton, 1982.

Boardman, Robert. *Britain and the People's Republic of China, 1949–1974.* London: Macmillan, 1976.

Bohlen, Charles E. *Witness to History: 1929–1969.* New York: Norton, 1979.

Boorman, Howard L. "Mao Tse-tung as Historian." In Feuerwerker, ed., *History in Communist China,* 306–29.

Borg, Dorothy, and Waldo Heinrichs, eds. *Uncertain Years: Chinese-American Relations, 1947–1950.* New York: Columbia University Press, 1980.

Brands, H. W. *Inside the Cold War: Loy Henderson and the Rise of the American Empire, 1918–1961.* New York: Oxford University Press, 1991.

Brandt, Conrad. *Stalin's Failure in China, 1924–1927.* New York: Norton, 1958.

Brownell, Will, and Richard Billings. *So Close to Greatness: A Biography of William C. Bullitt.* New York: Macmillan, 1987.

Buhite, Russell D. *Soviet-American Relations in Asia, 1945–1954.* Norman: University of Oklahoma Press, 1981.

Bullock, Alan. *Ernest Bevin: Foreign Secretary, 1945–1951.* New York: Norton, 1983.

Bundy, McGeorge. *Danger and Survival: Choices about the Bomb in the First Fifty Years.* New York: Vintage, 1988.

Burk, Robert. "Eisenhower Revisionism Revisited: Reflections on Eisenhower Scholarship." *Historian* 50 (February 1988): 196–209.

Cable, James. *The Geneva Conference of 1954 on Indochina.* New York: St Martin's Press, 1986.

Caridi, Ronald J. *The Korean War and American Politics: The Republican Party as a Case Study.* Philadelphia: University of Pennsylvania Press, 1968.

Carlton, David. *Anthony Eden: A Biography.* London: Allen Lane, 1981.

Chang, Gordon H. *Friends and Enemies: The United States, China and the Soviet Union, 1948–1972.* Stanford, Calif.: Stanford University Press, 1990.

_____. "To the Nuclear Brink: Eisenhower, Dulles, and the Quemoy-Matsu Crisis." *International Security* 12 (Spring 1988): 96–123.

Chen, Jian. "China's Changing Aims during the Korean War, 1950–1951." *Journal of American-East Asian Relations* 1 (Spring 1992): 8–41.

_____. "The Sino-Soviet Alliance and China's Entry into the Korean War."

Cold War International History Project working paper, No. 1, Woodrow Wilson International Center for Scholars. Washington, D.C., 1992.

Chen, King C. *Vietnam and China, 1938–1954.* Princeton, N.J.: Princeton University Press, 1969.

Chen Xiaolu. "China's Policy towards the United States, 1949–1955." In Harding and Yuan, eds., *Sino-American Relations,* 184–97.

Chennault, Anna. *A Thousand Springs: The Biography of a Marriage.* New York: Paul & Erickson, 1962.

Chern, Kenneth S. *Dilemma in China.* Hamden, Conn.: Archon Press, 1980.

Christensen, Thomas J. "Threats, Assurances, and the Last Chance for Peace: The Lessons of Mao's Korean War Telegrams." *International Security* 17 (Summer 1992): 122–54.

Clubb, O. Edmund. "Formosa and the Offshore Islands in American Policy, 1950–1955." *Political Science Quarterly* 74 (1959): 517–31.

Clutterbuck, Richard L. *The Long, Long War: Counterinsurgency in Malaya and Vietnam.* New York: Praeger, 1966.

Cohen, Warren I. "Acheson, His Advisers, and China, 1949–1950." In Borg and Heinrichs, eds., *Uncertain Years,* 13–52.

_____. "Ambassador Philip D. Sprouse on the Question of Recognition of the People's Republic of China in 1949 and 1950." *Diplomatic History* 2 (Spring 1978): 213–17.

_____. "Conversation with Chinese Friends: Zhou Enlai's Associates Reflect on Chinese-American Relations in the 1940s and the Korean War." *Diplomatic History* 11 (Summer 1987): 283–89.

_____. *Dean Rusk.* Totowa, N.J.: Cooper Square, 1980.

_____, ed. *New Frontiers in American–East Asian Relations.* New York: Columbia University Press, 1983.

Cohen, Warren I., and Akira Iriye, eds. *The Great Powers in East Asia, 1953–1960.* New York: Columbia University Press, 1990.

Colville, John. *The Fringes of Power: 10 Downing Street Diaries, 1939–1955.* New York: Norton, 1985.

Craig, Gordon A., and Alexander L. George. *Force and Statecraft: Diplomatic Problems of Our Time.* New York: Oxford University Press, 1983.

Cumings, Bruce. *The Origins of the Korean War: Liberation and the Emergence of Separate Regimes, 1945–1947.* Princeton, N.J.: Princeton University Press, 1981.

_____. *The Origins of the Korean War: The Roaring of the Cataract, 1947–1950.* Princeton, N.J.: Princeton University Press, 1990.

_____, ed. *Child of Conflict: The Korean-American Relationship, 1943–1953.* Seattle: University of Washington Press, 1983.

Dallek, Robert. *The American Style of Foreign Policy: Cultural Politics and Foreign Affairs.* New York: Knopf, 1983.

_____. *Franklin D. Roosevelt and American Foreign Policy, 1932–1945.* New York: Oxford University Press, 1979.

Dallin, David J. *Soviet Foreign Policy after Stalin.* Philadelphia: Lippincott, 1961.

Dalloz, Jacques. *The War in Indo-China, 1945–54.* Dublin: Gill & Macmillan, 1987.

Darby, Phillip. *Three Faces of Imperialism: British and American Approaches to Asia and Africa, 1870–1970.* New Haven, Conn.: Yale University Press, 1987.

De Santis, Hugh. *The Diplomacy of Silence: The American Foreign Service, the Soviet Union, and the Cold War, 1933–1947.* Chicago: University of Chicago Press, 1983.

DeSantis, Vincent. "Eisenhower Revisionism." *Review of Politics* 38 (April 1976): 190–207.

Dilks, David, ed. *The Diaries of Sir Alexander Cadogan, 1938–1945.* London: Cassell, 1971.

Dingman, Roger. "Atomic Diplomacy During the Korean War." *International Security* 13 (Winter 1988/89): 50–91.

Dittmer, Lowell. "China's Search for Its Place in the World." In Womack, ed., *Contemporary Chinese Politics in Historical Perspective,* 209–61.

Dobbs, Charles M. *The Unwanted Symbol: American Foreign Policy, the Cold War and Korea, 1945–1950.* Kent, Ohio: Kent State University Press, 1981.

Dockrill, M. L. "The Foreign Office, Anglo-American Relations and the Korean War, June 1950–June 1951." *International Affairs* 62 (Summer 1986): 459–76.

Dockrill, Michael, and John W. Young, eds. *British Foreign Policy, 1945–56.* New York: St. Martin's Press, 1989.

Domes, Jurgen. *Peng Te-huai: The Man and the Image.* Stanford, Calif.: Stanford University Press, 1985.

Donovan, Robert J. *Tumultuous Years: The Presidency of Harry S. Truman, 1949–1953.* New York: Norton, 1982.

Duiker, William J. *Vietnam: Nation in Revolution.* Boulder, Colo.: Westview, 1983.

Dulles, Foster Rhea. *American Policy toward Communist China: The Historical Record, 1949–1969.* New York: Thomas Y. Crowell, 1972.

Earl, Lawrence. *Yangtse Incident: The Story of HMS Amethyst.* London: Harrap, 1950.

Eden, Anthony. *Full Circle.* Boston: Houghton Mifflin, 1960.

Eisenhower, Dwight D. *The White House Years: Mandate for Change, 1953–1956.* Garden City, N.Y.: Doubleday, 1963.

———. *The White House Years: Waging Peace, 1957–1961.* Garden City, N.Y.: Doubleday, 1965.

Fairbank, John K., ed. *The Chinese World Order: Traditional China's Foreign Relations.* Cambridge, Mass.: Harvard University Press, 1968.

Fairbank, John K., Edwin O. Reischauer, and Albert M. Craig. *East Asia: Tradition and Transformation.* Rev. ed. Boston: Houghton Mifflin, 1989.

Fang, Percy Jucheng, and Lucy Guinong J. Fang. *Zhou Enlai: A Profile.* Beijing: Foreign Languages Press, 1986.

Farrar, Peter N. "Britain's Proposal for a Buffer Zone South of the Yalu in November 1950: Was It a Neglected Opportunity to End the Fighting in Korea?" *Journal of Contemporary History* 18 (April 1983): 327–51.

Fedorenko, N. "Recalling Zhou Enlai." *Far Eastern Affairs* 6 (1989): 93–100.

———. "The Stalin-Mao Summit in Moscow." *Far Eastern Affairs* 2 (1989): 134–48.

Ferrell, Robert H., ed. *The Diary of James C. Hagerty: Eisenhower in Mid-Course, 1954–1955.* Bloomington: Indiana University Press, 1983.

———, ed. *The Eisenhower Diaries.* New York: Norton, 1981.

———, ed. *Off the Record: The Private Papers of Harry S. Truman.* New York: Harper and Row, 1980.

Feuerwerker, Albert, ed. *History in Communist China.* Cambridge, Mass.: MIT Press, 1968.

Foot, Rosemary. "Anglo-American Relations in the Korean Crisis: The British Effort to Avert an Expanded War, December 1950–January 1951." *Diplomatic History* 10 (Winter 1986): 43–57.

———. "How Far to Push the Americans." In *New York Times Book Review* (August 21, 1988): 9–11.

———. "New Light on the Sino-Soviet Alliance: Chinese and American Perspectives." *Journal of Northeast Asian Studies* 10 (Fall 1991): 16–29.

———. "The Search for a *Modus Vivendi:* Anglo-American Relations and China Policy in the Eisenhower Era." In Cohen and Iriye, eds., *Great Powers in East Asia,* 143–63.

———. *A Substitute for Victory: The Politics of Peace Making at the Korean Armistice Talks.* Ithaca, N.Y.: Cornell University Press, 1990.

———. *The Wrong War: American Policy and the Dimensions of the Korean Conflict, 1950–1953.* Ithaca, N.Y.: Cornell University Press, 1985.

Fraser, T. G., and Peter Lowe, eds. *Conflict and Amity in East Asia: Essays in Honour of Ian Nish.* London: Macmillan, 1992.

Freeland, Richard H. *The Truman Doctrine and the Origins of McCarthyism: Foreign Policy, Domestic Politics, and Internal Security, 1946–1948.* New York: Knopf, 1972.

Gaddis, John Lewis. *The Long Peace: Inquiries into the History of the Cold War.* New York: Oxford University Press, 1987.

———. *Russia, the Soviet Union, and the United States: An Interpretive History.* New York: Knopf, 1978.

———. *Strategies of Containment: A Critical Appraisal of Post-War American National Security Policy.* New York: Oxford University Press, 1982.

———. "The Unexpected John Foster Dulles." In Immerman, ed., *John Foster Dulles and the Diplomacy of the Cold War,* 44–47.

Gallicchio, Marc S. *The Cold War Begins in Asia: American East Asian Policy and the Fall of the Japanese Empire.* New York: Columbia University Press, 1988.

Garthoff, Raymond L., ed. *Sino-Soviet Military Relations.* New York: Praeger, 1966.

Garver, John W. *Chinese-Soviet Relations, 1937–1945: The Diplomacy of Chinese Nationalism.* New York: Oxford University Press, 1988.

George, Alexander L., and Richard Smoke. *Deterrence in American Foreign Policy: Theory and Practice.* New York: Columbia University Press, 1974.

Gittings, John. *Survey of the Sino-Soviet Dispute: A Commentary and Extracts from the Recent Polemics, 1963–1967.* London: Oxford University Press, 1968.

Goldstein, Melvyn C. *A History of Modern Tibet, 1913–1951: The Demise of the Lamaist State.* Berkeley: University of California Press, 1989.

Goldstein, Steven M. "Chinese Communist Policy Toward the United States: Opportunities and Constraints, 1944–1950." In Borg and Heinrichs, eds., *Uncertain Years,* 235–78.

Goldstein, Steven M., and He Di. "New Chinese Sources on the History of the Cold War." *Cold War International History Project Bulletin* 1 (Spring 1992): 4–6.

Goncharov, Sergei N. "Stalin's Dialogue with Mao Zedong: Ivan Vladimirovich Kovalev, personal representative of Joseph Stalin to Mao Zedong, answers the questions of Historian-Sinologist S. N. Goncharov." Translated by Craig Seibert. *Journal of Northeast Asian Studies* 10 (Winter 1991–92): 43–76.

Gopal, Sarvepalli. *Jawaharlal Nehru: A Biography.* Cambridge, Mass.: Harvard University Press, 1979.

Gordon, Leonard H. D. "United States Opposition to Use of Force in the Taiwan Strait, 1954–1962." *Journal of American History* 72 (December 1985): 637–60.

Goulden, Joseph C. *Korea: The Untold Story of the War.* New York: McGraw-Hill, 1982.

Grantham, Alexander. *Via Ports: From Hong Kong to Hong Kong.* Hong Kong: University of Hong Kong Press, 1965.

Grasso, June M. *Truman's Two-China Policy, 1948–1950.* Armonk, N.Y.: M. E. Sharpe, 1987.

Greenstein, Fred I. *The Hidden-Hand Presidency: Eisenhower as Leader.* New York: Basic Books, 1982.

Gromyko, Andrei. *Memoirs.* New York: Doubleday, 1989.

Grunfeld, A. Tom. *The Making of Modern Tibet.* London: Zed Books, 1987.

Guhin, Michael A. *John Foster Dulles: A Statesman and His Time.* New York: Columbia University Press, 1972.

Gurtov, Melvin. *The First Vietnam Crisis: Chinese Communist Strategy and United States Involvements, 1953–1954.* New York: Columbia University Press, 1967.

Gurtov, Melvin, and Hwang Byong-moo. *China Under Threat: The Politics of Strategy and Diplomacy.* Baltimore, Md.: Johns Hopkins University Press, 1980.

Halberstan, David. *Ho.* New York: Random House, 1971.

Halliday, Jon, and Bruce Cumings, eds. *Korea: The Unknown War.* New York: Pantheon, 1988.

Hamby, Alonzo L. *Beyond the New Deal: Harry S. Truman and American Liberalism.* New York: Columbia University Press, 1973.

———. "The Mind and Character of Harry S. Truman." In Lacey, ed., *Truman Presidency,* 19–53.

Han, Yelong. "An Untold Story: American Policy toward Chinese Students in the United States, 1949–1955." *Journal of American–East Asian Relations* 2 (Spring 1993): 77–99.

Hao Yufan, and Zhai Zhihai. "China's Decision to Enter the Korean War: History Revisited." *China Quarterly* 121 (March 1990): 94–115.

Harding, Harry, ed. *China's Foreign Relations in the 1980s.* New Haven, Conn.: Yale University Press, 1984.

Harding, Harry, and Yuan Ming, eds., *Sino-American Relations, 1945–1955: A Joint Reassessment of a Critical Decade.* Wilmington, Del.: Scholarly Resources, 1989.

He Di. "The Evolution of the Chinese Communist Party's Policy towards the United States, 1944–1949." In Harding and Yuan, eds. *Sino-American Relations,* 31–50.

———. "The Evolution of the People's Republic of China's Policy toward the Offshore Islands." In Cohen and Iriye, eds., *Great Powers in East Asia,* 222–45.

———. " 'The Last Campaign to Unify China': The CCP's Unmaterialized Plan to Liberate Taiwan, 1949–1950." *Chinese Historians* 5 (Spring 1992): 1–16.

Heller, Francis H., ed. *The Korean War: A 25-Year Perspective.* Lawrence: Regents Press of Kansas, 1977.

Henderson, Loy W. *A Question of Trust: The Origins of US-Soviet Diplomatic Relations.* Stanford, Calif.: Hoover Institution Press, 1986.

Hermes, Walter G. *Truce Tent and Fighting Front.* Washington, D.C.: GPO, 1966.

Hess, Gary. "Redefining the American Position in Southeast Asia: The United States and the Geneva and Manila Conferences." In Kaplan, Artaud, and Rubin, eds., *Dien Bien Phu and the Crisis of Franco-American Relations,* 127–30.

Hooper, Beverley. *China Stands Up: Ending the Western Presence, 1948–1950.* Sydney: Allen & Unwin, 1986.

Hoopes, Townsend. *The Devil and John Foster Dulles.* Boston: Atlantic/Little, Brown, 1973.

Horne, Alistair. *Harold Macmillan: Volume II, 1956–1986.* New York: Viking, 1989.

Hosoya, Chihiro. "Japan, China, the United States, and the United Kingdom, 1951–2: The Case of the 'Yoshida Letter.' " *International Affairs* 60 (Spring 1984): 247–59.

Howe, Jonathan. *Multicrises: Sea Power and Global Politics in the Missile Age.* Cambridge, Mass.: MIT Press, 1971.

Hsieh, Alice. *Communist China's Strategy in the Nuclear Era.* Englewood Cliffs, N.J.: Prentice-Hall, 1962.

Hughes, Emmet John. *The Ordeal of Power: A Political Memoir of the Eisenhower Years.* New York: Atheneum, 1963.

Hunt, Michael H. "Beijing and the Korean Crisis, June 1950–June 1951." *Political Science Quarterly* (Fall 1992): 453–78.

_____. "Chinese Foreign Relations in Historical Perspective." In Harding, ed. *China's Foreign Relations in the 1980s*, 1–42.

_____. *Ideology and U.S. Foreign Policy*. New Haven, Conn.: Yale University Press, 1987.

_____. *The Making of a Special Relationship: The United States and China to 1914*. New York: Columbia University Press, 1983.

Hunt, Michael H., and Odd Arne Westad. "The Chinese Communist Party and International Affairs: A Field Report on New Historical Sources and Old Research Problems." *China Quarterly* 122 (June 1990): 258–72.

Immerman, Richard H., ed. *John Foster Dulles and the Diplomacy of the Cold War: A Reappraisal*. Princeton, N.J.: Princeton University Press, 1990.

Isaacson, Walter, and Evan Thomas. *The Wise Men: Six Friends and the World They Made*. New York: Simon and Schuster, 1986.

James, Robert Rhodes. *Anthony Eden*. New York: McGraw-Hill, 1986.

Jervis, Robert. "Hypotheses on Misperception." *World Politics* 20 (April 1968): 454–79.

_____. *Perception and Misperception in International Politics*. Princeton, N.J.: Princeton University Press, 1976.

Jervis, Robert, and Jack Snyder, eds. *Dominoes and Bandwagons: Strategic Beliefs and Great Power Competition in the Eurasian Rimland*. New York: Oxford University Press, 1991.

Johnson, U. Alexis. *The Right Hand of Power*. Englewood Cliffs, N.J.: Prentice-Hall, 1984.

Kalicki, J. H. *The Pattern of Sino-American Crises: Political-Military Interactions in the 1950s*. London: Cambridge University Press, 1975.

Kapista, M. S. *The CPR: Two Decades-Two Politics*. Arlington, Va.: Joint Publications Research Center, 1971.

Kaplan, Lawrence S., Denise Artaud, and Mark Rubin., eds. *Dien Bien Phu and the Crisis of Franco-American Relations, 1954–1955*. Wilmington, Del.: Scholarly Resources, 1990.

Kaufman, Burton I. *The Korean War: Challenges in Crisis, Credibility, and Command*. New York: Alfred A. Knopf, 1986.

Keeley, Joseph. *The China Lobby Man*. New Rochelle, N.Y.: Arlington House, 1969.

Keith, Ronald C. *The Diplomacy of Zhou Enlai*. New York: St. Martin's Press, 1989.

Kennan, George F. *Memoirs: 1925–1950*. Boston: Little, Brown, 1967.

_____. *Memoirs: 1950–1963*. Boston: Little, Brown, 1972.

Kennedy, Paul. *Strategy and Diplomacy, 1870–1945*. London: Allen & Unwin, 1983.

Khong, Yuen Foong. *Analogies at War: Korea, Munich, Dien Bien Phu, and the Vietnam Decisions of 1965*. Princeton, N.J.: Princeton University Press, 1992.

Khrushchev, Nikita S. *Khrushchev Remembers: The Last Testament*. Translated and edited by Strobe Talbott. Boston: Little, Brown, 1970.

_____. *Khrushchev Remembers: The Glasnost Tapes.* Boston: Little, Brown, 1990.

Klein, Donald W., and Anne B. Clark, eds. *Bibliographical Dictionary of Chinese Communism, 1921–1965.* 2 vols. Cambridge, Mass.: Harvard University Press, 1971.

Kusnitz, Leonard A. *Public Opinion and Foreign Policy: America's China Policy, 1949–1979.* Westport, Conn.: Greenwood Press, 1984.

Lacey, Michael J., ed. *The Truman Presidency.* New York: Cambridge University Press, 1989.

Lacouture, Jean. *Ho Chi Minh: A Political Biography.* New York: Random House, 1968.

Lam, Truong Buu. "Intervention versus Tribute in Sino-Vietnamese Relations, 1788–1790." In Fairbank, ed., *Chinese World Order,* 165–79.

Lamb, Alastair. *Britain and Chinese Central Asia: The Road to Lhasa, 1767 to 1905.* London: Routledge and Kegan Paul, 1960.

Leary, William M., Jr. "Aircraft and Anti-Communists: CAT in Action, 1949–52." *China Quarterly* 52 (1972): 654–69.

_____. *Perilous Mission: Civil Air Transport and CIA Covert Operation in Asia.* Tuscaloosa: University of Alabama Press, 1984.

Lebow, Richard Ned. *Between Peace and War: The Nature of International Crisis.* Baltimore, Md.: Johns Hopkins University Press, 1981.

Leffler, Melvin P. *A Preponderance of Power: National Security, the Truman Administration, and the Cold War.* Stanford, Calif.: Stanford University Press, 1992.

Levine, Steven I. "A New Look at American Mediation in the Chinese Civil War: The Marshall Mission and Manchuria." *Diplomatic History* 3 (Fall 1979): 349–76.

Lewis, John Wilson, and Xue Litai. *China Builds the Bomb.* Stanford, Calif.: Stanford University Press, 1988.

Li Haiwen. "A Distortion of History: An Interview with Shi Zhe about Kovalev's Recollections." Translated by Wang Xi. *Chinese Historians* 5 (Fall 1992): 59–64.

Lie, Trygve. *In the Cause of Peace: Seven Years with the United Nations.* New York: Macmillan, 1954.

Liu Shaoqi. *Collected Works of Liu Shaoqi, 1958–1967.* Hong Kong: Union Research Institute, 1968.

Louis, Wm. Roger, and Hedley Bull, eds. *The "Special Relationship": Anglo-American Relations since 1945.* Oxford: Clarendon, 1986.

Louis, Wm. Roger, and Roger Owens, eds. *Suez 1956: The Crisis and Its Consequences.* Oxford: Clarendon, 1989.

Lowe, Peter. "An Ally and a Recalcitrant General: Great Britain, Douglas MacArthur and the Korean War, 1950–1." *English Historical Review* 105 (July 1990): 624–53.

_____. "Challenge and Readjustment: Anglo-American Exchanges over East Asia, 1949–53." In Fraser and Lowe, eds., *Conflict and Amity in East Asia,* 143–62.

_____. *The Origins of the Korean War.* London: Longman, 1986.

_____. "The Settlement of the Korean War." In John W. Young, ed., *The Foreign Policy of Churchill's Peacetime Administration,* 207–31.

Luard, Evan. *Britain and China.* London: Chatto & Windus, 1962.

MacArthur, Douglas A. *Reminiscences.* New York: McGraw-Hill, 1964.

McAuliffe, Mary. "Commentary: Eisenhower, the President." *Journal of American History* 68 (December 1981): 625–32.

McCormick, Thomas J. *America's Half-Century: United States Foreign Policy in the Cold War.* Baltimore, Md.: Johns Hopkins University Press, 1989.

MacDonald, Callum. *Korea: The War Before Vietnam.* New York: Free Press, 1986.

MacFarquhar, Roderick. "The China Problem in Anglo-American Relations." In Louis and Bull, eds., *The "Special Relationship,"* 311–19.

McLane, Charles B. *Soviet Policy and the Chinese Communists, 1931–1946.* New York: Columbia University Press, 1958.

McLean, David. "American Nationalism, the China Myth, and the Truman Doctrine: The Question of Accommodation with Peking, 1949–50." *Diplomatic History* 10 (Winter 1986): 25–42.

McLellan, David S. *Dean Acheson: The State Department Years.* New York: Dodd, Mead, 1976.

McMahon, Robert J. "The Cold War in Asia: Toward a New Synthesis?" *Diplomatic History* 12 (Summer 1988): 307–27.

Macmillan, Harold. *Riding the Storm, 1956–1959.* London: Macmillan, 1971.

Mancall, Mark. *China at the Center: 300 Years of Foreign Policy.* New York: Free Press, 1984.

Mao Tse-tung. *Selected Works of Mao Tse-tung.* 5 vols. Beijing: Foreign Languages Press, 1965–77.

Marks, Sally. "The World According to Washington." *Diplomatic History* 11 (Summer 1987): 265–82.

Martin, Edwin W. *Divided Counsel: The Anglo-American Response to Communist Victory in China.* Lexington: University Press of Kentucky, 1986.

May, Ernest R. *"Lessons" of the Past: The Use and Misuse of History in American Foreign Policy.* New York: Oxford University Press, 1973.

_____. *The Truman Administration and China, 1945–1949.* Philadelphia: Lippincott, 1975.

Mayers, David Allan. *Cracking the Monolith: U.S. Policy Against the Sino-Soviet Alliance, 1949–1955.* Baton Rouge: Louisiana State University Press, 1987.

_____. *George Kennan and the Dilemma of U.S. Foreign Policy.* New York: Oxford University Press, 1988.

Melanson, Richard, and David Allan Mayers, eds. *Reevaluating Eisenhower: American Foreign Policy in the Fifties.* Urbana: University of Illinois Press, 1987.

Messer, Robert L. "Roosevelt, Truman, and China: An Overview." In Harding and Yuan, eds., *Sino-American Relations,* 63–77.

Miller, Richard Lawrence. *Truman: The Rise to Power.* New York: McGraw-Hill, 1986.

Ministry of Foreign Affairs of the Socialist Republic of Viet Nam. *The Truth about Vietnam-China Relations over the Last Thirty Years.* Hanoi: Ministry of Foreign Affairs, 1979.

Miscamble, Wilson D. *George F. Kennan and the Making of American Foreign Policy, 1947–1950.* Princeton, N.J.: Princeton University Press.

Morgan, Kenneth O. *Labour People: Leaders and Lieutenants, Hardie to Kinnock.* Oxford: Oxford University Press, 1987.

Mowry, George. "The Uses of History by Recent Presidents." *Journal of American History* 53 (June 1966): 6–16.

Munro-Leighton, Judith. "A Postrevisionist Scrutiny of America's Role in the Cold War in Asia, 1945–1950." *Journal of American–East Asian Relations* 1 (Spring 1992): 73–98.

Murfett, Malcolm H. *Hostage on the Yangtze: Britain, China, and the Amethyst Crisis of 1949.* Annapolis, Md.: Naval Institute Press, 1991.

Nagai, Yonosuke, and Akira Iriye, eds. *The Origins of the Cold War in Asia.* New York: Columbia University Press, 1977.

Nelson, Harvey. *Power and Insecurity: Beijing, Moscow, and Washington, 1949–1988.* Boulder, Colo.: Lynne Rienner, 1989.

Ngapoi Ngawang Jigmi. "On the 1959 Armed Rebellion." *China Reconstructs* 37 (March 1988): 25–29.

Nogee, Joseph L., and Robert H. Donaldson. *Soviet Foreign Policy since World War II.* 3d ed. New York: Pergamon Press, 1988.

North, Robert C. *Moscow and Chinese Communists.* Stanford, Calif.: Stanford University Press, 1953.

Oksenberg, Michel, and Robert B. Oxnan, eds. *Dragon and Eagle: United States–China Relations: Past and Present.* New York: Basic Books, 1978.

Ovendale, Ritchie. "Britain, the United States, and the Recognition of Communist China." *Historical Journal* 26 (1983): 139–58.

_____, ed. *The Foreign Policy of the British Labour Governments, 1945–1951.* Leicester, U.K.: Leicester University Press, 1984.

Panchen Lama. "Panchen Lama on 'Tibetan Independence.'" *China Reconstructs* 37 (January 1988): 8–15.

Panikkar, Kavalam M. *In Two Chinas: Memoirs of a Diplomat.* London: George Allen & Unwin, 1955.

Patterson, Thomas G. *Meeting the Communist Threat: Truman to Reagan.* New York: Oxford University Press, 1988.

Pelling, Henry. *The Labour Government, 1945–51.* New York: St. Martin's Press, 1984.

Pelz, Stephen. "U.S. Decisions on Korean Policy, 1943–1950: Some Hypotheses." In Cumings, ed., *Child of Conflict,* 93–132.

Pemberton, William. *Harry S. Truman: Fair Dealer and Cold Warrior.* Boston: Twayne Publishers, 1989.

Peng Dehuai. *Memoirs of a Chinese Marshal: The Autobiographical Notes of Peng Dehuai.* Beijing: Foreign Languages Press, 1984.

Phillips, Morgan. *East Meets West.* London: Lincolns-Praeger, 1954.

Pollack, Jonathan. "The Korean War and the Sino-American Relations." In Harding and Yuan, eds., *Sino-American Relations*, 213–37.

Porter, Brian. *Britain and the Rise of Communist China: A Study of British Attitudes, 1945–1954.* New York: Oxford University Press, 1967.

Pruessen, Ronald W. *John Foster Dulles: The Road to Power.* New York: Free Press, 1982.

Public Papers of the Presidents: Dwight D. Eisenhower, 1953–1961. Washington, D.C.: GPO, 1960–61.

Public Papers of the Presidents: Harry S. Truman, 1945–1953. Washington, D.C.: GPO, 1961–66.

Rabe, Stephen G. "Eisenhower Revisionism: A Decade of Scholarship." *Diplomatic History* 17 (Winter 1993): 97–115.

Randle, Robert F. *Geneva 1954: The Settlement of the Indochinese War.* Princeton, N.J.: Princeton University Press, 1969.

Rankin, Karl Lott. *China Assignment.* Seattle: University of Washington Press, 1964.

Reardon-Anderson, James. *Yenan and the Great Powers: The Origins of Chinese Communist Foreign Policy.* New York: Columbia University Press, 1980.

Reichard, Gary. "Eisenhower as President: The Changing View." *South Atlantic Quarterly* 77 (Summer 1979): 265–81.

Roberts, Frank. "Ernest Bevin as Foreign Secretary." In Ovendale, ed., *The Foreign Policy of the British Labour Governments,* 21–42.

Ross, Robert S. *The Indochina Tangle: China's Vietnam Policy, 1975–1979.* New York: Columbia University Press, 1988.

Rotter, Andrew J. *The Path to Vietnam: Origins of the American Commitment to Southeast Asia.* Ithaca, N.Y.: Cornell University Press, 1987.

Rovere, Richard H., and Arthur M. Schlesinger, Jr. *The MacArthur Controversy and American Foreign Policy.* New York: Noonday Press, 1951.

Ryan, Mark A. *Chinese Attitudes Toward Nuclear Weapons: China and the United States During the Korean War.* Armonk, N.Y.: M. E. Sharpe, 1989.

Salisbury, Harrison E. *To Peking and Beyond: A Report on the New Asia.* New York: Quadrangle, 1973.

Schaller, Michael. *The American Occupation of Japan: The Origins of the Cold War in Asia.* New York: Oxford University Press, 1985.

———. *Douglas MacArthur: The Far Eastern General.* New York: Oxford University Press, 1989.

———. "Securing the Great Crescent: Occupied Japan and the Origins of Containment in Southeast Asia." *Journal of American History* 69 (September 1982): 392–414.

Schlesinger, Arthur M., Jr. "The Ike Age Revisited." *Reviews in American History* 11 (March 1983): 1–11.

Schoenbaum, Thomas J. *Waging Peace and War: Dean Rusk in the Truman, Kennedy and Johnson Years.* New York: Simon and Schuster, 1988.

Schonberger, Howard B. *Aftermath of War: Americans and the Remaking of Japan, 1945–1952.* Kent, Ohio: Kent State University Press, 1989.

Schram, Stuart, ed. *Chairman Mao Talks to the People: Talks and Letters, 1956–1971.* New York: Pantheon Books, 1974.

———, ed. *Quotations from Chairman Mao Tse-tung.* New York: Bantam Books, 1967.

Shai, Aron. "Imperialism Imprisoned: The Closure of British Firms in the People's Republic of China." *English Historical Review* (January 1989): 88–109.

Shambaugh, David. "New Sources and Research Opportunities in the Study of China's Foreign Relations and National Security." *China Exchange News* 20 (Fall-Winter 1992): 24–27.

Shao, Kuo-kang. "Zhou Enlai's Diplomacy and the Neutralization of Indo-China, 1954–55." *China Quarterly* 107 (September 1986): 483–504.

Shao, Wenguang. *China, Britain, and Businessmen: Political and Commercial Relations, 1949–57.* London: Macmillan, 1991.

Sheng, Michael M. "America's Lost Chance in China? A Reappraisal of Chinese Communist Policy toward the United States before 1945." *Australian Journal of Chinese Affairs* 29 (January 1993): 135–57.

Shlaim, Avi, Peter Jones, and Keith Sainsbury. *British Foreign Secretaries Since 1945.* London: David & Charles, 1977.

Short, Anthony. *The Communist Insurrection in Malaya, 1948–1960.* London: Muller, 1975.

Shuckburgh, Evelyn. *Descent to Suez: Diaries 1951–56.* New York: Norton, 1986.

Sigal, Leon V. "The 'Rational Policy' Model and the Formosan Straits Crisis." *International Studies Quarterly* 14 (June 1970): 121–56.

Simmons, Robert R. *The Strained Alliance: Peking, Pyongyang, Moscow and the Politics of the Korean Civil War.* New York: Free Press, 1975.

Smith, Raymond, and John Zametica. "The Cold Warrior: Clement Attlee Reconsidered, 1945–7." *International Affairs* 61 (Spring 1985): 237–52.

Snow, Edgar. *Red Star Over China.* New York: Random House, 1938.

Spanier, John W. *The Truman-MacArthur Controversy and the Korean War.* Cambridge, Mass.: Harvard University Press, 1959.

Spence, Jonathan. *The Search for Modern China.* New York: Norton, 1990.

Spurr, Russell. *Enter the Dragon: China's Undeclared War against the U.S. in Korea, 1950–51.* New York: Newmarket Press, 1988.

Stairs, Denis. *The Diplomacy of Constraint: Canada, the Korean War, and the United States.* Toronto: University of Toronto Press, 1974.

Stolper, Thomas E. *China, Taiwan, and the Offshore Islands: Together with an Implication for Outer Mongolia and Sino-Soviet Relations.* Armonk, N.Y.: M. E. Sharpe, 1985.

Stueck, William W. [Jr.] "The Limits of Influence: British Policy and American Expansion of the War in Korea." *Pacific Historical Review* 55 (February 1986): 65–95.

Stueck, William W., Jr. *The Road to Confrontation: American Policy toward China and Korea, 1947–1950.* Chapel Hill: University of North Carolina Press, 1981.

Sulzberger, C. L. *A Long Row of Candles.* New York: Macmillan, 1969.

Swisher, Earl, ed. *China's Management of the American Barbarians: A Study of Sino-American Relations, 1841–1861, with Documents.* New Haven, Conn.: Yale University for the Far Eastern Association, 1953.

Tang, James Tuck-Hong. *Britain's Encounter with Revolutionary China, 1949–54.* New York: St. Martin's Press, 1992.

Thomas, John. "The Limits of Alliance: The Quemoy Crisis of 1958." In Garthoff, ed., *Sino-Soviet Military Relations,* 114–49.

Thorne, Christopher G. *Allies of a Kind: The United States, Britain and the War Against Japan, 1941–1945.* New York: Oxford University Press, 1978.

Thorpe, D. R. *Selwyn Lloyd.* London: Jonathan Cape, 1989.

Topping, Seymour. *Journey Between Two Chinas.* New York: Harper & Row, 1972.

Trevelyan, Humphrey. *Living with the Communists.* Boston: Gambit, 1971.

Truman, Harry S. *Memoirs: Years of Decisions.* Garden City, N.Y.: Doubleday, 1955.

_____. *Memoirs: Years of Trial and Hope.* Garden City, N.Y.: Doubleday, 1956.

Truman, Margaret. *Letters from Father: The Truman Family's Personal Correspondence.* New York: Arbor House, 1983.

Tsang, Steve Yut-sang. *Democracy Shelved: Great Britain, China and Attempts at Constitutional Reforms in Hong Kong, 1945–1952.* New York: Oxford University Press, 1988.

Tsou, Tang. *America's Failure in China, 1941–1950.* Chicago: University of Chicago Press, 1963.

_____. "Mao's Limited War in the Taiwan Strait." *Orbis* 3 (October 1959): 332–50.

Tucker, Nancy Bernkopf. "American Policy Toward Sino-Japanese Trade in the Postwar Years: Politics and Prosperity." *Diplomatic History* 8 (Summer 1984): 183–208.

_____. "China and America: 1941–1991." *Foreign Affairs* 70 (Winter 1991–92): 75–92.

_____. "Cold War Contacts: America and China, 1952–1956." In Harding and Yuan, eds., *Sino-American Relations,* 238–66.

_____. "A House Divided: The United States, the Department of State, and China." In Cohen and Iriye, eds., *Great Powers in East Asia,* 35–62.

_____. "John Foster Dulles and the Taiwan Roots of the 'Two Chinas' Policy." In Immerman, ed., *John Foster Dulles and the Diplomacy of the Cold War,* 235–62.

_____. "No Common Ground: American-Chinese-Soviet Relations, 1948–1972." *Diplomatic History* 16 (Spring 1992): 319–24.

_____. *Patterns in the Dust: Chinese-American Relations and the Recognition Controversy, 1949–1950.* New York: Columbia University Press, 1983.

U.S. Congress. *Congressional Record.* 1949–58. Washington, D.C.: GPO.

U.S. Department of Defense. *United States–Vietnam Relations, 1945–67.* Pentagon Papers. Washington, D.C.: GPO, 1971.

U.S. Department of State. *American Foreign Policy, 1950–1955: Basic Documents.* Washington, D.C.: GPO, 1957.

_____. *Department of State Bulletin.* 1949–58. Washington, D.C.: GPO.

_____. *Foreign Relations of the United States.* 1942–58. Washington, D.C.: GPO.

_____. *United States Relations with China, with Special Reference to the Period 1944–1949.* China White Paper. Washington, D.C.: GPO, 1949.

Ulam, Adam B. *Expansion and Coexistence: Soviet Foreign Policy, 1917–1973.* New York: Holt, Rinehart and Winston, 1974.

Unterberger, Betty M. *America's Siberian Expedition, 1918–1920.* Durham, N.C.: Duke University Press, 1956.

Van Ness, Peter. *Revolution and Chinese Foreign Policy: Peking's Support for Wars of National Liberation.* Berkeley: University of California Press, 1970.

Volokhova, A. "Zhou Enlai and Chinese Diplomacy." *Far Eastern Affairs* 5 (1988): 91–103.

Walker, William O., III. *Opium and Foreign Policy: The Anglo-American Search for Order in Asia, 1912–1954.* Chapel Hill: University of North Carolina Press, 1991.

Walt, Stephen M. *The Origins of Alliances.* Ithaca, N.Y.: Cornell University Press, 1987.

_____. "Testing Theories of Alliance Formation: The Case of Southwest Asia." *International Organization* 42 (Spring 1988): 275–316.

Wang Jisi. "The Origins of America's 'Two China' Policy." In Harding and Yuan, eds., *Sino-American Relations,* 198–212.

Warner, Geoffrey. "Britain and the Crisis over Dien Bien Phu, April 1954: The Failure of United Action." In Kaplan, Artaud, and Rubin, eds., *Dien Bien Phu and the Crisis of Franco-American Relations,* 55–77.

_____. "From Geneva to Manila: British Policy toward Indochina and SEATO, May–September 1954." In Kaplan, Artaud, and Rubin, eds., *Dien Bien Phu and the Crisis of Franco-American Relations,* 149–67.

_____. "The Study of Cold War Origins." *Diplomacy and Statecraft* 1 (November 1990): 13–26.

Watt, D. C. "Britain and the Cold War in the Far East, 1945–58." In Nagai and Iriye, eds., *Origins of the Cold War in Asia,* 89–122.

Weiler, Peter. "British Labour and the Cold War: The Foreign Policy of the Labour Governments, 1945–1951." *Journal of British Studies* 26 (January 1987): 54–82.

Weng, Byron S. "Communist China's Changing Attitudes Toward the United Nations." *International Organization* 20 (Autumn 1966): 677–704.

Westad, Odd Arne. *Cold War and Revolution: Soviet-American Rivalry and the Origins of the Chinese Civil War.* New York: Columbia University Press, 1993.

_____. "Rethinking Revolutions: The Cold War in the Third World." *Journal of Peace Research* 29 (1992): 455–64.

Whiting, Allen S. *China Crosses the Yalu: The Decision to Enter the Korean War.* Stanford, Calif.: Stanford University Press, 1968.

_____. *The Chinese Calculus of Deterrence*. Ann Arbor: University of Michigan Press, 1975.

_____. "Quemoy 1958: Mao's Miscalculations." *China Quarterly* 62 (June 1975): 263–70.

Wilbur, C. Martin, and Julie Lien-ying How. *Missionaries of Revolution: Soviet Advisers and Nationalist China, 1920–1927.* Cambridge, Mass.: Harvard University Press, 1989.

Wilson, Dick. *Zhou Enlai: A Biography.* New York: Viking, 1984.

Wolf, David C. " 'To Secure a Convenience': Britain Recognizes China — 1950." *Journal of Contemporary History* 18 (April 1983): 299–326.

Womack, Brantly, ed. *Contemporary Chinese Politics in Historical Perspective.* Cambridge: Cambridge University Press, 1991.

Xiang, Lanxin. "The Recognition Controversy: Anglo-American Relations in China, 1949." *Journal of Contemporary History* 27 (April 1992): 319–43.

Yang Kuisong. "The Soviet Factor and the CCP's Policy toward the United States in the 1940s." *Chinese Historians* 5 (Spring 1992): 17–34.

Yang, Yun-yuan. "Controversies over Tibet: China versus India, 1947–49." *China Quarterly* 111 (September 1987): 407–20.

Yergin, Daniel. *Shattered Peace: The Origins of the Cold War and the National Security State.* Boston: Houghton Mifflin, 1977.

Young, John W. "Churchill, the Russians and the Western Alliance: The Three-Power Conference at Bermuda, 1953." *English Historical Review* (October 1986): 889–912.

_____, ed. *The Foreign Policy of Churchill's Peacetime Administration, 1951– 1955.* Leicester, U.K.: Leicester University Press, 1988.

Young, Kenneth. *Negotiating with the Chinese Communists: The United States Experience, 1953–1967.* New York: McGraw-Hill, 1968.

Zhai, Qiang. "Britain, the United States, and the Jinmen-Mazu Crises, 1954–55 and 1958." *Chinese Historians* 5 (Fall 1992): 25–48.

_____. "China and the Geneva Conference of 1954." *China Quarterly* 129 (March 1992): 103–22.

_____. "Dulles, Wedge, and the Sino-American Ambassadorial Talks, 1955– 1957." *Chinese Historians* 2 (June 1989): 29–44.

_____. "Recent Chinese Writings on 1945–1955 Sino-American Relations." *The Society for Historians of American Foreign Relations Newsletter* 20 (December 1989): 75–84.

_____. "Transplanting the Chinese Model: Chinese Military Advisers and the First Vietnam War, 1950–1954." *Journal of Military History* 57 (October 1993): 689–715.

Zhang, Shu Guang. *Deterrence and Strategic Culture: Chinese-American Confrontations, 1949–1958.* Ithaca, N.Y.: Cornell University Press, 1992.

_____. " 'Preparedness Eliminates Mishaps': The CCP's Security Concerns in 1949–1950 and Origins of Sino-American Confrontation." *Journal of American–East Asian Relations* 1 (Spring 1992): 42–72.

Zheng Weizhi. "Independence Is the Basic Canon—An Analysis of the Principles of China's Foreign Policy." *Beijing Review* (January 7, 1985): 16–17.

Newspapers and Periodicals (1949–1958)

New York Times
Newsweek
Time

Unpublished Papers

Alcock, Christian. "Britain and the Korean War, 1950–1953." Ph.D. diss., Manchester University, 1986.
Browne, Blaine T. "A Common Thread: American Images of the Chinese and Japanese, 1930–1960." Ph.D. diss., University of Oklahoma, 1985.
Chen, Jian. "China's Road to the Korean War: A Critical Study of the Origins of Sino-American Confrontation, 1949–1950." Ph.D. diss., Southern Illinois University, 1990.
Harding, Harry. "The Domestic Sources of Foreign Policy: The Quemoy Crisis of 1954–1955 and 1958." Paper, Stanford University, 1970.
Jia, Qingguo. "Unmaterialized Rapprochement: Sino-American Relations in the Mid-1950s." Ph.D. diss., Cornell University, 1988.
Su Ge. "'A Horrible Dilemma': The Making of the U.S.-Taiwan Mutual Defense Treaty, 1948–1954." Ph.D. diss., Brigham Young University, 1987.
Wang, Richard Yuping. "The Joint Chiefs of Staff and United States Policy on China." Ph.D. diss., Mississippi State University, 1987.

Index

The Dragon, the Lion, & the Eagle

was composed in 10/13 Times on a Macintosh system with Linotronic output by Books International of Norcross, Georgia, and the bibliography was composed in 9-point Times by Central Typographers of Hong Kong. It was printed by sheet-fed offset on 55-pound Glatfelter Natural acid-free stock, notch case bound with 88-point binder's boards covered in Holliston Kingston Natural cloth, and wrapped with dustjackets printed in two colors on 100-pound enamel stock with polyester film lamination by Thomson-Shore, Inc., of Dexter, Michigan. It was designed by Will Underwood, and published by

THE KENT STATE UNIVERSITY PRESS
KENT, OHIO 44242